AGENTS OF CHAOS

Shadowrun Line Developer: Jason M. Hardy

Product Design & Development: Randall N. Bills, Jason M. Hardy, Philip A. Lee

Original Cue System Design: Matt "Golden Kumquat" Heerdt

Writing: Randall N. Bills, Patrick Goodman, Jason M. Hardy, Philip A. Lee, Aaron Pavao, O.C. Presley, Russell Zimmerman

Cover Art: Benjamin Giletti

Cover Layout: Matt "Golden Kumquat" Heerdt

Interior Art: Bruno Balixia, Gordon Bennetto, Daniel Comerci, Phillip Hilliker, David Hovey, Ian King, Michael Komarck, Ian Llanas, Alyssa Menold, Victor Manuel Leza Moreno, Kristen Plescow, Marc Sintes, Tony Shasteen, Takashi Tan, Iwo Widulinski

Interior Layout: Matt "Golden Kumquat" Heerdt

Proofreading: Mason Hart, Carl Schelin, Jeremy Weyand

Playtesting: Natalie Aked, Rob Aked, Armand Amonette, Brian Amonette, Mark Barraclough, Richard Brown, Jackson Brunsting, Paul Alexander Butler, James Carpio, Richard Clayton, Jacob Cohen, James Corbin, Raymond Croteau, Russell Davis, Karlene Dickens, Justin Diehl, Joel DiPippa, Joshua Dixie, Derek Dokter, Ben Dow, Beth Dow, John Dukes, Bruce Ford, Eugen Fournes, Joanna Fournes, Mable Friedman, Morgan Gould, Timothy Gray, Jerrod Gunning, Nicholas Honer, Martin Quincy Hall, Camille Jeanson, Kendall Jung, R.L. King, Ariel Licha, Mary Lindholm, Dave Lundquest, Berry Lyklema, Chris Maxfield, Carrie McIntosh, Stephen Mercer, Christina Mitton, Suzanna Powell, Patrick Lipper, Thomas Lomax Jr., Shane Mahon, Chris Maxfield, Mykal Merrill, Kim Morris, D. Casey O'Donovan, Geoff Raye, Richard Riessen, Matt Riley, Justin Schnider, David Scott, Mark Somers, Nathan Thiessen, Derek VanTilburg, Michael Vik, Troy Wieck, Clifton Wright, CZ Wright, Leland Zavadil, among others

Special Thanks: Rob Wieland, Paul Butler

PREFACE

RULES ARE MEANT TO BE BROKEN

It was the summer of 1989 when I was first exposed to *Shadowrun* via a four-page preview pamphlet at my local game store. A few weeks later and I had purchased the First Edition rulebook and taken the first steps on the path to what would become the greatest RPG love affair of my life. Wait, elves *and* cybernetics? Megacorporations *and* dragons? You can't do that!

I spent the next nineteen years running a campaign, and for most of it we were playing weekly, every Monday night. There are living, breathing stories and characters that only exist within the minds of the few people that sat around that table, and any one of them will happily regale you with tales of the duplicitous machinations of a dwarf fixer named Redeye or the tragic end of Eddie Garrett, ex-Lone Star cop turned reluctant shadowrunner.

Shadowrun occupies a very special place in my heart. The walls and shelves of my home are covered in *Shadowrun* books and art, and indeed sometimes I have to remind myself of the countless people who have fallen in love with the *Shadowrun* world not through the classic tabletop role playing game, but instead through one of the many *Shadowrun* video games, or any of the more than fifty published novels.

But everything ends. My beloved campaign came to a satisfying conclusion in the fall of 2008, and while I have kept up with the game's new editions and releases, and flirted with some short story arcs, it hasn't returned to my table in any meaningful way for a while. I find that my tastes have changed over the years, and while I have lost no love for the *Shadowrun* world, these days I prefer RPG game systems that are lighter on the rules and more focused on story and character. There has been a massive explosion of indie-style RPG game play in the last few years, and many people are engaging with the hobby in intriguing new ways. As a hobby-game retailer myself, I have also witnessed no shortage of gamers interested in playing tabletop *Shadowrun* but utterly intimidated by the massive rulebook. The fact of the matter is that that big black book isn't going anywhere, and there will always be players who want to joyously fiddle with every last glorious detail and chrome widget of rules found within those pages, and more power to them. I was one of them for a very long time.

Shadowrun has been part of our collective gaming consciousness for well over twenty-five years now, and it's been actively in print the whole time, something very few games can claim. It's been so long in fact, that what was a game of a speculative future has now become what is veritably an alternate *history* game! (Since magic did not, alas, return to the world in 2011. Although there's still a slim chance that my friend Warren might goblinize into an ork in 2018, as we've all long suspected he will, but that remains to be seen.)

Some of us shadowrunners are now getting long in the tooth, lacking the time to play or facilitate a game with such a robust and exhaustive rules set. Meanwhile, more collaborative storytelling-style RPGs and even gamemaster-free RPGs are seeing some real popularity as the hobby continues to grow and evolve.

That's where *Shadowrun: Anarchy* comes in. It's flexible enough to be played as a rules-light version of a traditional roleplaying game, or as a much more freeform "open table" style storytelling experience. I am incredibly pleased with what the Catalyst team has come up with here, and I think it has the potential to inject a

whole lot of new energy into the *Shadowrun* community. It's certainly going to get a new campaign to my table for the first time in years.

So if you're new to the Sixth World, welcome. Maybe you've always wanted to be an elf street ganger with an adrenal pump and a heart of gold. Or you've always entertained fantasies of summoning spirits from the back alley streets of Seattle by muttering arcane mysteries through your massive ork canine teeth. Or you're dying to see your *Shadowrun* video-game character come to

life in a tabletop pencil-and-paper RPG. There's plenty of room for all of us in the shadows.

If, like myself, you're returning to Mr. Johnson's table after a few previous jobs, you'll fit right in, but you'll find that the rules have changed a bit. But rules are meant to be broken.

Paul Alexander Butler
July 2016, Baltimore

TABLE OF

SYNCHRONICITY	4
INTRODUCTION	10
BLEEDING ON THE EDGE	12
EVERYTHING HAS A PRICE	12
DAYS THAT SHOOK THE WORLD	14
OPPOSITION REPORT	16
THE BIG TEN	16
ORGANIZED CRIME	20
GANGS	21
THE LAW	22
POLITICOS	22
MAGICAL GROUPS	23
LIFE IN THE SIXTH WORLD	24
GETTING AROUND	25
THE REST OF LIFE	26
RULES OF THE STREET	27
BEFORE THE GAME BEGINS	27
CHARACTER SHEET	29
SKILLS	31
SHADOW AMPS	32
PLAYING SHADOWRUN: ANARCHY	34
VEHICLE AND DRONE COMBAT	47
ADDITIONAL RULES	48
BUILDING STREET CRED	51
PLAYING ANARCHY	51
DIFFERENT WAYS TO RUN	52
CONTROLLING ANARCHY	55
PASSING THE MICROPHONE	55
KEEPING IT CIVIL:	56
SMOOTH TALKIN'	57
I COULD USE SOME HELP HERE	58

JUMPING THE TRACKS	59
LETTING THE LEAD FLY	60
FORCES OF CHAOS	61
CHARACTER CREATION	61
CHARACTER ADVANCEMENT	70
STREET PEOPLE	73
COYDOG	74
GENTRY	76
HARDPOINT	78
MS. MYTH	80
SLEDGE	82
ALYOSHA DUSKA	84
BIT-BUCKET	86
BORDERLINE	88
CHROME BISON	90
DAKTARI	92
FOURTH	94
FUSION	96
HAWK	98
JINN	100
KIX	102
KNOX	104
NINETAILS	106
RAIDER	108
RASPBERRY JAM	110
RAZZLE DAZZLE	112
REESE FRENZY	114
ROSE RED	116
RUCKUS	118
SHADES	120
STRIDER	122
THUNDER	124
TOMMY Q	126
VECTOR	128
WAGON	130
WHEEZER	132

NON-PLAYER CHARACTERS	134
BUG QUEEN	134
BUG SPIRIT	134
CORPORATE SECURITY	134
CORPORATE SUIT	134
DEVIL RAT	135
ENEMY DRONE (HEAVY)	135
ENEMY DRONE (MEDIUM)	135
ENEMY DRONE (SMALL)	135
ENEMY MAGE	136
GANGER	136
HELL HOUND	136
MR. JOHNSON (CORPORATE)	136
MR. JOHNSON (STREET)	137
RENT-A-COP	137
SECURITY SPIDER	137
SOLDIER	137
SPIRIT OF AIR	138
SPIRIT OF BEASTS	138
SPIRIT OF EARTH	139
SPIRIT OF FIRE	139
SPIRIT OF MAN	139
SPIRIT OF WATER	139
VAMPIRE	140
YOUNG DRAGON	140
THE SECRETS OF SEATTLE	141
HAPPENING WORLD	153
BE CAREFUL WHAT	154
BLACK STAR RISING	155
FOOD FIGHT	156
DON'T KNOW MUCH	157
ONTO THE PATH	158
SNATCH AND GRAB	159

CONTENTS

LET YOUR FLAG FLY	160
HONG KONG CANNON	161
NERPS RUN	162
DATA/STEEL	163
PUYALLUP PROBLEMS	164
THE HALLOWEENER	165
THE LIGHT WITHIN	166
URBAN BRAWL	168
UNKNOWN STUNTMAN	169
IS THAT A BUG	170
ASSASSIN'S GREED	171
CLEANING HOUSE	172
STREET SWEEPER	173
TRIAD TAKE-OUT	174
TRUCKING WITH THE FAE	175
ONE FOR ALL	177
COMPANY TOWN	178
MY FAIR LADY	179
FREE-FOR-ALL	180
LEAKS AND PLUMBERS, PT. 1	181
LEAKS AND PLUMBERS, PT. 2	182
BENEATH THE SANDS, PT. 1	184
BENEATH THE SANDS, PT. 2	185
ARABIAN KNIGHTS, PT. 1	186

ARABIAN KNIGHTS, PT. 2	187
ARABIAN KNIGHTS, PT. 3	188
ARABIAN KNIGHTS, PT. 4	189
UN-SEELED FATE, PT. 1	191
UN-SEELED FATE, PT. 2	192
UN-SEELED FATE, PT. 3	193
UN-SEELED FATE, PT. 4	195

ANARCHY & FIFTH EDITION	**197**
ANARCHY AND SHADOWRUN, 5E	**197**
MOVING FROM SR5 TO ANARCHY	198
MOVING FROM ANARCHY TO SR5	200
ANARCHY CATALOG	202
INDEX OF ANARCHY	**208**
SHADOW SLANG	**212**
CHARACTER SHEET	**213**

First Printing by Catalyst Game Labs, an imprint of InMediaRes Productions, LLC
PMB 202 • 303 –91st Ave. NE, E-502
Lake Stevens, WA 98258

Find us online:
info@shadowruntabletop.com
(Shadowrun questions)
http://www.shadowruntabletop.com
(Catalyst Shadowrun website)
http://www.shadowrun.com
(official Shadowrun Universe website)
http://www.catalystgamelabs.com
(Catalyst website)
http://shop.catalystgamelabs.com
(Catalyst/Shadowrun orders)

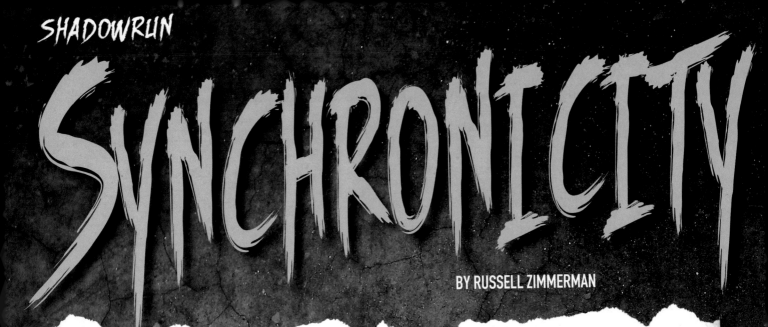

SHADOWRUN

SYNCHRONICITY

BY RUSSELL ZIMMERMAN

"I don't like it," Sledge said into their huddle, casting a wary glance clean over Hardpoint's head.

"You don't like anything," Gentry said, then stuck his tongue out. "It's barely even worth saying any more."

"Boys." Coydog shot a glance between the two of them, quirking an eyebrow.

"Listen here, you little squi—" Sledge started in, but got himself cut off.

"*Boys*," Ms. Myth's troll-deep voice ended the argument before it really got started. "We need in the building to get the focus. They need in the building, too. There's no need for two teams to be at odds with each other, is there? They're short on technical support, so we've got an advantage if things go sideways, and Sledge's worst fears come true."

"M'not scared," the big ork mumbled to nobody in particular.

"It just makes sense," Hardpoint cut in with dwarven certainty. He didn't speak up as often as the others, and when he did, they listened. "I say aye."

"Aye," Gentry nodded, shooting a glance at a particularly leggy member of the other team.

"Aye," Coydog nodded with a bright smile.

"Nay," Sledge crossed his blocky cyberarms over his broad chest.

Myth spoke last, like she so often did.

"Ayes have it, not even countin' mine, sweetie. If they're in, we're in."

"I don't like 'em." Lefty shot the larger group a concerned look, glaring a bit at the decker who kept staring at her. Her chromed-up left hand flexed and straightened with tension. Her right hand—her shooting hand—didn't move.

"You rarely do," Alyosha teased, the good-natured dwarf shooting her a smile that took the edge off.

"I know Myth," Tiny's bass rumbled. The troll easily doubled Alyosha's height and even loomed over the elf-lanky Lefty. "She's a righteous tusker. An' I've heard good things about her crew. They'll do fine."

"Yeah, but what will they be fine at *doing*? I heard 'em say they're after some magical doohickey—"

"A focus," Alyosha said, since he was the one who was supposed to know magic for the rest of them.

"*Doohickey*," Lefty doubled down. "And this isn't a retrieval job for us, as you two well know. We can't let 'em slow us down. In and out, maximum speed, minimum time, that was our plan."

Alyosha sighed. Precision was great, right until the moment that it interfered with actually getting the job done.

"Well without 'em, I'm our only way through the front fraggin' door, Left-o, and same with every other stinkin' door we come across. That's gonna slow us plenty, right? Highball's still down, can't run off-site info-tech for us. Without a decker, we're hosed, and they got a decker."

Lefty peered over at Gentry, who smiled at her.

"Some decker," she grumbled.

"I and great Bear," Alyosha Duska gestured everywhere and nowhere in particular, as he often did when talking about the spirits he could call, "Vote aye."

"Aye," Tiny's massive head shifted in a nod.

"Nay," Lefty pouted. "Fat lot of good it'll do me. Fine. If they're in, we're in."

She glared over at Gentry who lifted a hand to wave.

"But I'll be using an 'I told you so' later."

"Hey." Sledge introduced himself to the massive troll—massive even compared to Ms. Myth, who was partic-

ularly proud of her girlish figure—with open hostility and only grudging civility. The ork carried a sleek assault rifle and had a *Neil the Ork Barbarian* reproduction mono-sword over his shoulder.

"Yo." Tiny looked down at the chromed-up ork, showing wry amusement. His weapons, his arms, his style, was visibly and overtly lower-tech. Sledge knew the type, runners who thought older, simple stuff was more reliable. Tiny rippled with trollish mass, and his most obvious weapon was an absurdly heavy chopping blade, a machete writ large and in bold.

The two sized each other up, then fell into a tense silence, just waiting at the front of their pile-up for the rest of their teams to get in line. Everybody on both crews knew who'd take point. The two of them filled the alley, regardless, it would've been tough for anyone else to get past them to be in front of they'd tried.

"<In position.>" Hardpoint's voice came through both teams' commlinks, lacking inflection as was always the case when the dwarf rigged. He'd stay in the van, but—sure enough—shortly after his announcement, a pair of low-flying hoverdrones zipped into view, stubby autorifles held aloft on whirring gyroblades.

"Neat!" Coydog clapped her elf-thin hands as Duska finished his quiet, guttural, chanting and a ripple of power flowed from him. Nobody else on either team was Awakened, nobody else had their eyes open to the astral and the tricks of power the two shamans could pull, but the elf seemed impressed with his summoning work.

"Your turn," the dwarf said with a wry smile, only to tilt an approving eyebrow a moment later. There was, again, no obvious display of power as Coydog finished her crooning call, but a light breeze teased at her long, dark, hair, and apparently her own incantation was complete.

"Nice. Multi-spirit support," Lefty grudgingly admitted.

"Hey! Uh, you want me to take a look at your firewall?" Gentry sidled up, trying his friendliest smile. "I heard your usual Matrix dude wasn't—"

"Nope." She started screwing her oversized silencer into place on her long rifle, not even looking at him. "I'm good."

"Oh. Yeah. Okay, *raé*, I feel ya." Gentry looked halfway cool for about a second. "But what about the latest patches on your smartlink software, though? I bet my download speed is pretty wiz. I've got this sweet Sony Cybe—"

"I'm good." Her tone was chillier this time, a boxy magazine slapped home with a metallic *snick-snack* of finality.

"Yeah, okay, cool I'm just gonna, uhh …" And then he was in a hurry to be somewhere else.

Sledge grunted in amusement. Tiny shook his shaggy head. Alyosha chuckled openly. Coydog giggled and of-

fered Lefty a long-distance fist bump. Hardpoint's metallic, far-off *heh heh heh* rang into earbuds and cyberaudio suites across both teams. Gentry's cheeks flushed red, and he was abruptly very busy with something in augmented reality.

Myth split the night with a big-palmed clap and a bright smile. Lefty took off up a fire escape, long gun barely slowing her down. Gentry slunk past the motherly troll, who reached out to tousle his hair, easing the sting of yet another elven rejection.

"Okay runners," she said, nodding toward the door. Lefty clambered into her sniper's nest, Hardpoint's drones whirred and climbed. Tiny and Sledge readied their weapons.

"Let's get running."

Lefty leaned and twisted to swing her scope around and watch their progress. Hardpoint's gun-drones spread to cover each flank, the shamen huddled next to Myth in the middle of the group, the street muscle—ork and troll—waited at the door, ready to commit terrible violence as needed.

Gentry handled the camera just below the glowing Wuxing logo, then the door just below the camera, then the camera just inside the door. The human might not be all that socially adept—especially around elves—but Lefty had to admit he was good at his job.

No security assault team came boiling out to welcome them. Lefty didn't have to kill any welcoming party, didn't have to line up her old-fashioned sights and cutting-edge smartscope, didn't have to adjust the rifle's front-end with her inhumanly precise cyberlimb and squeeze with her flesh-and-blood trigger-finger for the exactly two pounds, five ounces, that would smear some idiot guard's grey matter all over the nice, clean, feng-shui-fancy facility walls.

Good.

She watched the last of them go in—did that Coydog girl shoot her a thumbs up?—and then Lefty swung her scope to scan upward, toggling through light-amplification mods and looking through what windows she had access to.

"There's been some gang activity, though, Chipped Razors," Duska worried, voice carrying more than Sledge liked, "So I'm a little worried about leaving Lefty alone out there. Perhaps I should have left my spirit out there to protect her?"

"She seems nice," Coydog smiled, then straightened her features, "I mean, for a professional killer and all. Very competent and professional. I'm sure she'll be fine."

"You two are gonna get us killed," Sledge turned his head over his shoulder to grumble. Omni-directional grumbling wasn't something he'd had implanted—it was just a natural knack.

"Shh," Coydog glowered, "We're communicating and coordinating between teams. Transparency is important in a healthy relationship."

Duska lifted an intrigued eyebrow. Tiny winced on Sledge's behalf. Myth snorted in a supremely unladylike fashion. Gentry snickered, but kept hacking the elevator controls.

"And besides, I have a spirit concealing us." Coydog timed it just right so her explanation coincided with Sledge opening his dumb mouth to say another dumb thing. "Nobody'll hear anyways."

"<Heh heh heh,>" Hardpoint weighed in via audio-link.

Sledge wisely stayed quiet.

"Ninth floor's us," Sledge stepped out as the elevator doors slid open, sweeping one side of the hallway with his Raiden assault rifle. At his back, Tiny swung the other way, huge blade up.

"You sure you're okay, boss?"

Myth gave them both a warm smile. "We'll be fine without you. Tenth floor's where Coy does her magic."

Sledge's cyberoptics had already slid off of the troll leader, though, and he cast a worried look at Coydog. Gentry pointedly looked away.

"Go cover Tiny while he does his job. I've got Myth and Gentry and Alyosha and—oh yeah!—fraggin' Bear and Coyote coverin' me while I do mine. I'm good."

She didn't blow him a kiss or shoot him a wink or call him sugar-wooger-noogums. Sledge's cheeks still flushed, though, Myth still stifled a smile, Gentry still looked away.

The elevator doors closed, and the car kept lifting.

"<Still clear. Hostiles on floors four and way up on twenty,>" Lefty said through the microphone built into her cyber-wrist, near enough her face in her prone shooting position. "<Proceed as planned.>"

She emphasized the *planned* enough to make Tiny roll his eyes and Alyosha to feel a little guilty, but nobody else seemed to pick up on it.

Just like she didn't seem to pick up on the pair of gangers whispering at one another, blades out, as they climbed up the fire escape behind her.

Coydog moved fast, squeezing out of the elevator ahead of Myth and even Gentry, Duska in her wake. The facility—the whole megacorporation—was well-known for

meticulously arraying every little thing just so, aligning their offices with the flow of chi energy that surrounded and enveloped metahumanity, whether they were aware of it or not. Some attributed it to ley lines, others to emotional claptrap, others to simply nature's will; what mattered was that Coydog could see it, could *feel* it, and she followed this tenth-floor's flow of power to her target.

Duska was just a step behind her, the spirit whisperer as attuned to the supernatural as Coydog, in his own way. Gentry chewed at his lip and hurriedly wiped cameras as he trailed them, and Myth took up the rear of the group, her shadowy bulk reassuring at their six.

"Ooh," Coydog finally smiled, casting a glance at Gentry and knowing the decker would already be working on that last security door. Through the thick safety glass, inside the central experimentation chamber of this floor of the building, an ornate metal bracer veritably blazed with power.

"What's it do?" Duska whispered.

"Somethin' neat," Coydog shrugged. The mundane security was Gentry's job. The wards, inlaid into the floor, were hers. "Johnson's paying a pretty penny, that's all we really know."

"Orichalcum?" The dwarf peered over on his tip-toes. The magical metal was phenomenally powerful, and equally expensive.

"The inlays for sure." Coydog nodded, "And maybe some of that big stuff, too."

Her wrinkled nose and gesture took in not only the gorgeous bracer they were here to steal, but also larger, heavier pieces. Broken lengths of pillar, an ancient-looking section of wall covered in runic carvings, a lovely marble statue that looked to be wearing metallic jewelry.

"I think so, too," Duska sighed. None of the heavier items would leave the room, he was sure. "They're beautiful. That's too bad."

Sledge stalked the cubicle walls with paramilitary precision, his move-by-wire upgrades making every footfall sure and certain, his street-earned experience keeping his gun steady.

"So what's with 'Tiny,' anyways?" he grunted.

"Hmm?" Tiny didn't look up from his satchel.

"It's ironic, right? Call the big guy 'Tiny,' I mean?"

"Prob'ly," the troll shrugged, busy.

Sledge grunted back, then the pair moved most of the way across the room. They were near the central area, ducking from cubicle to cubicle.

"So, uh," Sledge tried to remember Coydog and Myth's lessons on the importance of small talk. "How'd you meet Myth?"

"Hmm?" Tiny was halfway under a desk again, shoulders too broad to fit, stretching out one long arm to reach something.

"Myth." Sledge tried not to sound grouchy. He really, really tried. "How d'you know her?"

"School," Tiny said as they moved to their fourth such pit-stop. His big machete was never quite in the way, he seemed as practiced at moving with it as Sledge was with his rifle and sword.

"Like a … a tech school or something?"

Tiny looked up, clambering to his feet after wedging himself beneath this last desk.

"Why?"

Sledge shrugged.

"Figure smoothies won't let a troll into most schools. Thought, like, a vocational school or whatever might've been it. Myth there as some long con, you lookin' for work before The Man kicked you out …"

"<Movement!>" Lefty interrupted them, a heartbeat before Hardpoint's static-crackling voice did the same, a split-second before his gun-drones started firing a floor above them. Lefty sounded out of breath. Sledge didn't notice it. Tiny did.

The pair of them began to move—straight at the stairwell, running toward the trouble—but then flashlights split the darkness of the work-stations behind them. Underbarrel-mounted flashlights, carried on guns, carried by guards.

"Go help the others," Sledge dropped to one knee, bracing his Raiden against a flimsy wall, half-concealing himself and ready to open fire on the first guard that stepped fully into view. "I'll hold 'em here, you finish the gig."

"I will."

Tiny ran for the stairwell, and Sledge—firing a tight burst into an armored guard—didn't notice that the troll went *down*, not *up*, the stairs.

The guards had a security mage. *Had.*

Gentry's Colt snapped off quick shots whenever the decker wasn't ducked behind something and hacking furiously. Myth's Ingram Smartguns let out long roars of autofire as she sprayed and drew fire, hollering orders to the rest of the team over the chattering guns. Hardpoint's drones swooped and roared, laying down suppressive fire or flying up to flank a hunkered-down guard. Occasionally a window got a neat little hole blasted in it, and somewhere across the room, as if by magic, a security thug went down, as—across the street—Lefty shifted her aim for another shot.

Coydog and Duska? They had to handle the mage.

The young combat magician, fresh-faced enough he looked like a fuzzy-cheeked recent graduate of Something Or Another Tactical Sorcery Academy, had started strong. Very strong. Too strong. Coydog had barely countered the Fireball he'd decided to open with, and the elf's features turned grim when she thought about what would've happened had she not snuffed out the spell.

Going straight to a loud combat-casting like that was a rookie move. It showed impatience with the ebb and flow of combat, a lack of willingness to wait for the right moment, an inability to pause and survey the opposition. It showed an eagerness to prove oneself to peers or superiors. Pulling out a big gun so early showed immaturity, maybe even fear.

Most of all? It showed that you were the mage.

The young Wuxing caster got hit with a tornado, essentially, sucked into a raging whirlwind of Coydog's current air spirit, dashed against the ceiling, then the floor, then cast aside.

Then, getting shakily to his feet, glowing with power—again—as he mustered up a healing spell to try to repair his bruises and cracked bones, he got mauled by a rather unexpected bear.

Duska shook his head sadly as the team's fighting withdrawal continued.

"So young." The dwarf's glowing blue bear spirit roared and clawed and charged off toward some heavily armored troopers that had Gentry pinned down. Duska sighed, "You should've stayed down, my boy."

Lefty saw Tiny first, the massive wall of troll-meat smashing the front security doors open—the wrong way—with a battering ram—more precisely, a dwarf in now-cracked Wuxing combat armor. The troll's big machete was wet with blood, and Lefty suppressed a shudder as she lined up a shot and squeezed for a hair over a kilo.

Hardpoint's van rushed onto the scene next, a GMC Bulldog, as customized as you could hope for. Security came spilling out of a side door, but the van slewed to a sideways halt just in time for its armored hide to deflect incoming fire. The doorway was covered as Alyosha, Myth, and the rest came stumbling out, fighting a rear-action.

No, Lefty lined up a headshot, applied another kilo of pressure, and ended a life. But not all of them. She checked the chronometer in her heads-up display.

"<Tick, tock,>" was all she said, and all she had to.

"<Sledge!>" Tiny went rushing back down the hallway for just a few seconds, and when he came back out, there weren't any more guards firing from inside the building. "<Sledge, you gotta get outta there, big guy.>"

Lefty shifted, squinted, saw figures still moving on the ork's ninth floor, muzzle flashes still barking.

She wondered—another squeeze, another fallen guard—if Tiny or Alyosha had ever told Myth's crew why they were here.

"<Frag off,>" Sledge's fire didn't cease, but Lefty watched his bulkier silhouette move sidelong down a hallway. Moving and shooting, never standing still. A real pro. It'd be a shame if he didn't leave soon.

"<You bein' tech-school buddies with Myth don't mean you get to tell me—>"

"<It wasn't technical school, sweetie. Not that there's anything wrong with that,>" Myth cut in as she reloaded, then she leaned back around the van to lay down another whole magazine of fire. "<Sledge, Tiny's got his Master's. He's a structural engineer.>"

The twin-team's commlinks buzzed with a hurried image message, a photo showing a detonator and a dwindling countdown, a tiny-looking electronic device held in Tiny's massive off-hand.

"<You really should jump soon, Sledge-a-roonie,>" Tiny growled.

"<Or don't.>" That earned Gentry a punch from Coydog.

Everything's easier with a running start.

Sledge chewed at the nearby wall with a long burst, emptying his Yamaha Raiden in the process. The mirror-shined windows gave way, splitting the night air with jagged edges. He ran, built up speed, and leaped. His cyberarms cleared the way for him, battering aside the last brittle edges, and the few small cuts that got through to his meat were nothing compared to the fact he was leaping from a ninth-floor window.

Got a job to do, gravity or not.

The ork twisted, kicking his feet to bring his body around, flailing to orient himself as his move-by-wire kicked in and time slowed down. He got his Ingram in his hand as the ground—and the knot of Wuxing security troopers that had his team pinned down—loomed up at him.

Falling straight at them, Sledge lined up his smartlink targeting pip and let fly. His Smartgun barked and bucked, a long, nonstop, burst, and Wuxing guards fell dead, shot at from an unlikely angle, no cover to be found.

No reason not to try.

His free hand groped over his shoulder for his sword—a wiz blue-glowing replica from *Neil*'s latest tridflick, but also a monofilament-sharp blade in its own

right—and Sledge tried to angle his fall to land on one last drekhead. Might as well take one more with him.

Sorry Coyd—

Suddenly a tornado hit him, and Sledge was falling sideways instead of down. The world turned into a bouncing, shuddering, shower of sparks and bruises as the street rose up to meet him and he skipped along the pavement.

The rear of Hardpoint's van loomed at him, the inside cramped full of too many shadowrunners. Myth and Tiny took up half the space back there, and Alyosha ducked, and there was Coydog by one door, and at the other was Gentry, and then this weird shaggy-looking blue glowing thing—and then the world turned black, because Sledge was out cold.

Lefty watched the ork skip like a stone once, twice, and then slam right into the back of Hardpoint's van. Or, rather, into a shaggy bear-spirit who'd tried to soften his landing, and then into Gentry, and then into the van. Neither of the two meatheads got back up before the doors were slammed shut by gale-force winds and the van started to peel out, and Lefty scrambled up from her shooting position—again—and hurried to the edge of the building.

She stepped over a pair of Chipped Razors, a local gang that had, according to recent reports, about a seventy percent chance of trying to pull some drek tonight. They had tried. The two corpses were mauled terribly, almost looking like one of Alyosha's ursine spirits had done a number on them.

One hadn't.

Lefty's chromed-up arm was sticky with blood as she used it to help her vault off the roof of the building, even though all her blades had been tucked back into their concealed positions. She fell right down onto a three-point landing—rifle slung over one shoulder, safe from the impact—atop Hardpoint's van.

She gave the Bulldog a thump-thump with her metal fist and they sped away.

Just before they rounded the next corner, she looked back and saw the Wuxing facility split in half by a fireball. It then crumbled, folding at the mid-point like a pocketknife. Tiny'd been right; the judicious application of controlled explosives *would* disrupt the flow of chi in a pretty long-term way.

Two teams, one facility … *almost* one job.

WELCOME TO ANARCHY, CHUMMER!

INTRO

We're going to start with a simple statement of fact: *Shadowrun* is awesome. Elves hack the Matrix, trolls sling fireballs, dwarfs channel magic into the ability to punch through a brick wall, orks charm their way past security while carrying a massive firearm in case their words don't work, dragons run globe-spanning megacorporations—the list of compelling characters and fascinating story possibilities in the Sixth World could go on forever.

Which is the goal of this book. *Shadowrun: Anarchy* is all about giving players a chance to let loose a flood of stories in the *Shadowrun* universe, to chase your imagination into whatever dark corner or distant swamp it wanders into, and to see just what kind of chaos you can unleash. *Anarchy* serves as a complement to *Shadowrun, Fifth Edition;* while *SR5* offers opportunities for detailed simulations of your character's choices using rules with significant depth, in *Anarchy* the story comes first. There are still plenty opportunities to throw dice, because we love doing that, but those opportunities exist to help the story move forward. And in *Anarchy*, every player's contributions to the story can stretch beyond the actions of their characters. They have the chance to add elements to the story, from the appearance of new characters to the existence of strange magic to descriptions of strange objects and more. They get to challenge each other, but most of all they get to throw in ideas that will make the game exciting and memorable, and that will help them experience the things that have made *Shadowrun* one of the most enduring role-playing settings of all time.

This book is all you need to play *Shadowrun: Anarchy* (with the exception of some six-sided dice, but you can dig some of those up, right?), and it is designed to make it easy to jump into the game. Here's what you'll find: First, you'll see **The Bleeding Edge**, your guide to *Shadowrun*'s Sixth World setting and the role your character will play in it. **The Rules of the Street** gives you everything you need to resolve situations and conflicts in the game, so you know which dice to roll and when—and what to look for when you roll. The next two chapters give some advice for playing the game, as well as some alternate rules to suit different styles. **Building Street Cred** focuses on players and what they can do to make the game as fun as possible, while **Controlling Anarchy** is advice for gamemasters about how to help build exciting and memorable stories. While the book includes many pre-generated characters to help you dive into the action, **Forces of Chaos** guides you through the process of creating your own character to be just what you want it to be, as well as how to develop that character as it gains experience. **Street People** has that aforementioned collection of pre-generated characters, with a wide array of people such as a human razorgirl, an ork illusionist, a troll bruiser, and a dwarf parkour adept. It also has non-player characters and beasts that can be easily dropped into any job.

Speaking of jobs, the next two chapters have resources needed to set runners out onto the streets to get their work done. **The Secrets of Seattle** gives the background of the most iconic city in the Sixth World, the shadowrunner haven of Seattle, with places for runners to go, people to meet, and plot hooks to fuel their adventures. **The Happening World** is a collection of Contract Briefs, plotlines gamemasters can use to send the group out on a job, giving them the tools they need to get the game moving and provide some plot twists on the way. Finally, *Anarchy and Shadowrun, Fifth Edition* talks about how the two current rule sets work together, and how to move characters from one rule set to another. It also has a list of gear, spells, weapons, and more for ease of reference.

That's what the book has. Check it out, get a feel for it, then get ready for make your own characters, tell your own stories, and build your own legends on the mean streets of the Sixth World. *Shadowrun* may be awesome, but you're about to make it better.

BLEEDING ON THE EDGE

The first thing that you need to know about the Sixth World is that what you don't know absolutely will kill you. So will what you do know. In fact, it's safe to assume that anything and anyone you see or don't see has both the potential and the desire to kill you.

That's good info to know, but not enough to keep you alive. If you're going to run in the shadows, you're going to do the kind of drek that can make everyone in the world—law enforcement, corp security, some average dude who doesn't like the way you look—angry and/or scared, and they'll often react to that anger/fear combination by trying to take you out. If you want to stay alive and keep getting hired to run the shadows, you need to know how the world works. So here's a rundown of what the Sixth World is, how it got there, and some of the power players who make sure a few people stay on top while the vast majority of the people wriggle uncomfortably under their mighty thumbs.

EVERYTHING HAS A PRICE

Read the sentence in the header there. Read it again. Got it? Good. Because if that's the only thing you take away from this, if that's the only thing you learn, then you'll still be getting something valuable about the world you live in. You walk around this world, you'll see a lot of heaps, and each one of them's got someone perched on top of it. Every megacorporation has its CEO, governments have their chief executive, gangs have their lieutenant or head man or chief head basher or whatever the hell they decide to call it. Even that one block in the barrens that has nothing more than a rusty dumpster, an abandoned car, and a shed whose roof has caved in

has a scary-eyed guy named Rastool who scared off all the other scary-eyed guys so he can claim that spot as his own. Each of them figured out what they would have to pay to get to the top of that particular heap, and each one of them ponied up when the time came and paid it.

So this is what you need to know. If we're going to talk about payments, we need to talk about currency. What I mean is, we need to look at the things you might need to give up in order to get ahead.

MAGIC: PAYING WITH YOUR MIND

When magic came back into the world in 2011 (didn't know about that? Better check the timeline further down) and elves, dwarves, orks, and trolls started scratching and clawing for power alongside humans, it didn't take too long for people to start trying to get a handle on how to use all the new mana floating around for themselves. Turned out some people had a knack for it. While the rest of us were wondering what they were looking at with glazed eyes and weird expressions, they were figuring out how to channel and shape streams of mana—a sort of magic energy that seems to be just about everywhere. Turns out, if you can suss how it's done, you can use mana to set the air on fire, make people do things they'd never do, or other truly esoteric and/or insane things. And mana wasn't just for the spells and stuff we think of as magic. It gave some people the strength to punch through walls, others can shame a cobra with their reflexes, and there are some who can outrun a cheetah; and that's just scratching the surface. And you know all those magic goodies from legends and fairytales and myths? We got 'em all. Enchanted swords, magic rings, wands, amulets, mojo bags, every potion you can think of all exist. Not that they always work the way they did in the stories. Don't just grab the sword of a legendary warrior and expect to slice and dice like she did, for example. But, magic is out there, and people are using it. It's not easy—it can be draining, physically and mentally, and some people push themselves to the point where their sanity drips out of their ears in a nice, steady trickle. That's the price, and it's often gladly paid.

CORPORATIONS: PAYING WITH YOUR SELF

The way corporations work in the Sixth World isn't really anything new. It's just the latest iteration of the might-makes-right way of doing things. There's a lot of legal history we could cover to help you see how things got to this point, but in the end it boils down to one word: extraterritoriality. That's the word that allows corporations to say that whatever happens in their holdings, on the buildings and lands they own, is subject to their laws—and no one else's. Gaining extraterritorial status was a long-held dream of many of the world's largest corporations, and when judicial decisions in nations across the world gave it to them, they spent several years pissing on themselves and each other in utter delirium. Then they figured out their infighting was cutting into their bottom line, so they cut back on fighting each other and concentrated on pissing on the rest of us.

Not every corporation in the world has extraterritorial status. To understand who does, you have to know about the Corporate Court, the body the megacorporations created when they realized they were spending too much time solving their disputes by ravaging entire small countries. The Corporate Court is sometimes mocked as a toothless entity, a puppet of the world's largest megacorps, but its thirteen justices manage—usually—to keep open warfare between the corps from breaking out, and that's at least worth something.

As part of its duties, the Court has created a ranking system to tell you how big and powerful a particular corp is. At the top is the Big Ten, the AAA-rated, corps, the most powerful megacorps in the world. The main thing you need to understand is that these guys are bigger than big. Think of the world's largest manufacturer of computer equipment. Then add in a powerful magic supplies broker. Throw in a few banks, an insurance firm, an entertainment conglomerate, and a snack-food giant, and you're still not a tenth of the way to forming one of the Big Ten. They employ millions and control trillions of nuyen. Each and every one of them owns a piece of land within one hundred kilometers of you, unless you're in the Sahara, the Amazon, or at the bottom of the ocean. And maybe even then. These are the people in the world who have the nuyen, and we want it, which means they

determine what the rules of the game are. We just play it—and see how far those rules can bend.

AUGMENTATIONS: PAYING WITH YOUR SOUL

Every bit of who you are can be improved with the right piece of gear. Think you've got quick reflexes? You can be quicker, thanks to an artificial neural network that'll make you faster than a nervous jackrabbit. Think you're strong? Switch out the muscles you were born with for a set that's been custom-grown for power and efficiency, and you'll take strong to a whole new level. Think you're charming? Implant a set of specialized pheromone dispensers, and people will swoon when you walk by and nod enthusiastically when you talk.

And that's just for starters. You can put actual plates of armor on your skin, or lace your bones with metal so your fists and legs deliver crushing blows. You can make your senses sharper, your brain faster, and you can implant knowledge you never learned in school. (Possibly because you never went to school). You can replace entire pieces of your body with artificial replicas full of extra strength, nimble agility, secret compartments, and hidden weapons that provide very unpleasant surprises at just the right time.

But it's not free. And we're not just talking money; there's a higher price to pay. All this stuff is useful and great, but it's artificial, and your body knows it. Each time you get one of these augmentations, you give up a piece of yourself. You lose something inside of you, the essence of metahumanity. We don't quite understand what "it" is, but we know this much—the more artificial you make yourself, the farther you get from actual life. If you get too far, whatever animated you is going to disappear, until all the gear you bought just collapses and becomes indistinguishable from any other pile of silicon, steel, and chrome. So go ahead and get yourself augmented up, but understand that each time you do this, another piece of your metahumanity slides away.

LIFE IN THE SHADOWS: PAYING WITH YOUR BLOOD

The megacorporations of the world prefer a docile population, a world of people who do whatever work they're told, build anything, carry anything, sacrifice anything for the mega, and then spend all their money in the company store and be glad they got it so good. Sheep. That's how megacorps see metahumanity: a vast herd of sheep they have to keep in line to serve their purposes.

Which means the rest of us face a stark choice: Accept their drek. Or not.

For some of us, corp life is not a life. The megacorps own enough in the world. They don't need to own us. So we drop out and find another way. We do the jobs corps won't parcel out to their regular employees, the things they don't want connected back to them. Espionage work; missions of theft, sabotage, and assault—maybe even assassination, if you swing that way. That's how we survive. We still have to dance to the corporate tune to some degree, but if we live right and build up our skills, we can become the best at what we do and get paid what we deserve. Then, maybe, instead of being one of us, scrambling under the heels of the powerful, we can be one of them, and remake a small part of the world in our image.

But if we're going to survive, we have to find work. There are dozens, hundreds, thousands of jobs out there. You can make money off them, but each one will cost you something. You'll get a scar from a bullet that should have killed you. A leg that aches in the cold 'cause you broke it crashing your motorcycle on one of your less-perfect getaways. A missing arm because you were standing just a bit too close to a bomb going off, and a working cyber model is pricy. A fried brain lobe from lingering in the Matrix a second too long with security closing in on you. And that's just what will happen to your body. You'll be double-crossed, betrayed, and abandoned. You'll see trusted friends turn on you and watch others die right in front of you. You'll have every last bit of you tested in ways you can't imagine just to see how much you can endure.

And if you succeed? If you stay alive? Money, first of all, but more. You become a legend. You join the ranks of the people we tell stories about, the shadowrunners whose names we all know. Dirk Montgomery. FastJack. Sally Tsung. The Smiling Bandit. You'll have lived your own life, survived, and even thrived. You'll have stuck it to every man the Sixth World has to offer.

As long as you can pay the price.

DAYS THAT SHOOK THE WORLD

You know how when you meet some piece-of-drek punk ganger in an alley, and he's all full of mouthy attitudes and sucker punches, and you find yourself thinking how if you looked into that little dirtball's past and learned more about his parents and upbringing, you'd understand how he became such a bastard? Well, our world is a lot like that. I'll give you some of the highlights from the past that made the world into the snot-nosed asshole we all know and barely tolerate.

2001

The infamous Shiawase Decision in the United States Supreme Court gives multinational corporations the same rights and privileges as sovereign governments. The era of national governments as the chief drivers of global events comes to an end.

2002

Realizing they had only been half-heartedly exploiting Native Americans for the past century or so, the U.S. government puts their whole heart back into the job and lets corporations run roughshod over the resources found in Native American reservations during the so-called Resource Rush. This leads to unrest and resistance with serious consequences.

2010

Virally Induced Toxic Allergy Syndrome (VITAS) appears in New Delhi, India. Eventually it kills a quarter of the world's population.

2011

The Awakening, or at least the beginning of it. Dragons appear, people develop talents and abilities that can only be described as magic, babies are born in ways that exactly resemble elves and dwarfs of legend, and the world reveals itself to generally be much weirder than anyone ever suspected.

2018

After the Great Ghost Dance of the previous year, in which Native American shamans spurred natural disasters such as earthquakes and volcanic eruptions across the globe, the United States and Canada agree to the Treaty of Denver, in which large portions of both nations are given to aboriginal populations to become the various states that make up the Native American Nations of the Western Hemisphere.

2021

In a process known as Goblinization, some adults spontaneously mutate into creatures that become known as orks and trolls (a wider range of forms emerge as time passes). People react with fear and loathing, which, after more than half a century, has generally eased to fear and extreme distaste—though some people prefer to stick with loathing. Dwarfs, elves, trolls, orks, and the like are collectively labeled "metahumanity," though sometimes the label is broadened to include all forms of human-like life, including humans themselves, which irks the troll-haters to no end.

2029

The Matrix, the interconnected wonder of the computer world, crashes, and crashes hard. The virus that caused the Crash takes years to eradicate, and the whole dynamic sets the stage for cyberwarfare in the years to come.

2030

After losing a lot of territory to the Native American Nations, the remnants of the United States and Canada merge to form the United Canadian and American States (UCAS). In subsequent years, the Free State of California, the Confederation of American States, and the Caribbean League claim parts of what used to be the United States. This mirrors political fracturing and re-alignment occurring around the world.

2039

The fear and loathing against elves, dwarfs, orks, and trolls (particularly the latter two groups) comes to a head in the Night of Rage, a worldwide series of riots targeting metahumans and their families. The pain and scars inflicted that night still linger, nearly forty years later.

2055

After a cult known as the Universal Brotherhood introduces the vile creepies known as bug spirits to the world, Chicago became the most infested city on the planet. When containment didn't seem to be solving the problem, the Ares Corporation set off a nuke in the city, an event known as the Cermak Blast. The combined infestation of bugs, removal of anything resembling law and order, and destruction levied by the nuke made central Chicago the blasted wonderland it is today.

2057

The citizens of the UCAS collectively throw their hands in the air, say "What the hell?", and elect a dragon named Dunkelzahn as president. Dunkelzahn serves for just under ten and a half hours before being blown to kingdom come. A huge astral rift hovers at the scene of the assassination for years.

2061

Halley's comet passes by and shakes up the world. It initiates the Sudden Unexplained Recessive Genetic Expression (SURGE) event, bringing changelings to the world as some people take on animal characteristics. A new dragon named Ghostwalker emerges from the rift left by Dunkelzahn's assassination and decides to take up residence as the tyrant of Denver. For good measure, increased storms, earthquakes, and volcanic eruptions keep the entire population of the world on their toes.

2064

The combination of a massive corporate IPO, the machinations of a crazed artificial intelligence, and an assault by a terrorist group known as Winternight bring about the Second Matrix Crash, or Crash 2.0. A new Matrix emerges in its wake, bringing wireless accessibility to all. Also emerging: technomancers, who can access the Matrix with nothing more than their mind. This causes many to freak out.

2075

After campaigning for years about the lack of security in the wireless Matrix, activist and philanthropist Danielle de la Mar convinces the corporations of the world to revamp Matrix protocols to be stricter, less open, and more subject to corporate control. Because that was something they really needed to be talked into doing.

2076

A new condition known as cognitive fragmentation disorder (CFD) is spotted, where people suddenly and abruptly completely change their personalities, or become a battleground for warring personalities. A hybrid technological/biological virus is identified as the source, developed by artificial intelligences held captive for megacorporate research as a way to gain freedom for copies of themselves, if not their actual selves.

2077

Spread of the CFD virus continues, with an especially aggressive strain leading to most of Boston being quarantined. While infections finally eased toward the end of the year, the lockdown in Boston remained, and the next step in the AIs' aggression toward humanity is uncertain.

OPPOSITION REPORT

You know there are going to be people trying to stop you from doing the job you've been hired to do—if there weren't, you wouldn't be making nuyen one, because any simpleton could take care of the work. Lots of shadowrunners have ended up dead in an alley somewhere because they underestimated the strength of the opposition, or because they didn't understand all the interests involved in a run, and just who might be coming after them. The next few sections will help you not be like them, telling you about the wide range of people and things that might get in your way as you try to get drek done.

THE BIG TEN

The Big Ten megacorporations of the world control vast amounts of the world's resources and cash, along with employing a large percentage of the planet's population. They make the world keep spinning—and have the power to make it stop in short order. Any runner who lasts for more than a week or two is going to end up working for or against one or more of them, so it's best to know what you're up against. Here's a rundown:

ARES MACROTECHNOLOGY

Corporate Court Ranking (2078): 9
Corporate Slogan: "Making the World a Safer Place"
Corporate Status: AAA, public corporation
World Headquarters: Detroit, UCAS
President/CEO: Damien Knight
You Know Them For: Making your favorite gun, arresting you for using your favorite gun.

Most shadowrunners know Ares from their Ares Arms division, and with good reason. The Ares Predator is the staple sidearm for the discerning runner. Run by wealthy playboy Damien Knight, the corp has a reputation as a very "American" outfit: gung-ho, militaristic, patriotic, and individualistic— Mom and apple pie, in other
words. Don't let that fool you—sure, they're one of the better megas to work shadow ops for, but keep your eyes open, because they can be as underhanded as the

rest. And lately, they have an edge of desperation. The complete failure of the Ares Excalibur gun was the first visible symptom, but as time as past it has become clear that there is a rot at the heart of Area, an ongoing war that is claiming some of their best talent. Whether they will survive this war and regain their swagger or be weakened to the point that their many enemies start tearing them limb from limb is not yet clear.

Ares specializes in law enforcement, military hardware and arms, aerospace (they have five orbital habitats), entertainment, automotive (the former General Motors is also part of the Ares family), and smaller divisions in many other areas. Oh, and they own Knight Errant, one of the largest private law enforcement firms on the planet.

ARES TAGS

• Autos • Big bangs • Bug spirits • Damien Knight
• Detroit • Heavy machinery • Knight Errant
• Space travel • UCAS corp • Weapons

AZTECHNOLOGY

Corporate Court Ranking (2078): 4
Corporate Slogan: "The Way to a Better Tomorrow"
Corporate Status: AAA, private corporation
World Headquarters: Tenochtitlán, Aztlan
President/CEO: Flavia de la Rosa
You Know Them For: Great PR, selling microwave burritos at thousands of worldwide locations. Also, ruthlessness and blood magic, but they keep those under wraps.

If you've bought any kind of consumer goods recently, chances are you've contributed to Aztechnology's bottom line. Sixty percent of the goodies you find at your local Stuffer Shack come from the Big A—and plenty of the material that went into building it came from them, too. They make everything from chemicals to trideo-game software to military goods and magical supplies. They've got their fingers in more pies than just about any other mega, to the point that they essentially own an entire nation, the large bridge between North and South America known as Aztlan. On top of that, their public relations campaigns are second to none. Which is good, because they're also all about blood magic and evil conspiracies. Allegedly. Just don't say anything about that within earshot of the Big A's ferocious legal team.

The corp also has a gift for attracting—or attacking—powerful enemies. From the war they fought against Amazonia to the grudge that Ghostwalker, the tyrant dragon of Denver, has against them, they boast some of the most powerful enemies in the world. Since their enemies can

sling around some pretty serious mojo, Aztechnology's magic research work has focused on how they can outpace anyone and everyone in the magic department. Just don't expect to see headlines about that sort of work, since it's not the sort of thing that's done in the public eye.

AZTECHNOLOGY TAGS

• Aztlan • Blood magic • Central America • Jaguar warriors
• Path of the Sun • PR masters • Stuffer Shack • Teocalli

EVO CORPORATION

Corporate Court Ranking (2078): 7
Corporate Slogan: "Evo Is Acceptance"
Corporate Status: AAA, public corporation
World Headquarters: Vladivostok, Russia
President: Yuri Shibanokuji
You Know Them For: A billion commercials pitying you for not being awesome enough to sport their entire line of enhancements and augmentations

"EVOlve," they say in all their ads. Let's be fair, they are a megacorp that looks to the future. Their CEO is  an ork and their largest stock-holder is a free spirit. They focus a lot on transhumanist projects ranging from bioware cybernetics, anti-aging experiments, and other even more out-there projects designed to take metahumanity to the next stage of evolution. On top of that, they're the first megacorp to successfully set up a base on Mars. Evo leads the megas in goods and services designed with orks, trolls, elves, dwarfs, changelings, and other non-human people in mind. Their corporate culture is pretty touchy-feely, but don't freak—they can be as cold and calculating as any other mega. As one of the two corps conducting research on artificial intelligences that eventually led to the CFD outbreak, Evo is facing anger from the rest of the world, including their AAA peers, making their current work treacherous. The recent death of their CEO Anatoly Kirilenko at the hands of shadowrunners shows just how treacherous it can be.

EVO TAGS

• Acceptance • Augmentations
• Buttercup (free spirit shareholder) • CrashCart • EVOlution
• Monads • Russia • Transhumanism • Vladivostok

HORIZON GROUP

Corporate Court Ranking (2078): 10
Corporate Slogan: "We Know What You Think"
Corporate Status: AAA, private corporation

World Headquarters: Los Angeles, PCC
President/CEO: Gary Cline
You Know Them For: Your favorite trid shows, your favorite music, and your favorite off-book bunraku parlors offering the services of people who look like your favorite performers.

Horizon is based in the midst of media wonderland Los Angeles, and they've managed to score many exclusive contracts for dealing with the development of California. With charismatic ex-simstar Gary Cline at the helm, Horizon specializes in anything that can be used to manipulate opinion (media, advertising, entertainment, social networking, etc.), along with consumer goods and services, real estate and development, and pharmaceuticals. Its corporate culture is "people-centered," and employees are well taken care of and encouraged to develop their talents and pursue their interests on company time—as long as the corp reaps the profits. They had been renowned as being technomancer friendly, but a series of events culminating in a massacre in Las Vegas helped people understand that even the nicest of megacorps can spin out of control. They have redesigned the complicated software called the Consensus that helps them shape their decision-making process, with the hope they will not go so far astray again. Seeing weakness in two of their peers due to the CFD crisis, they are leading a PR charge that they hope will boost their standing in the Big Ten.

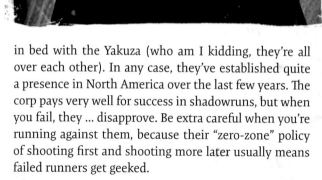

HORIZON TAGS

- Big data • Charisma Associates • Consensus
- Entertainment • Gary Cline • Livestreaming • Los Angeles
- Public relations • UCAS corp • Technomancer massacre

MITSUHAMA COMPUTER TECHNOLOGIES

Corporate Court Ranking (2078): 1
Corporate Slogan: "The Future Is Mitsuhama"
Corporate Status: AAA, public corporation
World Headquarters: Kyoto, Japanese Imperial State
President/CEO: Toshiro Mitsuhama
You Know Them For: The cold feeling of fear in your heart whenever you hear the words "Mitsuhama Zero-Zone."

This Japanacorp is basking in the glory of rising up to the spot of largest corporation in all the world, and they're not looking to slow down. The common perception is that they're all about the computers. Robotics, heavy industry, you name it—but it's less well known that they're one of the biggest manufacturers of magical goods around. There's a rumor going around that they're

MITSUHAMA

in bed with the Yakuza (who am I kidding, they're all over each other). In any case, they've established quite a presence in North America over the last few years. The corp pays very well for success in shadowruns, but when you fail, they … disapprove. Be extra careful when you're running against them, because their "zero-zone" policy of shooting first and shooting more later usually means failed runners get geeked.

MITSUHAMA TAGS

- Aggressive acquisition • Honor and respect • Electronics
- Japanacorp • Magic • Parashield • Technomancer research
- World's largest corp • Yakuza • Zero-Zone

NEONET

Corporate Court Ranking (2078): 8
Corporate Slogan: "Tomorrow Runs on NeoNET"
Corporate Status: AAA, public corporation
World Headquarters: Boston, UCAS
CEO: Richard Villiers
You Know Them For: Rising and falling more times than a phoenix.

Richard Villiers has helmed two previous corps that made their way to AAA

N·E·O·N·E·T

status, and twice he rescued them from possible collapse and re-invented them into something new. The question now is whether he can pull off the same trick a third time, as NeoNET seems to be teetering on the brink of disaster. If there is a spot between "reeling" and "free-falling," that is where NeoNET resides. Along with Evo, the corp is taking the blame for the CFD virus, and unlike Evo they have not been able to adapt to the challenges they are facing. With many key personnel and facilities lost in the Boston quarantine, NeoNET is bleeding, and plenty of megacorporate sharks are looking to feed on them. How or if they survive is an open question. They are not without resources, though—NeoNET is the primary power behind the Grid Overwatch Division, and they practically invented the wireless Matrix. Needless to say, they're heavily invested in Matrix infrastructure, along with cyberware, electronics, software, biotech, aerospace, small arms, and many other areas. To survive, NeoNET will have to draw on these strengths and unite a sometimes-divided corporation, which has major factions controlled by a long-time corporate raider, a reclusive dwarf, and the great dragon Celedyr. Runs for or against NeoNET are a grab-bag, now more than ever. Randomness can be fun, until that time you end up reaching in the bag and pulling out a scorpion.

NEONET TAGS

- AI research • Boston quarantine • Celedyr (great dragon)
- CFD • Miles Lanier • Richard Villiers
- Survival and adaptability • Wounded and desperate

RENRAKU COMPUTER SYSTEMS

Corporate Court Ranking (2078): 3
Corporate Slogan: "Today's Solutions to Today's Problems"
Corporate Status: AAA, public corporation
World Headquarters: Chiba, Japanese Imperial State
CEO: Inazo Aneki (Honorary)
You Know Them For: That big, flat-topped pyramid in Downtown Seattle that sends a chill through your heart every time you see it. Also, computers.

The revamped Matrix and the troubles of other members of the Big Ten have helped Renraku shake off the torpor of recent years and put itself on aggressive footing. Partnering effectively with its fellow Japanacorps, Renraku is looking to gain market share anywhere and everywhere, using as much ruthlessness as it takes to climb up the corporate ranks.

Renraku controls the world's largest data repository, and they own almost all of Asia's local grids. And when nobody knows what kind of useful (or incriminating) information you've got squirreled away in your datastores, it's going to take some strong motivation to risk messing with you. They've got a seriously traditional Japanese culture, and their Red Samurai military units are universally feared. Not respected, feared.

RENRAKU TAGS

- Anti-metahuman history • Business services
- Electronics • Loyalty • Japanacorp • Red Samurai
- Retail and wholesale • Tradition

SAEDER-KRUPP HEAVY INDUSTRIES

Corporate Court Ranking (2078): 2
Corporate Slogan: "One Step Ahead"
Corporate Status: AAA, private corporation
World Headquarters: Essen, Allied German States
President/CEO: Lofwyr
You Know Them For: Perhaps being single-handedly responsible for the adage: "Never cut a deal with a dragon."

Saeder-Krupp Heavy Industries can be summed up in one word: Lofwyr. The great dragon owns nearly one hundred percent of this German-based megacorp, and he rules it with the kind of attention to detail that only one of his kind can maintain. It's not impossible to put one over on Lofwyr, but it's very difficult—and usually fatal. The wyrm doesn't suffer fools gladly, and shadowrunners who go against him (or fail in one of his jobs) might just find themselves on his list—which is probably also his lunch menu.

If anyone in S-K is lacking for motivation these days, all they have to do is look at their Corporate Court ranking. That number two next to their name burns cold fire in their hearts, building a steely determination to reclaim the top spot they held for so long. They have plenty of areas in which to try to regain market share. Their primary areas of focus are heavy industry, chemicals, finance, and aerospace, but they have at least one finger in every pie the world has to offer, and they are extremely anxious to start cutting themselves larger pieces.

SAEDER-KRUPP TAGS

- Aetherlink • Allied German States • Cybernetics
- Hans Brackhaus • Heavy industry • Lofwyr
- New European Economic Commission • S-K swagger

SHIAWASE CORPORATION

Corporate Court Ranking (2078): 5
Corporate Slogan: "Advancing Life"
Corporate Status: AAA, public corporation

апtop草

World Headquarters: Osaka, Japanese Imperial State
President/CEO: Korin Yamana
You Know Them For: Their desperate attempt to get as cozy with the Japanese Imperial State as Aztechnology is with Aztlan.

The oldest of the megas, Shiawase was the first corp to claim extraterritorial status. A classic Japanese zaibatsu, Shiawase is run in a traditional "family" style, with most employees signing lifetime contracts and even marrying within the corp. Families, however, tend to squabble, and plenty of runners have made good cash in the course of these quarrels. As for what they do, what don't they do? Either directly or through subsidiaries, Shiawase has its hands in nuclear power, environmental engineering, biotech, heavy industry, technical service, minerals, military goods, and a whole lot more. They also sell lots of medkits to shadowrunners, which means they sometimes see shooting runners as a business investment, because every hit may mean another kit sold.

SHIAWASE

SHIAWASE TAGS

• Agriculture • Envirotech • Honor • Imperial connections • Japanacorp • Market Information and Forecasting Department • Sensei Snacks vending machines • Sokaiya

WUXING INCORPORATED

Corporate Court Ranking (2078): 6
Corporate Slogan: "We're Behind Everything You Do"
Corporate Status: AAA, public corporation
World Headquarters: Hong Kong, Free Enterprise Enclave
President: Wu Lung-Wei
You Know Them For: Making you move several times during your meetings so you don't mess up the feng shui of that particular room.

The only Chinese player on the megacorp scene, Wuxing owns a sizeable chunk of the Pacific rim. The corporation is quiet and conservative, the stealthiest of the Big Ten. Their employees are steeped in Chinese culture, even those who've never been within a thousand clicks of Asia. Traditionally focused on finance and shipping concerns, Wuxing also specializes in magical services and goods, vying for the top spot of most mystic megacorp. Wuxing has also expanded heavily into other markets, including agriculture, engineering, consumer goods, and chemicals.

WUXING

WUXING TAGS

• Arcane experts • Feng shui • Finance • Hong Kong • Mana flow • Shipping • Wu quintuplets • Weapons

ORGANIZED CRIME

A lot of shadowrunners will tell you the only real difference between what we do and organized crime is the organized part. There's some truth in that. Shadowrunners have occasionally formed organizations, like the legendary Assets, Inc., but as a rule it's not something we do. People like us, we don't take orders well. We don't like to share with anyone outside of our team (or often inside it, for that matter), not to mention the fact that regimentation, hierarchical organization, and all that lock-step discipline are pretty much poison to us. Organized crime, on the other hand, thrives on that stuff. Organized crime does the things large numbers of people do well: deals narcotics and other addictives; runs protection rackets; operates gambling rings—just about anything that requires an army and turns a profit. This means organized crime can often be found deeply entwined with legitimate, respected businesses. In some cases, it's hard to tell where the crime ends and the business begins.

Despite their violent reputations, the organizations that make up organized crime eschew pyrotechnics whenever possible. Firefights bring police attention and could result in important people getting killed or otherwise indisposed. As a general rule, the work they do goes better when no one is looking, so they put a lot of effort into keeping a low profile. But don't be confused—and don't get stupid. Just because they'd rather keep their guns holstered and the money flowing, don't think for a minute they won't get down and dirty when they need to.

The **Mafia** is an extensive and significant presence in every major North American city, most European cities, and a lot of cities everywhere else. They like cities. They usually don't work closely with the megacorporations because, let's face it, they *are* a megacorporation. The main difference between the recognized corps and the Mafia is that when there's infighting between Mafia's divisions, it's slightly more likely to involve high body counts.

The **Yakuza**, by contrast, have tied their fortunes to Mitsuhama Computer Technologies. This is not to say that every Yakuza rengo has a connection to Mitsuhama—they don't, and some rengos fight tooth and nail against those who do. But the Yakuza and MCT are inextricably tied together. As in four high-ranking Yakuza between them own about forty-five percent of the megacorporation. Mitsuhama uses Yakuza foot soldiers to do their dirty work, while the Yakuza uses MCT as the greatest money-laundering organization the world has ever seen. The corporate association gives the Yakuza a ruthless efficiency; anyone who deals with them watches their manners.

The **Triads** have their origins in what used to be China and differ from the other major crime networks in that they are decentralized—they have no central leadership, no supreme commander or high council or arbitration committee. This can mean a whole new set of protocols when you move from one Triad's turf to another; what kept you alive in one place might kill you in the next. Their lack of central leadership means conflict resolution within the Triads is often bloody and brutal—though they are capable of considerable restraint and finesse if the situation calls for it. The lack of central control also makes them more flexible in adapting to—and taking over—new territories. If they ever got over their cultural prejudice against women in authority and non-human metatypes in general, they'd own a lot bigger piece of the pie. The Triads have the usual gambling, drugs, and prostitution operations, but their specialty is Awakened drugs. For some reason the Triads attract a disproportionate percentage of mages, which makes them very efficient at finding, testing, and preparing the drugs with the best street value.

Remember when I told you organized crime liked to keep a low profile, avoid the spotlight, and keep attention off itself? I was not talking about the Russian **Vory v Zakone**. They can't match the money and manpower of the other major syndicates, so their primary public relations tool is intimidation. Their go-to negotiation technique is blunt brutality; the first indication the Vory have entered a new area is usually the bodies of criminals who thought it was their turf. The Vory want to shake things up, and they hit every confrontation at a full charge, loud and raging. It doesn't always work, but I'll tell you this—no one ever likes to see these guys coming.

In the Hopi tradition, Koshare is the spirit of overdo- ing things—gluttonous, disruptive, and irreverent, the uni- versal cautionary example. Koshare does all the things people should not do, illustrating why they should never do them. Which is why the network of Native American organized crime rings call themselves the **Koshari**. They do all the things you would expect an organized crime outfit to do, but they're especially skilled at talislegging, the illicit smuggling of magical reagents and telesma. If you're a t-bird pilot in the western half of North America, depending on the impression you make on the Koshari, you'll either be recruited, warned off their territory, or shut down hard.

GANGS

We don't have the room or the time to fill you in on all the gangs that are banging around whatever sprawl you're sitting in right now. Small places seem to get by with just one gang, but get much over two thousand locals and you're probably going to have two or more

GANGS TO KNOW ABOUT

Gangs vary from sprawl to sprawl, but there are four notable names to watch out for, since they can be major obstacles—or, if you're lucky and/or persuasive, useful tools.

The **Ancients**, as mentioned in the main text, is an all-elf gang of surprising resources and sophistication. Militaristic in structure as well as fighting strength, they are not a group that should be crossed, especially by orks.

The Awakened rainforest of South America is a prime source of new-wave drugs, and **Comando Verde** has assumed the role of bringing those drugs to the world. They are not well organized but they are legion, and if you are in a poverty-stricken area of a city where they are influential, beware of the death by a thousand cuts.

The **Cutters** are like one of those corporations that grew to a behemoth, only instead of hard work and ingenuity, they succeeded with sociopathy and improvised blades. They have a board of directors, high-ranking executives, and everything, along with tremendous access to a whole rainbow of illicit goods and a legion of knife-wielding goons to protect it.

While they're not as large as the others on this list, the **Halloweeners** are notable for the sheer chaos they create. Their ruthlessness is not focused on building a narcotics-based empire or anything like it—they just want to watch the world burn. Or more to the point, they want to set it on fire. Their garish costumes and attention-grabbing attacks help them appear larger and more powerful than their actual numbers.

gangs. Over a million locals, and you're talking a healthy gang network. You should take the time to figure out that network—doing one gang's work on another's turf is more likely to get you killed if you don't know that's what you're doing.

There are two types of gangs, and by and large as a runner you're most likely to come across versions of both types pretty regularly. **Street gangs** are all about territory. A few broken blocks, a handful of abandoned buildings, the streets around their favorite dive, fifteen different piles of brick, a neighborhood, you name it. Whatever they've got, it's theirs. They don't always know what to do with it—maybe deal minor drugs or run half-assed protection rackets—but they'll defend it against all comers. Which usually means hanging out and challenging anyone they don't know to a fight. There are street gangs that aren't all about the territory. Some gangs are racially based, like Seattle's elf-only Ancients; some are bound together by a common interest, like the Halloweeners, who dress up like ghouls to terrify and assault civilians unfortunate enough to cross their path. As a general rule, gangers are young, raw, untrained, unpredictable, quick-tempered, and eager to mix things up. So yeah, if the needs of whatever job you're on do not require you to deal with them, avoid gangs. Unless you think your evening would be much improved by a fistfight.

What street gangs do to a collection of sprawl blocks, **go-gangs** do to highways. Riding around on souped-up cycles and choppers, these gang members look for any driver who shows a milligram of fear. The least hesitation, such as looking like you're thinking things over, can trigger an attack. This could be a ram, or it could be a game of head-on chicken against a foe with a sawed-off shotgun propped on his handlebar. There's no point to their attacks—the attack *is* the point. They are random, indiscriminate, and leap to violence the way a frog leaps to water. Know where the go-gangs in whatever sprawl you're in and avoid them.

THE LAW

The most annoying thing local politicos can do is sic local law enforcement on you, because local ain't local anymore. Back in the day, law enforcement was a tangle of local, state, and federal authorities doing their own things—barely talking to one another and almost never sharing data. Oh sure, if you were a serial killer they'd spread the word and be on the lookout, but if you were a burglar or practiced any other illegal trade, you could pretty much move from one jurisdiction to the next and get a fresh start with no one being the wiser.

These days things are both worse and better. The bad part is most sprawls save their limited budgets by privatizing law enforcement—which means cops are corps. The two big boys are Lone Star, an independent corp that boasts about its tradition of no-holds-barred Texas justice (i.e., brutality), and Knight Errant, a division of Ares Macrotechnology. These two compete for big-ticket contracts; Knight Errant recently wrestled the plum of Seattle from Lone Star's hands. Other major security providers include Sakura Security, which has a large presence in Japan, German security giant Sternschutz, France's Esprit Industries (a subsidiary of Aztechnology), and Mitsuhama's one-two punch of Parashield and Petrovski Security. These companies have international reach, and their centralized databases are everywhere they are; do something in one jurisdiction and all the others know about it. So stay out of the database. Give them nothing—your name, your picture, your favorite make of whiskey, anything—because some smart cop, or smarter program, can use that anything to finger you. The good part is that while law-enforcement corps share all data internally, it's in their best interest to make their rivals look as inept as possible—which means they never tell each other anything. So as long as you know who's covering what turf, you can still find cracks to fall into.

But don't get cocky. Law-enforcement contracts can change hands in a blink; what's Knight Errant territory one day may be Lone Star the next. Meaning you may be an unknown free agent one day and an actively sought fugitive the next. And be aware that many sprawls have multiple security companies in their borders—Knight Errant may have the city contract while Lone Star covers residential or maybe corporate compounds. Make sure you know who's patrolling which streets when, and who might be looking for you.

POLITICOS

Politicians may not have the clout they did back in the day, but there are still taxes to be collected, laws to enforce, infrastructure to be maintained, and careers to be made. Most government crap goes on way over your head. You don't need to worry about who's president or king of whatever nation you're in and almost all state and regional objectives require resources and man-power beyond any runner team's inventory. What you want are the local officials—mayors, aldermen, trustees, that sort of thing—who enforce the laws, collect the taxes, fund emergency and rescue services, and try to ensure everything works. These local leaders may not be as powerful as the corps, but as long as you're on their turf, they've got a lot of ways to help you or hinder you. Good news is they're far enough down the food chain that there's a chance you can afford whatever it takes to buy their momentary cooperation. They're easier to blackmail, too. Ask around, look around, figure out whom you need to know and what you need to know about them—you never know when you're going to need them.

Besides the actual politicians, the other people you need to know about are the policlubs. If there is any cause in the Sixth World that two or more people can agree on, they'll form a policlub around it. Sometimes the point of the club is to, you know, actually participate in politics. Other times the clubs are a cover for illegal activities, and a lot of them are just an excuse for people to get together and get wasted. Most of these groups wield no discernible power; you can pretty much ignore them. There are a few you should pay attention to.

One is the **Humanis Policlub**. Elves, dwarfs, trolls, and orks have been in the world for more than five decades, but for some people that hasn't been long enough to get used to the idea or to like having them around. Especially the orks and trolls. Following the proud tradition of racist groups since the dawn of time, Humanis is dedicated to putting a friendly face on hate. They're not against anyone, they'll tell you, they're just pro-human. They don't want to take anything away from the other metatypes, they just want to make sure humans get their fair share (which is pretty much everything).

MAJOR POWERS

Nation-states aren't the major powers in the world anymore, but they're not entirely without power, either, so they keep popping their heads up and causing problems for shadowrunners. At the very least, they have borders that they tend to watch, and at the most, they play power games with elections and legislation that lead to plenty of extralegal action.

The **United Canadian and American States** do not dominate the globe like the former United States once did, but they still have enough wealth and military might to make people pay attention when they flex their muscles. Thanks to international gerrymandering, the major sprawl of Seattle is part of the UCAS, contributing a lot of economic heft—and a good supply of shadowrunning talent.

Just to the south of the bulk of the UCAS is the **Confederation of American States**. Sometimes people feel like the CAS can be ignored as the lesser younger sibling of the UCAS, but it has the right combination of wealth, spunk, and long-held grudges to rise up and get attention when it wants to.

The western portion of North America is dominated by the Native American Nations, including the **Sioux Nation** in the heart of the continent, the **Salish-Shidhe Council** to the northwest, and the **Pueblo Corporate Council** in the southwest. These nations do not always share a common interest, but they are capable of working together often enough to keep nearby nations nervous.

Central America is dominated by the nation of **Aztlan**, which nicely connects North and South America. The nation is essentially a subsidiary of Aztechnology, serving as a breadbasket and labor-generating machine to help the corp move forward.

The largest nation in South America is **Amazonia**, ruled by the dragon Hualpa. With severe restrictions on corporations and a respect for nature, Amazonia is seen as a paradise by some, but its shadows run as deep as those of any other nation.

In Europe, the **Allied German States** are an economic powerhouse, thanks in large part to the overwhelming strength of Saeder-Krupp. The nation is also home to the Free City of Berlin, a hotspot of new-anarchist and anti-corporate activity.

While the AGS has one megacorp, the **Japanese Imperial State** has three, including the newly anointed largest megacorp in the world. With the three megacorps working together outside of Japan's borders, the strength of the nation touches every part of the world.

In Africa, **Kenya** has gained significant strength thanks to the Kilimanjaro Mass Driver and the corporate interest surrounding it. The ghoul kingdom of **Asamando** has gained a different sort of strength, serving as one of the few places where the Infected are welcomed and recognized as citizens.

Humanis serves as a nexus for a whole range of like-minded groups, from the unpleasant and aggressive **Alamos 20,000** to the ultra-violent **Hand of Five**. If you're a non-human, if you like a non-human, or if you're going to be traveling anywhere non-humans are going to be, you need to be aware of what Humanis and its ilk are up to. They could pop in and mess things up at any time. Be warned.

The whole Newtonian thing about action causing reaction works with people, just like it does in physics. There are some notable pro-metahuman groups, from powerful lobbyists and organizers of the **Ork Rights Commission** to the radical and violence-prone **Sons of Sauron**. Like the anti-meta groups, these organizations are capable of causing distractions or chaos wherever you may be. And if you get pro-meta and anti-meta groups in the same place at the same time—well, I hope your contingency plans can deal with random explosions and scattered bodies.

In addition to racists of various flavors, you also need to keep an eye out for the various iterations of neo-anarchist policlubs. Sometimes they go by that name, just with capitals ("Neo-Anarchist"); but depending on the location and the situation they might call themselves the **Panopticans** or the **Lambeth Martyrs** or the **People's Party** or anything that sounds symbolic, sincere, and all about the little guy. Individual groups under the neo-anarchist policlub banner come in a variety of flavors. Some are wild-eyed bomb throwers who think everything should be reduced to rubble before trying to build something new; some think everything should be reduced to rubble and nothing built; some are earnest reformers, working within existing systems; some want to change how nations work; some want an end to all nations; some like coffee; some like tea. What unites these disparate agendas and the people who love them is a to-the-core distrust of centralized power in all its forms and wiles. We're talking both megacorps and big government. They're all about individuals controlling their own lives, and families and communities living the way they want to live. That is enough to make them radicals in the eyes of anybody with any authority. They are outsiders, often criminalized by the people in power. Just like us. Which makes them natural allies—provided you have a high tolerance for rhetoric.

MAGICAL GROUPS

Only a small percentage of the world's population has Awakened with magic talent, and it's an even smaller group that has the kind of ability that can really make an impact. This is good and bad for spellcasters and adepts. The good news is that they generally are in demand and can find a wide variety of work options. The bad news is that, as carriers of significant and unpredictable power, the Awakened are sought after by the powers of the

world in an effort to gain some control over their talents—or make sure they eliminate the competition. It's tough to survive in a world where there seem to be a hundred reasons for people to geek the mage first.

Magicians, then, band together for a lot of reasons—shared research on spells, conversation about common areas of interest, protection, information on powerful magical reagents and artifacts, and so on. Belonging to one of these groups can bring big benefits, but running into one of them in the course of a run can cause big headaches.

One of the two largest magic-focused organizations in the world is the **Draco Foundation**, the organization started by the late dragon Dunkelzahn's estate to execute his will and carry out his wishes. These wishes included bequests related to the disposition obscure magical artifacts and the creation of the Dunkelzahn Institute of Magical Research. The foundation has become a tremendous repository of knowledge, full of the type of people who are so dedicated to the pursuit of knowledge that they sometimes are blind to other concerns, including the well-being of people who are not them.

The second large magical organization is the **Atlantean Foundation**. It's older than the Draco Foundation and a bit more eccentric, with its belief that all magic in the Sixth World ties back to the ancient vanished civilization of Atlantis. While there is some competitiveness between the two foundations, the Atlantean Foundation received five billion nuyen from Dunkelzahn's will, which helps keep things from getting too hostile. If you're in the business of digging into rare artifacts or other strange magic, know that one or both of these organizations might be on your tail, offering stiff competition.

Shadowrunners know that spellslingers and adepts sometimes let their powers go to their head, and no organization reflects this more than the **Illuminates of the New Dawn**. They believe magic and those who wield it can lead metahumanity into a better future, and they are very persistent in working to make that future happen. From running for public office to recovering artifacts that might help them build their power, they are a very active and energetic. They are smaller than the two foundations, but the magic power and financial resources of the leader means they remain a force to be reckoned with.

On the darker side is Ordo Maximus. They appear to be a group of wealthy people, mostly in Europe, who share magic research and look for ways to build their power. Not exactly a humanitarian organization, but also not vastly different than most organizations on the planet. What makes them worse is the small group of vampires at the core of the group. Most people don't know about those Infected members, but those who do worry severely about vampires gaining and extending their powers.

LIFE IN THE SIXTH WORLD

The world you live in may not be pleasant, but it's still the one you wake up in each morning, and it's where you need to figure out how to live your life. Here are some of the keys to surviving, and even occasionally enjoying, those waking hours.

THE MATRIX

When you want to amuse yourself in your downtime, this is where you start. Music's on there, movies are on there, sports broadcasts, virtual nightclubs, chat rooms, epic battles on twisted landscapes, and so on and so forth.

The Matrix is around most of us every minute of every day, so much that we don't think about it much. We just use it. Most of the time we use it as augmented reality (AR), an overlay that adds information and occasional glitz to the world around us in the form of augmented reality objects, or AROs. You can also go whole-hog and dive into virtual reality (VR), leaving your meat body behind for a trip into the realm of pure information. While the speed of VR is convenient for hackers, most people like the ability to use the Matrix while carrying on with their lives at the same time.

With AR, the Matrix is constantly around you. As long as you've got the right gear, messages from friends pop up as floating windows hovering in your field of vision, moving as you move. Stores you walk by tell you about their current sales customized to your preferences. Music and video samples are everywhere, waiting for you to open them with a quick gesture to see if there's anything you like.

How do these music and movies match up to your taste, and how do they know where to find you? The magic of corporate control. You see, the Matrix has gone through two major Crashes, and been re-invented after each one. After the second one, back in 2064, the Matrix made the leap to wireless, and along with that it moved into a neo-anarchist ideal of freedom and openness, a network open and accessible to anyone with the tools to log on. That lasted a good decade until the corps realized there was a resource out there they weren't exploiting. After confessing that sin to their respective clergy and saying a few Hail Marys, the corps went about setting that mistake right, instituting more controls over the Matrix so that they can better shape what goes where. Naturally, their best customers get the best bandwidth, while the less resource-endowed are left to deal with spotty access and slow traffic.

Unless we know how to play the game. The clampdown of corporate control has re-ignited the battle between hackers and the overseers of the Matrix, as shadowrunners look to exploit the weaknesses of the new system and stay one step ahead of security. With the Matrix being almost entirely cloud-based, storage is vast and information is everywhere, but that doesn't mean it's easy to find. Exclusive, protected hosts keep unwanted visitors out and carefully watch those who are there, and the agents of the Corporate Court's Grid Overwatch Division are everywhere. If you want to try something illicit on the Matrix, remember that GOD is watching.

But that's mostly another topic. For now, just know that everyone and everything is on the Matrix, but the easiest things to find are the things programmers are betting you want to buy.

MATRIX MUSTS

You don't log on to the Matrix—you live on it. It's there all the time, woven into everything you do. But there are some things that are more effective and interesting to do than others—here's a couple.

Watching **sports** on the Matrix is a completely immersive experience. Sure, you can just watch the trid like it's some old flatvid or something, but you can also get right into the game, placing yourself on the field with AR players all around, seeing what they see, watching plays unfold around you, hearing the crowd cheer like it's cheering for you. It finally makes you feel justified when you use "we" when talking about your favorite team. This can be particularly intense when watching sports like urban brawl (a kind of ultra-violent, city-based capture the flag) and you walk into an ambush the same time your favorite player does.

Clubbing options abound in the Sixth World thanks to the Matrix, as your can virtually attend any nightclub in the world—provided, of course, you can get access to some of the private hosts. Dante's Inferno in Seattle has long been popular, but it has become even more so thanks to the international clientele that visits nicely and moves to the best of the hottest acts in town.

For general knowledge, **Aetherpedia** is a must. It may not always be definitive, but the speed of updates makes up for that. If you need some background about some part of the world, check there first—just remember that it's a first step to finding more info, not a comprehensive compendium of all knowledge.

GETTING AROUND

One thing you need to always remember in the Sixth World—after "Everything has a price"—is corporations love predictability and live to control. Take GridGuide, marketed as the ultimate convenience for the commuter. It's a programmed control system for your personal vehicle that takes you where you want to go with little input from you, the driver. And by golly, traffic flows more smoothly when everyone uses GridGuide and you can do other things while you drive, so it's great. Of course, GridGuide only works where the corps want it to work, which is fine for corporate drones on their daily commutes, but no good at all if you need to go into the barrens or a not-generally-open-to-the-public industrial area. And even if you're in approved areas, GridGuide doesn't respond well to emergencies, like evasive maneuvers or quick getaways. In fact, if you try to do anything GridGuide doesn't think is wise or safe, the system is going to drag you down. (But doesn't it always?) If you ever intend to go off the beaten path, or to maybe do something out of the ordinary, you're going to need to learn how to drive, and you need to have a vehicle that does not depend on the power of the grid.

If you're traveling from city to city or country to country, you can rely on your personal vehicle, but there are other modes of transportation available. Trains and buses are available in most sprawls, and they can take you from sprawl to sprawl. The security in intra-city transit is pretty light; if you have the nuyen, you can ride. You may need to pass through security, and your SIN will be checked for longer trips, but on trains the scanners are cheap and easily fooled. Plus, you get to ride a bullet train, which tends to be awesome. If they remembered to clean it.

If you opt for air travel, you've got three choices: regular, suborbital, and semiballistic.

Semiballistic is the fastest and the most expensive; it can get you from Europe to North America in less than an hour, and you'll pay through the nose for the privilege. Security is tight. SIN scanners are top-of-the-line and nearly impossible to fool. All weapons will be checked (don't even think about explosives), and all cyberware must be deactivated.

Sub-orbitals are slightly slower, slightly cheaper, and slightly easier to infiltrate. Slightly. Sub-orbital passengers are usually megacorporate clients, and the corps want them to feel safe. Security is tight, and violations will be dealt with harshly.

Regular air travel is for regular people. Security is present, but quality varies from provider to provider; if your fake SIN and forged documentation are good enough, you should do fine.

Of course, if you want to avoid public transportation altogether, there are ways to get around. Hitch a ride in the back of a cargo van, or in a container ship, or as part of a drone convoy. And then there's the almighty t-bird, the favorite choice of smugglers, spies, and anyone else involved in illicit border crossings. There are several different types of t-birds, but they have a few common characteristics: they're small, maneuverable, capable of landing in tight spots, and able to fly low to avoid radar. Learn how to pilot one of these babies well, and you'll never lack for work. Or anti-aircraft fire from folks you've pissed off.

THE REST OF LIFE

PAYING YOUR WAY

If you live in a civilized part of the world, you likely have not ever held actual cash in your hand. Money is transferred between bank accounts (usually in the form of nuyen, which is the world's leading currency) to settle debts; on those occasions when people want to severely limit access to their accounts, they use credsticks, small pieces of plastic with a specified amount of nuyen encoded on them. That's how you pay for things; if you use cash, you're either in some backwater part of the world without Matrix access, or you're a time traveler from the distant past.

While the nuyen is the most common currency in the world, some nations have their own currency, though they generally use the nuyen alongside it. Larger corporations, including the Big Ten, also have their own corporate scrip, which can only be used in their holdings. Corps love paying in scrip, as it means the money they put out will eventually come back to them, but shadowrunners hate it, as no one wants their spending options limited.

ENTERTAINMENT

The Matrix is a lot of things, but to most of the general populace, it's the greatest anti-boredom measure ever developed. The vast amounts of trideo streams, music, games, and what-not available on the Matrix could distract any individual for several lifetimes. Comedies like the Cree & Dido series, fantasy adventure like Neil the Ork Barbarian, action like the Water Margin series, classic music from Concrete Dreams and Maria Mercurial, new music from Christy Daee and CrimeTime—all that is out there, and more. There is a constant war between corporations trying to find ways to wring more money out of the Matrix and consumers trying to get as much as they can for free. With the new, more controlled Matrix, the corps have gotten the upper hand in this battle, but there is still enough free or low-cost entertainment to keep the public sufficiently anesthetized.

FOOD

Soy. The food scene is about soy. The different textures and tastes it can be given have turned out to be quite wide-ranging, which is good, because soy is all most of us can afford. Actual meat is an expensive luxury, so when the masses need something that has both texture and protein, we eat soy. It's omnipresent, even in our pick-me-up beverages, as soykaf is much more commonly available than genuine coffee. It's not bad, especially since most of us have never experienced the real alternative.

RULES OF THE STREET

Gameplay in *Shadowrun: Anarchy* revolves around two things (besides leaping into bad craziness for a handful of nuyen, which in *Shadowrun* is a given): *Building the Story* and *Rolling Dice*. But first, let's talk about some of the important things you'll need to be ready for the game.

Note: For ease of reference, important terms will be bolded when they are first detailed to make them easy to find. Additionally, the rules may reference the "Cue System." This is a general name for this unique rules system, while "*Shadowrun: Anarchy*" or "*Anarchy*" represents this entire volume, meaning the Cue System rules with the *Shadowrun: Anarchy* twist, or liquid *Shadowrun: Anarchy* poured over the rocks of the Cue System. Choose whichever drink-based analogy suits you.

DICE

As noted in the **Introduction**, *Shadowrun: Anarchy* uses six-sided dice; anytime "D" is used, as in "D6," it's shorthand for "die" or "dice," so 4D6 means 4 six-sided dice. Rolled dice are scored individually instead of being added together. *Shadowrun: Anarchy*, like regular *Shadowrun*, uses six-sided dice pretty much exclusively.

BEFORE THE GAME BEGINS

Here are some of the basic things, besides dice, that you will need to make a game of *Shadowrun: Anarchy* work.

CHOOSE OR CREATE A CHARACTER

Each **Character Sheet** (starting on p. 74) consists of an illustration and all the pertinent information for a *Shadowrun: Anarchy* character. To make sure you choose a character you'll like, you'll have to understand the different parts of a sheet. For an in-depth look at Character Sheets, see p. 29.

NOTE

Players can easily grab a character sheet and leap into action based on the name of a character, their Tags and Cues, or even just the artwork. But it can help to know how the game is going to work, and what you are going to be wielding when it's time to throw down. If you want that info, check out the **Rolling Dice** portion of this section (p. 37) before selecting their character sheets.

DESIGNATE A GAMEMASTER

In most tabletop roleplaying games, there is someone in charge—in this game, it's a **gamemaster** (GM). This person acts as the mastermind behind the game, creating the plots and stories the players will interact with.

The GM is in charge of establishing the setting and running the game world the players interact with, but they do not have the sole responsibility for introducing story elements and moving them forward. In *Shadowrun: Anarchy*, storytelling is a shared experience. Players apply their creativity to a variety of story elements, not just their characters' actions. They work with the GM

to build something entertaining and fun for everyone involved. This means that the GM's job is more about facilitating the story—keeping it moving and giving the players what they need to make the story fun—than it is about controlling it. See *Building the Story* on p. **35** for more information on how this works.

SELECT A CONTRACT BRIEF

On the mean streets of the Sixth World, there's no such thing as a typical shadowrun. Whether a Mr. Johnson sends you to steal a prototype, deal with freedom fighters in a bush war, guard (or geek) a VIP, or any number of other odd jobs, the possibilities of what your team will end up doing is endless. Flip through the **Happening World** section (see p. 153) and you can check out a huge variety of possibilities, jobs from cities or small towns that range from action-oriented combat to stealthy intrigue, and more. Pick your poison, and there's a vial ready to drink down at the gaming table.

Contract Briefs supply all the information you need to start playing, quick and easy. Each Contract Brief includes many points that players can use to play the job, and multiple Contract Briefs can be connected to make a Campaign (see p. 153). Here are some of the sections that will generally be found in the briefs.

- **Context:** A short overview of what the Contract Brief will be about, what the goal will be, and what opposition the characters can expect to find. This often is presented as in-universe text, something a character in the game universe might come across and read. These can be military documents, historical texts, security briefs, intercepted personal communications, local newspapers, and so on. This section is intended to help the GM establish some background for the story and establish the right feel.
- **Mr. Johnson's Pitch:** This section represents the team's meet with the Mr. Johnson who is contracting the shadowrunners' services, and it is usually read aloud to the group to kick off the Mission.
- **Objectives:** The Objectives list a set of goals or accomplishments that characters are expected to do, though they aren't mandatory—plots may twist, turn, and take runners in strange places.
- **Tags:** Tags give short descriptions of the Contract Brief to give players the gist of the adventure—for example, when trying to skim and find a specific flavor for a contract to run—or to aid the creation of a longer campaign.

- **The Setting:** The Setting is a description of the area where the characters find themselves at the beginning of the Contract Brief. The GM can read this aloud to players at the beginning of the job.
- **Enemies/Obstacles:** Finally, the Enemies/Obstacles section gives the opponents and obstacles that the characters may have to defeat or overcome to successfully complete the contract.
- **Scenes:** Each part of the job is considered a Scene, or section, of the overall Contract. For ease of use, each Scene includes suggested NPCs to use from the book. However, those are just suggestions. Use whatever NPCs your group thinks will make the job rattle and hum. Scenes may also offer special-case rules or GM advice for ways the players can tackle that particular Scene.

Like pretty much every part of *Shadowrun: Anarchy*, lots of the information given in a Contract Brief is up to the discretion of the players. Want to add your own NPCs? Go for it! Want to change parts of the Scene? No problem! Want to change the Objectives? No one's stopping you! Raise the fun factor high, keep the plot moving, and you're golden.

LOCK AND LOAD!

Once you've chosen characters, a GM, and Contract Brief, grab some dice and jump into the action.

CHARACTER SHEET

Your character sheet contains all of the information you'll need to tackle any problem, be it physical, magical, or virtual.

ILLUSTRATION/PERSONAL DATA

The character sheet includes an illustration of the character, along with Personal Data—name, metatype, age, that sort of thing. This section also includes a set of one-word **Tags** that immediately provide an at-a-glance grasp of what defines this character.

This section also includes a brief character description and some **Dispositions**, which are easy-to-review sentences that make a character who and what they are. This information, along with the **Cues** and **Qualities** on the second page, provides everything the player needs

to quickly get inside the head of their character and leap into the action. As a quick guide, Dispositions cover a character's motivations and rules of conduct, Cues cover things they might say, and Qualities cover some aspects of themselves that make them especially good at some things, less good at others.

ATTRIBUTES AND ATTRIBUTE DICE

Beginning at the top of the second page of the character sheet, you'll see the different **Attributes** and the number of dice that represent those stats (**Attribute Dice**).

Strength: It's how strong you are. Duh. Also represents your constitution, a measure of your physical health and resiliency. Strength determines your Physical Condition Monitor—the amount of damage you can absorb—as well as the amount of damage you inflict in close combat, so if you plan on punching a lot, this helps you punch harder.

Agility: It's not just about power—it's how you use it. Agility is a combination of hand-eye coordination, flexibility, balance, and reaction—reflexes and awareness of situations. This Attribute covers how good a person is in combat, whether ranged, close quarters, hand-to-hand, or even vehicle-to-vehicle.

Willpower: When you're slogging through a muddy ruined building in the barrens while acid rain is dissolving your coat, do you plug along or go home and make some nice, hot tea? Willpower helps determine the answer. It's a combination of your character's desire to push through adversity under any condition and that gut-instinct voice that anticipates an ambush or tells you when it's time to cut and run. Willpower determines how many boxes are in your Stun Condition Monitor, which measures the amount of punches (and other such damage) you can take before sagging to the grind in blank, unconscious submission

Logic: This corresponds to the mental faculties of the character, whether street smarts, learned science, or just plain inherent brilliance. Helps you quickly come up with an answer to the ever-present question, "If you're so smart, why are you still on the streets?"

Charisma: You don't need to out-shoot someone if you can talk them out of pulling on you. Charisma is your character's ability to talk their way out of a situation—your presence as you walk into a room and take charge.

Essence: In a technological world dominated by the need to be faster and stronger to survive, many people willingly carve away pieces of their metahumanity to stay one step ahead of the bullet with their name on it. Essence is a measure of how much of a character's metahumanity remains. See *Essence Loss* on page 33 for more information.

Edge: Edge is a very special number for each character. Unlike the other Attributes, it does not correspond to a number of dice, but instead it can be spent to gain some much-needed help for a particularly difficult roll (see *The Core Mechanic*, p. 37). Edge only replenishes at the beginning of each game session, so spend it wisely.

SKILLS

Skills represent the knowledge and abilities a character has developed while running the shadows. Skills cover a wide variety of topics, from the ability to shoot a gun, hack a Matrix system, or keep a teammate from bleeding out. Skills work hand in hand with Attributes when determining how many dice to roll for a given Test.

Skills are covered in detail on page 31.

SHADOW AMPS

The *Shadowrun* universe is a dystopian future where man meets magic and machine. From casting spells to augmenting physical attributes via magic to cyberware and bioware enhancing bones, flesh, and muscle, to chips that allow for bare-brained interactions with the worldwide Matrix, to complex forms used by technomancers, a myriad of ways exist to augment flesh and blood. **Shadow Amps** (short for Shadow Amplifications, often shortened further to simply "Amps") represent those more-human-than-human improvements and advantages, and they are covered in detail on page 32.

KARMA

In the Sixth World, what goes around comes around. **Karma** is a measure of the experience and resources your character has accumulated, for good or for otherwise, and it is used for improving your character (see **Character Advancement**, p. 70). A space is provided on the character sheet to keep track of how much Karma your character has earned.

CUES

In the center of the sheet are the character's **Cues**. Cues are statements or quotes that help define the character, whether it's attitude, capabilities, or personality. Each Cue can help form the basis of a **Narration** (see p. 34).

QUALITIES

Below the Cues are **Qualities**, which round out your character's personality and affect certain actions. These often are built off of a character's Disposition, providing concrete rules for how a character will react in various circumstances, whereas Tags define what your character is.

Each character has three Qualities—two positive and one negative.

WEAPONS

Most shadowrunners who plan to stay alive carry at least one weapon. The **Weapons** section lists these tools of the trade, the damage they inflict on a successful hit, and their range. In many instances, additional rules are included for the effects of the weapon.

Weapons are covered in more detail on p. 40.

ARMOR

The **Armor** track gives the number of Armor dots the character has. Armor is a generic term that covers things like a Kevlar jacket, military-grade body armor, an Armor spell, and extreme agility. Anything that might keep someone from being hit by an attack is in this category.

If a Skill or Amp provides a permanent Armor boost (as opposed to, say, an Armor spell that must be cast), it will be reflected in the Skill or Amp's text.

Armor helps absorb damage during **combat** (see p. 40).

CONDITION MONITOR

The **Condition Monitor** track defines the character's health status. Once a character's Armor (or any spell or Shadow Amp that acts as Armor) has been depleted by damage, further damage will accumulate on the appropriate part of the Condition Monitor.

There are two different types of damage, **Physical** and **Stun**, which are tracked separately. Different weapons and effects can either be Physical or Stun damage.

As injuries pile up, a character will suffer negative performance effects (see **Dice Pools**, p. 37).

GEAR

While a good shadowrunner trusts her abilities, she also carries some tools and supplies, which are listed in the Gear column of the character sheet. Unlike weapons, gear in *Shadowrun: Anarchy* has no set stats. Take a stimpatch, for example. Sure, it could just be a standard painkiller. But what if right in the middle of an escape, the GM drops a Plot Point to say that the stimpatch a shaman slaps on to overcome some wounds is from a bad batch laced with a custom-tailored street drug? What might happen?

In such instances, the player may have to answer those questions during gameplay with a clever Narration (see p. 34).

Gear generally falls into two categories:

Noncombat Gear: This is stuff that's (generally) not for killing people. What will Coydog use her shamanic lodge materials for? Does she have anything personal on her Meta Link commlink, or is it just a cheap burner unit?

Contacts: As the saying goes, "You are who you know," and your contacts can mean the difference between life and death in the shadows. The variety of contacts can help inspire unique approaches to otherwise sticky situations. Who is Coydog's contact Granny Smith? What's her deal? How could she help the team solve the problem at hand? Answering these sorts of questions can make for a great story.

NPC CHARACTER SHEET

Finally, there are two types of character sheets: those for fleshed-out player characters, and those for less-important individuals, like henchmen or supporting characters, or even for certain types of gear with their own damage tracks and weapons, such as vehicles and drones. These **non-player character** (**NPC**) sheets take up a third of a page and contain much less information than player character sheets. Gamemasters can also modify the NPCs in the **Street People** section (see p. 73) to expand the number of enemies for a given contract.

SKILLS

Each character has a unique set of **Skills** that showcase the actions that character excels in. Every Skill has two parts: a dice value and the specific Attribute the Skill is linked to. Whenever a player uses that particular Skill to accomplish an action, the value of the Skill is added to the linked Attribute to determine the base number of dice rolled. See **Rolling Dice**, p. 37, for more information on using Skills.

The name and description of each Skill (see **Skills List**, p. 32) provides a guideline for some ideas for what the Skill can do, but ultimately it'll be up to the player, the GM, and the roleplaying group to determine the limits of what each Skill can accomplish. Most Skills are broad enough to cover several different options for an action, such as the Hacking Skill, which can be used

to brute-force your way into a Matrix node, set a data bomb, engage in cybercombat with IC or spiders, and so on. If a player wants a given Skill to do something that might fall slightly outside the guidelines of that Skill and there is no other specific Skill in the Skills List that would govern the action, the GM may allow the action, generally allowing the player to simply roll the value of the Attribute normally linked to the Skill (magical skills are the exception to this rule).

SPECIALIZATIONS

Some Skills contain additional text in that Skill's box. These represent **Specializations**, meaning the character has further honed their proficiency in that Skill in a specific direction of focus, such as a particular weapon or a certain area of study. Specializations generally allow the player to gain extra dice when using that Skill in a Test. However, if the conditions of the Specialization are not met, you receive no bonus dice for the Test.

For example, on Shades' character sheet (see p. 121), the Specialization text on the Pistols Skill is "Pistols +2." This means that when Shades uses her Firearms Skill to fire a pistol, she receives two additional dice for the Test. However, when she's shooting any other type of gun, she won't roll the bonus Specialization dice.

SKILLS LIST

The following list shows which Attributes link to which Skills, and provides some examples of what kinds of actions each Skill can accomplish. For quick reference, each Skill on a character sheet shows a letter denoting the linked Attribute.

STRENGTH

Though Strength is not linked to any Skills, this Attribute determines the Physical track on the Condition Monitor (see **Damage, Armor, and the Condition Monitor**, p. 42), and it increases the damage of Close Combat actions (see **Combat**, p. 40).

AGILITY

Athletics: Running, jumping, swimming, and acrobatics.

Close Combat: Armed melee combat, unarmed melee combat, and martial arts.

Projectile Weapons: Bows, crossbows, throwing weapons, and certain critter attacks.

Firearms: Pistols, shotguns, submachine guns, and rifles.

Heavy Weapons: Machine guns, assault cannons, missile launchers, and grenade launchers.

Vehicle Weapons: Vehicle-mounted weapons, drone-mounted weapons, and pintle mounts.

Stealth: Sneaking, palming, and pickpocketing.

Piloting (Ground): Cars, trucks, bikes, even tanks. Wheeled and tracked drones too.

Piloting (Other): Boats, planes, and pretty much anything that moves on something besides ground.

Escape Artist: Escaping bindings, contortionism, and shaking a tail.

WILLPOWER

Conjuring: Summoning and banishing spirits. Magicians only. Cannot use untrained.

Sorcery: Spellcasting, ritual spellcasting, enchanting, and counterspelling. Magicians only. Cannot use untrained.

Astral Combat: Astral/spirit combat. Astral plane only. Magicians only.

Survival: Wilderness survival, navigation, and fasting.

Close Combat: When attacking spirits only.

LOGIC

Biotech: First aid, medicine, and cybertechnology.

Hacking: Computer hacking and cybercombat.

Electronics: Computer hardware and software, cyberdeck repair.

Engineering: Auto repair, aircraft repair, and boat repair.

Tasking: Summoning sprites, threading complex forms, and other Matrix tasks. Technomancers only. Cannot use untrained.

Tracking: Physical tracking, Matrix tracking, and shadowing.

Knowledge Skills: Languages, interests knowledge, and professional knowledge.

CHARISMA

Con: Con artistry, acting, performance, and etiquette.

Intimidation: Influence, interrogation, and torture.

Negotiation: Bargaining, contracts, and diplomacy.

Disguise: Camouflage, cosmetics, costuming, and digital alteration.

SHADOW AMPS

Shadow Amps (or just Amps) is a catchall term for certain advantages, spells, and modifications that can benefit a character. Amps is an umbrella term covering a huge swath of possibilities. From spells players can sling at opponents, to body modifications that make a character stronger or capable of sustaining damage, to implants that make a character smarter—almost anything is possible, if you're willing to pay the price.

Much like how Skills supplement Attributes, Amps also enhance related actions by granting certain effects. For example, one Shadow Amp might allow rerolls of certain dice that failed to score a hit, another might grant a bonus die in certain situations, and another might act like a Cue to a Narration instead of enhancing a die roll, and so on. Amp effects are listed on the character sheet. See **Rolling Dice** (p. 37) for more information on how Amps can factor into gameplay.

TYPES

Shadow Amps come in several different types. Here are a few examples of each type:

Spells: Magicians can manipulate mana to cast spells. Characters must be Awakened (see p. 63) to cast spells.

The Invisibility Spell allows the player to reroll one die that failed to score a hit on their Stealth Test, and the Improved Invisibility Spell allows two failed dice to be rerolled.

Telesma: Enchanted magical items can impart special bonuses when bound to a magician.

A weapon focus is an imbued melee weapon that

RULES OF THE STREET

can be used in astral combat, and a low-grade spirit focus allows the reroll of one die on a failed Conjuring Test.

Adept Powers: Instead of casting spells, adepts use mana to perform physical magic.

The Killing Hands adept power allows the player to deal Physical damage instead of Stun damage when using the Unarmed weapon in a Close Combat roll, and the Missile Parry power allows the character to pluck arrows or knives out of the air by negating one hit when targeted by a Projectile Weapons attack.

Cyberware: Cyberware represents technological implants in the body.

Wired reflexes 1 gives the player 1 extra attack action per Narration (see *Attack Limits*, p. 40). Wired reflexes 2 gives 1 extra attack per Narration and 1 Plot Point (see *Plot Points*, p. 35) at the beginning of each Scene.

Bioware: Bioware represents biological implants and genetically engineered improvements on the metahuman body.

Tailored pheromones allow the character to influence others. Rating 1 allows the reroll of one failed die on any Charisma-related Test, whereas Rating 3 rerolls 3 dice.

Cyberdecks: Unless you're a technomancer, you'll need some hardware to hack into the Matrix. Cyberdecks are what you need.

A cheap cyberdeck like an Erika MCD-1 will allow the reroll of one failed die on a Hacking Test, but a high-end cyberdeck, like a Shiawase Cyber-5, will allow three failed dice to be rerolled. Cyberdecks also have a Firewall rating and a Matrix Condition Monitor, which are both used in cybercombat (see *Hacking and Cybercombat*, p. 44).

Programs: If you want to be successful in the Matrix, you'll need some (possibly illegal) programs to massage data.

An Armor program reduces the amount of damage taken in cybercombat by 1, and a Biofeedback program lets you use neural feedback to damage a hostile decker's Condition Monitor instead of the cyberdeck's. See *Hacking and Cybercombat*, p. 44.

Critter Powers: Some nonmetahuman NPCs have special abilities that can be used in Tests, combat rolls, and general Narrations.

The spirit of earth's Concealment power lets it grant a +1 modifier, while a spirit of fire's Fear power inflicts a –1 modifier to opponents.

ESSENCE LOSS

Many Shadow Amps, most notably cyberware and bioware implants, require the character to trade away part of their metahumanity, and this results in Essence loss. The more you push the boundaries of what your body can do, the more you lose your metahumanity in the process.

Not all Amps include an Essence loss, however. For example, many magical Amps do not diminish your Essence. If a Shadow Amp includes an Essence loss, it will be noted as such on that portion of the character sheet, e.g., "[Cyberarms: Essence –1]."

If a character's Essence is low enough to incur any penalties, that fact is noted on the character sheet next to the Essence value. Low Essence imposes a dice-pool penalty on hits on magic- and healing-related Tests.

PLAYING SHADOWRUN: ANARCHY

Once each player has some dice and a character sheet, a Contract Brief has been selected, and a GM chosen, your group is ready to get started.

Shadowrun: Anarchy play is divided into a series of segments that build on each other: *Turns and Narrations, Scenes, Missions,* and *Campaigns.*

TURNS AND NARRATIONS

Shadowrun: Anarchy gameplay is divided into a series of turns. Each turn, every player has a chance to play out and describe their character's actions, along with other elements of the story going on around them. These descriptions are called **Narrations**, and as the game progresses these Narrations build on each other and form the story of the game.

A Narration gives a player a chance to describe what their character does as well as add and describe other story elements. Other players may have things to say during a Narration—their characters may react somehow, or players may offer commentary, ideas, or observations—but the primary thrust of the Narration should be directed by the player whose turn it is. The Narration usually only covers a few minutes of out-of-game time (and probably less in-game time) before moving to the next player, to keep things flowing quickly and giving everyone a chance to stay involved in the ongoing story. In combat, a Narration will typically last as long as it takes to execute a single Combat Action (see p. 40); in non-combat activities, the length of the Narration might be more variable. The general guideline is for it to last as long as the game needs to stay lively and keep everyone involved.

GAMEMASTER

Each turn begins with the GM and continues with the player on the GM's left until all players have had a turn

at Narration (though check the **Talk Time** sidebar and **Spending Plot Points: Gamemaster**, p. 36, for some exceptions to this).

The GM begins the turn by giving a narrative of the current situation and advancing the plot, as described under **Select a Contract Brief** (see p. 28). The GM also makes any actions or die rolls for enemies the characters may encounter.

Once all players have had a chance to narrate their character's actions, the turn ends and a new turn begins.

TALK TIME

For most Scenes and Turns, taking turns will work best, as it will keep the story moving, give people a chance to be creative on their turn, and also provide a structure where people can use Plot Points. Sometimes, though, the turn-based structure might interfere with the flow of conversation when runners are doing something like meeting with Mr. Johnson, questioning a witness, or other activities where multiple people might want to be engaged in conversation. In these circumstances, conversation moves around too quickly for it to be clear whose turn it is, and keeping track of turns becomes a hassle. To make life easier, the GM or the players can, with agreement of others at the table, initiate Talk Time, where the turn-based structure is suspended and players can engage in free-wheeling conversation. Once the conversation gets beyond mere talk and into tests, though—like when someone starts a serious Negotiation and Intimidation—it's time to let the story proceed through turns again.

SCENE

A Scene is defined as the start and finish of a given section of time within a Contract Brief. A Scene contains a number of turns, which vary depending upon what's occurring within a given Scene.

For example, take a look at *Be Careful What You Search For* (see p. 154). Each of the three descriptions of the Enemies/Obstacles found in that Event Brief is a Scene. There is no hard and fast rule on how many turns are in a Scene. Instead, that will be based on how many players are involved, their style of play, and their Narrations, which ultimately leads to how quickly (or slowly) they're able to accomplish the goals of a given Scene.

CONTRACT BRIEF

A Contract Brief usually constitutes a single game session, and the session ends when all of the Scenes within a Contract Brief are completed. The number of Scenes required to finish an Event Brief is detailed in each Event Brief, but this can be modified by the player group.

For example, one player group may decide after accomplishing the three Scenes laid out in *Be Careful What You Search For* that the Event Brief is done, and their time running the shadows is over for the day. However, another group playing the same Contract Brief might decide to add in a new fourth Scene that helps close up some of the plot threads that grew through players' Narrations, so they keep playing. A third group might not have as long to play as the other groups, so they actually split the Event Brief up into two different days of gaming sessions. Whatever works for each playing group is just fine.

BUILDING THE STORY: NARRATION AND FLOW

Giving a Narration is quite easy. All a player has to do is describe what his or her character is doing, such as engaging in a firefight, exploring a Matrix host, or summoning a spirit, as well as adding some descriptions about what happens around them when they do what they do.

If any action has a chance of failure, then a dice-rolling test is made to determine whether the action succeeds. See **Rolling Dice**, p. 37.

Many Narrations are based on Cues provided on character sheets or Mission Briefs.

CUES

Cues are building blocks players can use as a basis for Narrations. Cues are both suggestions and descriptions. They can be positive and negative and never have to be narrated the same way twice. If a player draws a blank or wants to make sure he's staying on-topic, he can look at a list of Cues and choose an appropriate one to base a Narration around.

MOVING THE STORY FORWARD

Collaborative narration is about creating a story and moving it forward. *Shadowrun: Anarchy* is about making impossible choices, facing terrifying challenges, and overcoming them in fantastic and fun ways. It is all about saying "yes" to fun, not "no" to something unexpected.

So when you are faced with the impossible, you smile and say, "Yes, and …" Then you make it up! There is no wrong way in *Shadowrun: Anarchy*. Want to have the characters swallowed by a magical alchera while running the shadows of Los Angeles? Then do it! But be ready for

the GM to have a metaplanar entity show up and try to force you out. After all, the rule is "Yes, and …" Respect other players' choices, don't use your Narrative to make an overly easy way out or an impossible challenge, and you'll be building a fun story.

PLOT POINTS

The most exciting plots include twists you never saw coming—a twisted water spirit emerging from a swamp, experimental security countermeasures appearing right in the middle of your firefight, a strange subsystem in a Matrix node that gets activated, or a vicious paracritter breaks free from its laboratory cage.

In gameplay, these twists can come about through Plot Points, which can be employed in many ways. They are used to interrupt or alter another player's Narration—a method of adding a twist to the game. They can also be used to change player turn order, add a glitch die, or gain back a point of Physical or Stun damage. The ways players utilize Plot Points are only limited by how creative they want to be.

Players will be earning and spending Plot Points throughout the game, and using some type of tokens (such as poker chips or pennies) is the best method to track them. However, players are free to use whatever system works best, whether it's chips, dice, noting them down on paper, tablet, or smartphone, and so on.

EARNING PLOT POINTS: PLAYERS

Players begin the game with three Plot Points each and may be awarded more points by the GM for particularly good Narrations. Players may have a maximum of five Plot Points at any time, and only one point may be awarded to a player at a time. Certain Shadow Amps give players a bonus Plot Point at the start of combat.

The GM is the only person who may award Plot Points, though some Shadow Amps tell them when this should happen.

EARNING PLOT POINTS: GAMEMASTER

The GM also receives Plot Points into a pool of their own. The GM starts a Contract Brief with one Plot Point, and every time a player spends a Plot Point (see below), the GM receives that point.

Unlike the players, the GM has no limit on how many Plot Points they can have.

SPENDING PLOT POINTS: PLAYERS

No matter what effect you want to cause, the cost is one Plot Point, and the change is immediately made to the

game. Players may not spend more than one point at a time in an attempt to maximize the twist, though they can spend multiple Plot Points during any player's Narration (whether their own, or another player's).

Example things to do with Plot Points:

- **Live dangerously:** Add a Glitch Die to a player's roll, including your own (see **The Glitch Die**, p. 39).
- **Shake it up:** Change turn order by making a Narration and taking actions when it isn't your normal turn.
- **Double time it:** Take two movement actions to close on—or get away from—an opponent (See **Character Movement**, p. 42).
- **Surprise threat:** Unseen corporate security guards show up!
- **First aid:** Heal a point of Physical or Stun damage
- **Malfunction:** A character's spirits/devices/etc. suddenly stop working for a short period of time.
- **Take the hit:** If a weaker or injured character is successfully hit by a combat action—i.e., the target rolled fewer hits than the attacker—then a player can spend a Plot Point to take the hit instead. The original target's defense roll is ignored, and the interrupting player rolls their own defense dice against the attacker's hits.
- **A dish best served cold:** Immediately take one free attack action against the NPC who just attacked you. This attack does not count as a Narration.

If you come up with another creative use for Plot Points, go for it! Plot Points are meant to change the game in fun and interesting ways, so don't be afraid to use your imagination.

Just remember, Plot Point use doesn't always mean a positive change. Often plot twists are a negative event—something goes wrong that must be fixed or adapted to by the characters.

SPENDING PLOT POINTS: GAMEMASTER

Like players, the GM can spend Plot Points in any fashion they choose, with the following caveats:

- With the exception of adding a Glitch Die (see p. 39), Plot Points can only be spent to aid NPCs or create plot twists; they cannot be spent to directly aid or hinder a player.
- The GM can only spend one Plot Point per turn, unlike the players who can spend more than one per turn.

- Instead of using a Plot Point to go first, the gamemaster can spend one to change how turn order works for a round. They can select to go in reverse order (starting with the player to the GM's right), or they can roll a die to randomly determine a new starting player for that round. This can be especially useful to shake up patterns players develop in a game or keep players on their toes.

TROUBLESHOOTING

In an improv-style game such as *Shadowrun: Anarchy*, the single greatest issue that can suck the life and energy out of a gaming session is if players start spending too much time deliberating over their actions and Narrations. If you've ever watched an improv play, when a character pauses too long trying to follow up with what's just been said, you're thrown out of the action and the energy is gone.

If this starts to occur, players should work together as a group to help a player feel more at ease with this style of play. This could be practice sessions outside of a game, or something as simple as finding an enjoyable improv play to watch that can provide an example of how this style can unfold. Gamemasters can also do a lot to help by asking specific questions (e.g., "What are you going to tell that ork who's making a series of exceptionally rude gestures?" rather than a basic "What happens next?") and by making sure turns keep moving at a good clip, so that players do not struggle too much with making the story move forward. Don't force players to come up with something if they are blanking on ideas, or make them feel too much pressure. Keep it light, keep turns moving, and keep it fun! The **Controlling Anarchy** chapter (p. 55) has more advice on how to keep the game moving.

ROLLING DICE

At some point, characters are going to attempt something difficult, awesome, or nearly impossible, because those are the sorts of things characters are supposed to do. At those points, it's time to roll the dice, so here's info on how many to roll and what kind of numbers you want to see.

HITS

The main goal when making any die roll is to score **hits**. When rolling dice, any die that comes up as a five or six are counted as hits. When you spend a point of Edge, dice that roll a four, five, or six are counted as hits.

THE CORE MECHANIC

Shadowrun: Anarchy uses a simple dice-rolling mechanic to resolve **Tests** and **Combat**.

Any time your character (or an acting NPC) wishes to perform an action where the success is in doubt, you need to make a Test to see whether the action was successful. Your main job is to figure out how many dice you are going to roll, then roll them and count up hits. The gamemaster decides on a difficulty for the roll and rolls an opposing dice pool, or rolls an opposing dice pool generated by an NPC. After making your roll, apply any Shadow Amp effects (if any), count up your final number of hits, and compare them to the number of hits rolled by the opposing dice. If your hits equal or exceed the hits scored by the opposing dice, then your action was successful. If you score zero hits, the Test automatically fails, even if the opposing dice also rolled zero hits.

This means that the mechanic for resolving all Tests looks like this:

Skill Dice + Attribute Dice + Modifiers (if any) + Shadow Amps effect (if any) vs. **Opposing Dice**

DICE POOLS

These are the elements that go into deciding how many dice you're going to roll:

Skill Dice: If you possess a relevant Skill for the action, then your Skill dice form the base of your dice pool. If you have a Specialization for that Skill, and the Specialization applies for the current action, then you also add the bonus dice as noted on the Skill.

Attribute Dice: The Skill used to perform an action denotes the Skill's linked Attribute with a letter. Find the appropriate Attribute and add that Attribute's dice to the dice pool. A list of Skills and their related Attributes can be found on p. 32.

Modifiers: Modifiers represent good or bad situational circumstances that take an ordinary situation and make it extraordinary. Such as: you're trying to hack into a keypad while being attacked (a negative modifier), you're wounded (a negative modifier), and you're getting additional help (this also could be a positive or negative modifier depending upon the Logic value of the player trying to help). Some negative modifiers are clearly set out by the rules, such as:

- **Injuries:** The more damage on your Condition Monitor, the higher the modifier will be. See **Damage, Armor, and the Condition Monitor**, p. 42.
- **Essence Loss:** The lower your Essence, the more negative modifiers are applied to certain Tests.

See Essence Loss, p. 33.

- **Qualities:** Positive and negative Qualities can affect certain actions by adding or subtracting dice from a roll. Check your character sheet to see if any of these apply.
- **Assistance:** Sometimes you just can't do it alone. These modifiers represent being helped by a teammate, a spirit, a Matrix sprite, or some other form of aid. See **Teamwork Tests**, p. 39.

Beyond that, the gamemaster might impose additional modifiers based in variable conditions. These modifiers (alone, not counted with the modifiers listed above) should never go beyond +5 or –5, and the highest (or lowest) level should apply only very rarely.

- **Environment:** Light, darkness, weather. This can also include things like the ground on which people are operating, surfaces they are trying to climb, and so on.
- **Attitude:** Social situations may be affected by the attitude of the non-player character, the overall situation, and the existing relationship with player characters.
- **Distractions:** Characters may be trying to drive and shoot at the same time, or fight while sustaining a spell, and the effort of doing multiple things makes them less effective performing at least one of them, so they take a penalty due to the distraction.

Shadow Amp Effects: The text on a Shadow Amp will note whether it can affect the outcome of a Test, such as allowing the reroll of dice that failed to score a hit or reducing the number of opposing dice rolled, negating hits, adding pips to dice (that is, making the roll one number higher), and so on. Make sure to apply a relevant effect before comparing hits with the opposing dice. Only one Shadow Amp can affect a roll's outcome; if two or more could apply to the Test, you must choose one effect to apply. See **Shadow Amps**, p. 32.

Opposing Dice: In some cases, the opposing dice are determined by making dice pools of an opposing player. For example, if a non-player character is being attacked, they will roll a defensive test of Agility + Logic, just like a player character.

In other circumstances, there will not be an opposing dice pool from another person (like when a player character is trying to climb a wall). In those cases, the number of opposing dice that are rolled depends on the difficulty of the action:

- **Very Easy:** 4 dice
- **Easy:** 6 dice
- **Average:** 8 dice
- **Hard:** 10 dice
- **Very Hard:** 12 dice

Different circumstances generally dictate a certain difficulty level. For example, a maglock at a securing the back door of a mom-and-pop store would likely fall into Very Easy difficulty (rolling only 4 dice against the player's dice pool), but a maglock in an ultra-secure Mitsuhama Zero Zone would certainly be Very Hard (12 dice). If the difficulty is not readily apparent or there is too much deliberation over the difficulty, the gamemaster can never go wrong with Average difficulty.

ATTRIBUTE TESTS

There are two types of occasions when you might exclude Skill dice from a Test and only roll Attribute dice.

Untrained: If you want to try a specific action but are untrained in that action—i.e., the appropriate Skill is not on your character sheet—then determine what the linked Attribute is for the missing Skill (see **Skills List**, p. 32), and then use that Attribute's dice for the Test. In a few limited circumstances, such as Magic-based actions, Untrained actions cannot be taken. If a Skill cannot be used untrained, that is noted on the Skills list.

Attribute-Only Tests: Some Tests only apply to a specific Attribute and don't need a related Skill. In those cases, either add two Attributes together, or add one Attribute to itself. For example, lifting a heavy object would require a Strength + Strength Test; catching a thrown object would require Agility + Agility; resisting torture, Willpower + Body; remembering a specific detail, Logic + Logic; judging someone's intentions, Charisma + Charisma; and so on. One of the most common Tests of this nature is **Perception**, which is Logic + Willpower; for more information on Perception, see below. Shadow Amp effects apply to Attribute-only Tests when appropriate.

PERCEPTION

As noted above, **Perception** Tests are made with Logic + Willpower. When a character is looking at inanimate objects, the opposing roll is based on the gamemaster's idea of the difficulty of the roll, per the listing for **Opposing Dice** on this page. If the character succeeds at such a Perception Test, rather than simply tell the character what they see, give the player a chance to detail what it is they discover, as this can bring the player into the fun of shaping the story.

If a character is trying to see a sapient being that may be trying to sneak past them, the Perception Test generally would be opposed by Stealth + Agility of whatever the character is trying to see. In this case, the gamemaster should feel free to tell the character who or what they see if they are successful.

EDGE

When you need a boost on a test, you can spend Edge in one of two ways. First, you can announce you're spending Edge before you roll a test; when you roll the dice, you get to add an extra die to the roll and count fours, fives, and sixes as hits, instead of just fives and sixes. Second, after you roll the dice, you can spend a point of Edge to re-roll all of the dice that were not fives and sixes. When spending Edge this way, you still only count fives and sixes as hits. If you want the benefit of having fours be hits, plan ahead!

You can spend a number of Edge points in a single gaming session equal to your Edge rating. Once you've spent them all, you're done using Edge until the next session.

TEAMWORK TESTS

Good shadowrunning requires teamwork, and sometimes that means pitching in as a team to get a single task done. When appropriate and sensible, players can help each other on a Test, making a **Teamwork Test**. A player can suggest a Teamwork Test on their Narration, or other players can mention they would like to help. Making the assist rolls do not require any change in whose turn it is; players can make an assist roll even when it is not their Narration, but the leader must make a roll during their Narration.

To assist, players choose a leader who will be doing the main work of a Test. The other players make the appropriate Skill Test. Any hits they make become additional dice for the player taking the lead on the Test, to a maximum of the leader's Skill level (or the higher of the two Attributes, if it is an Attribute-only Test).

Certain circumstances are not appropriate for assistance. Spellcasting, conjuring, and most combat tests cannot use Teamwork Tests. Gamemasters and players should use their judgment as to when other Teamwork Tests will be appropriate or not. Generally, characters need to be in the same place and able to function in a helpful way (meaning they are, you know, conscious and mobile) at a minimum.

THE GLITCH DIE: GLITCHES AND EXPLOITS

Even when a shadowrun is going right, sometimes a quirk of chaos manages to worm its way in and make things go south really, really fast—or provide just the lucky break you needed. In *Shadowrun: Anarchy*, game-

masters and players can represent this manifestation of fate, or whatever you want to call it, by introducing the Glitch Die into a roll.

To use the Glitch Die, the GM or a player must spend a Plot Point before a roll is made. The player spending the Plot Point gives the rolling player a die that is noticeably different from the other dice being rolled. This die can be a different color, style, or size—whichever the players prefer.

GLITCHES

If the Glitch Die comes up as a 1, then a Glitch has occurred, and the universe has once again attempted to screw you.

In the event of a Glitch, the player who made the roll must detail their stroke of bad luck in their Narration of the attempted action they were rolling for. For example, a player who Glitches an unarmed Close Combat roll could miss a kick and fall; a Glitched Hacking Test could accidentally delete the wrong file; a Stealth Test could draw the attention of a corporate security hellhound; a Firearms action could jam the gun; and so on.

A Glitch will still occur even if the Test itself is successful, thanks to the other dice rolled. For example, if you are trying to make a flying dive into cover and you succeed in a Gymnastics Test but roll a 1 on the Glitch Die, then maybe you dive for cover successfully but land wrong, jam your elbow on the ground, and take 1 point of Stun damage. Or maybe you Glitch on a successful Hacking Test: perhaps you grab the file you need, but you trip security in the process and alert some intrusion countermeasures. How the Glitch manifests is completely up to the imagination.

Regardless of how the Glitch occurs, it shouldn't be life threatening unless the affected player wishes it to be, for the sake of drama. Instead, a Glitch should represent unforeseen complications that really throw a spanner into the works. The best Glitches help move the story forward in new and interesting directions, so feel free to let your creative flag fly right in the face of bad luck.

EXPLOITS

If the Glitch Die rolls a 5 or a 6, then it counts as an **Exploit**.

When an Exploit occurs, the player has made fate their plaything, and something went really right for a change. This windfall of good luck can take any form the gamemaster deems appropriate for the action taken, such as bypassing the target's armor during an combat action, stumbling on an incriminating Matrix file that you weren't looking for, an attacking spirit suddenly and mysteriously backs down, and so on.

An Exploit can also occur if the roll failed. As long as the Glitch die rolled a hit, the Exploit reveals a silver lining to your failed action. For example, a failed swerve to maneuver your Harley-Davidson Scorpion out of danger might distract one of the people you're chasing, or an accidentally tripped Matrix alarm might spontaneously reset itself due to a scheduled maintenance routine.

As with Glitches, the best Exploits are those that inject some unexpected fun into your story.

COMBAT

Combat is when the time comes to bash heads, shoot people in the face for money, or what have you. It works in similar fashion to other Tests. Regardless of whether the action is ranged, melee, magical, or otherwise, the attack is resolved the same way. The basic dice-rolling mechanic for all combat is:

Skill Dice + Attribute Dice + Modifiers (if any) + Shadow Amp/Weapon Effects (if any) vs. **Agility Dice + Logic Dice + Modifiers + Shadow Amp Effects (if any)**

As shown, combat is a straightforward contest between the attacker's and defender's hits. If the attacker equals or exceeds the defender's hits, then the defender takes damage. The difference between the attacker' hits and defenders hits—called **net hits**—is added to the damage of the attack. If the attacker rolls fewer hits than the target, then the attack fails and inflicts no damage. If the attacker rolls zero hits, the attack automatically fails, even if the defender also rolled zero hits.

MODIFIERS

As with Test rolls, combat rolls can have a variety of situational modifiers added, all of which are decided upon by the GM. Certain spells, range penalties, and environmental effects are common modifiers seen in combat rolls.

In addition to those listed on p. 37, here are common modifiers that apply to combat rolls:
- **Weapon Dice:** Some weapons offer bonus dice when used in combat rolls.
- **Range:** Certain ranges incur dice penalties. See Weapons on this page.

SHADOW AMP/WEAPON EFFECTS

Some Shadow Amps can be used in combat, and some weapons have additional effects when used, such as allowing the reroll of dice that failed to score a hit or reducing the number of opposing dice rolled. Make sure to apply a relevant effect before comparing hits with the opposing dice. Only the weapon used and one Amp can affect a roll's outcome; if two or more Amps could apply to the combat roll, you must choose which effect to apply. See **Shadow Amps**, p. 32.

In combat rolls, if the defender possesses any Amps that apply to defense, such as a type of reaction enhancer or the physical adept power Missile Parry, then those effects get applied to the defender's roll before comparing hits.

ATTACK LIMITS

A character can only take a single attack action during their Narration. What is an Attack action? An action that intentionally and directly damages another living being (including NPCs, critters, spirits, and whatever). Want to debate the meaning of Attack action beyond that? Have fun, and we'll be here for you when you're ready to play!

Reaction Enhancers: The notable exceptions to this rule are the various types of reaction enhancers. For example, wired reflexes and the Increase Reflexes spell allow characters to take a bonus attack action. See **Seizing the Initiative**, p. 44.

WEAPONS

Weapons come in all shapes, types, and sizes. You name it, and one of the megacorps undoubtedly sells it—and in a variety of chic designer colors and styles to boot.

Most *Shadowrun: Anarchy* characters start each Mission with a default set of weapons. These are listed on the character sheet along with the amount of damage they do when used successfully against a target, their range brackets, and any special effects or bonuses their use confers.

Here's what you need to know when using weapons:

Ranges: All weapons list three general range brackets:
- **Close:** Melee weapons, unarmed combat
- **Near:** Short-ranged weapons, such as pistols and shotguns
- **Far:** Long-ranged weapons, such as rifles and heavy weapons

Each range bracket on a weapon listing can have three possible notations:
- **OK:** The weapon can be used at this range without penalty.
- **–X:** The weapon can be used at this range, but with a –X modifier.
- **—:** The weapon cannot be used at this range.

For example, Sledge's Ares Predator V has the following range notation: Close OK, Near –2, Far —. This means it can fire at Close range targets without penalty, suffers a –2 modifier at Near range, and cannot affect targets at Far range. Which makes him sad, but he'll just have to get another gun if he wants to shoot far.

There are no precise definitions for Close, Near, and Far ranges, mainly to prevent the game from being bogged down in specific measurements. The basic definitions are that Close is within reach of a sword or similar melee weapon, either by swinging it where you are or taking a few quick steps toward a target. Near is farther than that, going far enough outward that you start reaching the limits of where pistols have a reasonable chance to hit. Being generous, that range is around 100 meters, without being precise. Far is any distance beyond that. Remember that it is rare for any weapon that's not artillery or something to fire more than half a kilometer, and going a full kilometer is rarer still. Just because a weapon is capable of firing to the Far range does not mean it can hit something on the other side of the sprawl. When in doubt, the gamemaster makes the call if someone can be hit by weapons fire.

Unarmed Combat Damage: Your Strength determines the damage you do when engaging in unarmed combat. The damage you inflict is Stun damage equal to half Strength (rounded up), noted as (STR/2)S. Some Shadow Amps may increase this damage, or turn it into Physical damage.

Close Combat Damage Bonus: Close Combat weapons start with the same (STR/2) basic damage and usually add a bonus to that. Some of them, particularly blunt weapons, do Stun damage; others, like blades, do Physical damage. The type of damage a weapon does is indicated by a P or S after the base damage.

Carry Limits: Character sheets have six slots for weapons, so that's generally how many characters can have. If they want more, can figure out a way to list them, and have GM approval to have more, then go for it!

If a character has a Skill that requires the use of their hands, then the character can't use that Skill if they are holding a weapon (or gear) in that hand. If there is the slightest doubt about how the character uses said Skill, before gameplay begins, the players and gamemaster will need to determine for their games whether a particular Skill requires a free hand to use it.

Ammo and Reloading: *Shadowrun: Anarchy* doesn't require players to track things like ammunition, shots fired per turn, firing modes, reloading speeds, and so on. This is an action movie—all reloading is assumed to happen when the camera isn't pointed at you, if it happens at all.

Secondary Effects: Generally speaking, *Shadowrun: Anarchy* doesn't assume weapons have any other effects beyond straight-up damage as noted on the various character sheets. Those weapons with additional effects are specifically noted, of course. However, like the equipment also noted on the character sheets, players and gamemasters are free to come up with additional effects from a weapon, provided they can make a good Narration for it.

For example, Sledge has an Ares Predator V on his character sheet (see p. 83). The player choosing Sledge could pitch to the group that this is a custom mod of that pistol. The modification would allow the weapon to fire riot rounds that always knock the target down after dealing its damage. The gamemaster feels that's too powerful for a gun that small and decides that the weapon can't be used at Close range, and further, if the weapon scores a hit, the target will make a Strength Test with a modifier determined by the gamemaster. If the target succeeds, he or she withstood the extra effects of getting hit with such a large riot round; if the target fails, he or she is immediately on their back until they can spend a Narration to stand back up.

Meanwhile, in another situation, the gamemaster may decide Coydog's survival knife is actually an enchanted weapon focus. When it hits, that weapon's mystical powers partially numb the target, so the target applies a –1 modifier to any actions for the next two turns.

And so on. As usual, unleash your imaginations at the table!

Making the Game More or Less Lethal: The weapons on the character sheets are geared toward a good mix of play speed and fun combat action that'll span multiple turns of dice rolling to resolve a given situation. However, some groups may decide they want to switch things up to suit their style of play.

- **Less Lethal:** If a player group decides they want more dice rolling and heavier combat-oriented play, simply lower all Damage Values by 1, or even cut Damage Values in half. If weapons have a D6 for their Damage Value, change that to D6 – 1 damage.
- **More Lethal:** If another group wants quicker combat and more cinematic style where the good guys can take out the bad guys in a single swipe, reduce armor by half or more. The more armor goes away, the quicker people go down.

CHARACTER MOVEMENT

In *Shadowrun: Anarchy*, there are no hard-and-fast rules for walking and running speeds, and weapon ranges are abstracted. This places the focus on story and action. In many circumstances, the ranges are just approximations, and the gamemaster can provide a ruling of the current range, and the players can move on. There are times, though, when more tactical movement may be needed, so here are some rules for closing or expanding ranges in such situations.

Movement is based on the three different range brackets: Close, Near, and Far. See the *Weapons* section for more detail on how range brackets work.

Movement from Close to Near, or Near to Close, requires a single movement when on foot. Moving on foot from Near to Far, or Far to Near, requires three movements. Note that these can be divided among multiple people involved in maneuvering around each other. For example, let's say a player and an NPC are at Far range, and both of them decide they want to be Near. The player uses their movement to get closer, and the NPC does the same. That's two movements (the gamemaster should track the progress of these movements), so if on the player's turn they decide to move closer again, they'll be in Near range. Just in time for the NPC to shoot. Oops.

Note that characters can spend a Plot Point to take two movement actions to make this process go faster.

There is one exception to this rule. If you moved from Far to Near or Near to Far, in the very next turn you can decide to move back to the range you left. If you don't make that move in the next turn, the opportunity is lost; it's assumed that others move or the universe realigns in some way that requires the three movements to get from Near to Far or vice versa.

DAMAGE, ARMOR, AND THE CONDITION MONITOR

Whenever a fight occurs or a dangerous situation is encountered, there's a chance a character could take damage on the Condition Monitor.

Damage: On every character sheet, there's a Weapons column that lists the weapons the character started the game with and its **Damage Value**. Whenever a character takes damage, the damage from the weapon is first applied to the Armor column of the character sheet. Once all Armor circles are marked off, damage then begins to apply to the Condition Monitor. If that happens, it's time for some serious heroics before true disaster strikes.

Physical Damage vs. Stun Damage: There are two types of damage on the Condition Monitor: Physical and Stun. Physical damage represents potentially lethal damage: gashes and gouges, burns and breaks, and so on. Stun represents nonlethal damage: bruises, fatigue, synaptic overload, certain spells, and so on. Weapons with a

P notation in their Damage Value apply their damage to the Physical column on the Condition Monitor once armor has been depleted, and weapons with an **S** notation damage the Stun column.

Condition Monitor Flowchart: The Physical and Stun columns on the Condition Monitor of the character sheet take the form of flowcharts. Players start at the top, left-hand box of the damage column for the damage type and move to the right until the first row is marked off, then move to the left-hand box of the second row and move to the right until the second row is marked off, and so on.

- **First Row:** When the first row of boxes is filled, the character immediately applies a –1 modifier to all future die rolls.
- **Second Row:** When the second row of boxes is filled, a –2 modifier is applied to all die rolls. This replaces the –1 modifier from the first row instead of being cumulative.
- **Third Row:** When the third row of boxes is filled, a –3 modifier is applied to all die rolls. This replaces the –2 modifier from the second row instead of being cumulative.
- **Fourth Row (if applicable):** When the fourth row of boxes (if available) is filled, a –4 modifier is applied to all die rolls. This replaces the –3 modifier from the third row instead of being cumulative.
- **Staggered:** When all of the boxes of either Condition Monitor are filled, the character simply cannot give anymore and may take no actions (he does not give any more Narrations until he's healed; he cannot spend any Plot Points either). However, there are instances in which a spell or Skill could still be in effect even if the character is Staggered; the final call on whether an action or Skill is still active while a character is Staggered is up to the GM.
- **Knocked Out (Stun track only):** If the character is damaged again with Stun damage after being Staggered on the Stun Condition Monitor, they are Knocked Out; they are out of commission until they receive healing.
- **Killed in Action (Physical track only):** If the character receives Physical damage again after being Staggered on the Physical Condition Monitor, they are at risk of being killed. They must make an Edge + Edge Test, starting at Very Easy difficulty and increasing in difficulty by one step each time more damage hits. If they fail this test, the character is dead; for more details, see **Character Death**, p. 44.
- **Cumulative Wound Modifiers:** If a character has a wound modifier on both the Physical damage

track and the Stun damage track, the highest modifiers on each track are added together for a single modifier. For example, if a character has suffered enough damage to have a –1 modifier on the Stun track and a –2 modifier on the Physical track, then the character incurs a total wound modifier of –3 for any die rolls until enough damage has been healed to reduce one or both of the modifiers.

Regaining Armor/Condition Monitor Damage: Fortunately, there are many ways to repair Armor and heal Physical and Stun damage. A player could spend a Plot Point to regain a circle of Armor or Physical/Stun damage. Some characters carry first aid kits as equipment, which can restore Physical or Stun damage. Additionally, some characters are medics or magicians and can use an appropriate Skill to fix armor or heal a teammate, with each hit on the appropriate Skill Test healing a box of damage. Biotech can be used to heal damage to people, Electronics to repair damage to cyberdecks, and Engineering to repair damage to armor. Note that each person, device, vehicle, armor, or other piece of gear can only have one attempting healing or repair test per period of combat; you can't just make test after test until all damage is healed or repaired.

Some gear or spells may instantly repair damaged armor circles immediately after a combat; otherwise, armor, cyberdeck, and Condition Monitor damage are assumed to completely repair once the player has the equivalent of a night's worth of downtime. In this time, it is assumed that they put on a new piece of armor from storage or buy a replacement and are ready to roll.

In some cases, though, players may need more rapid or more thorough repair of their bodies, their gear, or their armor. In this case, characters will need to find someone who repairs armor and then offer them some form of payment. Since *Anarchy* does not have cash, a simple transfer of nuyen is not possible. Instead, armor repair must be paid for in one of the following ways:

- Pay 1 Karma for full armor repair. It's steep, yeah, but what good's Karma when you're dead? Sometimes you need to pony up to stay alive.
- Promise a favor. This means that the gamemaster gets to select the next Contract Brief, and the player must accept that job without negotiating the compensation. This can be one of the pre-generated Contract Briefs, or any other one the gamemaster has. If a player has a pending favor, they cannot take on another one until they have at least started the Contract Brief that is part of the favor. It is possible that multiple members of the team

may owe favors at the same time, leading to a string of favors they have to repay. In this case, the gamemaster determines which Contract Brief will fulfill the favor, but the team can decide between them which job they'll do first, second, and so on.

CHARACTER DEATH

As noted under **Damage, Armor, and the Condition Monitor** (see p. 42), the standard rules for the game allow a character to die. *Shadowrun: Anarchy* is a roleplaying game about the mean and gritty shadows of the Sixth World, and here, when a character dies, they stay dead.

That being said, some players may agree that a Killed In Action character isn't truly dead, but there should still be some consequences for a character running roughshod over his or her whole Condition Monitor. Or maybe the player was Killed In Action far too early in an evening's gaming session due to bad luck, and they don't want to sit out for the rest of the session. For these situations, here are a few options players can use to provide more depth of play:

The players should decide as a group which of these options are allowed and which option a player will use if a character is Killed In Action during a game. For each of these options, the character heals one box on their Physical Condition Monitor and is ready to move—hopefully out of harm's way.

- **Don't count me out just yet:** The character spends all but 1 of their available Plot Points to avoid being Killed In Action and suffer no further effects. If the character has only 1 available Plot Point to spend, this option cannot be chosen and another option must be chosen instead.
- **Just give me a minute:** In addition to the standard wound modifiers for damage on the Condition Monitor, the character will suffer an additional –1 modifier on all Tests and Combat rolls for his next 2 Narrations.
- **I'll never be the same:** Permanently reduce the character's total Physical and Stun Condition Monitor boxes by 1. Strength and Willpower remain unaffected.
- **I've had better days:** Permanently lower one random Attribute by 1. If Strength or Willpower is the affected Attribute, use the new value to reduce the character's total Physical or Stun Condition Monitors as per standard character creation rules (see p. 61). The Attribute can subsequently be improved as normal through Character Advancement rules (p. 70).

SEIZING THE INITIATIVE

When you're wired to the gills or amped up on reflex-enhancement magic, the world seems to slow down around you. You gain a fly-like perception, which often allows you to spot the perfect place to jump into the action to take the right shot or save someone's life.

To accomplish these kinds of feats, many characters who have Shadow Amps that improve their reaction are given a number of Plot Points at the beginning of each Scene. This can help them in combat, and may make these speedy characters more likely to perform actions such as **Take the hit** or **A dish best served cold** (see p. 52)

USING GEAR

Some characters carry a variety of gear that might be helpful during or after a fight. The uses of many of the different items may be obvious: a medkit would help treat a character who's been injured, or a tool kit could be used to repair armor or other devices. The intended application of other gear may be obscure or even totally unknown. In many cases, this is intentional and gives the players a chance to decide exactly what that gear does, based on the name. Gear is there to fuel Narrations and open up possibilities for storytelling, rather than carry specific mechanics.

HACKING AND CYBERCOMBAT

Since its introduction, the virtual data network of the Matrix has become a ubiquitous aspect of life for metahumans around the world, and deckers the world over ride the electrons to keep information free. The following rules provide guidelines on how to hack into systems and engage in cybercombat within the virtual world of the Matrix.

AR vs. VR: Deckers can access the Matrix in two ways: via AR (augmented reality) or VR (virtual reality). When using AR, you interact with the Matrix via a software window, viewing your persona, files, and other Matrix objects as icons in the window. However, when you're using VR, you dive into the virtual world, putting your whole awareness into the Matrix: you *become* your persona.

Accessing the Matrix via AR does not confer any bonuses, but going full VR confers a +1 bonus to any Hacking Tests. This bonus is noted on Shadow Amps that allow VR connection, such as datajacks and trodes, and it always applies in VR, even if another Amp is used to affect a Test while in VR.

However, when in VR, you cannot take any actions or use any Skills that would require the use of your physical body (gamemaster's discretion), and cybercombat (see below) can be more lethal.

Hacking: Now that you've gotten access to the Matrix, you probably want to start doing something that the ever-vigilant Grid Overwatch Division deems illegal. To defy GOD, you'll need your trusty Hacking Skill. Anything you want to access or control—be it a security camera, an electronic keypad, a secure system, a certain file, any Matrix-connected device, and so on—will require you to hack into the virtual Matrix object that represents it.

To make a hacking attempt, roll a standard Hacking Test and apply an applicable Shadow Amp effect or a bonus conferred by a cyberdeck. Failure might not necessarily trigger an alarm, but you are certainly free to narrate one if you think it will benefit the storytelling. If the Test is successful, you have succeeded in putting a mark—your persona's digital signature—on the Matrix object and can now access it. Certain objects, such as hostile Matrix objects like IC, sprites, and other personas cannot be marked and instead must be defeated in cybercombat.

Cybercombat: When a decker accesses the Matrix either via AR or full VR, all combat that takes place there will be cybercombat between their virtual persona and various Matrix threats, such as hostile personas and sprites, intrusion countermeasures (IC), and so on. Cybercombat represents using brute force in the Matrix, by sending data spikes and malicious code intended to crash the targeted threat.

To engage in cybercombat, the attacker must spend an attack action (see **Attack Limits**, p. 40). Use the Hacking Skill and an applicable Shadow Amp, such as a program, to aid the attack. Sprites and other Matrix constructs will use an appropriate Skill. Defense dice roll Logic + Firewall. Thus the dice-rolling mechanic for cybercombat is:

Hacking Dice + Logic Dice + Modifiers (if any) + Shadow Amp Effect (if any) vs. **Logic Dice + Firewall Dice + Modifiers (if any) + Shadow Amp Effect (if any)**

Stun damage to a decker using a cyberdeck is applied to the Condition Monitor of the cyberdeck itself, regardless of whether the target is using AR or VR (a cyberdeck's Condition Monitor is [(Device Rating / 2) + 8]. Physical damage, when using VR, is applied directly to the character's Condition Monitor, bypassing any armor worn; if using AR, apply Physical damage to the cyberdeck's Condition Monitor instead. When a cyberdeck's Condition Monitor is completely filled, the user is kicked out of the Matrix, and the cyberdeck is severely damaged, requiring the expenditure of 1 Karma to get working again, which not only makes it functional but fully repairs the Condition Monitor.

The Electronics Skill can be used to repair cyberdeck damage. See **Damage, Armor, and the Condition Monitor**, p. 42.

DIVING DEEP INTO THE MATRIX: OPTIONAL MATRIX RULES

For the ease of *Shadowrun: Anarchy* play, the mechanics for hacking the Matrix are intended to be simple and straightforward to keep action high; however, many players may wish to add an additional level of depth and intrigue to their Matrix experience. Here are a couple of optional guidelines that deck cowboys and virtuakinetics can include in their games if they wish.

Marks: In standard rules, only a single mark is needed to gain access to a Matrix object. When using advanced rules, the number of marks needed is determined by the GM. This number can vary depending on the security level and the difficulty of the Hacking Test. For example, hacking into a coffin motel's vending machine would be Very Easy (4 opposing dice) and only require a single mark. Spoofing a security camera at your local McHugh's might have a difficulty of Easy (6 opposing dice) and need two marks to gain access to it. But if you're trying to sleaze into a file vault at a high-security Renraku data farm, then the difficulty might ratchet up to Hard (10 opposing dice) and require three or four marks to gain access.

Noise: Standard rules assume that you will have a perfect connection between your cyberdeck and the system or device you are attempting to sleaze or brute-force your way into. However, in reality, this is rarely the case. A veritable soup of ARO spam (AR objects), electronic countermeasures, and so forth create an ever-worsening signal-to-noise ratio that only degrades further the greater the distance away from your target you are.

To determine noise, treat all Hacking actions as though you are using a weapon with the following range brackets: Close OK, Near –2, Far –4. (See **Weapons**, p. 40, for more about ranges). For example, if the system or device you are attempting to access is in Near range, you would apply a –2 modifier for any Hacking Tests made for or in that system.

Technomancers: Technomancers, a.k.a. virtuakinetics, are those rare few who can use a poorly understood ability to wirelessly access the Matrix directly with their own brains, without the need for a cyberdeck, a commlink, or any form of hardware or software. By using their own brains like computer software, a technomancer can experience the Matrix in AR or full VR.

The following rules govern the use of technomancers in *Shadowrun: Anarchy*.

- **Complex Forms:** Technomancers have no cyberdeck to hold programs. Instead they possess complex forms, Shadow Amps that replicate the effects of certain cyberdeck programs. These are applied in Matrix-related Tests and cybercombat just like standard Shadow Amps.
- **Cybercombat Defense:** Technomancers have no hardware to rely on in cyber combat, so they roll Logic x 2 against the attacker's dice when defending in cybercombat.
- **Matrix Damage:** Technomancers use their bare brains with no buffer against malignant computer code. Damage a technomancer suffers in cybercombat is applied directly to the appropriate track on the character's Condition Monitor, regardless of AR or VR. Any Shadow Amps that reduce cybercombat damage can be used to lower the damage received. When a technomancer's Condition Monitor reaches Staggered, Knocked Out, or Killed In Action, their persona is kicked out of the Matrix.
- **Sprites:** The constantly flowing data streams have also given rise to strange virtual entities known as sprites. Only technomancers can use the Tasking Skill to compile sprites from the Resonance, the energy streaming throughout the Matrix; deckers cannot compile sprites.

Compiling a sprite costs a full attack action. Success on a Tasking Test summons one sprite of the chosen type. A successfully conjured sprite acts like an NPC and has its own NPC sheet, but unless the gamemaster says otherwise, the player who compiled a sprite narrates the sprite's actions and rolls the sprite's dice during their own Narration.

A player may only have one compiled sprite at a time. To compile another, the player must first either decompile it with a successful Tasking Test (upon which it will return to the Resonance) or let its last Condition Monitor box get damaged.

Sprites are Matrix entities and thus can only be damaged in cybercombat or by another technomancer using the Tasking Skill to decompile the sprite.

Decompiling a sprite into harmless, random lines of code costs a full attack action. Use the Tasking Skill in a cybercombat roll against the sprite's defense dice. If the roll succeeds, deal the sprite a number of damage equal to the technomancer's Logic.

SPELLS, SPIRITS, AND ASTRAL COMBAT

Mana is a constant, everyday reality in the Sixth World, and knowing its ins and outs is a good way to stay alive. The following rules provide guidelines on how to cast spells, conjure and command spirits, and engage in astral combat on the astral plane.

Spells: Spells in *Shadowrun: Anarchy* fall into two categories: combat spells and effect spells. Combat spells inflict damage, either Physical or Stun; effect spells accomplish some form of non-damaging effect.

Casting a spell counts as an attack action for your Narration (see **Attack Limits**, p. 40). To cast a spell, make a Sorcery Test (opposed by the target, as listed with the spell, and use the Shadow Amp effect for the chosen spell. Success means the spell was cast successfully: a noncombat spell's effect occurs, or a combat spell applies its damage.

The damage and defense dice for a combat spell is listed in its description. Net hits by the attacker are either added as damage or have some other effect, based on the spell.

For example, let's take a look at Coydog's Lightning Bolt spell:

Lightning Bolt (Spell): 6P/AA
Reroll one failed die
Defense: S + W

The Shadow Amp effect lets Coydog reroll one die, and the defender will roll Strength and Willpower (S + W) against Coydog's hits. If Coydog wins the roll, then the defender will take 6P damage; the AA stands for Armor Avoidance, which means that any net hits on the spellcasting test do not add to the damage as normal, but rather indicate damage that bypassed the target's armor. So if Coydog rolled 4 hits and the target rolled 2, she has 2 net hits, meaning she did 6P damage total, and 2P of that bypasses the target's armor and goes right to the Condition Monitor. If a spell with Armor Avoidance has more net hits than the total amount of damage inflicted by the spell, all damage avoids armor, and the extra net hits have no further effect.

Combat spells are instantaneous; the spell immediately ends once its damage has been applied.

Effect spells last for as long as the spellcaster and story requires the spell to last. When the caster's next Narration arrives, the player can simply declare they are sustaining the spell they cast last turn; no Sorcery Test is needed. A character may only sustain one spell at a time. Depending on the complexity of the spell and/or how many turns the player has sustained the spell, the gamemaster may impose a negative modifier for any rolls the player makes while sustaining a spell.

Spirits: Players and NPCs can use the Conjuring Skill to summon spirits. Success on a Conjuring Test summons one spirit of the chosen type. Spirits are listed as NPCs on p. 138 to make things easy for both players and gamemasters. If a player wants to summon a particularly powerful spirit, the GM should increase the difficulty of the opposed roll and then give more powerful spells or effects to the spirit should the Conjuring Test succeed. A successfully conjured spirit acts like an NPC and has its own NPC sheet, but unless the gamemaster says otherwise, the player who conjured a spirit narrates the spirit's actions and rolls the spirit's dice during their own Narration.

Conjuring a spirit costs an attack action. Under normal circumstances, a player may only have one conjured spirit at a time. To conjure another, the player must first either dismiss the existing spirit with a successful Conjuring Test (upon which it will vanish), let it reach Knocked Out or Killed In Action, or wait until the spirit vanishes at dawn or at dusk.

Spirits are resilient and can only be easily damaged by spells, weapon foci, the Conjuring Skill, and the Astral Combat Skill (only in astral space: see *Astral Combat* below). However-er, it is possible to hurt a spirit by putting the force of one's will into a physical strike. To attack a spirit in this way, use Close Combat + Willpower (instead of Agility) with a –2 modifier. If successful, apply the attacker's Unarmed weapon damage to the spirit.

Banishing a spirit severs the mystical connection between the spirit and its summoner. Use the Conjuring Skill in a combat roll against the spirit's defense dice. If the roll succeeds, deal the spirit a number of Stun damage equal to the magician's Willpower.

Astral Projection: A magician can visit the astral plane by undergoing astral projection. This is accomplished by voluntarily detaching your essence and leaving your corporeal body behind in meat space. No test is needed for leaving your body or for returning to it later. However, if you return to find out your body has been moved in the interim, you have a different set of challenges to face.

Astral Combat: All combat that takes place on the astral plane is astral combat. On the astral plane, char-acters can battle against spirits, dual-natured critters (which inhabit both the physical and astral planes simultaneously), wards and other astral phenomena, other astrally projecting magicians, and so forth.

To engage in astral combat, the attacker must spend an attack action (see **Attack Limits**, p. 40). Use the Astral Combat Skill (or just Willpower, if untrained), and you may apply an applicable Shadow Amp, such as a damaging spell or a weapon focus, to aid their attack. Spirits and other astral denizens will use an appropriate Skill to engage in astral combat.

Any damage characters and NPCs take in astral combat is applied to the Stun track of the Condition Monitor.

VEHICLE AND DRONE COMBAT

Between the constant threat of go-gangs, police chases, military campaigns, and other vehicular shenanigans, there's bound to be some pedal-to-the-metal action in *Shadowrun: Anarchy*. Vehicle and drone combat is handled in the same way as standard Tests and combat rolls. Here are a few specific clarifications to help you burn rubber.

AR vs. VR: Vehicles and drones equipped with a Rigger Interface can be piloted either via AR (augmented reality) or VR (virtual reality). When using AR, you either control the vehicle manually or with a remote-control rig via an AR window. When you're using VR, you put your whole awareness into a vehicle or drone: you *are* the vehicle. Piloting a vehicle via AR does not confer any bonuses, but jumping into the vehicle and piloting via VR confers a +1 bonus to any Piloting or Vehicle Weapons Tests. This bonus is noted on the Control Rig Shadow Amp, and it always applies in VR, even if another Shadow Amp is used to affect a Test while in VR. When in VR, you cannot take any actions or use any Skills that would require the use of your physical body (GM's discretion).

Vehicle Movement: A character piloting a vehicle can move that vehicle from Far to Close with regards to a person on foot in a single action. They can also slow it down and move it from Far to Near in a single action (the reverse of these two actions also apply). This only applies in relation to a character on foot; if a character is in a vehicle, the normal movement rules apply.

Maneuvering and Stunts: Normal driving or piloting tasks like changing speeds and ranges don't require dice rolls, just a good Narration. However, if you want to attempt something risky—a hairpin turn, weaving through traffic, sliding your bike under a semi truck, driving a car on two wheels through a narrow alley, ramming another car, avoiding knocked-down debris, or some other dangerous moving violation—make a standard Test using the appropriate Piloting Skill (or just Agility, if untrained) and any modifiers the gamemaster deems applicable. If you are successful, the maneuver executes as planned; if you fail, you'd better hope you're wearing a helmet and/or have an up-to-date DocWagon contract: see *Crashes* below.

Attacking from a Vehicle or Drone: A character attempting an attack while inside or top of a vehicle or while piloting a drone makes a combat roll as normal, using an appropriate Skill. Due to the nature of fighting from on or inside a vehicle, appropriate modifiers apply to the attack. Most modifiers are up to the gamemaster, but here are some examples:

- **Passenger firing a personal weapon from a moving vehicle:** –1 or –2, depending on speed
- **Firing at a stationary vehicle:** +3
- **Firing at a vehicle moving at top speed:** –3.

Note that these modifiers do not apply to riggers using Shadow Amp drones or vehicles; they are assumed to have the skill to adapt to the movement of their equipment, and they simply receive the bonus as noted by the Amp. A character who attacks with any vehicle- or drone-mounted weaponry cannot use their own individual weapons during that same Narration.

Attacking a Vehicle or Drone: Combat actions against a piloted vehicle or drone are resolved like normal combat rolls, but the defender rolls the Agility + Logic of the pilot or driver controlling the targeted vehicle.

Damage to Vehicles and Drones: Vehicles and drones both have a number of Armor circle representing how much damage they can take. Successful attacks against a vehicle damage the vehicle's Armor pips and not the passengers. Once a vehicle's armor is depleted, the vehicle is out of commission and probably totaled, depending on the situation. Vehicle armor can be repaired in the same manner as character armor. When Shadow Amp drone lose all of their armor, they are not lost, but the Amp cannot be used until at least one Armor circle is repaired.

Crashes: If a vehicle crashes due to a failed Piloting Test or vehicle damage, the vehicle, pilot, and passengers will take damage equal to Damage Value of the vehicle's Ramming weapon. If the vehicle does not have Ramming, apply Physical damage equal to the vehicle's Durability divided by 2.

Storytelling: How damage to a vehicle affects its movement, weapons fire, and so on is absolutely up to the plot and how the storyline is developing: just remember that any vehicle is as strong—or not—as the plot needs it to be (though some Mission Briefs will provide specifics to help things alone). Instead of tracking the nitty-gritty details of damage effects to a vehicle, the gamemaster should weave that type of information into the narrative: engine sputtering and billowing smoke; tires shredding; explosive decompressions (if in space), or flooding with water (if underwater); ammo exploding (if in a military vehicle); abrupt one-thousand-meter drops in altitude (if flying); power system fluctuations and failures. The sky is the limit for the fun and challenging scenarios you can throw at players to overcome during such a conflict.

ADDITIONAL RULES

The Cue System is not rules heavy. Instead, it's about creating a framework off of which players simply spin up their imaginations through improv play to work through whatever characters, environments, and terrain they may come across. However, the very nature of magic and machine—not to mention exotic places like ghoul realms, magical disaster areas, the toxic northern beaches of the Allied German States, or any other unusual locale populating the Sixth World—means players might stumble a bit here and there.

For those that would like a few more guidelines when dealing with extreme situations, use the following rules. Of course, these can be used to craft further rules that will cover a variety of other circumstances and locales a player group may encounter.

BREATHING

Various situation and environments, such as toxic areas, being underwater, or running out of oxygen in a space environment, may threaten a character's ability to breathe.

A character can hold their breath for a number of Narrations equal to their Strength divided by three, rounded up. Once this period expires, the character will suffer 1 point of Stun Damage (ignoring Armor) until they can safely take another breath. Once a character has been reduced to Knocked Out status, he will take 2 boxes of Physical damage until breathing can resume or all Condition Monitor boxes are crossed off.

ENVIRONMENTAL CONDITIONS

The following rules for environmental conditions are optional and should be agreed on before gameplay. In all

instances, as usual, final adjudication for what does or doesn't work under these circumstances falls under the GM's purview.

- **Darkness:** A dim room or fighting at night inflicts a –1 modifier to all die rolls; complete darkness conveys a –3 modifier. Numerous characters or NPCs might ignore this due to various gear (night vision goggles), an appropriate Kiken Aug (cybereyes), or natural abilities (a dwarf or troll with thermographic vision).
- **Acid and toxic waste:** Coming in contact with acid, toxic waste, or other corrosive substances will cause a lasting damage effect. Any such substance initially inflicts 2 points of damage to armor, or 1 point of Physical damage if armor is depleted. Unless the substance can be immediately washed off or treated with a repair kit (for armor damage) or some form of healing (for Physical damage), the substance will inflict the same amount of damage for another two Narrations (or turns for NPCs without Narrations) before rendering itself inert.
- **Liquid Metals/Rocks:** There are numerous situations where characters might encounter magma or molten metals, such as a foundry in a Saeder-Krupp factory or active volcanoes in the Kingdom of Hawai'i. Coming in contact with such a substance causes 3 points of armor damage and 1 point of Physical damage as the character starts to cook. Incidental splashes of such substances only cause 1 armor damage.
- **Hot/noxious gas:** Hot/noxious gas affects visibility by imposing a –2 modifier when a character or NPC is trying to attack into or through a cloud of gas. Moving through a jet of gas causes 2 points of Physical damage, regardless of how many armor circles the character has remaining (i.e., no armor circles are reduced).
- **Underwater:** Due to the difficulty with moving while submerged in water, ranged weapons suffer a –1 modifier, and melee weapons incur a –3 modifier.
- **Airless vacuum:** Treat any airless situation as forcing characters to hold their breath (see **Breathing**, p. 48).

MIND CONTROL

Various enemies and characters may have the ability to take over a character and control her actions, via a Mind Control spell, chemical coercion, brainwashing, spiritual possession, or other nefarious means. When this occurs, the following rules are in effect.

When a character or NPC is under the effects of mind control, the controlling player dictates that person's actions during the character or NPCs appropriate Narrations rather than the controlling player. Successful mind control will remain in effect until the affected character resists the control or the controlling enemy is Staggered or Knocked Out.

A successful mind control attempt will last a minimum of one of the affected character's Narrations. Every subsequent Narration, the affected character must take a Willpower + Logic Test; succeeding in the Test ends the mind control.

An NPC controlling a character may not make the character perform any actions that would result in her own death or the death of her companions; she will disbelieve those actions so strongly that the enemy cannot force her to take them. In other words, a mind-controlled character cannot shoot herself in the temple, shove a character out a window, and so on. However, groups who prefer a more realistic and gritty campaign may agree to allow such potentially lethal actions.

BUILDING STREET CRED

PLAYING ANARCHY

Shadowrunners know that it's one thing to know what you're supposed to do on a run, but it's another to know how to pull it off with style. You've seen the basic rules for playing *Shadowrun: Anarchy*; here now are some tips for playing it well, making the game go smoothly, and pulling off runs you'll be talking about long after the game is played.

WHEN IT'S YOUR NARRATION

It's great when you can do something extraordinary, unusual, or hilarious on every Narration, but remember—one of the reasons a Plot Point is awarded for a particularly good Narration is that such Narrations do not happen every turn.

What this means is that while players should always be looking for opportunities to do the extraordinary, they should not feel too much pressure to come up with something amazing every turn. Your first job is to let everyone know what your character is up to and provide details about what is happening around them; accomplish that much, and the story will keep moving. Anything you add to that is gravy.

Here are some things to consider when building your Narration that can help add unusual twists or other elements that will keep the game interesting.

HOW CAN YOUR CHARACTER KEEP THE OPPOSITION ON THEIR TOES?

There are always obstacles in the Sixth World—people and things trying to keep you from earning your much-needed Karma. Good shadowrunners know how to stay a step or two ahead of them. When your Narration comes up, other people, both PCs and NPCs, will be doing things, and so much of what you will be doing is responding to them (on the simplest level, if they shoot, you shoot back). If you can do more than just react, though, and can make a move that will stymie the opposition, or anticipate their next move, or just plain confuse them, you'll not only put yourself in good position for whatever happens next, but you'll take the story in interesting directions.

Some examples: If you see you're being followed, the simplest thing is to try to shake the tail. But more advanced techniques include changing your destination and leading the tail to somewhere you did not intend to travel, or creating an illusory car to make an extra challenge for the pursuers. Another example is having a security guard ask to see your clearance. You may attempt to pass with genuine or fake credentials, but if you want to throw security a curveball, confess your complete lack of credentials, then work to weave a narrative that will make security want to let you in anyway ("There's a team of shadowrunners in your facility *right now*, and your best chance of stopping them and maybe *saving your fraggin' job* is to let me back there!").

HOW CAN YOU SHOW THE ELEMENTS THAT MAKE YOUR CHARACTER DISTINCT?

Each character in the **Street People** chapter has some trait or characteristic that make them unusual and different from the rest of the pack. These are embodied in the Dispositions, Cues, and Backgrounds, and they can provide guides for characters to respond to challenges in ways that are in character and unique. Use them to take actions that will bend the story in compelling directions.

For example, let's say a corp exec is the target of an unwilling extraction, and in her effort to hold off the shadowrunners, she has taken a hostage. Different shadowrunners have potential responses that could take the story in interesting directions. Shades' background (p. 120) in a corporate environment might make her want to opt for reason, helping the exec understand her position and why it might be good to go along—and let the poor hostage go. Knox (p. 104), on the other hand, has a chip on her shoulder and a willingness to use force to mix things up, so she might decide that the hostage situation is best resolved with some fast punches to the head. Let the characters' natures add twists to the stories.

WHAT'S COOL IN THE SIXTH WORLD?

This is a loaded question, because the answer is: a lot. Between magical alchera—vaguely material bridges to other dimensions—ferocious critters, savage toxic shamans, crazed gillettes and razorgirls, drakes working in the service of their draconic masters, enigmatic free spirits, and much more, there are a ton of elements out there that can be thrown in to a story. If the game you're in needs something to juice it up, reach into the *Shadowrun* bag of tricks and pick out an element that you really like, especially if it's something that hasn't been in your game for a while. Nothing like a roaming free spirit to shake the game up!

WHAT WILL MAKE THE GAME BETTER FOR OTHER PLAYERS?

This is always a good guideline, but some specific applications of it can help the game move well. Is there a player who has not had a chance to use their best skills recently? Steer the story in a way that will give them something to do. Did a player introduce a new element? Build on it to make sure it becomes part of the story. Look for opportunities to make sure everyone is included and interesting things keep happening, and the game will go better for all.

This guideline can also help you know how long to make your narration, paying attention to how others are reacting, how involved they are, and how anxious they are for their turn to begin. Paying attention to such elements will make you a better player.

WHEN IT'S NOT YOUR NARRATION

Just because it's not your turn doesn't mean you have nothing to do at the table. Planning for your Narra-

tion, including how your character will react to unfolding developments, is part of what you can do, but far from the only things. Interactions between players is one of the best parts of role-playing, and *Anarchy* works best when that continues. The player conducting the Narration will be moving the story forward, but other players are free to contribute thoughts, advice, quick character responses, and of course the occasional smart remark. The guideline is the same as the last question asked above: What will make the game better? Keeping the Narration from moving forward, interrupting too much, or criticizing the choices of the player will likely not help make the game work well. Adding ideas and humor will. Support the Narration in the way you want your Narration supported!

DIFFERENT WAYS TO RUN

One of the advantages of the *Anarchy* game model is that it's flexible. The default Turns and Narration structure allows for turn order and the use of Plot Points to be its initiative structure; the storytelling and initiative are intertwined in order to make for a more narrative-focused experience. Some groups may prefer different playing styles, though, so tweaking a few elements can adapt it to suit their playing styles. This section offers a few tweaks that some groups might want to use: a way to concentrate most gamemaster powers in a single person at the table, and two alternate initiative systems—one that is more mechanically based, rather than the default narrative-based initiative system, and another that is more free-flowing and cinematic.

A MORE FOCUSED GAMEMASTER

Rotating the shared elements of the gamemaster back into a single GM is primarily about limiting how Plot Points may be spent so that they fit more traditional player roles. This means that player uses of Plot Points would include the following:

- **Double time it:** Take two movement actions to close on—or get away from—an opponent
- **First aid:** Heal a point of Physical or Stun damage.
- **Take the hit:** If a weaker or injured character is successfully hit by a combat action—i.e., the target rolled fewer hits than the attacker—then a player can spend a Plot Point to take the hit instead. The original target's defense roll is ignored, and the interrupting player rolls their own defense dice against the attacker's hits.

- **A dish best served cold:** Immediately take one free attack action against the NPC who just attacked you. This attack does not count as a Narration.
- **Glitch Die:** The Glitch Die can be used, but it is no longer applied to other players (though the GM can of course still apply it as they feel appropriate). Instead, players can pay a Plot Point to include a Glitch Die on one of their own rolls in the hopes of getting an Exploit (p. 39). If they roll a Glitch (p. 39) the player can either accept it as is, or spend two Plot Points to avoid the Glitch. Remember the Narrative nature of *Shadowrun: Anarchy*, however, and if the player manages to create a memorable Narration to explain how the glitch was avoided, the gamemaster should award the player a Plot Point back (meaning that in effect, it only cost 1 Plot Point to avoid the problem).

Each player group that selects this rule will ultimately need to come to a consensus on what a player can and can't spend Plot Points on and how much that can affect GM-like events.

Gamemaster: When using this rule, the following additional rules apply to how the gamemaster may spend Plot Points:

- A GM can spend a number of Plot Points per turn equal to the number of players. However, only two Plot Points may be spent on the same player a turn.
- A GM earns two Plot Points for every Plot Point spent by a Player.

One other change that needs to be made to play with a more traditional gamemaster is to make Perception Tests (p. 38) more traditional—that is, instead of having the player describe what they see if they win the test, the GM gives them the information, with more information coming based on how many net hits the player rolled.

ROLLING INITIATIVE

Shadowrun: Anarchy's initiative system is based on two primary things—the position of people at the table and the use of Plot Points. It is built to be non-intrusive and fast-moving. Some groups, though, might want a more mechanically oriented system—so we have one!

In this system, players roll for initiative to determine who goes first. Generally speaking, initiative should be rolled at the beginning of each Scene, and then would stay consistent for the whole Scene. Depending on the

group's tolerance for rolling dice, initiative could be rolled before each combat starts, or even at the beginning of each round of combat.

To use this system, follow these steps:

- Each player should start building their Initiative Dice Pool using the following number of dice based upon their Game Level (see p. 62): Gang = 4 dice; Street Runner = 6 dice; Prime Runner = 8 dice.
- For each element of a character sheet that provides additional Plot Points (such as Shadow Amps or Qualities), that player adds a D6 for each bonus Plot Point they would receive. For example, Improved Reflexes 2, among other things, provides a +1 Plot Point per Scene, which means that player would add 1D6 to their Initiative Dice Pool. (In that instance, the Shadow Amps still provides the Plot Point generation during game play.)
- Finally, each player may spend any amount of Plot Points they have at the start of a Scene to add dice to their Initiative Dice Pool; one Plot Point equals 1D6.
- All players roll their Initiative Dice Pool; characters with the highest number of successes go first in the round, moving down to those with the least. Ties are broken by looking to see which of the tied players have the highest Edge. If Edge ratings are the same, break the tie with Agility. If ties remain, simply us the order tied players are seated, starting from the GM's left and ending with the GM. The GM should track initiative order and tell players when it is their turn to act. Players with extra Combat Actions from Shadow Amps may still use them.
- At the start of the next Scene (or combat or round), repeat.

CINEMATIC INITIATIVE

For groups that want a more cinematic or freestyle method of handling Initiative and Narrations, use the following:

The first Narration when combat starts is handled in an intuitive, narrative fashion based on an agreement of the players (who sprang the ambush, who escalated the staredown by going for a gun, who has the highest appropriate Attribute, or a Shadow Amp related to speed or perception, and so on). When that player is finished, they choose who goes next based on what makes sense for the story or, when in doubt, where a hypothetical camera would be watching the fight if it were an action movie (meaning the first player to act might be a teammate attempting to coordinate with their fast friend, or it might go to the enemy that was just attacked, so that the action stays focused on the characters locked in close combat, for instance).

Narrations proceed, with the group choosing who goes next after each Narration, until every character has gone once. NPCs may be grouped together to speed this process up (so that a small group of low-level guards could act all at once, while their more dangerous security officer might have her own spot in this rotation). Plot Points may still be used to jump forward in line if a player so chooses, though naturally this will happen less due to the way initiative is established. Still, as events unfold in combat, some unexpected things may happen, leading to a player wanting to move their turn forward.

The character that acts last in a round then gets to choose who goes first in the next round. If it's what makes sense, it can even be them! Narrations continue in that vein until everyone has acted for the second time, then you repeat the process as long as the action keeps up, round after round.

CONTROLLING ANARCHY

Whether you're a veteran of the *Shadowrun* universe or just starting out on your adventures with the Cue System, gamemasters can benefit from some advice on how to help their *Shadowrun: Anarchy* games run smoothly and keep the enjoyment factor high. The following sections cover a number of topics and situations that gamemasters might encounter in their games.

PASSING THE MICROPHONE: TRADITIONAL ROLEPLAYING GAMES VS. THE CUE SYSTEM

One thing that makes *Anarchy* different from many other RPGs is that players do not describe only their actions, with the gamemaster describing the rest of the world around them and making the plot move forward. In *Anarchy*, players have more free rein to introduce NPCs, describe their actions, add in other elements, and describe the setting. While this may take some adjusting for GMs accustomed to traditional RPGs, this style can be seen as a great opportunity for GMs that puts less of a burden on them. They do not have to plan the whole story or have a roster of NPCs that they intend to introduce to the adventure. Their role is less about creating a master design at the outset of an adventure or campaign, and more about responding to the elements the players introduce while throwing interesting ideas of their own, helping the story move along while making sure all the players have a chance to shine. This role can involve some quick thinking and adaptability, but tapping into the creativity of the group can spread that work around, meaning the gamemaster will primarily be looking at keeping the story moving and making sure players and their characters feel like they have something useful to do.

In *Anarchy*, players are still going to primarily see the game from the perspective of their characters, so significant parts of their Narrations will focus on what their characters do and how they respond to events around them. They also might decide to describe the actions of some NPCs, or add twists to the environment around them (such as introducing a sudden burst of acid rain, or a wild critter wandering close to the characters). This means that during another player's Narration, the GM no longer has total control over the story or the game. During another player's Narration, the GM's main responsibilities are as follows:

- Deciding whether an action requires the player roll a Test
- Declaring what modifiers (if any) apply to a Test
- Determining what Attribute(s) applies to an Attribute-only Test
- Roleplaying NPCs
- Making defense rolls for NPCs
- Knowing the information in the Contract Brief
- Arbitrating rules discussions
- Declaring that a player's Narration is finished (such as if a Narration has lasted for too long)

Many other elements that might be considered traditional RPG gamemaster duties—describing the scene, detailing what NPCs are doing, having enemies appear, and so forth—fall to the player who is currently giving a Narration. The GM's main role in relation to these elements is to listen carefully and to see how to use the events and plot twists the characters are using in the ongoing story.

When you're the GM and another player is giving a Narration, you might be tempted to jump in and correct them or do something out of turn. However, think of a Narration as a microphone: only the person holding the mic can describe what is going on in the game itself. You, the GM, start the turn with the mic. Once you set the scene for the turn, you pass the mic to the next player, and then it's their time to speak. When other players have the mic, just kick back and let them have their moment, keeping in mind the "Yes, and …" improv spirit of the Cue System. The only time you need to interject is for one of the conditions in the list above.

For those who are more familiar with traditional-style RPGs, it may help to think of Narrations in this way: When a player is giving their Narration, they act like a "micro-gamemaster" for the game, but only during their Narration. When the next player gives a Narration, they act like a micro-gamemaster for that Narration, and so on.

Because each player helps craft the story on their turn, the goal of *Anarchy* games is collaborative storytelling; in the end, the players and GM should be working together to create something memorable and fun.

KEEPING IT CIVIL: PREVENTING ABUSE

One of the GM's duties is to make sure the game runs smoothly and that everyone has fun. Here are a few suggestions to prevent players from abusing the game or keeping other players from having fun.

REFEREEING

One of the double-edged swords of the Cue System is control. The players enjoy a lot more control over the game during their Narration, but they can seize too much control if the GM doesn't apply the brakes now and then. The only inherent limit for a Narration is that each player can take one combat-related action (see p. 40), but everything else, such as giving descriptions, roleplaying, and taking non-combat Tests, is up to the player giving the Narration. The Narration ends when the player decides it ends, such as on a nice cliffhanger for the next player to riff off of. Every player should have an equal amount of time in the spotlight, however, so if one player's Narration seems to be taking an exorbitant amount of time in comparison to other players, it can suck some of the fun out of the game, especially if someone's been waiting for their Narration for a long while. If one player is going on for too long and not showing any signs of letting up any time soon, feel free to exercise your GM authority to have the player wrap it up—or in the worst instances, you may declare that the Narration is over right then. If that player has not yet taken their combat-related action by that point, then the action is forfeited—clearly, the character was busy with too many other things to get in an attack.

BUILDING UP INSTEAD OF TEARING DOWN

Shadowrun: Anarchy works best when everyone around the table listens to one another and builds on the story elements that players and gamemasters introduce. Sometimes, players or GMs might be tempted to use their Narrations to circumvent problems introduced by another player, or to cut off storytelling branches that they do not find appealing. Alternately, players might use their Narrations to heap difficulties on one or more other players, constantly throwing obstacles at them or neutralizing their abilities while letting themselves off easy.

All of these go against the spirit of collaborative storytelling, and it is up to the gamemaster to keep the story moving forward, instead of watching it do a constant back-and-forth as one player introduces plot elements that are immediately negated by another. Some strategies to help with this include:

- **Set the tone right from the start:** Make sure players know that they are supposed to build on each other's ideas, not tear them down, at the outset of the game with a quick review of how the game works.
- **Plan on how to work other players' suggestions into the story:** When looking over a Contract Brief before a game, consider ways that NPCs suggested by the players might be worked into the story—different roles they could fill in the larger plot. Then, when a player introduces a new NPC, you can smoothly integrate them into the storyline.
- **Intervene when players move to negate other players' contributions:** If one player introduces, say, a traffic pileup on the interstate in front of the players, then another player has some air spirits swoop in to quickly clean up the rubble without it affecting the story, that's the time to gently intervene and suggest that the players let the wreck become part of the story, rather than have it canceled out. Intervening quickly will help make sure players listen to one another rather than work at cross-purposes.
- **Ask questions tied to newly introduced story elements:** As discussed in the **Ask Good**

Questions section (p. 58), a directed and specific question can help focus a player's thoughts about how to respond to a newly introduced element. The way the question is phrased and the tone of voice the gamemaster uses can help build excitement for the new story elements.

ENCOURAGING PLAYER OPTIONS

Sometimes a player will keep using the same high-damage spell or the same highly effective weapon turn after turn. While this repetition is not against any rules, it may end up with one or more characters dominating the game to the detriment of other players. Also, performing the same action repeatedly doesn't add a lot of story interest to what is at heart a game that focuses on storytelling. If the players tend to simply spam the same spell or weapon or Skill every single Narration, here are a few options to encourage them to try something different.

Target Tokens: Any time a player repeats an action more than once in consecutive Narrations—firing the same gun without moving, casting the same spell, etc.—then that player earns a Target Token. These can be any type of marker, but they should be easy to differentiate from Plot Points. Once a player has earned three Target Tokens, the GM can cash those in for a +3 modifier to an NPC's action against that player. Target Tokens do not carry over from one combat to the next.

Cooldown: Before play begins, the GM can decide that certain actions have a cooldown period. An action that has a cooldown period simply means the player may not perform that same action on two consecutive turns. This represents a Gear item needing to recharge, a heavy weapon that has a complex reloading system, a spell that needs a lot of energy and concentration to cast, and so on. If a player with a cooldown action wishes to perform that action again in the next turn, they must spend a Plot Point to ignore the cooldown requirement.

SMOOTH TALKIN': INTERACTIONS BETWEEN PLAYERS

Due to the pass-the-microphone nature of *Shadowrun: Anarchy*, players might wonder how much they are allowed to interact with each other during another player's Narration (See **Passing the Microphone**, p. 55). After all, the person giving the Narration essentially has the microphone, so interrupting that player would be considered rude, *neh*?

Here are a few guidelines for handling player interactions during a player's Narration.

YOU'RE GONNA LOVE THIS!

If a player has a great idea or suggestion for advancing the story, but it's not their turn, they can spend a Plot Point to interject and offer their contribution, essentially pausing the current player's Narration. This contribution, be it a small detail or a large one, should be short, limited to one or two sentences max, and then the current player can continue their Narration.

ROLEPLAYING BANTER

During a player's Narration, other players are encouraged to roleplay their characters if and where appropriate, such as by responding to a question or adding to a discussion. Players should feel like they can participate in general roleplaying banter when it's not their own Narration, but the GM should strive to prevent any one player from stealing the limelight from the player who is giving their Narration. For a more freeform option to roleplaying, see *Talk Time* below.

TALK TIME

For most Scenes and Turns, each player giving a Narration one at a time will work best, as it will keep the story moving, give people a chance to be creative on their Narration, and also provide a structure where people can use Plot Points. Sometimes, though, the turn-based structure might interfere with the flow of conversation when runners are doing some group activity, like meeting with a Mr. Johnson, questioning a witness, or engaging in other activities where the whole group might want to participate in the conversation. In these circumstances, the GM can declare—or players can request—Talk Time, where the turn-based Narration structure is temporarily suspended while players engage in free-wheeling conversation. However, once the conversation gets beyond mere talk and into Tests—like when someone starts a serious Negotiation and Intimidation—it's time to let the story proceed through turns again. If Talk Time was requested during a player's Narration, that player can either choose to continue their Narration or opt to let the next player pick up from there.

I COULD USE SOME HELP HERE: OFFERING HINTS

Sometimes players might get stuck on their Narration and not really know what to do. This can come from inexperience with the Cue System or the *Shadowrun* universe

in general, lack of confidence in their role-playing abilities, or any number of other factors. If a player is having trouble coming up with something for their Narration, they should first look to their Cues, Skills, Gear, Contacts, and so forth. Each character sheet has a wealth of options for a Narration. However, if none of those seem to spark any ideas, the player can request outside help, or another player can offer to step in and assist.

GMs can use the following options to help a struggling player.

ASK GOOD QUESTIONS

One of the strongest things gamemasters can do to help shape Narrations and inspire ideas is to ask a good question to start off the Narration. Rather than simply saying "It's your turn" or asking "What do you do?", GMs can use questions as a prompt to help players focus on what they can do and how they might respond to the situations around them. Consider these strategies that can help generate questions that inspire action:

- **Offer a quick summary of events directly affecting the PC:** Something like "The ceiling of the underground lake is crumbling, your smuggler friend is urging you to get onto his submersible, and angry merrow are emerging from a flooded tunnel. How are you going to save your hoop?" can help players focus on matters of particular urgency that need their attention.
- **Remind them of plans they have made or goals they need to accomplish:** Players sometimes get so caught up in ongoing events that they lose focus on their larger goals, so reminding them of what they're supposed to be doing can help them move in a way that will keep the story on track. "How are you going to get past the security desk so you can infiltrate the corp exec's office?" or "You've located the gang's hideout—how are you going to approach the people inside so you can find the leader?" are examples of this approach.
- **Focus on particularly novel or interesting twists that you or other players have introduced:** This approach both gives players something interesting to focus on and rewards players for introducing compelling concepts during their narration. These questions can be something like "A strange blue mist just appeared over your head. What does it feel like to you?" or "Some 405 Hellhounds just rolled up next to you while you were cruising south. Want to shake them, ignore them, or something else?"

- **Prompt them with ways they could add a potential twist:** This doesn't mean suggesting specific plot twists, but rather suggesting possible areas where players could add something interesting. These questions could be something like "The stairway leads to a dark basement. What's hidden down there?" or "The exec's been acting nervous this whole time, and she looks like she has something to say. What is she going to tell you?"

OFFER A CLUE

Cues for what to do next can come from the GM or from other players.

From the GM: A struggling player can pay a Plot Point to ask the GM for some additional detail that might shake loose some ideas. The GM then provides a one- or two-sentence detail for the current events, and then it's all up to the narrating player.

The hint the GM gives doesn't necessarily need to come from what is outlined in a Contract Brief. The best hint prompts are those tailored to what is currently happening in the game. For example, if a player is in a room and can't decide what to do, then a good GM hint might be, "There's a spot of drywall that looks newer than the surrounding drywall," rather than some hint pointing toward the Contract Brief's ultimate goal. A prompt like this works better for the sake of immediacy than an an obscure clue trying to prod the story in the "correct" direction. (See *Jumping the Tracks* below.)

From Another Player: If another player sees a character struggling with a Narration, that player can spend a Plot Point to offer a one- or two-sentence detail as a prompt, in the same manner as outlined above. The GM may not spend a Plot Point to do this, only other players.

JUMPING THE TRACKS: HANDLING STORY DERAILMENT

The Cue System is all about telling a story, with each player building off what the previous player has added to the tale. The GM starts the story by using the Contract Brief as a guide: the Mr. Johnson's Pitch, the Setting, and the Scenes under Enemies/Obstacles all inform the GM as to the direction the story is initially intended to take. But what about those times when the players use their "micro-gamemaster" powers to make a Narration that swings the story in an unexpected direction that's completely opposite what the Contract Brief outlines? One of the strengths of the Cue System's style of story-

telling is that going off-rails from the as-written story is a feature, not a bug. Keeping that in mind, here are two approaches for handling a story that has jumped off the track. Depending on the situation, you may employ one or both of these options in the same game session.

BRING IT BACK AROUND

As the GM, you might feel that your role is to keep the story focused on what's written in the Contract Brief, and that's perfectly fine if that's the way your group wishes to play. But even when you as the GM are trying to ensure the story stays on track, player ingenuity, creative tangents, luck of the dice, and a number of other factors can potentially disrupt the story flow you intended. Minor derailments or subplots are to be encouraged due to the underlying improv nature of *Shadowrun: Anarchy*, but the major derailments, such as the ones that turn the story in the complete opposite direction, will often require some GM direction to steer back around.

The best method to bring the story back to its main focus is to first let the major derailment play out around the table until it comes back to your own Narration. (You may always spend Plot Points to affect the game before then, but doing so in such a blatant way may telegraph some of the secrets you are trying to keep under wraps.) You can then use your Narration and NPC actions (if any) to subtly align the story back toward what is written in the Contract Brief. Remember, though, that if you essentially override or nullify what another player has done, that player may get upset if the creative story development or awesome action they came up with is ignored or discarded out of hand, so if possible, try to work the derailment idea into the story direction that is outlined in the Contract Brief. This route preserves the direction of the story while also acknowledging that the other players' story accomplishments matter to the game.

For example, say one of the previous players killed the big bad NPC that the Contract Brief says is supposed to be the main villain of the piece. There was a big tussle on a suspension bridge, and the player shoved the NPC over the side and watched the lifeless corpse float on the ocean below. As the GM, you could easily invent some way to explain how this NPC didn't really die—you really need this NPC for a later scene!—even though the previous player's Narration was pretty specific, but going this route would essentially discard that player's story idea. A better way to bring the story back around to match the Contract Brief would be to let the death occur but then later introduce a new NPC who is either a relative or a close associate of the killed NPC, someone who intends to continue the deceased's agenda as outlined in the Contract Brief.

LET IT RIDE

If your group is not terribly concerned with playing out a specific story, the best method for handling a major story derailment is to simply sit back and let it stand, no matter how much it throws off the direction of the written story.

Unless a player sneaked a peek at the Contract Brief the group is playing, the GM is the only one who will actually know what is outlined in it, so none of the other players will ever know the story has gone too far off script. Depending on how far the story has strayed, it might even be beneficial to simply toss the Contract Brief as written and make a few notes on the fly for potential outcomes of this new story direction. Unless the new direction renders the Contract's written Objectives invalid or infeasible, the Objectives can still serve as a guide for what direction the story might go.

Once you've decided what parts of the Contract Brief to discard or keep (if any), then you can simply sit back and see where this new story goes. Letting it ride is a great way to discover unexpected story directions that could potentially lead to a multi-session campaign. Listen to the players—they will help shape the new story, with possibly only minor pushes from you.

LETTING THE LEAD FLY: COMBAT OPTIONS

There are a lot of ways to get maimed or killed in the Sixth World. If you are looking for some options to make combat a little faster, easier, or more survivable, here are some helpful options.

FALL BACK!

If the players are on the verge of having multiple characters Killed in Action or Knocked Out and they've already spent their allotment of Plot Points to keep themselves up and fighting, the best solution may be the hated retreat.

At the end of a round of Narrations, if all players agree, they can end the Scene. Any Plot Points remaining are forfeit (except those belonging to the GM, who receives an additional Plot Point). Additionally, the players cannot receive any Plot Points on their first two Narrations in the next Scene.

If the players failed to achieve any objectives in that Scene, then in addition to the restriction above, players will have a temporary maximum of 3 Plot Points (instead of the usual 5) for the duration of the next Scene.

JUST NEED A BREATHER

When using Cue System–style storytelling, the characters are likely to see their fair share of scrapes and bruises. Because of this, if the characters charge from one Scene to the next against tough NPCs without stopping to take stock of their condition, they're liable to get themselves killed pretty quickly.

In order to keep the game moving along at a brisk pace—even if the characters had to fall back because they were almost Killed in Action or Knocked Out—after each Scene, characters can automatically repair half of their damaged Armor or heal half of one Condition Monitor track for free, rounding up. All remaining damage must be recovered by normal methods, such as spending Plot Points, casting spells, or using medical or repair abilities.

THEY'RE JUST MOOKS!

There are many instances in stories where the protagonists lay down the hurt on a slew of mooks or henchmen that are all taken out in one fell swoop. While this shouldn't be embraced very often in an RPG setting, as that approach would most likely make an evening's gaming a tad too boring, the GM should be willing to embrace this type of scenario every now and then. Perhaps a character rolls an incredible surplus of hits on a combat roll, or maybe the player provides a fantastic Narration that is wonderfully creative and causes the whole group to explode into laughter. Whatever the instance, don't be afraid to let the "wall of mooks" go down when it feels right and makes that game all the more memorable. However, this option should be used sparingly.

FORCES OF CHAOS

CHARACTER CREATION

This book has a bunch of characters for players to pick up and jump into the shadows with, but one of the fun things about role-playing is designing characters just the way you want them and then watching them grow into awesome forces of nature. Or at least into people capable of surviving the drekstorms the Sixth World relentlessly conjures.

The following rules provide a framework for creating a shadowrunner. As with all aspects of *Shadowrun: Anarchy*, the framework is light and fast and designed for players to playfully and enjoyably create a character sheet that reflects the style they want to embrace in a game. If you don't like where your character is going at any time during the process, feel free to back up and start down the path that'll make it the most fun!

FOLLOW THE STEPS

Download and print out the blank character sheet from **shadowruntabletop.com** and proceed through the following steps to create your shadowrunner:

1. Create a Character Theme (Character Name)
2. Choose Game Level
3. Choose Metatype
4. Decide if your character is Awakened or Emerged
5. Assign Attribute Points
6. Assign Skill Points
7. Add Shadow Amps
8. Add Qualities
9. Assign Armor
10. Select Weapons
11. Select Gear
12. Create Cues
13. Create Character Background
14. Final Tweaking

1. CREATE A CHARACTER THEME

Imagine you're a casting director for your favorite TV show, and you've got a selection of walk-on characters you've got to fill for a new episode, characters who need to be cool and vibrant, even if they're only on-screen for a few minutes.

As you review the script you run into a list of concise character descriptions: male, late twenties, stoic and very tough, doesn't talk much; woman, early thirties, always smiling, with a devil-may-care attitude; male, teen, with a brooding anger that he fails to leash more often than not; and so on. In the role of casting director, you'll use those descriptions to find the right actor to convincingly fill that role in the episode.

In a similar fashion, as you work to create a shadowrunner, you need to find a short and flavorful description of the theme of your character. Do you want to play the juiced-up street samurai who follows a code and only fights for causes she believes in? Or do you want to play a shaman who sees the spirit world as a harmonious place that the urban sprawl of metahumanity is quickly ruining with pollution and greed? Or perhaps you'd rather be the brainy cyberdeck whiz who feels she's stuck in a world of imbeciles and who can hack any Matrix system on the planet without a single milligram of magic?

Anything's possible—the only limits come from your imagination. Well, and some of the practicalities of the game world, which might keep you from having a shadowrunner from Venus or something, but let's stay focused. Pick something that's interesting to you and that will inspire you to do amazing and challenging stuff as you play, and it will work out.

With that in mind, jot down a few descriptive words that outline your theme. Don't hesitate to fill a page if you're still trying to feel your way to what you want, knowing you're going to toss most of the concepts by the wayside as you zero in on your mark. Additionally, if you're still floundering a little, feel free to find out what everyone else in the group is playing and find a niche to fill: Is there room for a sarcastic, brooding, older doctor as a mentor-type for an up-and-coming tyro on your team? Jump in and see if that role fits you.

Once you've got your theme, you'll use that as the framework to help you make the decisions involved in the rest of the process.

CHARACTER NAME

While this step appears at the start of character creation, it can actually happen any time during the process.

Some players will find they've already got a character name they've been hanging on to for just such an adventure; the name itself drips with theme and will immediately lend itself to a certain flavor. If you say "Sledge," most people will likely have a preconceived notion of where the character creation process is going to take them: a burly, chromed-to-the-gills street sammie who can pound foes into the pavement.

Other players, however, may find they don't have a good name in mind and instead, even with a theme, may have to travel most, if not all, of the creation process before the right name presents itself. And of course don't forget to trawl through the sample characters for names that might spark your imagination to craft your own unique take on a given theme.

TAGS

While not a requirement for character creation, every sample character sheet includes a short list of one-word Tags, and these Tags are carried throughout most of the sections of the book. They're designed to give a very quick look at the theme/style of what you're looking at. In the case of characters, Tags define what a character *is*, as opposed to how a character would react in a given situation (see **Create Character Background**, p. 69).

EXAMPLE

Ash is playing *Shadowrun* for the first time, and she wants to go with a classic character—a street samurai. She decides to name her character "Sledge," as that exemplifies a hard-hitting nature. She thinks a tough kid from the Ork Underground would be fun to play, so she makes the following tags: Ork, Gruff, Fighter, Underground, Brash. She's got the first parts of her character ready to roll.

2. DETERMINE GAME LEVEL

The player group should decide what kind of overall power level the characters in the game will have. Are you interested in playing jumped-up gangers looking to carve a name for yourselves, or do you want to play veteran shadowrunners with rap sheets longer than the the polluted Mississippi River? Or maybe you wish to play somewhere in the middle, shadowrunners who are more seasoned than outright n00bs but still have a lot to learn? The selected level determines what each character will allocate to certain aspects of their shadowrunner.

GANG-LEVEL GAME

A gang-level game provides the following character-creation stats:

- **Attributes:** 12 Attribute points
- **Skills:** 10 Skill points
- **Amps:** 6 Shadow Amp points
- **Weapons:** 1 weapon (ranged or melee)
- **Gear:** Armor, 3 items, 1 contact

STREET RUNNER GAME

A standard game provides the following character-creation stats:

- **Attributes:** 16 Attribute points
- **Skills:** 12 Skill points
- **Amps:** 10 Shadow Amp points
- **Weapons:** 2 weapons (one ranged, one melee)
- **Gear:** Armor, 4 items, 2 contacts

PRIME RUNNER GAME

A prime runner game provides the following character-creation stats:

- **Attributes:** 20 Attribute points
- **Skills:** 14 Skill points
- **Amps:** 14 Shadow Amp points
- **Weapons:** 3 weapons (any)
- **Gear:** Armor, 5 items, 3 contacts

3. CHOOSE METATYPE

It may seem like a simple choice, but your character's metatype can shape several aspects of your character. Choose one of the following metatypes and apply the following bonuses:

Human: +1 Edge, +1 Skill point
Elf: +1 Agility, +1 Charisma
Dwarf: +1 Strength, +1 Willpower
Ork: +2 Strength
Troll: +2 Strength, +3 Armor circles, –1 Skill point

4. DECIDE IF YOUR CHARACTER IS AWAKENED OR EMERGED

Some abilities in the Sixth World are only available to people who qualify them. If you're not Awakened, you can't access mana to do amazing things like cast spells, summon spirits, or enhance your physical abilities. If you're not Emerged, you can't access the Matrix solely with the power of your mind, meaning you do not have access to technomancer abilities. If you want access to either of these areas (but not both—characters cannot be both Awakened and Emerged), you have to select that

option in this step and pay the cost. Check either the Awakened or Emerged box on your character sheet, and deduct 2 Shadow Amp points (see step 7)

5. ASSIGN ATTRIBUTE POINTS

Based on the chosen game level, each player has a number of Attribute points to assign to the five Attributes: Strength, Agility, Willpower, Logic, and Charisma. (Edge is a special Attribute that is covered under the **Select Shadow Amps** section, p. 65, and so is not improved in this step.) Each Attribute point assigned equals one point for that Attribute, and characters begin with all Attributes set at 1 (since 0 is not a rating that functional metahumans can have in any Attribute). That means that if you want a Strength of 5, you assign 4 of your allotted Attribute points to Strength to increase the base rating of 1.

If you have a metatype bonus to an Attribute, you add the bonus to how many Attribute points you spent on that Attribute to determine the final Attribute value. For example, dwarves gain a +1 bonus to Willpower, so if you spend 4 Attribute points on Willpower, you will have Willpower 6 (base rating of 1 + 4 spent + racial bonus 1 = 6).

FORCES OF CHAOS   63

ATTRIBUTE MAXIMUMS

METATYPE	STRENGTH	AGILITY	WILLPOWER	LOGIC	CHARISMA
Human	6	6	6	6	6
Elf	6	7	6	6	8
Dwarf	8	6	7	6	6
Ork	8	6	6	5	5
Troll	10	5	6	5	4

Your character's theme can help you decide how many points to assign to each Attribute. The only restriction on Attribute point allocation is that no Attribute can exceed its maximum for your character's metatype. The **Attribute Maximum** table shows the maximums for each metatype.

CONDITION MONITOR

The Strength and Willpower Attributes have a direct correlation to the damage tracks on the Condition Monitor. Use the following rules for determining the character's Condition Monitor:

Physical Damage Track: The Physical Condition is based on the Strength Attribute. Divide Strength by two, round up, and add eight, and that's how many boxes you get on your Physical Condition Monitor. Arrange those boxes in rows of three, with leftover boxes in the bottom row. So Strength 4 gives ten boxes—three rows of three and a bottom row of a single box.

Stun Damage Track: The Stun Damage Track is based on the Willpower Attribute. As with Strength in the Physical Damage Track, divide Willpower by two, round up, and add eight. Then make a condition monitor with three boxes per row, and any leftover boxes on the bottom row.

6. ASSIGN SKILL POINTS

Based on the chosen game level, each player has a number of Skill points to assign. Peruse the list of Skills on page 32, and choose a few of them that match your character's theme. Characters may only start with five skills. They should also select a Knowledge Skill (see below), which does not have a rating and thus does not cost Skill points.

Once you have chosen your Skills, distribute your Skill points until all of them have been assigned. There is nothing to be done with leftover Skill points, so you might as well use them all. Each Skill point assigned equals one point for that Skill. For example, if you want a Close Combat of 4, you assign 4 of your Skill points to Close Combat.

Skills must be assigned a minimum of 1 point, and the maximum value of any Skill during character generation is 5 (6 if you are doing a Prime Runner game).

Once all Skill points have been assigned, use the Skills list on page 32 and note which Attribute links to each Skill.

Knowledge Skills: These Skills represent things your character might know in-game. They can encompass a variety of subjects, including languages (e.g., Japanese, the elven language of Sperethiel, the ork language of Or'zet), interests (e.g., sculpting, online gaming, trog rock bands), or professional knowledge (e.g., police procedure, local gang info, corporate culture). Knowledge Skills are not listed in the Skills list on page 32—you can create your own, so use your imagination. Since they are so broad, they are not given a rating, and they typically do not add to dice pools—they should be used to further storytelling possibilities, rather than as a mechanism for tests. Check out the sample characters starting on page 73 for more examples of Knowledge Skills

Specializations: If you wish to narrow the focus of a Skill with a Specialization, choose the Skill, determine the Specialization's focus, and then apply the bonus dice to that Skill for that specific focus. For example, a Sorcery Skill Specialization can be a specific type of spell (Combat, Illusion, etc.), a Close Combat Specialization can be a specific weapon, and a Hacking Specialization can be a specific Matrix action, such as accessing maglocks. A Specialization to a Skill allows the player to roll two extra dice when using that Skill.

Choosing a Specialization for a skill costs 1 Skill point.

Players can begin with only one Specialization, but further Specializations may be obtained through Character Advancement (see p. 70). Skills with a rating of 1 cannot have a Specialization.

EXAMPLE

At the Street Runner level, Ash has 12 points to spend on Skills. She selects the five skills she wants first: Athletics, Close Combat, Firearms, Intimidation, and Stealth. She decides Close Combat and Firearms are most important, so they both get a rating of 3, costing 6 total points. She puts 2 points into Intimidation—Sledge needs to be able to stare punks into submission every now and again—and 2 into Athletics, as Sledge is tough physical specimen. Stealth gets 1 point, and the final point goes into a specialization. Ash wants Sledge to be handy with a katana, so she adds that specialization to Sledge's Close Combat skill.

7. SELECT SHADOW AMPS

Shadow Amps represent that additional power, that oomph of augmentation that catapults your shadowrunner to a level above your average guttertrash. Here is where you get that much-needed edge over the opposition.

Like many aspects of character creation, the best Shadow Amps are those that fit your character's theme, but don't hesitate to add a seemingly mismatched Amp if it might give your character that unique feel you're looking for.

You can add Shadow Amps in two ways, either by choosing one you like from the list on p. 202 or by creating one of your own. The maximum number of Shadow Amps a character can have is six. Empty slots can be filled by purchasing new Amps during **Character Advancement** (see p. 70). Existing Amps can be upgraded or replaced (also detailed in **Character Advancement**, p. 70).

The following rules cover how to add Shadow Amps to your character:

A. DETERMINE BASE COST

Whether you use a premade Shadow Amp or create one yourself, you must first determine its total cost. Consult the list of Shadow Amps and types on page 202, and decide

SHADOW AMP COST TABLE

TYPE	BASE COST
Adept Power	1
Bioware	2, –0.5 Essence
Cyberdeck*	2
Programs/Complex Forms	1
Cyberware	1, –1 Essence
Spell	1
Talisman	1
Gear	0

* Limit one per character; cyberdecks start with a Firewall 1, Matrix Condition Monitor 6, 1 reroll 1 on Matrix actions, may run 1 program at a time.

ADDED EFFECT	COST
Advanced/damaging/magical effect†	+1
Armor-piercing damage (spells only)	+1
Damage reduction	+1 per point of reduction (max 3)
Die effect (rerolls, healing hits, etc.)	+1 per die (max 3)
Reaction enhancement (see below)	+1 per level (max 3)
Additional dice pips (adding numbers to dice rolls)	+1 per level (max 3)

† May require approval of the GM and other players; see p. 207 for listing of effects.

REACTION ENHANCEMENT LEVEL	BENEFIT‡
1	+1 attack
2	+1 attack, 1 Plot Point per Scene
3	+1 attack, 2 Plot Points per Scene

‡ These are not cumulative. Choose the effect for the chosen level.

what type of Amp you wish to add or create. Then consult the *Shadow Amp Cost Table* to find the base cost for that slot type. This is the minimum Shadow Amp point cost for the slot and a simple, functional description of what the Shadow Amp does; no rules text, such as those described in the Added Effect list in the table are included in the base cost. That means the initial selection of a Shadow Amp is useful for story purposes, but not much else.

If you're fine with the basic description and aren't concerned about adding other effects, then you can stop there. Add the Shadow Amp to your character sheet and then continue to spend points on other Amps. But if you really want it to be useful, the Amp should do something. Which we'll cover.

B. DETERMINE ADDED EFFECTS

Standard Shadow Amps with simple descriptions can function like Cues during your Narration: for example, a spell or adept power with an interesting description might give you a unique idea on how to tackle a problem, or a piece of cyberware might let you approach something from a different angle. However, if you're looking for more than just standard mojo for a Shadow Amp, that's where added effects come into play.

Added effects allow you to customize Shadow Amps beyond a simple description. If you want to include an added effect, consult the Added Effects section of the *Shadow Amp Cost Table* and add the appropriate cost to the base cost of the Shadow Amp. Once you have added all of the desired effects, determine the total cost and allocate that many Shadow Amp points to that Shadow Amp.

If an added effect turns a Shadow Amp into a weapon—an implanted cyberware weapon, for example—make sure to list that in the Weapons section of the character sheet. See **Select Weapons**, p. 68, for more detail.

EXAMPLE

At the Street Runner level, Ash has 10 Shadow Amp points to spend on Sledge. She wants Sledge to have some gleaming chrome on him, so she starts with a cyberarm, which costs 1 point. She wants to be able to reroll two dice on Close Combat attacks, so she adds that ability, which costs two points. The cyberarm as a whole costs 3 Amp points and 1 Essence.

Next she adds some cyberspurs to the cyberarm. The effect she wants is to allow Sledge to do either Physical or Stun damage in unarmed attacks. This Amp adds an Amp level and increases the Essence cost of the arm.

Now she turns to the eyes. She selects a single effect for the eyes—the ability to ignore vision modifiers. This costs 2 points, and once again, she loses a point of Essence.

Finally, Ash is well aware that speed kills, so she needs something like wired reflexes. Or something that is wired reflexes. She gets it at the second level to get +1 attack and +1 Plot Point. Again, the price is 3 Amp points.

Altogether, Sledge has spent all 10 Amp points and has lost 5 points of Essence, making his Essence 1. He would have trouble casting magic, but Ash wasn't planning on having him do that anyway. The loss of dice on healing tests might make life difficult for Sledge, but Ash figures she'll deal with it by making sure Sledge takes out opponents before they hurt him too much.

C. DETERMINE ESSENCE EFFECTS

Each character starts with an Essence of 6, and cyberware or bioware Shadow Amps reduce a character's Essence according to the Shadow Amp's Essence cost listed in the *Shadow Amp Cost Table*. A character can never have an Essence of 0 or lower; 0.5 is the lowest allowable Essence. If a player wishes to add a Shadow Amp whose Essence cost would reduce the character to an Essence of 0 or lower, that Shadow Amp cannot be purchased.

A character's Essence value has the following effects on gameplay:

ESSENCE EFFECTS

RATING	EFFECT
6–5.5	No negative effects.
5–3.5	–1 modifier on Magic-related Tests and attempts to heal this character.
3–1.5	–2 modifier on Magic-related Tests and attempts to heal this character.
1–0.5	–3 modifier on Magic-related Tests and attempts to heal this character.

D. NOTE SHADOW AMP LEVEL

Count up the points spent on each Shadow Amp, and write that number in the upper left corner of the Shadow Amp box. That is the Shadow Amp level, and is needed to calculate upgrade costs in the future.

E. CONVERT LEFTOVER SHADOW AMP POINTS TO EDGE POINTS

Each character starts with an Edge of 1. If a player does not spend all of their allotted Shadow Amp points, the remaining points are added to the player's Edge Attribute (max 6). For example, if a player in a Prime Runner game chose to spend only 12 of their available 14 Shadow Amp points, the remaining 2 points would be added to their Edge, increasing it from 1 to 3.

EXAMPLE

Sledge doesn't have any leftover Amp points, so his Edge will stay at one. Ash could opt to have the cyberarm make only one reroll on Close Combat tests, saving a point there are transferring it to Edge, but she decides she wants the rerolls.

8. ADD QUALITIES

Each player must choose two positive qualities and one negative quality for their character.

Positive qualities generally add additional dice to a Skill, though they can also offer a myriad of other positive gameplay bonuses. Negative qualities generally subtract dice, but they can also double penalties, or cause a number of other negative gameplay challenges.

When choosing qualities, you can either pick one from the sample character sheets or you can create one.

To create a quality, choose whether you want it to be positive or negative. When providing a dice bonus, positive qualities add two dice; when providing a dice pool penalty, negative qualities subtract two dice from on Skill, Shadow Amp, or other effect. You can get more creative if you want (see listed qualities on p. 204 for other examples), but adding or subtracting two dice is the most straightforward way to make a quality.

9. ASSIGN ARMOR

Most characters do not have natural armor, so if they're not wearing armor, they get no armor protection. Trolls, though, are thicker and sturdier than other metatypes, so they get +3 circles as a metatype bonus.

If you want more armor than your natural armor—and if you want to survive more than a few minutes, you do—you want some wearable armor. Armor comes at three levels—6 circles, 9 circles, or 12 circles. To obtain armor value 9, you do not need to do anything but choose one of the basic armor types and add it to your gear list. To choose armor that gives 12 circles, subtract one skill point from your selected skills—if you are choosing to specialize in heavy combat protection, then you are less effective in other skills. To choose armor with 6 circles, give yourself a bonus Skill point to compensate for your decreased armor (if you're going to travel armor-light, it's clearly because you have some other skills to rely on).

Some armor might be selected as Shadow Amps to give bonuses besides straight protection. For example, chameleon suits can give bonus dice to Stealth Tests, or faewear may give bonuses to Con tests. These pieces of armor should be selected as Shadow Amps, with a base armor value of 9. In these cases, the armor value may be increased by 3 for an additional Shadow Amp point, to a maximum of 12.

Basic armor is as follows:

Synthleather jacket: 6
Actioneer Business Clothes: 6
Armor clothing: 6
Armor vest: 9

Lined coat: 9
Armor jacket: 12
Body armor: 12

EXAMPLE

While Ash wouldn't mind getting some extra armor for Sledge, she really doesn't want to lose a Skill Point. She decides to take an armor vest at the standard rating of 9, and perhaps get more when Sledge has earned some Karma.

10. SELECT WEAPONS

Characters can choose at least two starting weapons, not counting their Unarmed Combat stats or weapons granted by Shadow Amps. We recommend each player take one ranged weapon and one melee weapon, but this may vary, depending on the character's theme. If a player wishes to start with more than two weapons, the player group must approve this.

As with the Cues in a later step, selecting your weapons can be fun. You can simply copy the weapons from one of the sample character sheets, using the sample sheets like a shopping catalog. However, unleashing the lawbreaker inside can be far more enjoyable: just make up whatever cool name you want—the more cyberpunk-sounding, the better! What about a napalm arrow? Write that down. Or have you seen a weapon in the pages of a *Shadowrun* book and always wondered what name it might have? What about a monofilament cat o' nine tails? Write that down too. When it comes to your weapons, consider the theme of your character and embrace it.

To determine the stats of a newly created weapon, look at the gear catalog or find a comparable weapon in the sample character sheets, and use the Damage value and range brackets of the existing weapon. (Additional range brackets can be found in under the **Weapons** section of **Anarchy and Shadowrun, Fifth Edition** on p. 206.)

Regardless of whether you choose existing weapons or create your own, just remember that your character can only ever have a total of six weapons.

EXAMPLE

Ash knows Sledge needs a variety of weapons to deal with different conditions and ranges. First she selects a katana, since she wants that to be the ork's signature weapon. She adds in a pistol, the classic Ares Predator, for close range work. For longer ranges she goes with some two-handed firearms—a submachine gun and an assault rifle. Sledge will be ready for just about any combat situation.

11. SELECT GEAR

A player may choose up to four items of noncombat Gear and two Contacts.

As discussed under **Using Gear** (see p. 44), Gear in *Shadowrun: Anarchy* is not a set of hard rules and does not come with attached mechanics. Instead, they almost act as their own Cues, propelling the action forward without dropping into the minutiae of what exactly a piece of equipment weighs, what it does, and so on.

Use the few lines on the Gear section to accentuate the theme of your character, providing items you feel will be fun and enjoyable during game play. You don't even have to know what some of them do … one or two could just be crazy, fun-sounding names that you'll figure out on the fly. Or take a look at items on the sample character sheets and choose something that sounds like must-have equipment that you think might pull your hoop out of the fire at some point.

A chosen piece of Gear does not necessarily have to match your character's role, but a decker will likely get more use out of a piece of computer-related gear than a computer-illiterate shaman would. Also keep in mind that you're probably better off not worrying about mundane items such as ammunition and spare magazines. *Anarchy* doesn't concern itself with tracking how many bullets are left in a gun, so make sure you reserve your gear slots for more important items. Which means items that present interesting storytelling possibilities.

It's important to make clear that, due to the loose nature of these rules, it's all too easy for players to create wildly powerful/ludicrously small gear; e.g., a "pocket tactical nuclear warhead launcher." After all, "the rules didn't say I couldn't!" If your player group decides such a thing is cool and fits with what you want to see in your games, by all means allow it. But most player groups will realize that even within these rules, a limit needs to be set on the power of gear, and that limit is: Does the piece of Gear lead to a fun story for all the players? Player groups may want to police Gear during character creation to ensure it's within the limits they're all comfortable with … or be stuck with the GM having to say, "Yup, sorry, that nuke launcher you just spent a dozen playing sessions obtaining fizzles, spurts, and goes silent … It's a dud. And now the spirits in the area you tried to irradiate are *really* pissed."

Contacts: Contacts represent a special kind of Gear, namely the people your character knows. These can run the gamut from street lowlifes to people in corporate penthouses, and they'll be the ones your character gets in touch with when things go south, you need some information, or you just need a shoulder to bleed on.

You should choose Contacts that go along with your character's theme and background. For example, if your character grew up on the streets, then having an AA-rated corp exec as a Contact might be a hard sell to the player group, but a gang leader and BTL-chip dealer wouldn't be out of the question. Likewise, if you're playing an ex-cop, then maybe you'd have a police chief or a Knight-Errant beat cop for a Contact. That said, feel free to think outside the box, because sometimes people can know some surprising folks.

> **EXAMPLE**
>
> Sledge has two prime needs in Contacts: Someone to supply the weapons he uses to make chaos, and someone in law enforcement who can provide useful insider info and maybe smooth things over when Sledge gets into trouble. So Ash gives the ork a Contact named "Red Dot" Dottie, a weapons dealer, and Elkarra Johannsen, a beat cop who happens to be an ork, giving Sledge a little affinity with her.

12. CREATE CUES

As noted under **Cues** (see p. 35), these are phrases that can be bold statements a character might make in a given situation, or can be used to spark an idea of which direction a character might leap.

When creating Cues for your own character, use the same method you used when generating your character theme: jot down different phrases, sentences, or just saucy, juicy words that sound like something that would be fun to say during the action of the game. Then use the list to zero in on the best set of Cues.

You can also review the sample character sheets (see p. 74) to spark your own ideas for Cues. If you're having a difficult time, feel free to use catchphrases taken from your favorite comic books, movies, TV shows, and novels, just tweaked slightly to make them unique to your character. For example "That was totally wicked!" could be tweaked to "That was totally killin'!"

If you're still struggling, feel free to make the generation of Cues into a party game for all those who'll be involved in a game of *Anarchy*. Each player can write down two or three (or more) Cues based on your character theme, and then you can select some, none, or all of them. Even the craziest Cues could prove an interesting take on your character's personality under the right circumstances, so don't be so quick to toss the wilder concepts out.

> **EXAMPLE**
>
> Ash wants Cues that reflect different aspects of Sledge's nature. He's rough-and-tumble, temperamental, but with his own code and a dedication to keeping his word. So she writes the following Cues: "It's a street fight, not a boxing match!"; "You look at me cross-eyed again, I'll gut you, chummer"; and "We said we'd do the job, so we do the job." Those lines, along with a few others she comes up with, can provide prompts for how Sledge will react in a variety of situations, so she has some guides if she gets stuck and needs reminders of what kind of character she wants Sledge to be.

13. CREATE CHARACTER BACKGROUND

Now that your character is done, feel free to fill in some details of your character's background by using your character theme as a springboard. Take a look at some of the sample character sheets to get some inspiration for your character's background information. Here are some things you are encouraged to add to bring your character to life:

Personal Data: This represents vital statistics: metatype, age, sex, height/weight, and any other pertinent details you want to write down.

History: This is the meat of your character: who they are, where they came from, why they're running the shadows, and so forth.

Personality: This represents details about how your character reacts to and interacts with various circumstances. This can be as detailed as you want to make it.

Dispositions: Like Cues, your character's Dispositions should flow from how you're building your theme. Even the description you used when generating your theme could be turned into Disposition statements.

As previously noted under *Tags* (see p. 62), Dispositions define how a character will react given various stimuli and circumstances (as opposed to Tags, which define what your character is).

Again, review the sample character sheets, or ask for suggestions from your player group if you're struggling to define this aspect of your character.

14. FINAL TWEAKING

Once you've written down all of your character details on the blank character sheet, review the final character to ensure it's everything you want it to be. If you want to nip and tuck a little here and there, by all means, feel free.

Some of the places you can tweak characters are:
- Adjusting Armor up or down (make sure you pay or receive the requisite Skill Points for the change).
- Changing how a specific Shadow Amp works.

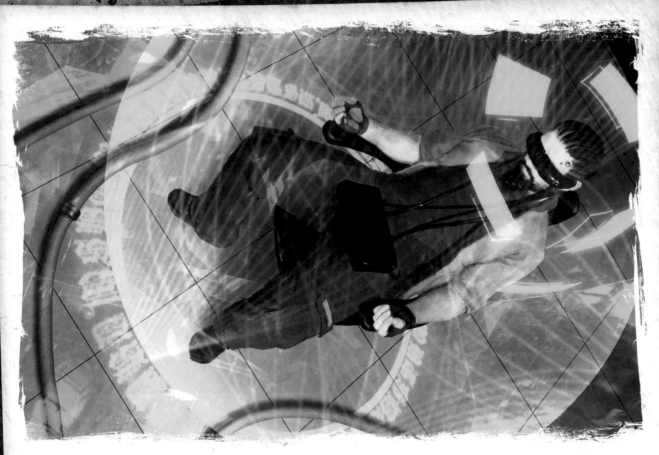

Such tweaking should be kept within reason. For example, you shouldn't change Attribute or Skill ratings up or down, as that has far too great an impact on the mechanics of gameplay. Make sure Attributes and Skills are where you want them to be, and take another look at Cues and Dispositions to make sure they convey the character the way you want them to be. With that, you're ready to roll!

CHARACTER ADVANCEMENT

Players may advance their characters by accumulating **Karma** earned during game play and translating points of Karma into improvements on their character sheets.

There are three ways to earn Karma:
- **Gameplay:** Every time a player finishes a Contract, their character earns the amount of Karma described in the Contract Brief for meeting particular objectives.
- **Gamemaster:** At the completion of a Contract, the gamemaster may award a bonus point of Karma to any players who they felt demonstrated extra cleverness, humor, bravado, or other positive qualities in the course of their Narrations.

In all cases, the players should remember to mark down their accumulated Karma points in the appropriate spot on their character sheet.

After noting accumulated Karma points after a successful Contract, players can then spend that Karma in the following ways:
- Improve an Attribute
- Improve/Add a Skill
- Improve/Add a Shadow Amp
- Remove a negative quality
- Improve Armor
- Buy/Improve Weapons and Gear

To make any of these changes, using the following rules (no other aspects of the character sheet change):

IMPROVING ATTRIBUTES

To increase an Attribute by 1 point, spend Karma equal to the chosen Attribute's new rating x 2. For example, to improve a Logic of 4 to a 5 would cost 10 Karma (5 x 2). Attributes can never exceed the maximum for the character's metatype (see the **Attribute Maximums** chart on p. 64).

If Strength or Willpower are improved, remember to adjust the Condition Monitor (see **Condition Monitor**,

p. 64) and melee weapon damage (see **Close Combat Damage Bonus**, p. 41) appropriately.

IMPROVING/ADDING SKILLS

Improve Skill: To increase a Skill by 1 point, spend Karma equal to the Skill's new rating. For example, to improve an Engineering Skill of 3 to a 4 would cost 4 Karma. The maximum value for Skills is 12.

Add a new Skill: If you have an open Skill slot on your character sheet, you can buy a new Skill at rating 1. (If you do not have an open Skill slot, you may not buy a new Skill unless the player group agrees to allow additional Skills.) To buy a new Skill, choose a Skill from the Skills list on page 32 and pay 2 Karma to get that Skill at rating 1.

Add a specialization: You may add a specialization to a Skill that does not already have one. To do so, pay 2 Karma, choose the specialization's focus, and note a +2 modifier for that Skill. Skills with a rating of 1 cannot add specializations.

IMPROVING/ADDING SHADOW AMPS

Improve a Shadow Amp: First, determine how you want to improve the Shadow Amp. Consult the **Shadow Amp Cost Table** on page 65 and choose the effect you wish to improve. For example, you could add the ability to reroll 1 failed die, or you could increase the damage reduction from 1 circle to 2 circles. Shadow Amps may only be improved one level at a time. For example, you cannot add 2 dice rerolls to a Shadow Amp that doesn't already have a die reroll effect, and you cannot increase the damage reduction from 1 to 3 circles.

Once you have determined the new effect, reference the small number in the corner of the Shadow Amp's box (the total level of the Amp). To improve the Shadow Amp, increase its level by 1, pay an amount of Karma equal to the new level, and add the chosen improvement to the Shadow Amp. For example, if a Shadow Amp has a listed level of 4, increase its level to 5 and pay 5 Karma for the improvement.

Add a new Shadow Amp: If you have an open Shadow Amp slot on your character sheet and can afford the Essence cost (if any), you can buy a new Shadow Amp for that slot. (If you do not have an open Shadow Amp slot, you can spend Karma to replace an existing Amp, but you may not add a new one unless the player group agrees to allow additional Shadow Amps.) To buy a new Shadow Amp, see **Select Shadow Amps**, p. 65, to determine the level for the Shadow Amp you wish to add, paying Karma equal to each level you purchase. That is, if you buy a new spell Amp, pay 1 Karma for that first level. Then, to add a new power, pay 2 more Karma for that level, making 3 Karma total.

If you wish to add a Shadow Amps that is listed on another character sheet, the cost for that is represented by a small number in the corner of the Shadow Amp's box. Once you have determined the cost, pay the required Essence cost (if any) and an amount of Karma equal to the Shadow Amp's cost, plus an amount equal to each level below it (for example, a level 3 amp would cost 3 +2 +1 = 6 Karma.

REMOVE A NEGATIVE QUALITY

If your character is constantly getting into trouble because of their negative quality, you can choose to spend Karma to remove it from your character sheet. But ridding yourself of a character flaw isn't easy. To remove a negative quality, pay 6 Karma. Detailing the story of how you overcame the negative quality to your group, just to add to the ongoing narrative of your player and their team.

Note that this option should be used with caution. While removing the negative quality may help a character mechanically, it removes some great storytelling options, and telling fun stories is what *Anarchy* is all about. Be cautious about taking away opportunities for characters to overcome challenges!

IMPROVE ARMOR

Some armor improvements might done using Shadow Amps, but in some cases characters might simply want to improve their Armor rating. This is a simple matter of spending 3 Karma for each 3-point improvement in Armor. Note that worn Armor can never increase to a rating of more than 12.

BUY/IMPROVE WEAPONS AND GEAR

Sometimes the weapons and Gear you have just aren't enough to get the job done, and you might need to find more ways to geek people and keep yourself from getting geeked. Due to the nature of the Cue System, the *Shadowrun: Anarchy* rules do not worry about tracking nuyen, the Sixth World's most common currency. Players are welcome to roleplay the exchange of funds when acquiring new items, but this is not necessary. Instead, acquiring or upgrading new toys simply requires an expenditure of Karma.

Buy new Weapons and Gear: At any time, even during a game session, a player may spend 2 Karma to acquire one of the following: 1 weapon, any 2 Gear items, or 1 Contact.

Customize a Weapon: To customize a weapon, choose a weapon effect, and spend 3 Karma. Here are some example weapon upgrades:

Accuracy: Add the reroll of one failed die. (Examples: laser sights, integral smartgun system)

Lethality: Increase Damage by 1. (Examples: flechette rounds, explosive rounds)

Range: Decrease the range penalty of a single distance by 1. A weapon with a "–1" in a given range bracket will change to an "OK." Range brackets with a "—" cannot be changed. (Sample customizations that might accomplish this: nightvision scope, high-caliber rounds)

Further sample weapon effects can be found on the characters included with this book.

EXAMPLE

Ash has racked up a nice total of 14 Karma. There are a number of ways to improve Sledge, and she wants the benefits to be spread through different areas. First, her street samurai character could use a little boost in Logic to help out on Perception tests, so she raises that Attribute from a 3 to a 4. This costs twice the new rating, meaning 2 x 4, or 8—more than half of her available Karma.

She also has decided that her rating of 1 in Athletics is keeping Sledge from being as dynamic as she wants him to be, so she boosts it to 2. That costs Karma equal to the new rating, meaning 2. She has now spent a total of 10 Karma.

Sledge's wired reflexes have a Shadow Amp level of 3. If she boosts them to 4, it will cost her 4 Karma. This will give her a second additional Plot Point per Scene, which she is eager to have. Sledge is improved but out of Karma, so it's time to round up a new job.

STREET PEOPLE

You've got the world and the rules; now it's time to populate it. Here are some characters and NPCs you can use to get running immediately. There's plenty of variety here, so find a person who suits your fancy and hit the streets!

CHARACTERS

Coydog, elf street shaman   p. 74
Gentry, human combat decker   p. 76
Hardpoint, dwarf security rigger   p. 78
Ms. Myth, troll face   p. 80
Sledge, ork street samurai   p. 82
Alyosha Duska, dwarf spirit whisperer   p. 84
Bit-Bucket, ork decker   p. 86
Borderline, human ganger razorgirl   p. 88
Chrome Bison, troll street samurai   p. 90
Daktari, dwarf street doc   p. 92
Fourth, ork reporter   p. 94
Fusion, ork rigger/ganger   p. 96
Hawk, human street samurai   p. 98
Jinn, elf brute force decker   p. 100
Kix, elf razorgirl   p. 102
Knox, dwarf street fighting adept   p. 104
Ninetails, human infiltration expert   p. 106
Raider, elf combat archaeologist   p. 108
Raspberry Jam, human arms dealer   p. 110
Razzle Dazzle, ork illusionist   p. 112
Reese Frenzy, ork rocker/face   p. 114
Rose Red, elf mystic adept   p. 116
Ruckus, troll bruiser   p. 118
Shades, human former company woman   p. 120

Strider, dwarf parkour adept   p. 122
Thunder, human vigilante   p. 124
Tommy Q, human former wage mage   p. 126
Vector, human technomancer   p. 128
Wagon, human combat medic   p. 130
Wheezer, troll gang leader   p. 132

NON-PLAYER CHARACTERS

Bug queen   p. 134
Bug spirit   p. 134
Corporate security   p. 134
Corporate suit   p. 134
Devil rat   p. 135
Enemy drone (heavy)   p. 135
Enemy drone (medium)   p. 135
Enemy drone (small)   p. 135
Enemy mage   p. 136
Ganger   p. 136
Hell hound   p. 136
Mr. Johnson (corporate)   p. 136
Mr. Johnson (street)   p. 137
Rent-a-cop   p. 137
Security spider   p. 137
Soldier   p. 137
Spirit of air   p. 138
Spirit of beasts   p. 138
Spirit of earth   p. 139
Spirit of man   p. 139
Spirit of water   p. 139
Vampire   p. 140
Young dragon   p. 140

COYDOG

ELF STREET SHAMAN

TAGS

• Elf • Coyote • Magician • Salish-Shidhe • Prankster

BACKGROUND

Coydog was born to a tribal Sinsearach elf and a Salish-Shidhe soldier, and she inherited traits of both. She inherited her mother's gracefully pointed ears, long limbs, and elven knack for charm. Her father made her a fighter.

While her brother, Scout-Who-Kills-Six-Times, embraced the streets of Seattle and fell in with the First Nations gang, the streets had another plan for Coydog. Her affinity for wind and weather erupted rather magnificently when trouble came calling one day, and before long she found herself studying with a shamanic mentor, Four-Paws-Laughing, on Council Island. As a follower of Coyote, she knew she could never settle for life as a corporate wage mage, and simple talismonger work or reagent hunting would be too boring for her. That left the shadows.

As a promising beginner to the Seattle shadowrun scene, Coydog has developed a name for herself already for innovation and talent. Falling in with—and forming an integral part of—"Myth's Crew," she's a creative, versatile shaman who'll only get better with experience. Coydog's a casual hooder, a runner who's in the shadows to do good, not just do good for herself. The young elf sometimes finds herself at odds with more mercenary runners, but so far her good nature and potent air spirits have seen her through, even when her morals might otherwise make her job more difficult. She chose the shadows because they offered her freedom, not wealth; only time will tell if she's able to walk her path as freely as she'd like.

COYDOG

☐ Emerged
☒ Awakened

STRENGTH	AGILITY	WILLPOWER	LOGIC	CHARISMA	EDGE
2	4	6	4	7	1

DISPOSITIONS

TOTAL KARMA | KARMA BALANCE

Cities are a natural habitat too.

Be flexible.

You can handle anything with your spirit friends.

Coyote's paths aren't always straight and narrow.

SKILLS

ASTRAL COMBAT	1+W	CON	1+C	CONJURING (AIR SPIRITS +2)	5+W
SORCERY	4+W	SURVIVAL	1+L	STREET GANGS	(K)

SHADOW AMPS   ESSENCE: 6   No penalties.

3 | **LIGHTNING BOLT (SPELL)**
Combat spell. Damage of 6P/AA, may reroll 1 Sorcery die, defense S + W.

3 | **PHYSICAL MASK (SPELL)**
Effect. Mass illusion/disguises, and targeted group may reroll 2 failed Disguise dice.

2 | **CONFUSION (SPELL)**
Effect. Target's senses are confused. Target rolls 1 less die per action.

CUES

Spirits are my friends, not my servants. But yeah, I'll ask him.

Maybe we could try something totally new.

Did I have to do that? No. But your expression made it worth it.

How about a plan that *doesn't* waste two hundred bullets?

Sorry, bro, I'm not that kind of elf.

Where's the fun in the easy way?

I'll have to twist mana in ways I've never done before. Perfect!

Five nuyen says you can't swipe his badge without him noticing.

You talk about "war bonnets" one more time and you'll wake up with feathers growing out of your hoop.

QUALITIES

MENTOR SPIRIT (COYOTE)
+1 die for Con tests, may reroll 1 die when casting illusion or control spells.

SPIRIT AFFINITY (AIR)
+2 dice summoning Air Spirits.

GREMLINS
When using high-tech items, always add a Glitch Die that cannot roll an Exploit.

WEAPONS

UNARMED	DAM 1S	CLOSE OK	NEAR —	FAR —

	DAM	CLOSE	NEAR	FAR		DAM	CLOSE	NEAR	FAR		DAM	CLOSE	NEAR	FAR
Survival Knife	2P	OK	–2	—	Browning Ultra Power Pistol	6P	OK	–2	—					
	DAM	CLOSE	NEAR	FAR		DAM	CLOSE	NEAR	FAR		DAM	CLOSE	NEAR	FAR

CONDITION MONITOR

ARMOR
TRIBAL-CHIC ARMOR CLOTHING

PHYSICAL
–1 –2 –3

STUN
–1 –2 –3 –4

GEAR
Fake SIN, broken Meta Link commlink, Toyota Gopher pickup truck, magical lodge materials, survival kit

CONTACTS
Scout-Who-Kills-Six-Times (ganger, big brother)
Four-Paws-Laughing (Coyote shaman, pain in the butt)

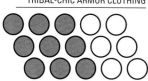

GENTRY

HUMAN COMBAT DECKER

TAGS

- Human • Hacker • Free Runner • Neo-Anarchist • Fanboy

BACKGROUND

Gentry may not be as good as he thinks he is, but then no one is as good as Gentry thinks he is. For a while, he had a rough time of it, but he's found steady work in Ms. Myth's crew in the Seattle shadows. Born a human in the elven "wonderland" of Tír Tairngire, Gentry's street name was a cruel joke; the Gentry are the lowest class of citizens there, and his handle served as a constant reminder that his rounded ears would keep him from ever climbing society's ladder. Working as a street-hacker and a data courier—including for rebel terrorists—Gentry's luck eventually ran out and he found himself tried for treason and locked up in a Tír prison.

He found his way out through an unexpected angle: professional sports. The hyperviolent game of urban brawl spread into the Tír, and they desperately needed to fill rosters. Convicts who seemed dangerous enough to put on a good show but harmless enough not to escape were offered work-release programs, and Gentry fit the bill. Pyscho-conditioned to ensure game-field obedience (and as further insurance against escape attempts), he leaped, vaulted, shot, and hacked his way to an early release—and an unceremonious dumping on the streets of Seattle.

His head may be a mess of crossed wires—literally as well as metaphorically—but Gentry's no slouch in the Matrix. He's athletic enough to handle the night-to-night hurdles of being a shadowrunner, smart enough to take care of the tech issues the life throws his way, and solid enough in a fight to hold his own. Bad luck has caught up with him a few times, and so has a habit of running his mouth and fawning over nearby elves, but he's found a niche with Ms. Myth and has started to make a name for himself in the Emerald Grid, Seattle's Matrix.

GENTRY

☐ Emerged
☐ Awakened

STRENGTH	AGILITY	WILLPOWER	LOGIC	CHARISMA	EDGE
4	6	3	6	2	2

DISPOSITIONS

TOTAL KARMA	KARMA BALANCE

Information wants to be free.

When in doubt, hack the world.

Frag the system, cuz the system fragged you.

Suck up to elves, they're pretty wiz.

SKILLS

ATHLETICS	3+A	ELECTRONICS	4+L	FIREARMS	2+A
HACKING	4+L	ELVEN CULTURE	(K)		

SHADOW AMPS

ESSENCE: 4.5 — −1 die to magic/healing tests.

3 SYNTHACARDIUM
Bioware. May reroll 1 die on Athletics rolls. −0.5 Essence

2 DATAJACK AND HEADWARE
Cyberware. May access the Matrix via full VR, +1D6 to Matrix actions. −1 Essence.

5 CYBERDECK 3 (SHIAWASE CYBER-5)
May reroll 2 dice on Matrix actions, Firewall +3, Matrix Condition Monitor 12, may run 2 programs

CUES

Frag off, then, and watch this.

If I can't hack it, I can shoot it. If I can't shoot it, I run.

Sledge, you put the "ork" in "dork."

I've been left for dead by people a lot smarter than you.

Cyber-5s don't grow on trees; I earned this thing.

Hey, stuff it, *goronagit*. Nobody asked you what you thought, *li ha*?

Sperethiel is just a more beautiful language!

This is nothing. Saw drek like this all the time in urban brawl.

What? *Of course* I can handle it. You do your job, I'll do mine!

QUALITIES

NATURAL ATHLETE
+2 dice for Athletics tests

CODESLINGER:
+2 dice when for Hacking tests.

ELF POSEUR
When making social tests with elves, always add a Glitch Die that cannot roll an Exploit.

WEAPONS

UNARMED	DAM	CLOSE	NEAR	FAR
	3S	OK	—	—

	DAM	CLOSE	NEAR	FAR		DAM	CLOSE	NEAR	FAR		DAM	CLOSE	NEAR	FAR
Stun Baton	7S	OK	—	—	Colt America L36 Pistol	5P	OK	−2	—					
	DAM	CLOSE	NEAR	FAR		DAM	CLOSE	NEAR	FAR		DAM	CLOSE	NEAR	FAR

ARMOR

URBAN EXPLORER JUMPSUIT

CONDITION MONITOR

PHYSICAL: −1, −2, −3, −4

STUN: −1, −2, −3

GEAR

Courier bag, fake SIN, Transys Avalon commlink, stim patch

CONTACTS

Signal (elven technomancer terrorist/freedom fighter)

Galadriel (elven madam)

HARDPOINT

DWARF SECURITY RIGGER

TAGS

• Dwarf • Corp-Trained • Wheelman • Pilot • Veteran

BACKGROUND

It's not easy being a "halfer" in one of the Sixth World's most traditional, conservative Japanese megacorps. Born to meta-mixed parents, Hardpoint was never really given a fair shake; discriminated against because of his Anglo heritage, treated unfairly due to being a metahuman, and repeatedly passed over for promotion and approval, his wasn't an easy childhood.

As a younger man he excelled in the corporation's structured athletics programs (dominating his weight class in non-combat-augmented grappling), scored top ranks in corporate academia, and stayed firmly in step with Mitsuhama's strict corporate culture. Eventually, he earned a spot only as a reserve combat rigger in MCT's fabled security corps. He was eventually driven from the corporation when an arranged marriage proved to be one insult too many; begging his father for forgiveness, he left the family business behind and jumped into the shadows.

Despite letting his hair down (and his beard out), Hardpoint has retained more than a few habits from his MCT days. Loyal to a fault, he'll never let his team down or betray a trust (which means he won't make an attack directly on MCT if he can help it). He's also a pragmatist, whose confidence is well-earned but grounded in reality. If Hardpoint can't finish a job, he won't take it. His teammates invariably appreciate his attitude as much as his ability. He's got a mellow nature that really only changes when his friends are hurt or someone is extraordinarily wasteful or cruel. Inefficiency still gets under his skin a little, though, and Hardpoint often works hard trying to improve his machines.

HARDPOINT

☐ Emerged
☐ Awakened

STRENGTH	AGILITY	WILLPOWER	LOGIC	CHARISMA	EDGE
5	6	3	6	3	1

DISPOSITIONS

TOTAL KARMA

KARMA BALANCE

MCT Seattle District Jiu-Jitsu champ, unaugmented division.

Precision is everything.

You've got a drone for that.

Mitsuhama puts out the best products.

SKILLS

CLOSE COMBAT (JIU-JITSU +2)	2+A	ENGINEERING 1+L	PILOTING (GROUND) 2+A
PILOTING (OTHER)	3+A	VEHICLE WEAPONS 3+A	SECURITY PROCEDURES (K)

SHADOW AMPS — ESSENCE: 3

−2 dice to magic/healing tests.

3 — CONTROL RIG 2
Cyberware. Control vehicles by VR, +1 die to vehicle actions, may reroll two dice on vehicle actions. −2 Essence.

2 — CYBEREYES
Cyberware. Ignore vision modifiers, may reroll 1 failed die with ranged attacks. −1 Essence.

3 — CUSTOMIZED MCT GUN-DRONES 2
Gain +2 attacks/movements (only with gun drones).

2 — MCT FLY-SPY AERIAL DRONES
+1 to Perception tests.

CUES

Faster?! Engines can only do so much!

If you hurt my team, *aho*, the whole world's my Zero Zone. No prisoners.

You've got to bring the right tool for the right job. Luckily, you've got me.

Well, at least we can sell it for scrap.

Hai, I really am that good.

We should put more guns on that!

Konichiwa. Vacate the area, the drones will begin firing in five seconds.

Chin up. We'll find a way through this. Probably with firepower.

QUALITIES

SPEED RACER
+2 dice for Piloting (Ground) tests.

COMBAT PILOT
+2 dice to Piloting (Other) tests.

STUBBORN
−2 dice when using a drone/vehicle that isn't MCT-crafted or that Hardpoint hasn't customized.

WEAPONS

	DAM	CLOSE	NEAR	FAR
UNARMED	3S	OK	—	—

	DAM	CLOSE	NEAR	FAR		DAM	CLOSE	NEAR	FAR
Ingram Smartgun. SMG	6P	OK	−2	—	Gun-Drone Mounted Rifle	8P	OK	OK	−2

DAM	CLOSE	NEAR	FAR		DAM	CLOSE	NEAR	FAR		DAM	CLOSE	NEAR	FAR

CONDITION MONITOR

ARMOR
LIGHT ARMOR JACKET

PHYSICAL
−1 −2 −3 −4

STUN
−1 −2 −3 −4

GEAR
Fake SIN, Transys Avalon commlink, mechanic toolkit, customized GMC Bulldog step-van

CONTACTS
Black (scrapyard owner/mechanic)

Quick Billy McCoy (smuggler)

SHADOWRUN ANARCHY

TALYST game labs

MS. MYTH

TROLL FACE

TAGS

• Troll • Shadowrunner • Professional • Negotiatior • Leader

BACKGROUND

Ms. Myth's father was a janitor who tried to teach his baby girl a work ethic, a willingness to clean every corner of a filthy building for honest pay, and corporate loyalty. Her mother was a restaurant server, who did her best to teach her daughter that sucking up paid well, long hours meant fair pay, and service with a smile beat service with good food.

Instead, Myth learned that sometimes you've got to get your hands dirty, that janitors have access to every nook and cranny of a secure facility, and that smiling made people more scared of you than frowning did.

She ran the streets, rather than letting the streets run her. Hustling, plotting, and planning were Myth's keys to urban success, and she only fell back on her trollish brawn when all else failed. Smarter than she looks and more charming than anyone ever expected, Myth's spent years navigating the Seattle shadows, playing multiple sides in the great game; sometimes working as a fixer, other times as a runner, and even others as a corporate freelance troubleshooter on mid-term retainer.

Myth will lie—with a smile—to almost the whole world to see a job done smoothly and professionally, with only a few exceptions. She's always honest and realistic when wooing an extraction target (kidnapping gigs aren't her style), and she'll never, ever, lie to her team. Myth's team knows she'll do what's best for them and shoot straight, and in turn Myth knows they'll always give her their best. And the best part is that she picked them herself, so she knows their best is pretty good.

MS. MYTH

☐ Emerged
☐ Awakened

STRENGTH	AGILITY	WILLPOWER	LOGIC	CHARISMA	EDGE
6	3	4	5	5	4

DISPOSITIONS

TOTAL KARMA	KARMA BALANCE

You protect your team—more than they know.

Plan all the time, talk when you can, fight when you must.

Use the right runner for the right job.

Improvisation is an ugly necessity in this line of work.

SKILLS

CON	3+C	FIREARMS	2+A	INTIMIDATION	2+C
NEGOTIATION	3+C	STEALTH	1+A	SAFEHOUSES	(K)

SHADOW AMPS   ESSENCE: 5.5   _No penalty._

3 — **TAILORED PHEROMONES 1**
Bioware. Reroll 1 die on all in-person Charisma-related tests. –0.5 Essence

2 — **I KNOW EVERYBODY**
Gain (Charisma rating) contacts.

2 — **TEAM PLAYER**
You may freely gift your own Plot Points or Edge to other players.

CUES

Shake my hand, let's both leave here happy.

No one's going to offer you a better deal.

Think this through. Let's be professionals about this.

You get tough jobs because you can handle them.

That's a nice plan. How about now we add some critical thought to it?

Trust me, you can do it!

Aww, drek. Go loud!

You think talk is cheap? Try using better words.

Don't mistake restraint for weakness.

QUALITIES

EXCEPTIONAL ATTRIBUTE (CHARISMA)
Increase your Charisma cap by +1.

SILVER TONGUE
May reroll two dice on Charisma tests.

COMBAT PARALYSIS
Act last on the first round of any combat (that isn't you specifically initiating an ambush).

WEAPONS

UNARMED	DAM 3S	CLOSE OK	NEAR —	FAR —

	DAM	CLOSE	NEAR	FAR		DAM	CLOSE	NEAR	FAR		DAM	CLOSE	NEAR	FAR
Fichetti Smartgun 600 Pistol	5P	OK	2	—	**Ingram Smartgun** SMG	6P	OK	–2	—					
	DAM	CLOSE	NEAR	FAR		DAM	CLOSE	NEAR	FAR		DAM	CLOSE	NEAR	FAR

CONDITION MONITOR

PHYSICAL   —1 —2 —3 —4

STUN   —1 —2 —3 —4

ARMOR

LIGHT URBAN CAMO SUIT

GEAR

Fake SIN, cheap burner commlinks, sharp suit, smoke grenade

CONTACTS

The Juggler (elven fixer); **Esmerelda Expertise** (Mr. Johnson); **Khayyim** (street doc); **Frankie the Fomori** (bartender); **Kelly Quick** (Cutters gang lieutenant); **Mr. Satou** (company man); **Bing-Lei "Billy" Shen** (triad lieutenant)

SHADOWRUN ANARCHY

CATALYST game labs

SLEDGE

ORK STREET SAMURAI

TAGS

• Ork • Gruff • Fighter • Underground • Brash

BACKGROUND

Life's tough in the Underground, so you've got to be tougher. Every young ork coming up in the dark knows the rules, and every one of 'em knows which ones can be broken. Sledge grew up hard and he grew up fast, feeling in his gut that the world was a bigger place than what he saw, and that he was meant for bigger things than Skraa-cha gang colors and fighting over turf. The Underground wasn't the only option out there; Seattle offered deep, dark, shadows, too. Shadows that would leave him more room to grow than tunnels.

Sledge's penchant for combat paid off in a big way, and instead of drinking away his first windfall or gambling with it, he went for a surer bet. Slowly but surely, he invested his low-level profits back into himself, getting stronger, tougher, and faster, so he could take on bigger challenges. The ork's especially proud of his arms—and he regularly has street docs work on them—and his fusion of chrome, courage, and consistency has made him a force to be reckoned with.

The backbone of Myth's crew, Sledge is as dangerous in close as he is at range. With a few trophies taken from high-profile gigs already—like his favorite Raiden autogun or his trademark *Neil the Ork Barbarian* sword—he's making a name for himself as a reliable, dangerous professional in a reliably dangerous profession. His code of honor is short but dear to him, and bloodshed's waiting for anyone who tries to make him cross a line.

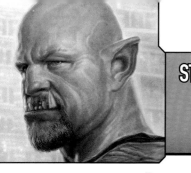

SLEDGE

☐ Emerged
☐ Awakened

STRENGTH	AGILITY	WILLPOWER	LOGIC	CHARISMA	EDGE
8	6	3	4	2	1

DISPOSITIONS

TOTAL KARMA

KARMA BALANCE

The streets have rules.

Backing down shows weakness.

Your word is your bond.

When in doubt, nail 'em.

SKILLS

ATHLETICS	1+A	CLOSE COMBAT	4+A	FIREARMS	4+A
INTIMIDATION	2+C	STEALTH	1+A	ORK UNDERGROUND	(K)

SHADOW AMPS

ESSENCE: 1 — −3 dice to magic/healing tests.

2 — **MOVE-BY-WIRE 1**
Cyberware. Gains +1 attack/movement. −1 Essence

3 — **CUSTOM CYBEREYES WITH SMARTLINK**
Cyberware. Ignore vision modifiers, may reroll 1 failed die with ranged attacks, +1 die to Firearms or Heavy Weapons rolls. −1 Essence

4 — **CUSTOM CYBERARM SUITE**
Cyberware. May reroll one die on Agility-related rolls, reduce all damage taken by 1, Unarmed attacks may do physical or stun damage, and may reroll 1 die with Close Combat attacks. −3 Essence

1 — **MORE WHERE THAT CAME FROM**
Gain 2 additional weapons.

CUES

We took the job, we do the job.

It's a street fight, not some Queensberry bulldrek!

I didn't mean you when I said that about elves, Coydog!

Shh! You're gonna get us all killed. Act like a fraggin' professional, would'ja?

You look at me cross-eyed again, I'll gut you, chummer.

I'm gonna need more ammo for this gig.

Hey, get a move on! We haven't got all night.

Everyone gets one chance to back down. You're spending yours right now.

QUALITIES

BIOCOMPATABILITY
Ignore 1 point of Shadow Amp Essence cost.

BRUISER
+2 dice to Intimidation tests.

DISTINCTIVE STYLE
Constantly upgrading and tinkering with custom cyberarms creates an easy-to-remember look.

WEAPONS

UNARMED	DAM	CLOSE	NEAR	FAR
	4S/4P	OK	—	—

Custom replica mono-katana	DAM	CLOSE	NEAR	FAR	Ares Predator V Pistol	DAM	CLOSE	NEAR	FAR	Ingram Smartgun SMG	DAM	CLOSE	NEAR	FAR
	6P	OK	—	—		6P	OK	−2	—		6P	OK	OK	—

Yamaha Raiden Assault Rifle	DAM	CLOSE	NEAR	FAR		DAM	CLOSE	NEAR	FAR		DAM	CLOSE	NEAR	FAR
	8P	OK	OK	−2										

CONDITION MONITOR

ARMOR

TACTICAL VEST

PHYSICAL   STUN

−1 −2 −3 −4 (physical)

−1 −2 −3 −4 (stun)

GEAR

Fake SIN, Renraku Sensei commlink, trauma patch, big old Harley combat bike

CONTACTS

"Red Dot" Dottie (weapons dealer)

Elkarra Johannsen (orkish beat cop)

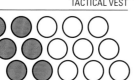

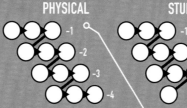

ALYOSHA DUSKA

DWARF SPIRIT WHISPERER

TAGS

• Dwarf • Shaman • Spirits • For Hire • Respectful

BACKGROUND

Organized crime isn't a life you choose so you can be a good parent. Alyosha knows that well. His father was Vory v Zakone, Russian mafia, and while Alyosha didn't feel much love as a kid, he learned a lot about the world's underbelly. The most important thing he learned was that the Vory wasn't for him. Crime itself was neutral, though. Laws were made up by metahumans and enforced, or not, by other metahumans. Spirits taught him a different path.

As a youth, Alyosha was visited by the Bear spirit, his only comfort in a house of violence and insecurity. The spirit taught him to live in cooperation with the world, not dominate it. It taught him how the spirit world works, how spirits speak to one another, and that his family is much broader than just blood. Bear was Alyosha's father, and Alyosha was Bear's shaman.

Because of his upbringing, Alyosha felt ill participating in violence. But the spirits around him did not feel the same way. Spirits would fight for him, if he asked. And he had a gift for asking. Sometimes spirits said, "no," but that was okay. Alyosha respected them and their wishes—there are always other spirits around, willing to help. Bear taught him that.

Alyosha pays the rent doing what he does best. As a Spirit Whisperer, he summons spirits for hire. Need a spirit to spy on a husband or wife? Protect a child? Clean your house? Alyosha is your shaman. But Alyosha loves the jobs that bring him back into the underworld, reminding him that this world's laws are nothing more than human words. In the end, he's always cared more about what the spirits have to say.

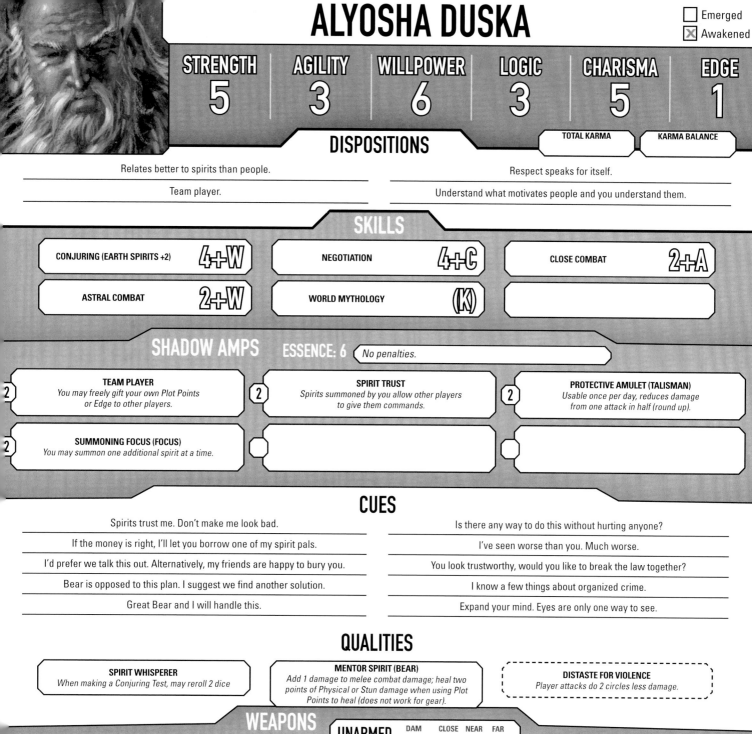

ALYOSHA DUSKA

☐ Emerged
☒ Awakened

STRENGTH	AGILITY	WILLPOWER	LOGIC	CHARISMA	EDGE
5	3	6	3	5	1

DISPOSITIONS

TOTAL KARMA | KARMA BALANCE

Relates better to spirits than people.

Team player.

Respect speaks for itself.

Understand what motivates people and you understand them.

SKILLS

| CONJURING (EARTH SPIRITS +2) | 4+W | NEGOTIATION | 4+C | CLOSE COMBAT | 2+A |
| ASTRAL COMBAT | 2+W | WORLD MYTHOLOGY | (K) | | |

SHADOW AMPS

ESSENCE: 6 — No penalties.

2 — TEAM PLAYER
You may freely gift your own Plot Points or Edge to other players.

2 — SPIRIT TRUST
Spirits summoned by you allow other players to give them commands.

2 — PROTECTIVE AMULET (TALISMAN)
Usable once per day, reduces damage from one attack in half (round up).

2 — SUMMONING FOCUS (FOCUS)
You may summon one additional spirit at a time.

CUES

Spirits trust me. Don't make me look bad.

If the money is right, I'll let you borrow one of my spirit pals.

I'd prefer we talk this out. Alternatively, my friends are happy to bury you.

Bear is opposed to this plan. I suggest we find another solution.

Great Bear and I will handle this.

Is there any way to do this without hurting anyone?

I've seen worse than you. Much worse.

You look trustworthy, would you like to break the law together?

I know a few things about organized crime.

Expand your mind. Eyes are only one way to see.

QUALITIES

SPIRIT WHISPERER
When making a Conjuring Test, may reroll 2 dice

MENTOR SPIRIT (BEAR)
Add 1 damage to melee combat damage; heal two points of Physical or Stun damage when using Plot Points to heal (does not work for gear).

DISTASTE FOR VIOLENCE
Player attacks do 2 circles less damage.

WEAPONS

	DAM	CLOSE	NEAR	FAR
UNARMED	4S	OK	—	—

	DAM	CLOSE	NEAR	FAR		DAM	CLOSE	NEAR	FAR		DAM	CLOSE	NEAR	FAR
Gnarled Staff	6P	OK	—	—	Boomerang	4P	OK	−2	—		DAM	CLOSE	NEAR	FAR
	DAM	CLOSE	NEAR	FAR		DAM	CLOSE	NEAR	FAR		DAM	CLOSE	NEAR	FAR

CONDITION MONITOR

ARMOR

ARMOR CLOTHING

PHYSICAL

−1 −2 −3 −4

STUN

−1 −2 −3 −4

GEAR

Fake SIN, magical lodge materials, Xiao Technologies XT-2G commlink, fifty drams of reagents

CONTACTS

Deadeye (transhumanist/smuggler)

Lazar Fedorov (Vory v Zakone Russian Mafia boss)

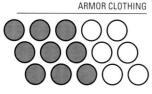

BIT-BUCKET

ORK DECKER

TAGS

• Ork • Hacker • Cocky • Greedy • Vexing

BACKGROUND

Bit-Bucket didn't get into hacking because he was a shy kid who loved electronics. He didn't get into hacking because he wanted to avoid the gang brawls common to his Ork Underground upbringing. He got into hacking for the simple reason that he understood that in the Sixth World, that's where the money is.

As a youth (by the name of Grralk), he and his friends did some minor smash-and-grabs in the Tourist Highway, and he was dissatisfied to walk away with a few pieces of fruit, or some cheap commlinks that he couldn't get anyone to buy for more than twenty nuyen. Tens of thousands of nuyen were flowing through the Highway each day, and at that point he could only figure out how to grab the smallest fraction of it.

He wasn't having any of that drek. The money was there, all around him, he just needed to figure out how to get his hands on it. He made his stealing more targeted, getting himself the tools he needed to learn how the Matrix worked and how he could break it. He learned how it was different from the meat world and how it was the same—how sometimes, bursting in with a flurry of noise and tumult was as good a strategy as any. He didn't have a teacher or mentor or anything; instead, he learned from books, from blogs, and from trial and error. He made a lot of mistakes, bricked a lot of 'links, but by the time the Matrix revisions of 2075 kicked in, he was ready to hack into a corporate database and have a new cyberdeck delivered to a PO box he rented. He didn't pay for either the deck or the mailbox.

Bit-Bucket's mark is an ork fist in a studded glove coming right at you, which is how he hacks. He is bold and showy, usually very willing for his targets to know who he is and what he is doing to them. He has developed a kind of one-sided rivalry with legendary shadowrunner Bull, known as "the best ork decker you never met," mainly because every time people found out he was an ork and a decker, they mentioned Bull, and Bit-Bucket decided he needed to show who out-ranked whom when it came to ork deckers. Primarily this involved hacking into Bull's restaurant and trash-talking Bull on Matrix forums, so nothing serious. Mostly, it's a way for Bit-Bucket to raise his profile, which he likes to do whenever possible.

BIT-BUCKET

☐ Emerged
☐ Awakened

STRENGTH	AGILITY	WILLPOWER	LOGIC	CHARISMA	EDGE
6	4	5	5	3	1

DISPOSITIONS

TOTAL KARMA | KARMA BALANCE

Data wants to be very, very expensive.

Tired as hell of living in decking legend Bull's shadow.

Never met a node he didn't think he could hack.

Has a big, precariously balanced chip on his shoulder.

SKILLS

CLOSE COMBAT	2+A
HACKING (CYBERCOMBAT +2)	5+L

ELECTRONICS	3+L
FAMOUS MATRIX PERSONALITIES	(K)

FIREARMS	1+A

SHADOW AMPS

ESSENCE: 5 — −1 die to magic/healing tests.

2 BIOFEEDBACK
Program. Deals cybercombat damage to his opponent's Physical or Matrix condition monitor.

2 DATAJACK AND HEADWARE
Cyberware. Can access the Matrix in full VR. +1 die to Matrix actions. −1 Essence

3 HAMMER
Program. Does +2 circles of damage in cybercombat.

3 NOVATECH NAVIGATOR
Cyberdeck. May reroll one die on Matrix actions. Firewall +2. Matrix condition monitor 9. May run one program at a time.

CUES

I'll show them who's the best ork decker!

Mister, that's one of the frostiest nodes I've ever seen. Gonna cost extra.

Ever been hit with Black Hammer? No? Then zip it and get me some aspirin.

Oh, that just ain't right!

Is that the best you can do?

Yeah, I'm a tusker with a deck. Deal with it.

Fished his commlink out of Puget Sound. Give me a few minutes, I'll fix it up.

Back off. Bypassing this maglock is more complicated than it looks.

QUALITIES

CODESLINGER
+2 dice for Hacking tests.

TOUGHNESS
All damage taken is reduced by 1 point per attack.

SINNER, CRIMINAL
Known to law enforcement; data available through the Global SIN Registry.

WEAPONS

UNARMED	DAM 3S	CLOSE OK	NEAR —	FAR —

	DAM	CLOSE	NEAR	FAR		DAM	CLOSE	NEAR	FAR		DAM	CLOSE	NEAR	FAR
Survival Knife	5P	OK	—	—	Ares Predator V Pistol	5P	OK	−2	—					
	DAM	CLOSE	NEAR	FAR		DAM	CLOSE	NEAR	FAR		DAM	CLOSE	NEAR	FAR

CONDITION MONITOR

ARMOR
LINED COAT

PHYSICAL
−1 −2 −3 −4

STUN
−1 −2 −3 −4

GEAR
Electronics toolkit, Erika Elite commlink, stim patches, Yamaha Growler motorcycle

CONTACTS
Tommy Vanns (electronics dealer)
Jerry Hauser (ork fixer)

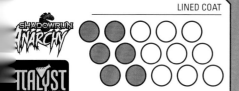

SHADOWRUN ANARCHY

CATALYST game labs

BORDERLINE

HUMAN GANGER RAZORGIRL

TAGS

- Human • Razorgirl • Anarchist • Barrens • Halloweeners

BACKGROUND

The Redmond Barrens define Borderline's existence. For most people, Redmond is somewhere to avoid at all costs. For her, it's home.

Growing up in the Barrens isn't all bad. There were times when the radiation over Glow City looked beautiful at night, romantic even. Or on Black Mondays when the Anarchist Black Cross would supply free medical care and food for everyone. Even the gangs sometimes stopped fighting so they could see doctors. But the happiest day of the year for Borderline was Halloween. That was when the Halloweeners would tear through Redmond, wearing wicked costumes, and turn the world upside-down.

When Borderline turned twelve, she marched over to the Jackal's Lantern and declared her desire to join the Halloweeners. It didn't turn out how she expected—but it made her strong. Strong enough to steal food for her siblings. Strong enough to deal with anyone who threatened her. Strong enough to blackmail a street doc into upgrading her body. After ten years of running with the 'Weeners, she was the baddest razorgirl in Redmond.

She stands on the edge of two worlds: the broken world of the Barrens and the world outside. Running the shadows has broadened her perspective. She still has ties to the Halloweeners, but her world has expanded beyond them. Shadowruns now take her all over Seattle, but she always comes back. Redmond is in her blood. It's where her family is. It's where her name means something. It's who she is.

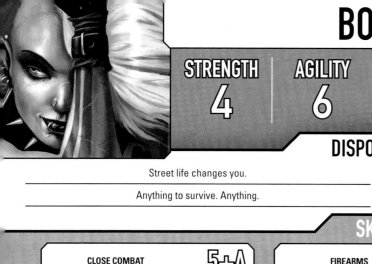

BORDERLINE

☐ Emerged
☐ Awakened

STRENGTH	AGILITY	WILLPOWER	LOGIC	CHARISMA	EDGE
4	6	4	3	4	2

DISPOSITIONS

TOTAL KARMA

KARMA BALANCE

Street life changes you.

Anything to survive. Anything.

Life never gives anything for free.

Trust doesn't come quick, if ever.

SKILLS

CLOSE COMBAT **5+A**	FIREARMS **2+A**	INTIMIDATION **3+C**
SURVIVAL (URBAN AREAS +2) **3+W**	LOCAL NEIGHBORHOODS **(K)**	

SHADOW AMPS   ESSENCE: 2.5   −2 dice to magic/healing tests.

4 | **WIRED REFLEXES 3**
Cyberware. +1 attack, 2 Plot Points per Scene. −2 Essence

4 | **BIOWARE ARMS 2**
Bioware. May reroll 2 dice on Agility-related rolls. −0.5 Essence

2 | **RETRACTABLE HAND RAZORS**
Cyberware weapon. Inflicts Physical damage with Unarmed attack, may reroll 1 die. −1 Essence

CUES

Trust you? I don't trust my own mother.

I knew they were gonna betray us.

Do what I tell you, and we'll get along fine.

When you're a Halloweener, you're a 'Weener all the way.

Safe? What does that mean?

Hope gets you dead. Focus on now.

I leave the Barrens all the time. But they never leave me.

In case you haven't heard, I like cutting things, so by all means, keep refusing.

I know a place we can lie low.

I'm a girl on the edge. And I like it that way.

QUALITIES

AMBIDEXTROUS
+2 dice when using two melee weapons.

HOME GROUND (BARRENS)
Gain +1 Plot Point when entering or waking up in the Redmond Barrens.

PARANOIA
Must reroll successes (max 2) when making social tests.

WEAPONS

UNARMED	DAM	CLOSE	NEAR	FAR
	2S	OK	—	—

	DAM	CLOSE	NEAR	FAR		DAM	CLOSE	NEAR	FAR		DAM	CLOSE	NEAR	FAR
Hand Razors	3P	OK	—	—	Katana	5P	OK	—	—	Cavalier Deputy Pistol	6P	OK	−2	—
	DAM	CLOSE	NEAR	FAR		DAM	CLOSE	NEAR	FAR		DAM	CLOSE	NEAR	FAR

CONDITION MONITOR

ARMOR

SYNTHLEATHER CLOTHING

CONDITION MONITOR

PHYSICAL   STUN
−1   −1
−2   −2
−3   −3
−4   −4

GEAR

Fake SIN, enhanced vision goggles, Sony Emperor commlink, metal restraints

CONTACTS

Carnevil (ganger lieutenant)

Jack the Ripper (retired shadowrunner/cybersecurity expert)

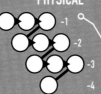
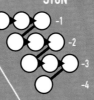

CHROME BISON

TROLL STREET SAMURAI

TAGS

• Troll • Tank • Salish-Shidhe • Dependable • Runner

BACKGROUND

The child who eventually became Chrome Bison spent years complaining to the elders about not having trideo. Her pleas for gaming consoles always fell on deaf ears. Whenever she begged her parents to let her try fast food, the answer was always the same. "We are not like the rest of the world. We are survivors and caretakers. That world you long for is a world of parasites."

She didn't know how much she would miss that sheltered childhood until she lost it forever. Rebellion took her into the "real" world. There, she learned about racism. She learned about injustice. She learned troll skin often stopped bears from hurting her, but it didn't stop explosive rounds. A good Samaritan with a fake SIN and a DocWagon contract got her out of there and paid for her cyber. Now, her body *could* stop explosive rounds. That was her introduction to the shadows. The price for her new 'ware was becoming a shadowrunner until she paid off her debt.

Once she had, she went back home, only to find that her tribe was gone, and in its place was a massive mining operation. The miners said her tribe had just moved on. She knew better. This corporation had been trying to buy their land for years. Now it looked like they just took it. Maybe if she had been there, she could have protected them. But she wasn't. Indulging her own desires instead of helping her people survive was a mistake. One that she will never repeat. She'll die before she lets anyone down again.

CHROME BISON

☐ Emerged
☐ Awakened

STRENGTH	AGILITY	WILLPOWER	LOGIC	CHARISMA	EDGE
8	4	5	3	3	1

DISPOSITIONS

TOTAL KARMA

KARMA BALANCE

Protective of team.

Honor means a great deal.

Uses humor as a means of redirection.

Doesn't trust easy, but likes being trustworthy.

SKILLS

CLOSE COMBAT	3+A
PROJECTILE WEAPONS	2+A

FIREARMS (HEAVY PISTOLS +2)	2+A
SALISH LANGUAGE	(K)

SURVIVAL	2+W

SHADOW AMPS   ESSENCE: 2   −2 dice to magic/healing tests.

3 | **ALUMINUM BONE LACING 2**
Reduce damage taken by 2. −1 Essence

3 | **DERMAL PLATING 2**
Reduce damage taken by 2. −1 Essence

3 | **SKILL WIRES 1 (FIREARMS)**
+1 die to Firearms rolls. −1 Essence

3 | **SMARTLINK**
+1 die to Firearms or Heavy Weapons rolls. −1 Essence

CUES

I just have big bones. Big, chrome, cyber-enhanced bones.

I could try smashing it until it opens …

I'll take the hits so you don't have to.

I like the city. But I was raised to respect nature.

You aren't my friend. But I'll still protect you.

Just because I got shot, doesn't mean I need a hospital!

You have a very shootable face.

No matter what, we all live through this. I promise.

Taco Temple sounds good about now.

I can't keep this up forever!

QUALITIES

HIGH PAIN TOLERANCE
Does not take dice penalties for damage until second row of damage boxes is filled.

GUTS
May reroll 2 dice when resisting fear or intimidation.

ALLERGY (SEAFOOD)
When affected by allergy (GM decision), −4 to all dice rolls.

WEAPONS

UNARMED	DAM	CLOSE	NEAR	FAR
	4S	OK	—	—

	DAM	CLOSE	NEAR	FAR		DAM	CLOSE	NEAR	FAR		DAM	CLOSE	NEAR	FAR
Defiance EX Shocker	6S	OK	−4	—	Ruger Super Warhawk	6P	OK	−2	—	Frag Grenade	12P	OK*	OK*	—
					Heavy Pistol					*Player(s) take damage as well at GM discretion				
	DAM	CLOSE	NEAR	FAR		DAM	CLOSE	NEAR	FAR		DAM	CLOSE	NEAR	FAR

CONDITION MONITOR

ARMOR

ARMOR JACKET, TROLL SKIN

PHYSICAL

−1
−2
−3
−4

STUN

−1
−2
−3
−4

GEAR

Fake SIN, Toyota Gopher, Transys Avalon Commlink, 3 fragmentation grenades

CONTACTS

Mr. Cogent (fixer)

Dr. Maplethorpe (street doc)

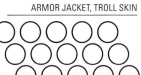

SHADOWRUN ANARCHY

CATALYST game labs

DAKTARI

DWARF STREET DOC

TAGS

• Dwarf • Magician • Healer • Conscientious • Pacifist

BACKGROUND

Steve Kiley thought he had it all. He had a great job with DocWagon, the premier private emergency medical care provider on the North American continent, if not the planet. He got to have an adventure every single day as his high-threat response team roared in to rescue another subscriber. Most importantly, he got to save lives, which since his youth had been his entire *raison d'etre*. He lost patients sometimes; all doctors do. But his successful treatment percentage was a credit to his corp, and his supervisors had recommended him for a promotion.

Naively, he thought that meant something.

On a high-threat response job into gang territory in Redmond, Steve had just worked a miracle. Their client was a shadowrunner who'd gotten in way over his head fighting the Death Heads, one of the newer gangs in the area. He'd taken a very big knife very close to the heart, and he had come perilously close to bleeding out before the knife was removed and Steve's magical treatment closed the artery and patched the hole in his lungs. As Steve and his partner were loading their patient into the waiting chopper, they came under fire from the gang. Steve was struck squarely in the chest, and while his body armor stopped the round, he was knocked out.

He came to sometime later and realized two things. First, the DocWagon High-Threat Response motto, "No one left behind," was a complete load of drek. Second, he was surrounded by more than a dozen gangers, most of them with varying degrees of injury. He traded his services to Fusion, the gang's leader, for the chance to leave Redmond intact. When he finally got back to a more civilized part of Seattle a few days later, he found that he'd been declared dead by DocWagon. Not feeling too charitable toward them anyway, he took that as a sign that it was time to move on. Since then, he's run a shadow clinic back in Redmond, where his skills are sorely needed, and taken the occasional contract as medical support on actual shadowruns.

DAKTARI

STRENGTH	AGILITY	WILLPOWER	LOGIC	CHARISMA	EDGE
6	4	5	5	3	2

DISPOSITIONS

TOTAL KARMA	KARMA BALANCE

Renders aid to anyone who needs it.

All life is sacred, and must be protected at all costs.

First, do no harm.

Willing to go to great lengths to save his patient.

SKILLS

BIOTECH	4+L	CLOSE COMBAT	1+A	CONJURING	2+W
FIREARMS	1+A	SORCERY (SPELLCASTING +2)	4+W	LOCAL MEDICAL FACILITIES	(K)

SHADOW AMPS   ESSENCE: 6   No penalties.

DIAGNOSE
Effect spell. Caster can determine the target's state of health. Each narration it's sustained reveals one specific problem per hit on the Sorcery test.

2 HEAL
Effect spell. Target character regains one box of physical damage per hit per Narration the spell is sustained.

2 STUNBOLT
Combat spell. Damage of 8S/AA. Defense = S + W.

SUSTAINING FOCUS
Talisman. Can maintain one additional spell.

CUES

Careful, Jack! Those meds don't exactly grow on trees!

Some days, I kinda miss my DocWagon days, when I just got *shot at* on the job.

I've operated in worse conditions.

Welcome back from the other side. You're welcome.

This is going to sting a little.

Take two NERPS and call me in the morning.

Your collarbone's broken in two places. You might also want to quit smoking.

Look, she's going to die unless I do something.
Quit pointing that at me and let me help!

QUALITIES

GUTS
May reroll 2 dice when resisting fear or intimidation.

MENTOR SPIRIT (BEAR)
+1 to melee combat damage; using First Aid doesn't cost a Plot Point.

COMBAT PARALYSIS
Act last on the first round of any combat (that wasn't specifically you initiating an ambush).

WEAPONS

				UNARMED	DAM 4S	CLOSE OK	NEAR —	FAR —				

	DAM	CLOSE	NEAR	FAR		DAM	CLOSE	NEAR	FAR		DAM	CLOSE	NEAR	FAR
Narcojet Tranquilizer Pistol	6S	OK	−2	—	Stun Baton	7S	OK	—	—					
	DAM	CLOSE	NEAR	FAR		DAM	CLOSE	NEAR	FAR		DAM	CLOSE	NEAR	FAR

ARMOR

ARMORED CLOTHING

CONDITION MONITOR

PHYSICAL
-1 -2 -3 -4

STUN
-1 -2 -3 -4

GEAR

AR glasses, GMC Bulldog stepvan (customized), Hermes Ikon commlink, high-end medkit

CONTACTS

Jenny Whitesleeves (DocWagon quartermaster)

Fusion (ork rigger/ganger)

FOURTH

ORK REPORTER

TAGS

- Ork • Journalist • Inquisitive • Crusader • Abrasive

BACKGROUND

Funny thing about the truth: Though it may take a thousand years, it will always find a way out. Fourth (as in the Fourth Estate) has dedicated herself to helping it escape into the wild at a substantially accelerated pace.

Likely as not, she wouldn't be out to make the lives of the rich and powerful so miserable now if that car hadn't hit her girlfriend. If the uber-rich corp exec's punk kid had stopped to render aid, Ashley might not have bled out in a Tacoma gutter. If Knight Errant had taken the death of a SINless ork girl seriously, they might have found out that she wasn't the first one to be hurt or killed at this punk's hands. It hadn't taken much to figure it out; a few questions here, a drink or two there, the occasional bare-your-tusks threat, and all the answers started coming together.

She'd taken everything that she'd learned to the Knights, and they did nothing. That was when she'd met Reyes. He was a reporter, looking up crime blotter stuff, sifting around for a story. He told her the way to defeat people like this corp kid wasn't through the rigged legal system, but through public outcry. One person couldn't get the system to change, but if they could create enough public outrage, the Knights would have to do something to quiet them down.

It worked. He could smell the story himself, and he offered to do it for her, but she knew she had to do this herself. Ultimately, he showed her how to work sources, gather info, and put out a story that pushed people to action. The first one took a couple of weeks to put together; the follow-ups took months. What her early work lacked in grace and sophistication, it made up for in passion. She made life a living hell for the punk, and it became a sufficient embarrassment to Knight Errant that ultimately they had to do something to make the protests stop. Justice was served.

Then the public forgot about it. By that time, though, Fourth had found another truth to set free. And then another. Her life's work unfolded before her.

STREET PEOPLE

FOURTH

☐ Emerged
☐ Awakened

STRENGTH	AGILITY	WILLPOWER	LOGIC	CHARISMA	EDGE
6	3	4	5	5	2

DISPOSITIONS

TOTAL KARMA

KARMA BALANCE

The truth is out there, and she must set it free.

The people deserve to know what is being done to them.

Raking the muck is sometimes part of the job.

Doggedly single-minded when pursuing a story.

SKILLS

FIREARMS	3+A
TRACKING	3+L

INTIMIDATION (INTERROGATION +2)	4+C
LOCAL NEWS OUTLETS	(K)

STEALTH	2+A

SHADOW AMPS

ESSENCE: 2.5 _−2 dice to magic/healing tests._

CYBEREARS
Cyberware. Can listen to conversations at both Close and Near ranges. May reroll 1 failed die on hearing-related tests. −1 Essence

(2) **CYBEREYES**
Cyberware. Ignore vision modifiers due to lighting conditions. May reroll 1 failed die on ranged attacks. −1 Essence

(2) **DATAJACK AND HEADWARE**
Cyberware. Can access the Matrix in full VR. +1 die to Matrix actions. −1 Essence.

TAILORED PHEROMONES
Bioware. Reroll 1 failed die on all in-person Charisma-related tests. −0.5 Essence

CUES

That's very interesting. And on the record too, right?

Long as they spell my name right on the byline, I don't much care.

Sometimes the truth is scary as hell—but it's all that matters.

I am forever missing deadlines because someone is shooting at me.

Congratulations, mister; you're tonight's lead story.

"Follow the money" _sounds_ easy, but people work hard to cover the trail.

I'd rather get this story the easy way, _omae_, but if you push me, I can play rough, too.

The story's gonna get out—the question is, will you help tell it?

QUALITIES

CATLIKE
+2 dice for Stealth tests.

SILVER TONGUE
May reroll 2 failed dice on Charisma-related tests.

COMBAT PARALYSIS
Act last on the first round of any combat (which wasn't specifically you initiating an ambush).

WEAPONS

UNARMED	DAM	CLOSE	NEAR	FAR
	3S	OK	—	—

	DAM	CLOSE	NEAR	FAR		DAM	CLOSE	NEAR	FAR		DAM	CLOSE	NEAR	FAR
Collapsible Baton	5P	OK	—	—	Colt America L36 Light Pistol	5P	OK	−2	—					
	DAM	CLOSE	NEAR	FAR		DAM	CLOSE	NEAR	FAR		DAM	CLOSE	NEAR	FAR

ARMOR

ACTIONEER BUSINESS CLOTHING

CONDITION MONITOR

PHYSICAL
-1 -2 -3 -4

STUN
-1 -2 -3 -4

GEAR

Ford Americar sedan, Hermes Ikon commlink, stim patches, white noise generator

CONTACTS

KSAF (trid news station)

Jenny Johnson (politician's personal assistant)

FUSION

ORK RIGGER/GANGER

TAGS

• Ork • Rigger • Redmond • Gang Leader • Death Heads

BACKGROUND

Fusion didn't plan on ever leading a gang. She was just an ork who loved her bike. That is, until she met Stubbs. She'd always had a thing for dwarfs. When he came riding around Downtown on his chromed-out street-cycle, she'll admit that she swooned a bit. When he came around the next day asking about bikers looking for money, she was in. When he told her he was putting a gang together to show the Ancients who was boss, she was first in line.

Her bike got chromed out to match the gang's colors, and she ended up spending all of her ill-gotten gains making her bike faster and tougher. A chrome skull tattoo, neural upgrades so she could rig into vehicles and drones, a wiz bike, and a cute bad boy dwarf. Life didn't get any better.

The gang became the Death Heads. She was in charge when the bosses were away doing their shadowrunner thing. But they weren't around when the Ancients came around looking for payback. That was when she realized that having a go-gang wasn't just about being a bad motherfragger on a wiz set of wheels. Lots of her closest chummers fell to the Ancients, and the rest high-tailed it to Redmond. The other gangs in the barrens weren't as mobile or organized as the Ancients, so that's where they laid down roots. And she told Stubbs the gang was hers now. She'd earned it.

The first year that Fusion and the Death Heads spent in Redmond was dedicated to upgrading their bikes for the broken Barrens terrain. The next year was spent dominating the roads. Now, she does whatever she wants.

FUSION

☐ Emerged
☐ Awakened

STRENGTH	AGILITY	WILLPOWER	LOGIC	CHARISMA	EDGE
4	5	4	5	5	1

DISPOSITIONS

TOTAL KARMA	KARMA BALANCE

Obsessive and protective about bike.

Enjoys her life: Being an ork/shadowrunner/gang leader becomes her.

Gang family comes first, everything else second.

Driven to push her own limits and the limits of her gear.

SKILLS

ENGINEERING	2+L	PILOTING (GROUND)	3+A	VEHICLE WEAPONS	3+A
FIREARMS	3+A	CLOSE COMBAT	2+A	REGIONAL GANGS	(K)

SHADOW AMPS   ESSENCE: 4   −1 die to magic/healing tests.

CONTROL RIG 3
Cyberware. Control vehicles by VR, +1 die to vehicle actions, may reroll 2 dice on vehicle actions. −2 Essence

[2] **GM-NISSAN DOBERMAN DRONE**
Gain +1 attack (only with Doberman drone)

[3] **2X MCT FLY-SPY AERIAL DRONE**
+2 dice to Perception tests.

HARLEY-DAVIDSON SCORPION
With Mounted Assault Rifle, Mounted Grenade Launcher

CUES

Touch not, lest ye be touched!

Hey! You aren't half bad. Wanna join my gang?

You aren't my type. Unless you're a dwarf, then let's party!

Street race! All right!

I have some people I can call for a diversion.

Three things make me happy: My bike, my gang, and bein' bad.

There's a simple solution. Burn it down!

Don't overestimate your skills. That's how people die.

They won't get away from me!

There's no such thing as fast enough.

QUALITIES

LEADER OF THE PACK
Add 1 group/organization/gang to list of contacts.

GEARHEAD
When pushing the limits of vehicles or performing difficult maneuvers, add +2 dice to roll.

EMOTIONAL ATTACHMENT (BIKE)
At GM discretion, must spend a Plot Point to avoid prioritizing her custom bike above anything else.

WEAPONS

	DAM	CLOSE	NEAR	FAR
UNARMED	2S	OK	—	—

	DAM	CLOSE	NEAR	FAR		DAM	CLOSE	NEAR	FAR		DAM	CLOSE	NEAR	FAR
Survival Knife	3P	OK	—	—	Ares Predator V Pistol	6P	OK	−2	—	Doberman Drone	8P	OK	—	—
Mounted Assault Rifle	8P	OK	OK	−2	Mtd. Grenade Launcher	12P	OK*	OK*	OK					

*Player(s) take damage as well at GM discretion

CONDITION MONITOR

ARMOR
SYNTHLEATHER JACKET

PHYSICAL
−1 −2 −3 −4

STUN
−1 −2 −3 −4

GEAR
Fake SIN, Harley-Davidson Scorpion bike, Transys Avalon commlink, goggles (image link, thermographic vision, magnification)

CONTACTS
Stubbs (dwarf decker/data thief)

Walturr (Silver Spoke bar owner)

Death Heads (Redmond go-gang)

HAWK

HUMAN STREET SAMURAI

TAGS

• Human • Soldier • Leader • Patient • Stern

BACKGROUND

His time in the UCAS Army taught Joseph Simmons a lot of things. It taught him how to shoot. It taught him how to work with a unit. It taught him to trust his fellow soldiers to do their jobs, because they were trusting him to do his. It taught him to lead, and to be patient. It took a street punk from Seattle and made him part of something bigger. It taught him to be better.

It also taught him that the brass further up the chain of command would stab you in the fragging back and not think twice about it. After ten years of faithful service, they exercised the early termination clause of his enlistment contract, and he found himself back on the streets of Puyallup. One afternoon, he was sitting at the counter of a diner, wondering how he was going to pay for the meal he'd just ordered and realizing that there weren't many career paths in the private sector for well-trained killers. He realized that he was lost without a unit around him.

An older-looking ork sat down next to him at the counter and asked, in a raspy voice, "You got any skills?"

That changed everything. There might not have been a lot of call for his skills in the private sector, but there was a great need for men with leadership skills in the shadows. Most shadowrunner teams don't have someone who can bring the best out of each member, and that was something at which he excelled.

So now he has a second career—and a new sense of purpose.

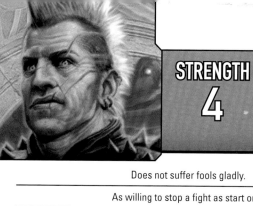

HAWK

☐ Emerged
☐ Awakened

STRENGTH	AGILITY	WILLPOWER	LOGIC	CHARISMA	EDGE
4	5	5	3	4	2

DISPOSITIONS

TOTAL KARMA | KARMA BALANCE

Does not suffer fools gladly.

As willing to stop a fight as start one.

Fights for his team.

Will wait as long as necessary for the right opening.

SKILLS

CLOSE COMBAT	2+A	FIREARMS	5+A	HEAVY WEAPONS	3+A
PILOTING (GROUND)	2+A	MERCENARY HOTSPOTS	(K)		

SHADOW AMPS   ESSENCE: 3   *−2 dice to magic/healing tests.*

CUSTOM CYBEREYES W/SMARTLINK
Cyberware. Ignore vision modifiers due to lighting conditions. May reroll 1 failed die on ranged attacks. Add +1 die to Firearms or Heavy Weapons rolls. −1 Essence.

[2] **MORE WHERE THAT CAME FROM**
Gain 2 additional weapons.

[2] **RETRACTABLE CYBERSPUR**
Cyberware. Additional melee weapon slot. −1 Essence

WIRED REFLEXES 1
Cyberware. Gains +1 attack or movement. −1 Essence

CUES

I have a clear shot.

That's one of my team, mister. I'd reconsider your next move if I was you.

Plan's fragged, people; I'm open to suggestions!

I have a backup plan, but it requires a lot of ammunition.

My team. My run. My rules.

This reminds me of the Yucatan. I fraggin' hate the Yucatan!

The brass ain't gonna watch out for us. That's our job.

You know, just once, I'd like things to go smoothly. Just once, to see what it's like.

QUALITIES

EXPERT SHOT
+2 dice for Firearms tests.

GUTS
+2 dice to resist fear and Intimidation attempts.

SINNER, NATIONAL (UCAS)
Legal citizen; data available through the Global SIN Registry.

WEAPONS

UNARMED	DAM	CLOSE	NEAR	FAR
	2S	OK	—	—

	DAM	CLOSE	NEAR	FAR		DAM	CLOSE	NEAR	FAR		DAM	CLOSE	NEAR	FAR
Ares Desert Strike Sniper Rifle	9P	−4	−2	OK	**Ares Predator V** Heavy Pistol	6P	OK	−2	—	**Colt M-23** Assault Rifle	8P	OK	OK	−2
Cougar Fineblade Combat Knife	5P	OK	—	—	**Cyberspur**	4P	OK	—	—					

CONDITION MONITOR

ARMOR

BODY ARMOR

PHYSICAL
−1 −2 −3 −4

STUN
−1 −2 −3 −4

GEAR

Erika Elite commlink, fake SIN, Harley-Davidson Scorpion motorcycle, survival kit

CONTACTS

Alicia Dietz (arms dealer)

Jerry Hauser (ork fixer)

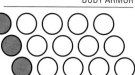

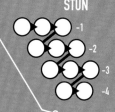

JINN

ELF BRUTE FORCE DECKER

TAGS

- Elf • Decker • Runner • Shiawase Enthusiast
- Islamic Renaissance Movement

BACKGROUND

Jinn grew up in Istanbul (the Free City of Constantinople, if you care to be official about it). As Sufis, his family found that Istanbul was a haven of tolerance for their beliefs compared to many of its neighboring states. Jinn grew to appreciate the diversity of his cosmopolitan home, growing more attached to culture and luxury as he grew. At an early age, he became fascinated with high fashion, so he learned how to navigate the Matrix, just to experience more of the culture he lacked. Seeing the male and female models in outrageous clothing inspired him like nothing else.

While attending a fashion show sponsored by Shiawase, young Jinn met Empress Hitomi Shiawase. The empress was in Istanbul to spread goodwill on behalf of Shiawase Corporation and seeing a photo opportunity, she struck up a conversation with a local child—Jinn. Without knowing who she was, Jinn blathered away about the latest fashions and how he had to hack certain Matrix sites just to view feeds from Milan. Curiously, this impressed Hitomi, who gave Jinn his first cyberdeck (before the new Matrix regulations) and offered him a job at Shiawase when he got older.

Jinn never forgot that meeting, and his love for fashion and decking now included a passion for Shiawase products. Jinn never did take the job offer at Shiawase, as he discovered his gift for hacking allowed him to make nuyen far easier than being a wageslave. He loves the finer things in life, and for him, that means superb fashion, Shiawase tech at his fingertips, and forcing the Matrix to do his bidding.

JINN

☐ Emerged
☐ Awakened

STRENGTH	AGILITY	WILLPOWER	LOGIC	CHARISMA	EDGE
3	4	4	6	6	1

DISPOSITIONS

TOTAL KARMA | KARMA BALANCE

Looking good while doing bad.

Hit hard, hit quick, and jack out before they know what hit them.

Compliments draw out the good nature in others.

Shiawase products or nothing.

SKILLS

HACKING (CYBERCOMBAT +2)	5+L	ELECTRONICS	3+L	FIREARMS	2+A
NEGOTIATION	2+C	HIGH FASHION	(K)		

SHADOW AMPS

ESSENCE: 4 — −1 die to magic/healing tests.

2 | **DATAJACK AND HEADWARE**
Cyberware. May access the Matrix via full VR, +1 die to Matrix actions. −1 Essence

4 | **SHIAWASE CYBER-4 CYBERDECK**
May reroll 2 dice on Matrix actions, Firewall +3, Matrix Condition Monitor 9, may run 1 program at a time.

2 | **SMARTLINK**
Cyberware. +1 die to Firearms or Heavy Weapons rolls. −1 Essence

2 | **HAMMER (PROGRAM)**
+2 damage in Cybercombat.

CUES

It is not bragging, my friend. I am that good.

Summon me in the Matrix and I will grant your wishes.

Faith and technology have created something perfect. Me.

The first step to making art is knowing how to see it.

Perhaps the civilized people among us should talk this over?

That is an exceptional outfit! At least you will lose looking sharp.

Because Shiawase products are the best, that's why.

There are many bad deckers, but no excuses for personas that tacky.

Hosts that want me to pay to enter are so adorable.

QUALITIES

DISTINCTIVE STYLE (HIGH FASHION)
Always seen wearing high-fashion clothing, particularly shades of red and purple.

BRAND LOYALTY (SHIAWASE)
+1 die when using Shiawase gear. −2 dice when making a test using gear not produced by Shiawase.

GO BIG OR GO HOME
−2 dice when making a cybercombat test, but may re-roll all misses once.

WEAPONS

	DAM	CLOSE	NEAR	FAR
UNARMED	2S	OK	—	—

	DAM	CLOSE	NEAR	FAR		DAM	CLOSE	NEAR	FAR		DAM	CLOSE	NEAR	FAR
Shiawase Arms Stun Staff	7S	OK	—	—	Shiawase Arms Monsoon	8P	OK	OK	−2					
	DAM	CLOSE	NEAR	FAR		DAM	CLOSE	NEAR	FAR		DAM	CLOSE	NEAR	FAR

ARMOR

HIGH FASHION ARMORED CLOTHING

CONDITION MONITOR

PHYSICAL −1 −2 −3 −4

STUN −1 −2 −3 −4

GEAR

Fake SIN, Shiawase Karuma sportscar, Shiawase Kawaii Shugenja commlink, Shiawase Wellington briefcase

CONTACTS

Mara Ariel (former Israeli Mossad operative, physical adept)

Nabila Al'Kajit (luxury clothing dealer)

SHADOWRUN ANARCHY

TALYST game labs

KIX

ELF RAZORGIRL

TAGS

• Elf • Augmented • Slasher • Adrenaline Junkie • Prickly

BACKGROUND

Puyallup's got some of the meanest streets in Seattle, and Seattle's got some of the meanest in the Sixth World. Kix came up from there, deep in the Puyallup Barrens, near enough to the elven ghetto of Tarislar to have ugly neighborhood race relations, but not deep in the heart of the pointy-eared district where her metatype would bring safety in numbers. She had the worst of both worlds, and it didn't take long until she knew the only way out was to stop taking it and start dishing it out.

She started with knives, the gutter-cheapest way to escalate a confrontation wildly past the level of an open hand or closed fist. Her quickness made her a natural, and her eagerness to inflict damage married nicely to her physical ability. It wasn't long before she opted for implanted blades—she'd never be disarmed or disadvantaged again—and once the augmentations started, they didn't stop until she was the leanest, meanest thing on the streets.

She eventually settled on Kix as a street handle—short for Kickstand, since aside from her slicing and dicing, she's mean on a bike—and it didn't take her long to build a name and a rep. Scorning the romantic notions of honor and etiquette that street samurai cling to, she's purely a Barrens-born pragmatist. She maintains no illusions of glory or nobility to her chosen calling—a job's just a job, a fight's just a fight, and someone's life is just nuyen waiting to be earned.

KIX

☐ Emerged
☐ Awakened

STRENGTH	AGILITY	WILLPOWER	LOGIC	CHARISMA	EDGE
5	7	2	4	3	1

DISPOSITIONS

TOTAL KARMA

KARMA BALANCE

Honor's for suckers and wannabes. Just win.

If you're not faster, you're stronger. If you're not stronger, you're faster.

Draw blood, get paid.

Your rep is all you've got. Live up to it.

SKILLS

CLOSE COMBAT	5+A
PILOT (GROUND) (MOTORCYCLES +2)	2+A

FIREARMS	2+A
COMBAT AUGMENTATIONS	(K)

INTIMIDATION	3+C

SHADOW AMPS   ESSENCE: 1

−3 dice to magic/healing tests.

4 **WIRED REFLEXES 3**
Cyberware. Gain +1 attack/movement, +2 Plot Points per scene. −3 Essence

6 **CUSTOM CYBERARM SUITE**
Cyberware. May reroll 2 dice on Agility-related rolls, Unarmed attacks may do physical or stun damage, may reroll 2 dice with Unarmed attacks. −3 Essence

CUES

You transfer the nuyen, I cut a fool. Simple.

Hey! Bet your life I'm faster'n you?

Streets are mean, chummer. I'm meaner.

Guns are alright, but blades never jam or need reloading.

You take that one, I've got the three on the right.

It's just biz.

I can take 'em. Whoever they are.

Walk away while you can.

Wait, he's offering us how much?!

You can cut your way through anything.

QUALITIES

EXCEPTIONAL ATTRIBUTE (AGILITY)
Increase your Agility cap by +1.

BIOCOMPATABILITY
Ignore 1 point of Shadow Amp Essence cost.

COMBAT JUNKIE
Must spend a Plot Point to avoid using violence as a first response to most problems.

WEAPONS

	DAM	CLOSE	NEAR	FAR
UNARMED	3S/3P	OK	—	—

	DAM	CLOSE	NEAR	FAR		DAM	CLOSE	NEAR	FAR		DAM	CLOSE	NEAR	FAR
Browning Ultra-Power Pistol	6P	OK	−2	—	**Defiance T-250** Shotgun (May attack 2 targets at half damage.)	9P	OK	−4	—					
	DAM	CLOSE	NEAR	FAR		DAM	CLOSE	NEAR	FAR		DAM	CLOSE	NEAR	FAR

CONDITION MONITOR

ARMOR

ARMORED CLOTHING

PHYSICAL

−1
−2
−3

STUN

−1
−2
−3
−4

GEAR

Fake SIN, Renraku Sensei commlink, Yamaha Rapier street bike, pocket full of recreational pharmaceutical slap-patches

CONTACTS

Chrissy Chrome (street doc, cybernetic eccentric)

Chance O'Reilly (Irish mobster)

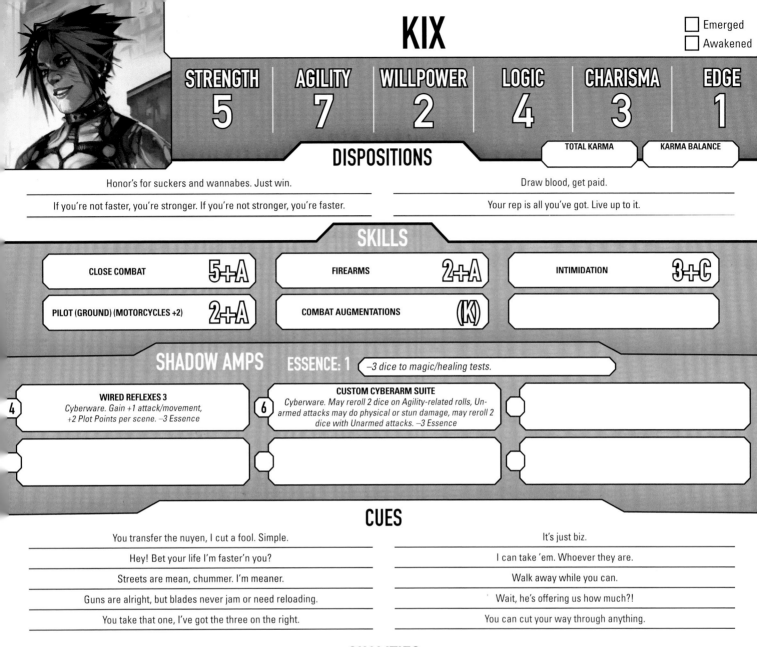
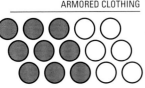

KNOX

DWARF STREET FIGHTING ADEPT

TAGS

• Dwarf • Adept • Mana Pits • Gladiator • Street Life

BACKGROUND

Growing up without a SIN meant that Knox never had access to the finer things in life. When most normal kids were playing with trideo games, watching the latest Desert Wars, or catching up with the latest Fragging Unicorns album, she was getting bullied by the other poor kids in her neighborhood. Being a dwarf wasn't easy in the Ork Underground, but it certainly made her tough. She learned that if she backed down, the fights kept coming. But when she fought back hard enough, even if she lost, kids stopped wanting to throw down.

That lesson served her well until she Awakened, and everything changed.

Now, her body was alive with power. Instead of being the victim, she chose big targets and picked on them instead. It was never enough. This was what she knew. Survival. Brawls. Blood. This is what made her feel alive. She'd never have to lose again. That's how she found the mana pits, pit fights where all of the fighters used magic. She finally had a challenge.

While fighting in the pits, a Mr. Johnson offered her a job making more nuyen than she'd ever seen. He said her skills in brawling were just what he needed. After joining up with him and bruising the people he wanted bruised, she found that punching people for money was great. Her dream job! She still fights in the mana pits when runs are scarce, and she thrives on those moments where she can indulge her aggression and get paid to do it.

KNOX

☐ Emerged
☒ Awakened

STRENGTH	AGILITY	WILLPOWER	LOGIC	CHARISMA	EDGE
4	6	6	3	4	2

DISPOSITIONS

TOTAL KARMA | KARMA BALANCE

Hit first. Then talk.

She can be reasonable. She chooses not to.

The only thing worth respect is winning.

Never give up. Never stop.

SKILLS

CLOSE COMBAT	5+A	SURVIVAL	2+W	INTIMIDATION	2+C
ATHLETICS	4+A	COOKING	(K)		

SHADOW AMPS

ESSENCE: 6 — No penalties.

3 | **CRITICAL STRIKE 2** — *Adept power. Add 2 damage to melee attack.*

3 | **IMPROVED REFLEXES 2** — *Adept power. +1 attack, 1 Plot Point per Scene.*

3 | **ATTRIBUTE BOOST 2 (AGILITY)** — *Add 2 dice OR 2 damage when using Agility.*

CUES

Did you see that? He looked at me funny! I'm gonna hit him!

Be careful. Your fingers don't mean nearly as much to me as they do to you.

I don't just punch things. I also take punches. And kicks. And bullets.

No. I don't want to see if we can sneak in.

Yes. I say we go in fast and loud.

I can't help it. Hitting is the only thing that makes me feel better.

I'm in total control. This is me in control.

I can take a lot of things. Your attitude isn't one of them.

No. I don't want to talk to them.

What did mercy ever do for me?

QUALITIES

TOUGH AS NAILS (PHYSICAL)
Add 1 to Physical Condition Monitor

TOUGH AS NAILS (STUN)
Add 1 to Stun Condition Monitor

COMBAT JUNKIE
Must use a Plot Point to avoid using violence as first response to any given problem.

WEAPONS

				UNARMED	DAM	CLOSE	NEAR	FAR
					2S(4S)	OK	—	—

	DAM	CLOSE	NEAR	FAR		DAM	CLOSE	NEAR	FAR		DAM	CLOSE	NEAR	FAR
Densiplast Knucks	3P(5P)	OK	—	—	Streetline Special Pistol	5P	OK	–2	—					
	DAM	CLOSE	NEAR	FAR		DAM	CLOSE	NEAR	FAR		DAM	CLOSE	NEAR	FAR

CONDITION MONITOR

ARMOR
SYNTHLEATHER CLOTHING

PHYSICAL
-1 -2 -3 -4

STUN
-1 -2 -3 -4

GEAR
Fake SIN, 3 stim patches, Meta Link commlink, survival kit

CONTACTS
Mr. Pink (negotiator/hitman)

Chandala (mana pit fight promoter)

SHADOWRUN ANARCHY

CATALYST game labs

NINETAILS

HUMAN INFILTRATION EXPERT

TAGS

• Human • Acrobat • Thief • Light Touch • Pack Rat

BACKGROUND

Life on the streets isn't easy, but it *is* simple: Take what you can, hold what you need, it's yours if you can keep it. It's true of syndicates and gangs battling for turf, it's true of hungry kids fighting over a devil rat corpse to eat, and it's true of everyone in between.

Ninetails? Ninetails is an expert on the "take what you can" part.

She started small, like most Barrens-brats. Simple cons, quick distractions, smooth palming tricks. Pick-pocketing escalated to snatch-and-grabs, snatch-and-grabs to burglaries, and burglaries—well, burglaries became something of a specialty.

Ninetails cuts through mundane security like a mono-filament knife through a soy patty. There aren't many locks she can't handle, many alarms she can't disable, many safes she can't crack. She's practiced at social engineering to get past what guards she can't avoid, and she's lean, mean, and augmented enough to handle anybody who forces the issue. With a little help for deep Matrix work or magical security, there aren't many places she can't get into, and she charges a premium for her elite skills.

As a specialist in intrusion and infiltration, she's a valuable asset for a shadowrunner team that can hire her. Tails isn't the ruthless killer some shadowrunners are. Her focus is on getting in unseen, retrieving a lucrative target, and escaping without notice. Violence is the last resort of the artless, and lethal violence just isn't her style.

NINETAILS

☐ Emerged
☐ Awakened

STRENGTH	AGILITY	WILLPOWER	LOGIC	CHARISMA	EDGE
3	6	2	5	5	2

TOTAL KARMA | KARMA BALANCE

DISPOSITIONS

You can go anywhere. Prove it to the world.

You want that. And that. And that.

Improvisation is everything.

Don't forget to have a little fun.

SKILLS

ATHLETICS	4+A	CLOSE COMBAT	3+A	CON	2+A
HACKING	1+L	STEALTH	4+A	SECURITY SYSTEMS	(K)

SHADOW AMPS

ESSENCE: 4.5 — *−1 die to magic/healing tests.*

3 BALANCE TAIL
Cyberware. Add +2 dice to Athletics rolls. −1 Essence

2 CUSTOMIZED LINED COAT (HIDDEN COMPARTMENTS)
10 armor, Perception tests are at −2 to spot items hidden within.

3 SYNTHACARDIUM
Bioware. May reroll 1 die on Athletics rolls. −0.5 Essence.

2 TOP-END B&E KIT
Reroll 1 failed die on lockpicking tests, safecracking tests, etc.

CUES

Ooh, shiny!

Pfft, sure I can get past that lock.

I dunno, 60/40 sounds more fair.

Magic's not my bag. I don't have to know what a focus does to know it's worth a lot.

There's always another way in.

I know a guy who'll pay good nuyen for that!

What do you mean, "It's just stuff?" "Stuff" is why we do this job!

The plastique's for the safe, ya psycho, not the load-bearing beams.

That stupid guard's high on soykaf and corporate loyalty. He won't know what hit him.

You guys keeps talking. I'm gonna go get something *done*.

QUALITIES

NATURAL ATHLETE
+2 dice for Athletics tests.

CATLIKE
+2 dice for Stealth tests.

LIFELONG THIEF
At GM discretion, you must spend a Plot Point to avoid prioritizing petty (or grand) larceny over other concerns.

WEAPONS

	DAM	CLOSE	NEAR	FAR
UNARMED	2S/2P	OK	—	—

	DAM	CLOSE	NEAR	FAR		DAM	CLOSE	NEAR	FAR		DAM	CLOSE	NEAR	FAR
Collapsible Stun Baton	7S	OK	—	—	Taser	6S	OK	−4	—		DAM	CLOSE	NEAR	FAR
	DAM	CLOSE	NEAR	FAR		DAM	CLOSE	NEAR	FAR		DAM	CLOSE	NEAR	FAR

CONDITION MONITOR

PHYSICAL −1 −2 −3

STUN −1 −2 −3

ARMOR

CUSTOM LONG COAT

GEAR

Fake SIN, Transys Avalon commlink, RFID-blocking messenger bag, Suzuki Aurora street bike, synthetic elf ears

CONTACTS

Charlene "Clean Charlie" Malone (fence, pawnbroker)

Felix (Cat shaman, cat burglar)

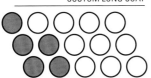
SHADOWRUN ANARCHY / CATALYST game labs

RAIDER

ELF COMBAT ARCHAEOLOGIST

TAGS

• Elf • Scholar • Explorer • Trouble Magnet • Curious

BACKGROUND

Ernie Talloak had one goal as a kid: Get the hell out of Tucumcari. It was hardly a unique goal; most every kid in Tucumcari had the same idea. For most of them, that involved getting some sort of job with a corp, maybe even the Pueblo Corporate Council itself. For Ernie, it meant studying his butt off and getting a scholarship to the university in Santa Fe, studying his butt off there, and *then* getting a nice, cushy corp job.

Long fascinated by the lore of his Navajo heritage, Ernie gravitated to history and archeology, and he excelled there. His professors took an interest in him, and soon he was out in the field with them, learning on-the-job in a way that was impossible in the classroom even with the best of Matrix simulations.

It was on one research expedition to an Anasazi cliff dwelling that Ernie discovered, completely by accident, a hidden entrance to a previously unknown set of chambers. He and his professors spent the next several days carefully examining the contents. He helped catalog everything, helped carefully pack relics for transport back to the university for further study—and then watched as they were shipped, not to the university, but to a PCC warehouse. They were to be sold off. No one would learn more about their heritage from them. Ancient mysteries would not be unraveled. They would become trinkets in some corp exec's private collection. Nothing would be learned. So he complained, vocally, to his professors.

It was at about that point that they tried to kill him.

Narrowly escaping death, Ernie found his career in academia abruptly ended. The shadows were there to catch him, though. Since then, he's been from the desert sands of Egypt to the jungles of the Yucatan. There was even a trip to Antarctica once. He's made many discoveries since he began. Some of them have wound up with the corps, but most have made it where they belong: In a museum, where they can provide knowledge and enlightenment.

RAIDER

☐ Emerged
☐ Awakened

STRENGTH	AGILITY	WILLPOWER	LOGIC	CHARISMA	EDGE
3	5	5	6	4	3

DISPOSITIONS

TOTAL KARMA	KARMA BALANCE

Knowledge is power.

Some discoveries are bigger than nations or corps.

There are things that are better off not being unearthed.

Sometimes you just have to dive in headlong and hope for the best.

SKILLS

ATHLETICS	2+A	CLOSE COMBAT	2+A	FIREARMS	2+A
SURVIVAL (NAVIGATION +2)	3+W	TRACKING	3+L	HISTORICAL LORE	(K)

SHADOW AMPS

ESSENCE: 4 — −1 die to magic/healing tests.

3 | **CEREBRAL BOOSTER**
Bioware. Reroll one failed die in Logic-related tests. −0.5 Essence

2 | **CYBEREYES**
Cyberware. Ignore vision modifiers due to lighting conditions. May reroll 1 failed die on ranged attacks. −1 Essence

3 | **ORTHOSKIN 1**
Bioware. Damage is reduced by 1 point per attack. −0.5 Essence

CUES

Okay, smart guy, you got down here. Got a plan for getting out?

This is usually the part where the artifact melts someone's face off.

Oh, look! Angry locals! I was wondering when they were going to show up.

I can't let them have this; they'd turn it into a dreadful weapon.

I know it's a cliché, but … that belongs in a museum.

There's never a big red "X" when you need one.

Watch your step! Put your foot on the wrong stone, and really bad things could happen!

Aztechnology on one side, hell hounds on the other … I should have stayed in bed.

QUALITIES

GUTS
May reroll 2 dice when resisting fear or intimidation.

HAWKEYE
+2 dice for Perception tests.

SINNER, NATIONAL (PUEBLO CORPORATE COUNCIL)
Legal citizen; data available through the Global SIN Registry.

WEAPONS

UNARMED	DAM	CLOSE	NEAR	FAR
	2S	OK	—	—

	DAM	CLOSE	NEAR	FAR		DAM	CLOSE	NEAR	FAR		DAM	CLOSE	NEAR	FAR
Cavalier Deputy Heavy Pistol	6P	OK	−2	—	Survival Knife	3P	OK	—	—					
	DAM	CLOSE	NEAR	FAR		DAM	CLOSE	NEAR	FAR		DAM	CLOSE	NEAR	FAR

CONDITION MONITOR

ARMOR
ARMORED CLOTHING

PHYSICAL −1 −2 −3 −4

STUN −1 −2 −3 −4

GEAR
Archeologist's tools, courier/sample bag, medkit, NeoNET Titan ruggedized commlink

CONTACTS
The Cordwainer Museum

Grace Palmer (university professor)

RASPBERRY JAM

HUMAN ARMS DEALER

TAGS

• Human • Arms Dealer • Downtown • Shameless • Lucky

BACKGROUND

Raspberry Jam is a second-generation gun runner. And not just guns. He's the kind of guy who can get you anything you want as long as the payment is good. His dad was never in the picture, so his mother became a wildly successful black-market dealer in Seattle. She was a sweet woman who never looked like an arms dealer, so she got away with murder, often literally. His momma taught him early never to trust anybody, but everybody deserves courtesy. As a result, Raspberry is extremely likable, even when he is trying to kill you.

He's always cracking a joke and is the first to say yes to something wild. His mouth never shuts off, and often he makes up words when his brain can't keep up. Business is just about the only thing that Raspberry Jam takes seriously. All the rest of the world is just a plaything, something to be enjoyed with the wealth he has earned. When it comes time to make a deal or get a job done, however, the smile stays on, but the gloves come off.

Growing up around mean, vile people, Raspberry learned to have a shut-off valve for his heart. He has one somewhere deep inside, though, and he loves to have people love him—a real life-of-the-party type. But he also thrives on danger. That's why, although his primary source of income is liberating illegal goods into the free market, he runs the shadows to get his adrenaline fix. It's not a bad way to test his product out, either.

RASPBERRY JAM

☐ Emerged
☐ Awakened

STRENGTH	AGILITY	WILLPOWER	LOGIC	CHARISMA	EDGE
4	4	4	4	5	6

DISPOSITIONS

TOTAL KARMA | KARMA BALANCE

Cannot lower his voice.

Likable, despite horrific disregard for life and law.

Proud of his poor, city heritage.

Luck will get him out of it, just like always.

SKILLS

CON	3+C
FIREARMS	3+A

INTIMIDATION (+2 DICE IF USING FIREARM)	3+C
CITY UNDERWORLD	(K)

NEGOTIATION	3+C

SHADOW AMPS   ESSENCE: 6   No penalties.

4 — CUSTOM LINED COAT
(Hidden compartments, bug scanner.) 10 armor. Perception tests are –3 dice for items in coat.

2 — MORE WHERE THAT CAME FROM
Gain additional 2 weapons. May trade melee weapon for additional ranged weapon.

CUES

I don't do discounts; I provide quality.

Information is power. Blackmail can get you things you never dreamed of.

I know a guy …

Hahahahaha. Just kidding. Let's do it.

This Monsoon packs quite a punch. I'll be able to sell tons of these.

Killing has nothing to do with personal feelings. It's just biz.

Like mamma Blackberry said, "Smiles don't cost a thing. But that's all you get for free."

Nah, I don't smoke what I sell. Clean living, chummers.

All right, so we amp up, break in, grab the snigfolferin and bejiggle out?

You wannit, Raspberry get it.

QUALITIES

BLACK MARKET PIPELINE (NARCOTICS)
Add a reliable fence for Narcotics to contacts*.

BETTER FEARED THAN LOVED
You have leverage on someone important. Add this blackmailed person to contacts.†

DISTINCTIVE STYLE (FLAMBOYANT PURPLE CLOTHING)
Stands out in every crowd with outlandish purple coats.

WEAPONS

UNARMED	DAM	CLOSE	NEAR	FAR
	2S	OK	—	—

	DAM	CLOSE	NEAR	FAR		DAM	CLOSE	NEAR	FAR		DAM	CLOSE	NEAR	FAR
Ares Predator V (Heavy Pistol)	6P	OK	–2	—	Uzi IV	6P	OK	OK	—	Shiawase Arms Monsoon	8P	OK	OK	–2
Defiance T-250 (Shotgun)	9P	OK*	–2	—										

Defiance T-250 Shotgun (By taking –2, may attack 2 targets at half damage each.)

ARMOR
CUSTOM LINED COAT

CONDITION MONITOR
PHYSICAL   STUN
-1, -2, -3, -4

GEAR
Fake SIN, area jammer, Leviathan Technical LT–2100 commlink, white noise generator

CONTACTS
Professor Birger Falkenrath (university professor/hermetic mage); **Guard-a-Manger** (fixer specializing in food/restaurant/catering/hospitality); * **Holla Gram** (narcotics dealer); † **Gregory Michael Deter** (blackmailed) (Head of Marketing for Ares Arms Seattle)

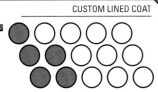

RAZZLE DAZZLE

ORK ILLUSIONIST

TAGS

• Ork • Magician • Showy • Pretentious • Sensualist

BACKGROUND

Rebecca doesn't remember a time when she didn't want something more. A little more food. Softer sheets. Shinier toys. Growing up near the Shattergraves, in the wrong part of Chicago, though, didn't make that very likely. She was smart enough to figure that out, however, and after she Awakened, she found her way out.

Magic was the escape she'd been longing for. No more ugly apartment or hateful home life for her; even if she didn't have pretty things, she could make the things she had look pretty. And that was enough, at least at first. Soon, she discovered that people were willing to pay her to cast her spells, and that was the real escape. She'd found her way out of the Shattergraves and into the shadows, and now she could actually buy—and occasionally steal—the soft and shiny things she'd always craved.

Her greatest skills revolve around illusions, and that serves her well in the shadows. She is frequently depended upon to provide a distraction so that the rest of the team could pull off the job. Growing up in the slums of post-Bug City Chicago, a dislike of insects both magical and mundane had been *de rigeur* in daily life; for Rebecca, it'd grown into active fear. Ironically, channeling this fear into some of her distractions has become a trademark.

Shadowrunning has given her the chance to travel the world and live in comparative luxury. But she still wants a little something more.

RAZZLE DAZZLE

☐ Emerged
☒ Awakened

STRENGTH	AGILITY	WILLPOWER	LOGIC	CHARISMA	EDGE
5	4	6	5	3	2

DISPOSITIONS

TOTAL KARMA   KARMA BALANCE

Loves the finer things in life.

Prefers the non-lethal approach.

Prefers wide open spaces to tight, confining ones.

The line between illusion and reality is quite thin.

SKILLS

CLOSE COMBAT	1+A	FIREARMS	1+A	PILOTING (GROUND)	2+A
SORCERY (SPELLCASTING +2)	5+W	STEALTH	2+A	MAGIC-FRIENDLY CLUBS	(K)

SHADOW AMPS   ESSENCE: 6   No penalties

2 ILLUSION
Effect spell. Target character sees and hears things that aren't there; target is distracted and suffers a −1 die penalty to all tests while the spell is sustained.

3 IMPROVED INVISIBILITY
Effect spell. Renders up to WIL characters invisible, targeted group may reroll 2 failed Stealth dice per Narration while the spell is sustained.

2 STUNBOLT
Combat spell. Damage of 8S/-A. Defense = S + W

CUES

Leave them unconscious, not dead. They won't come after us so hard later.

Did you see that?

Life's an illusion; I just make it more so.

Yes, I know we have to swim for it! Cats can swim.
But I don't like it, and I'll whine a lot.

Oh, feel how soft this is!

I would really rather not go in there, thanks for asking.

You think Mr. Johnson would mind if we held onto a couple of these?

Give me a sec, and I'll have this guy crying for his mommy.

QUALITIES

FOCUSED CONCENTRATION
May sustain two spells during a narration instead of just one.

MENTOR SPIRIT (CAT)
+1 die for Athletics or Stealth tests; may reroll one failed Sorcery die when using effect spells.

PHOBIA (ENTOMOPHOBIA)
Has an irrational fear of insects. When confronted by them, must succeed at an Average W+L test or suffer a −2 dice penalty to all rolls.

WEAPONS

					UNARMED	DAM 3S	CLOSE OK	NEAR —	FAR —				

	DAM	CLOSE	NEAR	FAR		DAM	CLOSE	NEAR	FAR		DAM	CLOSE	NEAR	FAR
Wizard's Staff	5S	OK	—	—	Yamaha Pulsar Taser	6S	OK	−2	—					
	DAM	CLOSE	NEAR	FAR		DAM	CLOSE	NEAR	FAR		DAM	CLOSE	NEAR	FAR

CONDITION MONITOR

ARMOR
LINED CLOAK

PHYSICAL
−1 −2 −3 −4

STUN
−1 −2 −3 −4

GEAR
Fake SIN, Hermes Ikon commlink, magical circle materials, Yamaha Rapier motorcycle

CONTACTS
Copperfield Society (illusionist initiatory group)
Boomer (street doc)

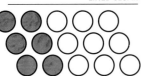

REESE FRENZY

ORK ROCKER/FACE

TAGS

• Ork • Musician • Activist • Fast Talker • For the People

BACKGROUND

Most shadowrunners find themselves rebelling against the system because it's the only thing they are good at. Well, that or because the nuyen is good. But not Reese Frenzy. Reese has everything someone like him could want. He was raised in a decent home, did all the right things growing up, and got a degree in biology from the University of Denver. As the front man for a Denver-based Sprawlpunk band, he has the respect of his peers. When he's not doing that, he works at a hospital as a nurse, using his degree in biology for something useful. So why would that kind of person run the shadows?

Injustice. Somewhere deep inside, a voice tells him that everything this world says is good—isn't. No matter what the corp news says, corruption and oppression based on race, gender, metatype, or what-have-you continue strongly today. Education liberated his mind, and now his conscience rages to free others. Now, when an opportunity comes up to do some bad for a good reason, he lives out the lyrics of his songs on the streets.

Having heard of shadowrunners all his life, he considered them gangsters, hostile, and dangerous. And to be fair, many of them are. But he also met some runners who were not in it for themselves. They were in it to change things, take down the corps, give people a fair chance at a free life. And that resonated with him. Now, when an opportunity comes up to do some bad for a good reason, he takes the lyrics in his songs and lives them out on the streets.

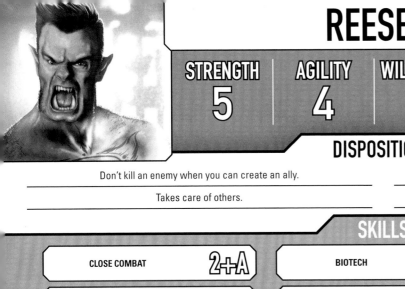

REESE FRENZY

☐ Emerged
☐ Awakened

STRENGTH	AGILITY	WILLPOWER	LOGIC	CHARISMA	EDGE
5	4	4	5	5	3

TOTAL KARMA	KARMA BALANCE

DISPOSITIONS

Don't kill an enemy when you can create an ally.

Takes care of others.

Saves anger for *the man*, not the people.

Opinions are meant to be shared. Loudly.

SKILLS

CLOSE COMBAT	2+A
ORK HISTORY	(K)

BIOTECH	2+A
NATIVE AMERICAN HISTORY	(K)

CON	5+C
ACTIVIST MOVEMENTS	(K)

SHADOW AMPS

ESSENCE: 3 — −2 dice to magic/healing tests.

3 | **SYNTHLINK**
Cyberware. Gains +2 dice to Con rolls. −1 Essence

1 | **AUDIO ANALYZER**
Cyberware. −1 Essence

3 | **DYNAMIC HANDPRINTS**
Bioware. Fingerprints can change to avoid leaving prints, or leave someone else's. −0.5 Essence

1 | **DYNAMIC FACIAL HAIR/TATTOOS**
Bioware. −0.5 Essence

CUES

I don't have to sing about injustice. I can yell about it instead!

I feel a frenzy coming on …

Band? Music? Sorry, you must have me confused with someone else.

You don't honestly believe those lies, do you?

I'm not going to let you hurt them.

Violent, untrustworthy, backstabbing, greedy? You just described corps, not me.

That looks painful, let me look at it. No really, I'm a nurse.

Sandwiches? Anyone want some sandwiches?

If this is "freedom," I don't want it.

QUALITIES

FAME (REGIONAL, MUSICIAN)
+2 dice to Charisma based tests if recognized.

COLLEGE EDUCATION
May choose 2 additional Knowledge skills.

SINNER (DENVER)
Character is a legal citizen. Their data is available through the Global SIN Registry.

WEAPONS

	DAM	CLOSE	NEAR	FAR
UNARMED	3S	OK	—	—

	DAM	CLOSE	NEAR	FAR		DAM	CLOSE	NEAR	FAR		DAM	CLOSE	NEAR	FAR
Heavy Guitar (Club)	6P	OK	—	—	**Yamaha Pulsar** Taser	6S	OK	−4	—		DAM	CLOSE	NEAR	FAR
	DAM	CLOSE	NEAR	FAR		DAM	CLOSE	NEAR	FAR		DAM	CLOSE	NEAR	FAR

CONDITION MONITOR

ARMOR

SYNTHLEATHER CLOTHING

PHYSICAL

-1
-2
-3
-4

STUN

-1
-2
-3
-4

GEAR

White noise generator, medkit, Microtronica Azteca Raptor commlink, area signal jammer

CONTACTS

Rev. Jürgen Barth (minister, Church of Unity and Justice)

Brave Saturn (Scum of the Earth ganger)

SHADOWRUN ANARCHY

CATALYST game labs

ROSE RED

ELF MYSTIC ADEPT

TAGS

• Elf • Mystic Adept • Runner • Neo-Anarchist • Operative

BACKGROUND

Not many people can say that shadowrunning is a moral step up from their last profession. But most other people didn't traffic in human beings. Together with her sister, Rose Red started off as a victim of trafficking herself, and she became one of her pimp's biggest money-makers. Along the way, she awakened and used her newfound powers to force others into bondage like she was. She became so good at it that she eventually killed her owner and took over the business.

Rose Red was notorious as a high-end madam for wealthy business people and politicians, first in Toronto, then branching out to Seattle. She eventually found her sister and convinced her to come work for her. Rose gave her sister the best jobs with the most influential clientele, while hiring gangers to kidnap other young metahumans to fill the ever-growing needs of her other clients. Everything was going according to her plans until one of those politicians was seen with her sister, and her sister became a liability. Unable to stop her sister from being killed to serve a politician's reputation, Rose fell apart. She walked away from her life and lived on the streets of Toronto for months, refusing to talk to anyone or use her powers.

Someone saved her life by inviting her to a local meeting of neo-anarchists. There, she discovered she had been a tool of the system. Broken and used by the powerful, only to be so brainwashed that she did the same to others. Without shaming her, they invited her to be a part of the solution, not the problem. Taking note of her powers, they referred her to Black Star, a group of neo-anarchist shadowrunners who work for the people, not the money. She's never looked back.

ROSE RED

☐ Emerged
☒ Awakened

STRENGTH	AGILITY	WILLPOWER	LOGIC	CHARISMA	EDGE
3	5	5	5	5	1

DISPOSITIONS

TOTAL KARMA

KARMA BALANCE

A sucker for people in need.

Take any chance to give authority a black eye.

Play well with others. Coalitions get things done.

Information is always useful.

SKILLS

SORCERY	3+W
DISGUISE	2+C

CLOSE COMBAT (BLADES +2)	4+A
PIRATE MATRIX BROADCASTERS	(K)

PROJECTILE WEAPONS	3+A

SHADOW AMPS

ESSENCE: 6 — *No penalties.*

2 — **IMPROVED REFLEXES**
Adept power. +1 attack.

2 — **CRITICAL STRIKE 1**
Adept power. Add 1 damage to melee attack.

2 — **STUNBOLT (SPELL)**
Combat. Damage of 8S/AA. Defense = S + W.

2 — **CONFUSION (SPELL)**
Effect. Target's senses are confused. Target rolls 1 less dice per action while spell is sustained.

CUES

I'm no Robin Hood. He never looked this good.

You hurt others because they can't stop you. I'll teach you how that feels.

Sure, I'll take corporate money. They're funding their own downfall.

You didn't need that hand, did you?

Free your mind, chummer. Here's the link to a neo-anarchist Matrix broadcast.

All of my power is worthless if I can't fix what's broken.

What did status quo ever do for me?

I can't stand when thugs like you pick on people.

Red is my color—the color of power, passion, shame, and blood.

We can't force people to be free.

QUALITIES

GUTS
May reroll 2 dice when resisting fear or intimidation.

INDOMITABLE (BLADES)
When attacking with Blades, may reroll exactly 2 dice.

DISTINCTIVE STYLE (RED CLOTHING)
Never seen without noticeable red outfits.

WEAPONS

	DAM	CLOSE	NEAR	FAR
UNARMED	2S(3S)	OK	—	—

	DAM	CLOSE	NEAR	FAR			DAM	CLOSE	NEAR	FAR		DAM	CLOSE	NEAR	FAR
Heirloom Blade Sword	5P(6P)	OK	—	—		Throwing Knives	3P	OK	−2	—					
	DAM	CLOSE	NEAR	FAR			DAM	CLOSE	NEAR	FAR		DAM	CLOSE	NEAR	FAR

CONDITION MONITOR

ARMOR

RED SYNTHLEATHER JACKET

PHYSICAL −1 −2 −3 −4

STUN −1 −2 −3 −4

GEAR

Suzuki Aurora motorcycle, fake SIN, Erika Elite commlink, locket necklace with sister's picture

CONTACTS

Cyber Sarah (professional escort/bodyguard)

Old Crow (informational anarchist, Raven shaman)

RUCKUS

TROLL BRUISER

TAGS

• Troll • Brawler • Thoughtful • Suspicious • Runner

BACKGROUND

Ruckus knows better than most how unfair the world can be. The first strike against him is that he's a troll. Sure, there are lots of trolls who make it just fine in life, but the others—the majority—don't. Second, he was abandoned as a child by his parents, who just didn't want a troll as a kid. Third, he was adopted by a nice old woman who was poor—which made him poor as well. Poor trolls without parents have very few options for gainful employment, and so Ruckus didn't bother to try.

The one thing he had going for him was that he was big, even for a troll. And that meant others saw him as valuable. Dropping out of school just seemed to make sense when he wasn't really good at it anyway, and there were always gangers willing to pay him just to back them up. Every once in a while, Ruckus had to hit someone. After a few months, that was his primary job.

His fortunes changed one day when the cops busted down his door and, although he didn't resist, they beat him and shot him in the leg. He didn't do what he was accused of, but after having his leg amputated, he spent a few months in jail anyway. The only thing he got out of it was a used cyberleg. When he got out, Nana Rickard, who had taken him in as a child, had died. Ruckus was hungry, angry, and aimless. He slept underneath the city streets until a ganger he used to know said he needed backup for a shadowrun. Ruckus didn't know what a shadowrun was, but after he got paid, he decided he wanted to do more of them.

RUCKUS

☐ Emerged
☐ Awakened

STRENGTH	AGILITY	WILLPOWER	LOGIC	CHARISMA	EDGE
9	5	3	2	3	4

DISPOSITIONS

TOTAL KARMA   KARMA BALANCE

Operates like inertia. Takes a while to rile him up or calm him down.

Usually calm, but can become feral in a fight.

Being a troll is far from easy.

No one uses authority to help you—it's always about keeping you down.

SKILLS

CLOSE COMBAT (CLUBS +2)	5+A
INTIMIDATION	4+C

FIREARMS	1+A
LOCAL CHARITIES	(K)

ATHLETICS	1+W

SHADOW AMPS   ESSENCE: 5   –1 dice to magic/healing tests.

3 | **CYBERLEG 2**
Cyberware: Gain 1 extra movement per narration, may re-roll 2 dice on athletics tests. –1 Essence

4 | **FEAR**
+2 dice to Intimidation rolls, melee opponents must roll 2 hits on CHA + WIL test or run away.

CUES

Aww, don't be like that. I didn't mean to break it!

I'm starving! If I hit enough bad guys, can we go to McHugh's?

Don't you pick on them!

Trolls are people, too.

I know where we can get some food. Come on.

Uh-uh. No. No cops. No way.

That was silly. Now you'll have to deal with Cosmo.

Nana hated it when I complained. So whatever is fine.

Say "trog" one more time, motherfragger.

I don't like killing. It's just a side effect of me hitting them.

QUALITIES

ANIMAL EMPATHY
+2 dice on any test involving influence or control of an animal.

INDOMITABLE (CLUBS)
When attacking with the Clubs Skill, may reroll 2 dice.

PHOBIA (LAW ENFORCEMENT)
When in the presence of any Law Enforcement, –2 to all dice rolls.

WEAPONS

	DAM	CLOSE	NEAR	FAR
UNARMED	5S	OK	—	—

	DAM	CLOSE	NEAR	FAR
Cosmo	8P	OK	–4	—
Lucky Baseball Bat (Club)				
	DAM	CLOSE	NEAR	FAR

	DAM	CLOSE	NEAR	FAR
Rocks	6P	OK	–2	—
For Throwing				
	DAM	CLOSE	NEAR	FAR

	DAM	CLOSE	NEAR	FAR
	DAM	CLOSE	NEAR	FAR

CONDITION MONITOR

ARMOR

SYNTHLEATHER, TROLL SKIN

PHYSICAL

–1
–2
–3
–4
–5

STUN

–1
–2
–3
–4

GEAR

Bag of large rocks, Meta Link commlink, crowbar, plastic restraints

CONTACTS

Rainbowsmite (paracritter trainer)

PuttDawg (heavy weapons specialist)

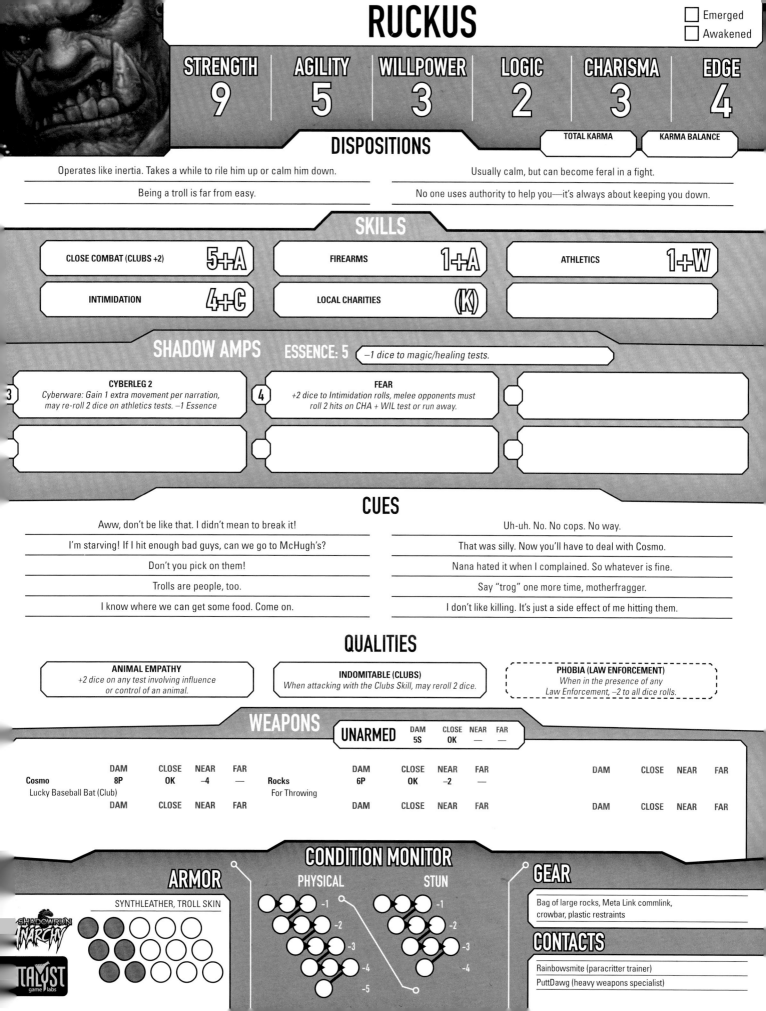

SHADES

HUMAN FORMER COMPANY WOMAN

TAGS

• Human • Professional • Experienced • Subtle • Mercenary

BACKGROUND

Shades never wanted to go independent. She never wanted to be uncertain about her next nuyen transfer. She never wanted to be a shadowrunner. She wanted to fight for her company and protect people.

Raised by corporate citizens to be a corporate citizen, she had her whole life planned out for her when she was young. She stuck with her plan, excelled in her studies, and worked her way up the corporate ladder out of uniformed security and into the high-responsibility life of being an executive protection specialist. Exec-protect came with perks, upgrades, and high-profile assignments, everything she wanted—until the time a job went wrong.

She took on one assignment too many—a mission as a proactive bodyguard, a corporate assassin—and eventually ran out of loyalty to her employers when they sent her after the wrong target. Shades took her skills, her attitude, and her augs and hit the road. Now working for the highest bidder, she brings a professional's touch and a keen eye to any team.

Augmenting her combat abilities with subtle recon drones, Shades serves a new master now: herself, by way of the almighty nuyen. She understands that in the shadows her reputation is of tremendous importance, and she's determined to put her nose to the grindstone in order to climb this new ladder. She's well aware of the importance of teamwork and is well-equipped to make the people around her better. She figures a little professionalism goes a long way, and friends can make all the difference in an ugly business.

Maybe here she can still fight for something. Maybe here she can still protect people.

SHADES

☐ Emerged
☐ Awakened

STRENGTH	AGILITY	WILLPOWER	LOGIC	CHARISMA	EDGE
3	5	5	5	3	4

DISPOSITIONS

TOTAL KARMA | KARMA BALANCE

Ask questions, formulate a plan, and carry it through.

If you keep a cool head, you can do the impossible.

Details matter.

You work short-term contracts now. Be selective who you sign with.

SKILLS

CLOSE COMBAT	2+A
PILOTING (OTHER)	3+A

FIREARMS (PISTOLS +2)	4+A
STEALTH	2+A

PILOTING (GROUND)	2+A
SECURITY PROCEDURES	(K)

SHADOW AMPS   ESSENCE: 4   −1 die to magic/healing tests.

2 CONTROL RIG I
Cyberware. Control vehicles by VR, +1 die to vehicle actions. −1 Essence

2 PLASTIC BONE LACING
Cyberware. Reduce all damage taken by 1. −1 Essence

2 SPY DRONE I
+1 to Perception tests.

2 TEAM PLAYER
You may freely share your Plot Points and Edge with other players.

CUES

Sir, get down!

Just relax. I've handled worse.

That's it, kid gloves are off.

I'm not on their payroll. Their call, not mine, so frag 'em.

The world sucks, but I don't have to.

Eyes in the sky are a go.

Let's make sure everyone's in one piece before we move on.

Trust me. I know what I'm talking about.

Just because you're making money doesn't mean you can't try to help.

QUALITIES

HAWKEYE
+2 dice for Perception tests.

GUTS
You may reroll 2 dice when resisting fear or intimidation.

SINNER, CORPORATE (ARES)
You're an Ares citizen, with data available through the Global SIN Registry.

WEAPONS

	DAM	CLOSE	NEAR	FAR
UNARMED	2S	OK	—	—

	DAM	CLOSE	NEAR	FAR		DAM	CLOSE	NEAR	FAR		DAM	CLOSE	NEAR	FAR
Shock Glove	6S	OK	—	—	Ares Predator V Heavy Pistol	6P	OK	−2	—					
	DAM	CLOSE	NEAR	FAR		DAM	CLOSE	NEAR	FAR		DAM	CLOSE	NEAR	FAR

CONDITION MONITOR

ARMOR
ACTIONEER BUSINESS CLOTHES

PHYSICAL
−1 −2 −3 −4

STUN
−1 −2 −3 −4

GEAR
Fake SIN, fake bodyguard/concealed weapons license, electronic-link glasses, armored sedan

CONTACTS
Michael Kristoff (Ares quartermaster)

Jules Sawyer (bodyguard)

SHADOWRUN ANARCHY

CATALYST game labs

STRIDER

DWARF PARKOUR ADEPT

TAGS

- Dwarf • Adept • Runner • Thrill-Seeker • Courier

BACKGROUND

The Puyallup district of the Seattle sprawl is loaded with hard-luck stories, but Strider has steadfastly refused to be one of them. Born a dwarf to human parents, she had to deal with prejudice and disappointment from an early age. She took solace in sports programs at school as she grew up, and in spite of her "stumpy dwarf legs," she excelled at track and field events. It was in school that she discovered the sport of parkour, or free-running, a discipline that turned obstacles into advantages. She fell in love with the sport and the philosophy almost instantly.

Running away from home at an early age, she made her living at odd jobs. She discovered her adept abilities while evading an assault, and immediately saw uses for them. She had always loved to run, and she knew that many people needed small packages and documents delivered quickly. She went into business for herself as a freelance courier.

Business was tough at first. Being SINless, more than a few of her deliveries were for less-than-savory types looking to save a few nuyen, as well as avoid licensed couriers and their reporting requirements. She didn't let that stop her, though, and she gained a reputation. One of the deliveries she made was ordered by the troll face called Ms. Myth, who hired Strider to deliver a package to private investigator Jimmy Kincaid. Both Kincaid and Ms. Myth were impressed with her, especially after learning that she had taken down a pair of thugs hired to steal her package while en route to Kincaid's office. Both have continued to use her services, and Ms. Myth has even contemplated taking her out in the field with her team.

STRIDER

☐ Emerged
☒ Awakened

STRENGTH	AGILITY	WILLPOWER	LOGIC	CHARISMA	EDGE
5	6	5	4	3	2

DISPOSITIONS

TOTAL KARMA | KARMA BALANCE

Always striving to beat her best time.

Streets and sidewalks are for ordinary people.

The package is sacred; it must arrive safely.

The riskier the delivery, the more fun it is.

SKILLS

ATHLETICS (RUNNING +2)	5+A
STEALTH	3+A
CLOSE COMBAT	2+A
LOCAL GEOGRAPHY	(K)
PROJECTILE WEAPONS	2+A

SHADOW AMPS   ESSENCE: 6   No penalties

3 — **IMPROVED REFLEXES 2**
Adept power. Gains +1 attack or movement, and +1 Plot Point per Scene.

3 — **LIGHT BODY**
Adept power. Gains +2 dice for jumping tests.

1 — **WALL RUNNING**
Adept power. Run up/across vertical surfaces during a movement.

CUES

Live to run, run to live.

I know a shortcut.

Catch me if you can!

Never been much for people; fortunately, running is a solitary pursuit.

Roadblocks just mean someone made a new path for you.

You're about to see my stumpy little dwarf legs up close, *omae*.

Can't get there from here. From up there, however …

Yeah, I'm one of Jimmy Kincaid's seven dwarfs. Ha ha ha. What of it?

Oh, I can get it there. It's your ability to pay that's the question.

QUALITIES

NATURAL ATHLETE
+2 dice for Athletics tests

QUICK HEALER
+2 dice to any test to heal this character

THRILL-SEEKER
Must succeed at an Average W+L test or take the most dangerous course of action

WEAPONS

	DAM	CLOSE	NEAR	FAR
UNARMED	3S	OK	—	—

	DAM	CLOSE	NEAR	FAR		DAM	CLOSE	NEAR	FAR		DAM	CLOSE	NEAR	FAR
Extendable Batons	5S	OK	—	—	Throwing Knives	5P	OK	−2	—		DAM	CLOSE	NEAR	FAR
	DAM	CLOSE	NEAR	FAR		DAM	CLOSE	NEAR	FAR		DAM	CLOSE	NEAR	FAR

CONDITION MONITOR

ARMOR
ARMORED CLOTHING

PHYSICAL
−1
−2
−3
−4

STUN
−1
−2
−3
−4

GEAR
Courier bag, fake SIN, Renraku Sensei commlink, stim patches (3)

CONTACTS
Alley Cat Express (free-runner/courier group)

Kevin Tranh (corporate secretary/receptionist)

SHADOWRUN ANARCHY

CATALYST game labs

THUNDER

HUMAN VIGILANTE

TAGS

• Human • Shaman • Mechanic • Protector • Religious

BACKGROUND

Born in the Clear Lake district of the Houston sprawl, Erica Krieger lived an uneventful, comfortable life as a child. Her parents both worked for AresSpace. When she was five years old, the Second Matrix Crash happened, and in the chaos, both of her parents were killed in an accident. Having no other family that anyone was aware of, Erica was taken in by Sid Morrow, a friend of her father. He raised her as his own daughter from that day on.

Her adopted brother Danny began teaching her the family business of automobile maintenance, and Sid cheerfully let her work in their shop in the Pasadena district when she was old enough. Before that happened, her sister Sophie was born. Not long after that, Erica Awakened as a mage. Her ability to fix vehicles magically was a help around the shop.

Sid and his wife Dinah died in a car accident when Erica was ten, and the shop was left to Danny. Erica spent a lot of her time taking care of Sophie, who had a learning disability. Years later, while Erica was running errands for Danny, several members of the Vaqueros street gang assaulted Sophie and killed Danny. The Lone Star investigation was cursory, at best, and Erica went after the gangers herself.

She met both Leland Dunn, a former shadowrunner turned street preacher, and her mentor spirit, Dragonslayer, on this journey. Leland taught her to fight, and Dragonslayer showed her the path he wanted her to take. Now she splits her time between the auto shop she inherited and patrolling the streets of her neighborhood, keeping the residents safe (or, at least, safer) from the gangs that plague the area.

THUNDER

☐ Emerged
☒ Awakened

STRENGTH	AGILITY	WILLPOWER	LOGIC	CHARISMA	EDGE
4	3	6	5	4	2

DISPOSITIONS

TOTAL KARMA	KARMA BALANCE

These are her streets, and she'll keep them safe.

Nothing is more important than family.

Never met a party she didn't like.

Still struggling with, and growing into, her faith.

SKILLS

CLOSE COMBAT	3+A	CONJURING	1+W	ENGINEERING	3+L
PILOTING (GROUND)	2+A	SORCERY (SPELLCASTING +2)	3+W	GANG IDENTIFICATION	(K)

SHADOW AMPS   ESSENCE: 6   *No penalties.*

2 — FIX
Effect spell. Target vehicle/device regains one box of damage per hit, per narration the spell is sustained.

2 — HEAL
Effect spell. Target character regains one box of physical damage per hit, per narration the spell is sustained.

2 — LIGHTNING BOLT (SPELL)
Combat spell. Damage of 6P/AA. Defense S + W.

2 — STUNBOLT
Combat spell. Damage of 8S/AA. Defense = S + W

CUES

Tonight, we slay the dragon of Boredom. And his first cousin, Thirst.

"Thou shalt not kill."

When was the last time you changed the fuel filter in this thing?

Got no use for gangs, and only a little more use for the Star.

Very not bad!

Leave her alone, *amigo*, and nobody has to get hurt tonight.

I don't worship Dragonslayer; he's not God. He's more like an angel.

I can do a lot of things with this bike, but I can't make it drive up walls. Sorry.

QUALITIES

GUTS
May reroll 2 dice when resisting fear or intimidation.

MENTOR SPIRIT (DRAGONSLAYER)
+1 die for combat spells; may reroll 1 failed die on Close Combat tests.

DEPENDENT (SOPHIE)
Must spend a Plot Point to avoid prioritizing her sister Sophie above anything else.

WEAPONS

	DAM	CLOSE	NEAR	FAR
UNARMED	2S	OK	—	—

	DAM	CLOSE	NEAR	FAR		DAM	CLOSE	NEAR	FAR		DAM	CLOSE	NEAR	FAR
Large Box Wrench	4S	OK	—	—	Sword	5P	OK	—	—					
	DAM	CLOSE	NEAR	FAR		DAM	CLOSE	NEAR	FAR		DAM	CLOSE	NEAR	FAR

ARMOR
LINED COAT

CONDITION MONITOR
PHYSICAL   STUN

-1, -2, -3, -4

GEAR
AR/motorcycle goggles, BMW Blitzen motorcycle, mechanic's toolkit, Renraku Sensei commlink

CONTACTS
Darryl Givens (beat cop)
Leland Dunn (human adept)

SHADOWRUN ANARCHY — CATALYST game labs

TOMMY Q

HUMAN FORMER WAGE MAGE

TAGS

- Human • Combat Hermetic • Tactician
- Clothes Horse • Perfectionist

BACKGROUND

Tommy's got Talent to spare—that's capital-T-Talent, the magical ability some are lucky enough to be born with. He was given great advantages from an early age: wealthy parents, magical potential, and the patronage (however distant) of one of the world's most potent forces.

But he always had a taste for shortcuts, too.

He squandered his good fortune every chance he got. He learned things he wasn't supposed to. He flaunted his abilities and made enemies instead of allies. He cut corners to augment his natural potential. He lied, he spied, and he stole.

Then he took everything he had and jumped to the shadows. Why live a life constrained by the restrictions of corporate rules and regulations? Freedom's where it's at! The streets are alive with magic and potential, the shadows are the way to choose your own path, and being an independent contractor is surely the path to unending wealthy and glory.

Tommy's not the easiest runner to work with, but he's good enough that most teams don't mind the chip on his shoulder. He's handy in a fight, quick with a spirit, and great at patching up an injured teammate, and arrogance is a fair price to pay for a corporate-trained combat mage. Tommy's only going to get better over time, and he hopes his hand-picked parting gift from his former employers helps him to improve all the quicker. He's not sure what the focus is meant to do, but he knows he'll figure it out sooner rather than later. Just a few more nuyen for reagents, and he'll be on his way to real power. Just ask him.

TOMMY Q

☐ Emerged
☒ Awakened

STRENGTH	AGILITY	WILLPOWER	LOGIC	CHARISMA	EDGE
3	3	6	6	3	4

DISPOSITIONS

TOTAL KARMA	KARMA BALANCE

There isn't much that scares you.

You're a professional; act like it.

If you want to be the best, you should only use the best.

Being direct works if you're good enough.

SKILLS

ASTRAL COMBAT	2+W	CONJURING	4+W	FIREARMS	3+A
SORCERY (COUNTERSPELLING +2)	4+W	HERMETIC THEORY & DRAGON LORE	(K)	SECURITY PROCEDURES	(K)

SHADOW AMPS

ESSENCE: 5.5 — No penalties.

3 — SYNAPTIC BOOSTER 1
Bioware. +1 action. –0.5 Essence

2 — STUNBOLT
Combat. Damage of 8S/AA. Defense = S + W

2 — HEAL
Effect. Target regains one physical damage per narration the spell is sustained.

FOCUS
A powerful magical item, but with abilities not yet unlocked.

CUES

I don't work for them any more. Don't worry about why.

Talent like this doesn't come cheap.

It's not as easy as I make it look.

You've got two seconds to take that back before I turn you to goo.

I could do that without a problem if it was *twice* as hard.

Affirmative, going loud!

What do you mean, "I don't need to know?" What are you hiding?

The corp made me smart, but the streets made me amazing.

QUALITIES

FORMAL EDUCATION
Gain two additional knowledge skills.

IRON WILL
May reroll two dice during Conjuring tests.

SINNER, CORPORATE (SAEDER-KRUPP)
Corporate citizen, with data available through the Global SIN Registry.

WEAPONS

UNARMED	DAM	CLOSE	NEAR	FAR
	2S	OK	—	—

	DAM	CLOSE	NEAR	FAR		DAM	CLOSE	NEAR	FAR		DAM	CLOSE	NEAR	FAR
Tactical Knife	3P	OK	–2	—	H&K CityLine V Pistol	6P	OK	–2	—					
	DAM	CLOSE	NEAR	FAR		DAM	CLOSE	NEAR	FAR		DAM	CLOSE	NEAR	FAR

CONDITION MONITOR

ARMOR

ACTIONEER BUSINESS CLOTHES

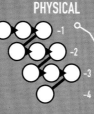

PHYSICAL

-1 -2 -3 -4

STUN

-1 -2 -3 -4

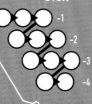

GEAR

Fake SIN, Fairlight Caliban commlink, Eurocar Westwind sports car, hermetic lodge materials

CONTACTS

Adriana Singh (talismonger, hermetic sorceress)

Rudolph "Nose" Bauer (company man, assassin)

VECTOR

HUMAN TECHNOMANCER

TAGS

- Human • Virtuakinetic • Freedom-Fighter
- Anarchist • Passionate

BACKGROUND

Nobody really seems to know what his name was before he took on the *nom du guerre* Vector, and he's quite comfortable with that. He's gone to great lengths to make sure this state of affairs is so.

Some who know him call him a freedom fighter, struggling to free those of his kind captured by various corps. Others skip over the niceties and call him a terrorist. Given the effort he's put into erasing his past, even his country of origin is uncertain. Those who have spoke with him believe they have detected a trace of a German accent in his voice, and the Free City of Berlin would be a likely home for someone so dedicated to anti-corporate actions.

Wherever he came from, his current home is Snohomish, an unlikely spot for a creature of the Matrix. It gives him a break from the flood of Matrix traffic that hits him in other parts of the sprawl, plus it provides seclusion from the many corporate forces eager to track him down. He hasn't executed any major datasteals or anything—what irritates the corps are the pranks he's pulled to cause chaos in various corp hosts, and the technomancers he's freed from corporate facilities. From changing AROs advertising clothing to display the faces of child laborers who ostensibly made it (with labels such as "Handcrafted with care by Aqib, age 12") to messing up the augmented reality directions at the massive Center House mall so no shoppers had any idea of where they were going. That sort of thing made Vector someone the corps would like to see punished, but it was freeing ten technomancers from a Mitsuhama facility and four from a NeoNET facility that really got Vector on the corps' drek list.

Far from being cowed or intimidated, Vector sees the target on his back as a call to arms and a push to do even more, to go bigger, and to make more of a splash. To some, that makes him dangerous to work with, but other runners see it s an indication that he's a kindred spirit.

VECTOR

☒ Emerged
☐ Awakened

STRENGTH	AGILITY	WILLPOWER	LOGIC	CHARISMA	EDGE
3	4	5	6	3	3

DISPOSITIONS

TOTAL KARMA

KARMA BALANCE

You're either with him or against him.

Corps are a modern evil, although an occasionally necessary one.

Technomancers are the future of the Matrix.

Dealing with non-technomancers can be trying for him.

SKILLS

CLOSE COMBAT	2+A
TASKING	3+L

FIREARMS	2+A
RESONANCE LORE	(K)

HACKING (CYBERCOMBAT +2)	5+L

SHADOW AMPS ESSENCE: 6 _No penalties_

1 — CLEANER
Effect complex form. Erase your last three Matrix actions; they can't be seen by GOD.

2 — EXPLOIT
Effect complex form. May reroll two dice on non-cybercombat Hacking tests.

2 — PULSE STORM
Effect complex form. Make a cybercombat attack against target. For each narration that the complex form is sustained, all target's actions are at –1 die per net hit.

2 — RESONANCE SPIKE
Cybercombat complex form. Matrix damage of 8. Defense = L + Firewall

CUES

The Lord said to Pharoah, "Let my people go." It's good advice for you, too.

The technomancers they're holding are just kids! I'm going in there!

I need a commlink because sometimes one must take phone calls.

Come, my little sprites; let's see what chaos we can wreak today.

The Resonance speaks to me.

Yes, I can hack the system from here and get you reservations at Dante's Inferno.

You have no idea what freedom is.

I'm using their over-reliance on tech against them.

QUALITIES

CODESLINGER
+2 dice for Hacking tests.

NATURAL HARDENING
Matrix damage taken is reduced by 2 points per attack.

PARANOIA
Must reroll successes (maximum of 2) when making social tests.

WEAPONS

UNARMED	DAM	CLOSE	NEAR	FAR
	2S	OK	—	—

	DAM	CLOSE	NEAR	FAR		DAM	CLOSE	NEAR	FAR		DAM	CLOSE	NEAR	FAR
Collapsible baton	4P	OK	—	—	Colt America L36 Light Pistol	5P	OK	–2	—					
	DAM	CLOSE	NEAR	FAR		DAM	CLOSE	NEAR	FAR		DAM	CLOSE	NEAR	FAR

CONDITION MONITOR

ARMOR
LINED COAT

PHYSICAL
-1
-2
-3
-4

STUN
-1
-2
-3
-4

GEAR
Hyundai Shin-Hyung sports sedan, medkit, Meta Link commlink, trauma patches

CONTACTS
Rose Red (Black Star operative)
Raptor (gang lieutenant)

SHADOWRUN ANARCHY

CATALYST game labs

WAGON

HUMAN COMBAT MEDIC

TAGS

- Human • Second-Gen Shadowrunner • Street Professional
- Backup • Healer

BACKGROUND

It's not easy raising a kid while you're both professional criminals, but Wagon's folks managed it. Born into the shadows and trained to run them, Wagon's a solid chummer who's welcome on almost any crew who's heard of him. His parents took a steady stream of low-risk, reasonable-reward work and ran the shadows for decades. Wagon has worked hard to build the same reputation for reliability, but only time will tell if he takes bigger gambles than they did.

Most of his formal education came from street docs and black-market clinics, and he took to the work like a fish to water. He's also a heck of a shot, with a real knack for gunplay. His steady nerves and hand-eye coordination shine whether he's wielding a laser scalpel or a laser sight, but Wagon's most valuable asset is his even temperament and willingness to compromise. A peacemaker by natural inclination, there aren't many better at keeping a team running smoothly, being everyone's friend, and providing that intangible *something extra* that can make a group of disparate criminals into a well-oiled machine.

Wagon's affable nature has left a trail of contacts behind him, from a wide variety of syndicates and sources, which multiplies his usefulness in the shadows. He's a startlingly fast learner, a great conversationalist, and a voracious reader, and he easily picks up new skills and new friends alike. While he's at his best patching up a teammate in need, his parents saw to it he'd always be ready to run the shadows, and he's never a detriment to his team.

WAGON

☐ Emerged
☐ Awakened

STRENGTH	AGILITY	WILLPOWER	LOGIC	CHARISMA	EDGE
3	5	4	5	4	6

DISPOSITIONS

TOTAL KARMA | KARMA BALANCE

Teamwork makes the dream work.

The team comes first, the job comes second.

You can break every rule but the golden one: Leave no one behind.

Be laid-back. Friends and contacts are better than corpses and enemies.

SKILLS

ATHLETICS	2+A	BIOTECH (FIRST AID +2)	4+L	FIREARMS	2+A
NEGOTIATION	2+C	STEALTH	2+A	SHADOWRUNNERS	(K)

SHADOW AMPS

ESSENCE: 6 — No penalties.

2 — I KNOW EVERYBODY
Add (CHA rating) contacts.

2 — TEAM PLAYER
You may freely gift your own Plot Points or Edge to other players.

2 — JACK OF ALL TRADES
When rolling an untrained skill, you may reroll 1 die.

CUES

Relax, it's just blood!

If you can't keep up, at least lay down some cover fire!

Some street docs actually work on the streets, you know.

Things don't have to get nasty, chummer. Let's talk about his.

Less stress, more success.

I've got your six.

Easy, chummer, I've got you. We've survived worse.

Small caliber. You'll be fine!

What happens if *I* get shot? I shoot back!

I probably know someone who knows someone who knows about that.

QUALITIES

EXPERT SHOT
+2 dice with Firearms.

DON'T YOU DIE ON ME!
+2 dice with Biotech.

MEDIC!
Must spend a Plot Point to keep from healing friendlies if they're injured (as long as active combat has ceased).

WEAPONS

	DAM	CLOSE	NEAR	FAR
UNARMED	3S	OK	—	—

	DAM	CLOSE	NEAR	FAR		DAM	CLOSE	NEAR	FAR		DAM	CLOSE	NEAR	FAR
Savalette Guardian Pistol	6P	OK	−2	—	**Ares Alpha** Assault Rifle	8P	OK	OK	−2					

ARMOR

TACTICAL VEST

CONDITION MONITOR

PHYSICAL −1 −2 −3

STUN −1 −2 −3 −4

GEAR

Fake SIN, Transys Avalon commlink, Jeep, professional medkit

CONTACTS

Monica Foster (DocWagon quartermaster); **Alexander Khan** (street doc); **Kanako Mori** (Yakuza safehouse operator); **High-ball** (Mafia combat decker); **Danielle "Danny" Kim** (Seoulpa lieutenant); **Doctor Sebastian Moritz** (trauma surgeon)

SHADOWRUN ANARCHY

CATALYST game labs

WHEEZER

TROLL GANG LEADER

TAGS

• Troll • Brawler • Practical • Vicious • Crude

BACKGROUND

When it came down to it, Darren Wilkes always kind of liked the streets—no ceilings to brush his horns on. He could even put his imposing physical stature to work. Pops had already disappeared, and Ma was having trouble feeding the twins, so he went to work doing what a troll kid from South Houston did best. He was a big, tough bastard and he scared people, and there were any number of gangs willing to employ these talents. He fell in with the Vaqueros and was soon earning his keep as the muscle for some of their protection rackets.

Ma was willing to take the money—she was a practical lady, if nothing else—but she didn't want the twins to follow their big brother into the gang. One failure, she said, was enough. So he left. He still sends money by, and she still takes it, but he hasn't seen her or the twins in years.

He's had more than his share of conflict with Lone Star over the years. One of the earliest run-ins left him with a throat injury that led to his street name. He can't muster much volume when he speaks, and his words sound like they're coming out of a leaking air compressor, but he'd never been one to say much anyway, so it didn't bother him much.

What did bother him was not getting what he thought was his due from the leaders of the gang. So he fought his way up through the ranks. For a while, he was content to be the top dog's lieutenant, but after a while, even that rankled. Everybody thought Duke would remain king of the mountain because he was a much better knife fighter, but Wheezer was bigger, tougher, and meaner than anyone—even the survivors of his ascent through the ranks—gave him credit for. Now he rules the gang with an iron fist. This occasionally brings him into conflict with Thunder, but the two have reached an accord of late. How that holds up remains to be seen.

WHEEZER

☐ Emerged
☐ Awakened

STRENGTH	AGILITY	WILLPOWER	LOGIC	CHARISMA	EDGE
8	4	5	3	3	2

DISPOSITIONS

TOTAL KARMA	KARMA BALANCE

These are *his* streets, and he *will* control them.

What's mine is mine, and what's yours is mine, too.

Strength is a virtue. So is fear.

Keeps his word, even when it's not in his favor.

SKILLS

CLOSE COMBAT	3+A

FIREARMS	2+A

INTIMIDATION	4+S

PILOTING (GROUND)	2+A

LOCAL LAW ENFORCEMENT	(K)

SHADOW AMPS

ESSENCE: 3 —2 dice to magic/healing tests.

4 **BONE LACING 2**
Cyberware. Damage taken is reduced by 2 points per attack. Unarmed damage becomes Physical. –1 Essence

3 **CYBEREYES**
Cyberware. Ignore vision modifiers due to lighting conditions. May reroll 2 failed dice on ranged attacks. –1 Essence

2 **WIRED REFLEXES 1**
Cyberware. Gains +1 attack or movement. –1 Essence

CUES

This is our turf, chummer; you've got to pay the toll.

You fraggers are in way the hell over your heads!

Don't need the Star; *we're* the fraggin' law around here.

Nice plan. Very subtle. You might've noticed that I don't do subtle.

We settle this the Vaquero way: trial by combat.

You have a problem with my decision, drekface?

Just like I told you: You won this round, you're free to go.

You hired us to handle the guards; we're handling the guards. Go do your thing!

QUALITIES

BRUISER
+2 dice for Intimidation tests; may link Intimidation to Strength instead of Charisma.

GUTS
May reroll 2 dice when resisting fear or intimidation.

SINNER, CRIMINAL
Known to law enforcement; data available through the Global SIN Registry.

WEAPONS

| | | | | | | UNARMED | DAM 4P | CLOSE OK | NEAR — | FAR — | | | | | |

	DAM	CLOSE	NEAR	FAR			DAM	CLOSE	NEAR	FAR		DAM	CLOSE	NEAR	FAR
Bowie Knife	5P	OK	—	—		Ares Predator V Heavy Pistol	6P	OK	–2	—					
	DAM	CLOSE	NEAR	FAR			DAM	CLOSE	NEAR	FAR		DAM	CLOSE	NEAR	FAR

CONDITION MONITOR

PHYSICAL

-1
-2
-3
-4

STUN

-1
-2
-3
-4

ARMOR

ARMORED VEST, TROLL SKIN

GEAR

Erika Elite commlink, fake SIN, Harley-Davidson Scorpion motorcycle, trauma patches

CONTACTS

Corwin Meese (crooked beat cop)

Vaqueros (street gang)

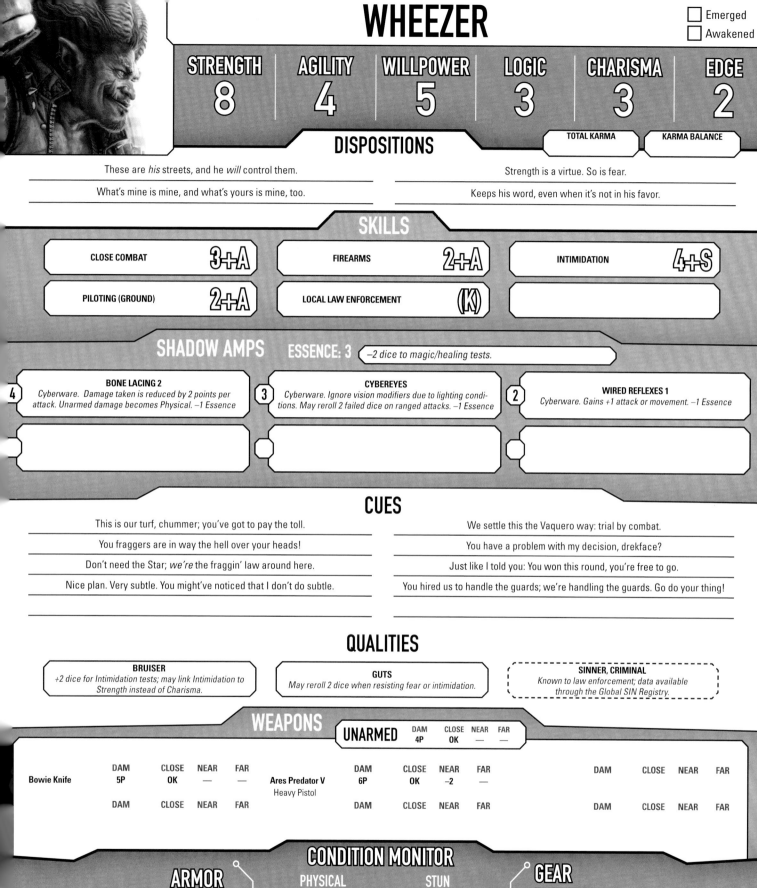

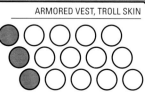

NON-PLAYER CHARACTERS

Note that some of the "characters" here are actually critters, beasts of the Sixth World with special powers that can cause havoc for shadowrunners, especially when they take up residence in urban environments. Critter Powers work similar to Spells, Adept Powers, and Technomancer Amps in that they can only be used by characters specifically designated as critters, in the same way that spellcasters and adepts are Awakened and technomancers are Emerged.

BUG QUEEN

STR	AGL	WIL	LOG	CHA	EDG
9	5	6	4	2	4

SKILLS: Athletics 5+A, Close Combat 6+A, Intimidation 4+C, Sorcery 3+W, Stealth 2+A, Tracking 3+L

SHADOW AMPS: Essence: 6 (no penalties)

Critter: Has access to critter amps.

Acid Spit (Spell): Combat. Damage of 6P/AA, +2 damage to Armor.

Insect Chemicals (Critter Power): Give +1 Plot Point/turn to ally bug spirit.

Immunity (Normal Weapons) 5 (Critter Power): Reduce damage taken by non-magical weapons by 5.

WEAPONS

	Damage	Close	Near	Far
Claws	6P	OK	—	—
Mandibles	8P	–2	—	—

Armor: 12 [Natural armor]
Condition Monitors (P/S): 13/11

BUG SPIRIT

STR	AGL	WIL	LOG	CHA	EDG
7	4	3	1	1	1

SKILLS: Athletics 3+A, Close Combat 4+A, Intimidation 3+C, Stealth 2+A, Tracking 2+L

SHADOW AMPS: Essence: 6 (no penalties)

Critter: Has access to critter amps.

Immunity (Normal Weapons) 2 (Critter Power): Reduce damage taken by non-magical weapons by 2.

WEAPONS

	Damage	Close	Near	Far
Claws	5P	OK	—	—
Mandibles	7P	–2	—	—

Armor: 6 [Natural armor]
Condition Monitors (P/S): 12/10

CORPORATE SECURITY

STR	AGL	WIL	LOG	CHA	EDG
4	4	3	3	2	2

SKILLS: Athletics 3+A, Close Combat 4+A, Con 1+C, Firearms 4+A, Intimidation 2+C, Piloting (Ground) 2+A

SHADOW AMPS: Essence: 4 (–2 modifier on Magic-related Tests and attempts to heal this character.)

Cybereyes 1: Cyberware. Ignore vision modifiers, may reroll 1 die on ranged attacks. –1 Essence

Reaction Enhancers: Cyberware. +1 Plot Point at the beginning of combat. –1 Essence

WEAPONS

	Damage	Close	Near	Far
Unarmed	2S	OK	—	—
Ares Predator V	6P	OK	–2	—
Stun baton	7S	OK	—	—

Armor: 9 [Armor vest]
Condition Monitors (P/S): 10/10

CORPORATE SUIT

STR	AGL	WIL	LOG	CHA	EDG
2	2	2	3	2	2

SKILLS: Electronics 2+L, Negotiation 2+C, Piloting (Ground) 1+A

SHADOW AMPS: Essence: 5 (–1 modifier on Magic-related Tests and attempts to heal this character.)

Datajack and Headware: Cyberware. May access the Matrix via full VR. +1 die to Matrix actions. –1 Essence

	Damage	Close	Near	Far
Unarmed	2S	OK	—	—
Yamaha Pulsar	5S	OK	–2	—

Armor: 0
Condition Monitors (P/S): 9/9

DEVIL RAT

STR	AGL	WIL	LOG	CHA	EDG
2	5	3	2	5	2

SKILLS: Athletics 5+A, Close Combat 5+A, Stealth 6+A, Tracking 5+L

SHADOW AMPS: Essence: 6 (no penalties)

  Critter: Has access to critter amps.

  Animal Control (ordinary rats, Critter Power): May give order to up to Charisma x 5 rats in Near range.

  Concealment (Critter Power): May reroll 3 dice on Stealth tests when not moving.

WEAPONS

	Damage	Close	Near	Far
Bite	2P	OK	—	—
Claws	1P	OK	—	—

  Armor: 0
  Condition Monitors (P/S): 9/10

ENEMY DRONE (HEAVY)

STR	AGL	WIL	LOG	CHA	EDG
10	6	0	6	0	0

SKILLS: Close Combat 3+A, Projectile Weapons 3+A, Vehicle Weapons 3+A

SHADOW AMPS: Essence: 0 (cannot be targeted with WIL or be healed)

  Armor Plating: Reduce damage taken by 1.
  Audio Analyzer
  Flying (optional)

WEAPONS

	Damage	Close	Near	Far
Melee Weapon Attack	8P	OK	—	—
Mounted Assault Rifle	8P	OK	OK	–2
Mounted Machine Gun	8P	OK	OK	OK
Mounted Grenade Launcher	12P	OK*	OK*	OK

Player(s) take damage as well at GM discretion

  Armor: 12 [Natural armor]
  Condition Monitors (P/S): 13/-

ENEMY DRONE (MEDIUM)

STR	AGL	WIL	LOG	CHA	EDG
6	8	0	6	0	0

SKILLS: Close Combat 3+A, Projectile Weapons 3+A, Vehicle Weapons 3+A

SHADOW AMPS: Essence: 0 (cannot be targeted with WIL or be healed)

  Armor Plating: Reduce damage taken by 1.
  Audio Analyzer
  Flying (optional)

WEAPONS (CHOOSE ONE FROM BELOW)

	Damage	Close	Near	Far
Melee Weapon Attack	8P	OK	—	—
Mounted Assault Rifle	8P	OK	OK	–2
Mounted SMG	6P	OK	OK	—
Mounted Grenade Launcher	12P	OK*	OK*	OK

Player(s) take damage as well at GM discretion

  Armor: 9 [Natural armor]
  Condition Monitors (P/S): 11/—

ENEMY DRONE (SMALL)

STR	AGL	WIL	LOG	CHA	EDG
4	10	0	6	0	0

SKILLS: Close Combat 3+A, Projectile Weapons 3+A, Vehicle Weapons 3+A

SHADOW AMPS: Essence: 0 (cannot be targeted with WIL or be healed)

  Armor Plating: Reduce damage taken by 1.
  Audio Analyzer
  Flying (optional)

WEAPONS (CHOOSE ONE FROM BELOW)

	Damage	Close	Near	Far
Melee Weapon Attack	8P	OK	—	—
Mounted Assault Rifle	8P	OK	OK	–2
Mounted Machine Pistol	6P	OK	–2	—
Mounted Grenade Launcher	12P	OK*	OK*	OK

Player(s) take damage as well at GM discretion

  Armor: 6 [Natural armor]
  Condition Monitors (P/S): 10/—

ENEMY MAGE

STR	AGL	WIL	LOG	CHA	EDG
3	4	6	5	4	2

SKILLS: Astral Combat 4+W, Athletics 2+A, Close Combat 2+A, Conjuring 4+W, Firearms 3+A, Sorcery 5+W, Stealth 2+A

SHADOW AMPS: Essence: 6 (no penalties)

Awakened: Has access to magical amps.

Control Thoughts 3 (Spell): Effect. +3 dice to Intimidation and Negotiation Tests

Fireball (Spell): Combat. Damage of 6P. Defense = A + L. Damages multiple targets.

Improved Invisibility (Spell): Effect. Mass invisibility, and targeted group may reroll 2 failed Stealth dice.

WEAPONS

	Damage	Close	Near	Far
Unarmed	2S	OK	—	—
Uzi IV	6P	OK	OK	—
Combat Knife	3P	OK	—	—

Armor: 9 [Lined coat]
Condition Monitors (P/S): 10/11

GANGER

STR	AGL	WIL	LOG	CHA	EDG
4	4	3	2	2	2

SKILLS: Athletics 3+A, Close Combat 3+W, Con 2+C, Firearms 3+A, Intimidation 2+C, Piloting (Ground) 2+A

SHADOW AMPS: Essence: 5 (–1 modifier on Magic-related Tests and attempts to heal this character.)

Cyberarms 1: May reroll 1 die on Agility-related rolls.

WEAPONS

	Damage	Close	Near	Far
Unarmed	2S	OK	—	—
Remington Roomsweeper	6P	OK	–2	—
Combat Knife	3P	OK	—	—

Armor: 9 [Armor vest]
Condition Monitors (P/S): 10/10

HELL HOUND

STR	AGL	WIL	LOG	CHA	EDG
6	4	4	2	3	3

SKILLS: Athletics 3+A, Close Combat 4+A, Heavy Weapons 4+A, Intimidation 3+C, Stealth 5+A, Tracking 5+L

SHADOW AMPS: Essence: 6 (no penalties)

Critter: Has access to critter amps.

Elemental Attack (Fire) (Critter Power): Combat. Damage of 6P/AA. Defense = A + L. +2 damage to Armor.

Enhanced Senses (Critter Power): Gain +3 dice to any Perception test.

Fear (Critter Power): May reroll 2 dice on Intimidation tests.

Immunity to Fire 4 (Critter Power): Reduce damage taken from fire by 4.

WEAPONS

	Damage	Close	Near	Far
Bite	5P	OK	—	—
Claws	3P	OK	—	—

Armor: 2 [Natural armor]
Condition Monitors (P/S): 11/10

MR. JOHNSON (CORPORATE)

STR	AGL	WIL	LOG	CHA	EDG
3	3	5	4	5	3

SKILLS: Athletics 2+A, Con 4+C, Electronics 2+L, Escape Artist 1+A, Firearms 3+A, Intimidation 2+C, Negotiation 4+C, Piloting (Ground) 2+A

SHADOW AMPS: Essence: 5 (–1 modifier on Magic-related Tests and attempts to heal this character.)

Synaptic Booster 1: Bioware, +1 action. –0.5 Essence

Tailored Pheromones 2: Bioware. Reroll 2 dice on all in-person Charisma-related tests. –0.5 Essence

WEAPONS

	Damage	Close	Near	Far
Unarmed	2S	OK	—	—
Ares Predator V	6P	OK	–2	—
Stun baton	7S	OK	—	—

Armor: 6 [Armor clothing]
Condition Monitors (P/S): 10/11

MR. JOHNSON (STREET)

STR	AGL	WIL	LOG	CHA	EDG
4	4	4	3	4	3

SKILLS: Athletics 2+A, Con 4+C, Electronics 2+L, Escape Artist 1+A, Firearms 3+A, Intimidation 1+C, Negotiation 3+C, Piloting (Ground) 2+A

SHADOW AMPS: Essence: 4.5 (–1 modifier on Magic-related Tests and attempts to heal this character.)

  Reaction Enhancers: Cyberware. +1 Plot Point at the beginning of combat. –1 Essence

  Tailored Pheromones 1: Bioware. Reroll 1 die on all in-person Charisma-related tests. –0.5 Essence

WEAPONS

	Damage	Close	Near	Far
Unarmed	2S	OK	—	—
Ruger Super Warhawk	7P	OK	–2	—
Sap	4S	OK	—	—

  Armor: 6 [Armor clothing]
  Condition Monitors (P/S): 10/11

RENT-A-COP

STR	AGL	WIL	LOG	CHA	EDG
4	4	4	3	2	2

SKILLS: Athletics 4+A, Close Combat 4+A, Con 1+C, Firearms 4+A, Intimidation 2+C, Piloting (Ground) 2+A

SHADOW AMPS: Essence: 5 (–1 modifier on Magic-related Tests and attempts to heal this character.)

  Reaction Enhancers: Cyberware. +1 Plot Point at the beginning of combat. –1 Essence

WEAPONS

	Damage	Close	Near	Far
Unarmed	2S	OK	—	—
Ares Predator V	6P	OK	–2	—
Stun baton	7S	OK	—	—

  Armor: 12 [Armor jacket]
  Condition Monitors (P/S): 10/10

SECURITY SPIDER

STR	AGL	WIL	LOG	CHA	EDG
2	3	4	5	3	2

SKILLS: Electronics 4+L, Firearms 1+A, Hacking 5+L, Tracking 3+L

SHADOW AMPS: Essence: 3.5 (–2 modifier on Magic-related Tests and attempts to heal this character.)

  Cyberdeck 3: May reroll 2 dice on Matrix actions, Firewall +3, Matrix Condition Monitor 12, may run 2 programs

  Datajack and Headware: Cyberware. May access the Matrix via full VR. +1 die to Matrix actions. –1 Essence

  Exploit (program): May reroll 2 dice of non-Cyber-combat hacking tests.

  Hammer (program): +2 damage in Cybercombat

  Track (program): May reroll 2 dice on Matrix Tracking tests.

WEAPONS

	Damage	Close	Near	Far
Unarmed	1S	OK	—	—
Colt America L36	5P	OK	–2	—

  Armor: 6 [Armor clothing]
  Condition Monitors (P/S): 9/10

SOLDIER

STR	AGL	WIL	LOG	CHA	EDG
4	5	5	3	2	2

SKILLS: Athletics 2+A, Close Combat 3+A, Firearms 4+A, Intimidation 2+C, plus one of the following: Engineering 2+L, Heavy Weapons 2+A, Piloting (Ground) 2+A, Tracking 2+L. For **ELITE SOLDIER**, use all skills, increase Close Combat, Firearms, and Heavy Weapons by 1 each.

SHADOW AMPS: Essence: 5 (–1 modifier on Magic-related Tests and attempts to heal this character.)

  Aluminum Bone Lacing 2: Reduce damage taken by 2. –1 Essence

WEAPONS

	Damage	Close	Near	Far
Unarmed	2S	OK	—	—
Ares Predator V	6P	OK	–2	—
Ares Alpha, assault rifle	8P	OK	OK	—

  Armor: 12 [Armor jacket]
  Condition Monitors (P/S): 10/11

SPIRIT OF AIR

STR	AGL	WIL	LOG	CHA	EDG
4	10	6	6	6	3

SKILLS: Astral Combat 3+W, Close Combat 3+A
SHADOW AMPS: Essence: 6 (no penalties)
  Critter: Has access to critter amps.
  Immunity (Normal Weapons) 3 (Critter Power): Reduce damage taken by non-magical weapons by 3.
  Engulf (Critter Power): Combat/Effect. Damage of 4S/AA. Defense = S + W. Target cannot move.
  Choose one:
  Elemental Attack (Cold) (Critter Power): Combat. Damage of 6S/AA. Defense = S + W. +2 damage to Armor.
  -OR-
  Elemental Attack (Electricity) (Critter Power): Combat. Damage of 6P/AA. Defense = S + W.

WEAPONS

	Damage	Close	Near	Far
Unarmed	2S	OK	—	—

  Armor: 6 [Natural armor]
  Condition Monitors (P/S): 10/11
  Note: For greater spirit of air, increase all Attributes by 2, increase Immunity by 2, choose both elemental attacks, and increase damage of all attacks by 2.

SPIRIT OF BEASTS

STR	AGL	WIL	LOG	CHA	EDG
8	7	6	6	6	3

SKILLS: Astral Combat 3+W, Close Combat 3+A
SHADOW AMPS: Essence: 6 (no penalties)
  Critter: Has access to critter amps.
  Immunity (Normal Weapons) 3 (Critter Power): Reduce damage taken by non-magical weapons by 3.
  Natural Weapon (Critter Power): Weapon (claws, teeth, tail) STR/2 +3P
  Animal Control: Mundane animals obey simple commands. Limited to swarm of tiny creatures, 3 dozen small creatures, or 6 large creatures).

WEAPONS

	Damage	Close	Near	Far
Unarmed	3S	OK	—	—
Natural Weapon	7P	OK	—	—

  Armor: 9 [Natural armor]
  Condition Monitors (P/S): 12/11
  Note: For greater spirit of beasts, increase all Attributes by 2, increase Immunity by 2, and increase damage of all attacks by 2.

SPIRIT OF EARTH

STR	AGL	WIL	LOG	CHA	EDG
10	4	6	5	6	3

SKILLS: Astral Combat 3+W, Close Combat 3+A
SHADOW AMPS: Essence: 6 (no penalties)
  Critter: Has access to critter amps.
  Immunity (Normal Weapons) 3 (Critter Power): Reduce damage taken by non-magical weapons by 3.
  Engulf (Critter Power): Combat/Effect. Damage of 4S/AA. Defense = S + W. Target Cannot move.
  Elemental Attack (Earth) (Critter Power): Combat. Damage of 8P. Defense = A + L.

WEAPONS

	Damage	Close	Near	Far
Unarmed	5P	OK	—	—

  Armor: 12 [Natural Armor]
  Condition Monitors (P/S): 13/11
  Note: For greater spirit of earth, increase all Attributes by 2, increase Immunity by 2, and increase damage of all attacks by 2.

SPIRIT OF MAN

STR	AGL	WIL	LOG	CHA	EDG
6	7	6	7	6	3

SKILLS: Astral Combat 3+W, Close Combat 3+A
SHADOW AMPS: Essence: 6 (no penalties)
  Critter: Has access to critter amps.
  Immunity (Normal Weapons) 3 (Critter Power): Reduce damage taken by non-magical weapons by 3.
  Accident (Critter Power): Effect. Each combat turn, may add 1 glitch die to (WIL rating) rolls.
  Control Thoughts (Critter Power): Effect. +3 dice to Intimidation and Negotiation Tests.

WEAPONS

	Damage	Close	Near	Far
Unarmed	3S	OK	—	—

  Armor: 9 [Natural armor]
  Condition Monitors (P/S): 11/11
  Note: For greater spirit of man, increase all Attributes by 2, increase Immunity by 2, and increase damage of all attacks by 2.

SPIRIT OF FIRE

STR	AGL	WIL	LOG	CHA	EDG
6	9	6	6	6	3

SKILLS: Astral Combat 3+W, Close Combat 3+A
SHADOW AMPS: Essence: 6 (no penalties)
  Critter: Has access to critter amps.
  Immunity (Normal Weapons) 3 (Critter Power): Reduce damage taken by non-magical weapons by 3.
  Elemental Attack (Fire) (Critter Power): Combat. Damage of 6P/AA. Defense = A + L. +2 damage to Armor.

WEAPONS

	Damage	Close	Near	Far
Unarmed	3P	OK	—	—

  Armor: 6 [Natural armor]
  Condition Monitors (P/S): 11/11
  Note: For greater spirit of fire, increase all Attributes by 2, increase Immunity by 2, and increase damage of all attacks by 2.

SPIRIT OF WATER

STR	AGL	WIL	LOG	CHA	EDG
6	8	6	6	6	3

SKILLS: Astral Combat 3+W, Close Combat 3+A
SHADOW AMPS: Essence: 6 (no penalties)
  Critter: Has access to critter amps.
  Immunity (Normal Weapons) 3 (Critter Power): Reduce damage taken by non-magical weapons by 3.
  Elemental Attack (Water) (Critter Power): Combat. Damage of 8S. Defense = A + L.

WEAPONS

	Damage	Close	Near	Far
Unarmed	3S	OK	—	—

  Armor: 9 [Natural armor]
  Condition Monitors (P/S): 11/11
  Note: For greater spirit of water, increase all Attributes by 2, increase Immunity by 2, and increase damage of all attacks by 2.

TECHNOMANCER SPRITE (BASIC)

STR	AGL	WIL	LOG	CHA	EDG
—	—	2	2	2	1

SKILLS: Electronics 3+L, Hacking 3+L, Tracking 3+L
SHADOW AMPS: Essence 6 [no penalites]; Choose one Techomancer Amp, p. 203
    Armor: 6 [natural armor]
    Condition Monitors (P/S): —/9

VAMPIRE

STR	AGL	WIL	LOG	CHA	EDG
5	5	5	5	5	3

SKILLS: Astral Combat 4+W, Athletics 3+A, Close Combat 3+A, Conjuring 6+W, Firearms 3+A, Intimidation 4+C, Negotiation 5+C, Sorcery 6+W, Stealth 5+A
SHADOW AMPS: Essence: 6 (no penalties)
    Awakened: Has access to magical amps.
    Essence Drain (Critter Power): If used on incapacitated enemy, permanently lowers essence of target by 1.
    Immunity (Age, Pathogens, Toxins) (Critter Power)
    Infection: If an Essence Drain action would take the target to 0 essence, target is infected with the same virus as the attacker.
    Mist Form (Critter Power)
    Regeneration (Critter Power): Every combat turn, Critter regains 2 pips of damage, in the following order: stun, physical, armor (if Natural Armor).
    Control Thoughts (Critter Power): Effect. +3 dice to Intimidation and Negotiation Tests.
    Animal Control: Mundane animals obey simple commands. Limited to swarm of tiny creatures, 3 dozen small creatures, or 6 large creatures)
    Vampire Sorcery (Critter Power): Optional. Vampires may choose from any spell in the list of Spell Amps.
    Weaknesses (Sunlight): When in sunlight, vampires take -4 damage/turn, which cannot be regenerated.
    Weaknesses (Wood): When attacked with wooden weapons, add 4 damage, which cannot be regenerated.
    Dietary Requirement (MetahumanBlood)

WEAPONS

	Damage	Close	Near	Far
Unarmed	2S	OK	—	—
Natural Weapon	6P	OK	—	—
Ares Predator V	6P	OK	-2	—

    Armor: 9 [Lined Coat]
    Condition Monitors (P/S): 11/11

YOUNG DRAGON

STR	AGL	WIL	LOG	CHA	EDG
15	10	9	9	9	6

SKILLS: Astral Combat 6+W, Close Combat 6+A, Conjuring 6+W, Intimidation 4+C, Projectile Weapons 6+W, Sorcery 8+W
SHADOW AMPS: Essence: 6 (no penalties)
    Critter: Has access to critter amps.
    Immunity (Normal Weapons) 3 (Critter Power): Reduce damage taken by non-magical weapons by 3.
    Elemental Attack (Fire) (Critter Power): Combat. Damage of 6P/AA. Defense = A + L. +2 damage to Armor.
    Natural Weapon (Critter Power): Weapon (claws, teeth, tail) STR/2 +3P
    Animal Control (Critter Power): Mundane animals obey simple commands. Limited to swarm of tiny creatures, three dozen small creatures, or six large creatures)
    Dragonspeech (Critter Power): May speak and be understood without the use of audible words.
    Enhanced Sense (Critter Power)s: +3 dice to any perception roll.
    Fear (Critter Power): +3 dice to intimidation rolls, melee opponents must roll 3 hits on CHA+WIL or run away.
    Dragon Sorcery: Dragons may choose from any spell in the list of Spell Amps.

WEAPONS

	Damage	Close	Near	Far
Unarmed	8S	OK	OK	—
Natural Weapon	11P	OK	OK	—

    Armor: 15 [Natural armor]
    Condition Monitors (P/S): 16/13

THE SECRETS OF SEATTLE

POSTED BY: SOUNDER

If you're a mountain climber with any prets at all, you don't look for the easy way up a slope. You don't climb a mountain that's "kind of" high. You go big, just to see if you can. And to show the world you can take it. If you're a combat biker, you may tool around in the minors a little, making a name for yourself and putting some scratch together for a proper bike, but your sights are set on the majors. You want to show what you can do, and you want to do it at the top, in the big time. Being the best in the minors is the same as not being good enough.

Seattle is the major leagues. The big time. Yeah, there are a lot of places in the world to run, and lots of challenges. Neo-Tokyo is swimming in cash, Mumbai spins East and West together into dizzy intoxication, GeMiTo seems to pack everything in the world in its vast sprawl, and Lagos finds more ways to kill you than you ever believed existed. But Seattle, the Queen City, sits on top of them all. This place is full of legends—the Ork Underground that started as an outlaw refuge and made itself into an official district of the city; Dante's Inferno, where the hottest people in the city and the hottest icons across the Matrix mingle; the Arcology Commercial and Housing Enclave, a vast, mostly empty building still trying to shake off the ghosts of its past; Glow City, a melted-down nuke plant where only the truly desperate find shelter; and many more. You can run in lots of places in the world and make a decent living (assuming you stay alive), but there's only one city where, when you tell people you've run there, they widen their eyes and sit a little straighter without knowing they're doing it. That's Seattle.

So, wanna run at the top? Here's some essential info you'll need to know about the Emerald City.

THE WHOLE CITY

The way Seattle hits you depends on how you enter. Come from the air, and the first thing you notice is Mount Rainier, especially if you're coming in on a low-flying t-bird and the mountain peak is higher than you. It lords over the sprawl like an ancient Greek god; the lights and the pavement of urbanity may have stretched across the region for dozens of kilometers, but most of Rainier remains untouched. You quickly find out how vast the sprawl is, but you never shake that first impression of it being dwarfed by a massive peak.

Come by land, and odds are you are assaulted by green. Unlike some sprawls in the heart of North America, the Seattle skyline is not a distant beacon that can be seen from any slightly elevated position within fifty kilometers. You don't see it until you are already in the sprawl, so the outlying areas hit you first. The evergreen trees, the emerald-green road signs, and (assuming you are a normal, AR-using person) the green AR overlay that tints everything. It's the color of perpetual life, which is what the civic leaders want you to think, but it also holds a longstanding connection to the color of money.

Enter by water and the first thing you see is the purple glow in the sky as you round the western peninsula and make your way into Puget Sound. Then the obstacles move out of your way, and you see that skyline looming over the reflective water, the lights and neon looking pristine and clean from a distance. It is every urban wonderland you ever dreamed of, it holds all the possibilities in the world, and it dares you to come closer and attempt to find a flaw. You approach, because you cannot help it, even though you know that the lights and beauty are very likely a trap, and once you're in you'll be caught in a grasp that will not easily let go.

All of these impressions are true, and all of them are incomplete. Any single impression of Seattle is going to be inaccurate, because one impression cannot contain a city as large as this. Every type of person you can conceive of is here—unimaginably rich business magnates, master thieves, staunchly judgmental law-enforcement officers, relaxed neo-hippies, shamans looking for deposits of toxic sludge to bury themselves in, brilliant inventors, equally brilliant patent thieves, gangs looking to build power for themselves, gangs looking to burn everything down, mobsters who would shoot their own brother and sell their own mother, pimps, muggers, robbers, murderers, assassins, every possible kind of sinner, and precious few saints.

That variety helps make Seattle the shadowrunning capital of the world. Other cities may have more devastated barrens, wealthier corporate headquarters, or more magical resources, but no city has it all like Seattle does. Its location, an isolated UCAS island surrounded by the Salish-Shidhe Council and not far from the Tír Tairngire, ensures that government tensions will always be part of the city's mix, while its North American location and historically high traffic and immigration from Asia means that all the megacorps feel they have a key population base there (Aztechnology and Saeder-Krupp may have the least claim on the city but still compete fiercely in its borders, partly out of habit). The sheer amount of wealth involved in these battles attracts all variety of organized crime. And on top of that, dragons have taken root in the city, adding to the powers attempting to claim the sprawl for their own.

The equation is simple: bright lights of power combined with the need to perform dark, illicit deeds makes shadows everywhere.

The money is high, the stakes are higher, so the competition is fierce. One reason Seattle shadowrunning is so dangerous is not just the array of powers lined up to double-cross or trip you up—it's also the other shadowrunners who will wait for you to show a sign of weakness and then make you pay so they can take your place on the ladder. That's the real trick of the city, knowing that any gun, even the one on the hip of your best chummer, may be pointed at you at any second. Living with that possibility is exhausting. Surviving it is exhilarating.

THE SHAPE OF THE CITY

Like any sprawl, the underlying land shapes what happens on top of it. To understand what's happening on the streets, you need to understand what they're built on.

Seattle is nestled between mountains on the east and the Sound to the west. The protection of the mountains and the ocean currents keep the climate mild though often cloudy. Most things about the climate tend to be gentle. Seattle has more rainy days than New York, but less total rainfall. On-and-off rain is very common (especially in Everett), as is morning rain that fades to afternoon sunshine and then returns in the evening.

Metahumanity contributes some of the cloudiness of the area. Air sometimes has trouble moving past those mountains to the east, and all those trash fires in the Barrens, along with industry all across the sprawl, has a cumulative effect. Fog is a frequent morning-and-evening visitor, and often it has odors making it clear it is not simply water vapor floating around. It's great for giving cover to covert nighttime operations, but not so good for more basic purposes like breathing. Tacoma is the part of the sprawl most notable for its range of unpleasant odors, but bad smells can be found anywhere in the sprawl.

The good news about the climate is temperature extremes are rare. You don't see too many summer days above the mid-thirties, and most winter days get at least a few degrees above the freezing line, if not all the way to ten. That means that the sizable portion of the population without reliable heat and cooling (or luxuries such as a roof) can usually find a way to survive without the elements killing them.

While Seattle is not immune to the general rule that wealth flows toward waterfronts, it's not a perfectly reliable rule because Seattle has so much shoreline. The Sound runs on almost the entire western border of the sprawl, and while this includes the luxuries of Downtown, it also includes less-glamorous locales like Tacoma and Everett. The well-to-do residents of Bellevue have Lake Washington on which to build palatial estates, but just east of that is Lake Sammamish, where residents of the Redmond Barrens dump trash, shopping carts, and corpses. Water is used many ways across the city—Lake Youngs in Renton is tree-lined and welcoming to strolling residents, while the artificial reservoir known as Lake Tapps in Auburn provides hydroelectric power, a source of cooling for local industries, and a place to dump chemicals. One of those bodies of water is a lot more pleasant to be around than the other.

> ◈ Don't be fooled into thinking Lake Tapps is a good spot to dump a body. Yeah, it's toxic, but also a preservative. Bodies don't dissolve; they more mummify, or embalm. If those are verbs. Anyway, they don't go away.
> ◈ Cayman

Another part of the appeal of Seattle is that its greenery and temperate weather can lull you into

a sense of safety, a feeling that while bad things may happen, true disaster is distant. Hurricanes don't hit it, tornadoes are rare, it's usually too damp for wildfires, and volcanoes are generally too far away to directly harm the city, especially if there's no Great Ghost Dance going on. Earthquakes are a real threat, but big ones manage to occur so infrequently that they don't weigh on people's minds. People may die, the feeling goes, but the city will live.

One of the curses of being a shadowrunner is you see enough under the fabric of society to know the lie behind that sentiment. The Matrix Crashes were excellent examples of how a seemingly stable infrastructure can rip apart at the seams and throw everything into chaos, and the Matrix is not the only part of daily life that could break. Shutting down the ports, taking out bridges over the Snohomish River, keeping planes from landing at SeaTac—any one of those things would be painful. All of them at once might be ruinous. Get control of the minds of some financial leaders, have them make a few nightmarishly bad decisions, and the bottom falls out of the city's business infrastructure. Complete disaster and ruin are waiting on the other side of the next shadowrun; sometimes they're waiting on the other side of the street. If you run in Seattle for a long time, you are balancing on a knife blade for years on end. Doing that without losing a significant amount of blood is an accomplishment indeed.

> ◉ This is just one of the reasons why, if people know you ran in Seattle, you'll go up a notch or two in their esteem. Of course, then they'll wonder why you aren't there anymore.
> ◉ Traveler Jones

THE CULTURE

Let's start this with admission that defining a single culture in a city of millions is a fool's errand. There are a thousand micro-cultures in the city, sub-groups of people in neighborhoods butting against each other, or different cultures from floor to floor in a megacorporate complex. So yes, this is written with the knowledge that anyone reading this could pick out dozens of people they know in Seattle who don't really reflect these elements at all. What we're talking about is a tendency, an inclination in a certain direction that flows through the various residents of the city.

That said, there are certain characteristics of Seattle that it's good to know about if you're going to run there, if only so you don't appear like a complete rookie when Mr. Johnson is sizing you up.

Change: There used to be a time when certain Seattle residents were resistant to change, talking about how things used to be ten, twenty, fifty years ago, and offering suggestions on how the city could reclaim its past. Some of the older residents were called mossbacks, because they had settled in the area like a large, moist rock.

That doesn't happen much anymore. The sprawl has a way of beating people's resistance to change right out of them. At the top of the sprawl's social pyramid, you have people who have millions or billions of nuyen at their disposal and a government built to facilitate their desires. If they want to bulldoze a neighborhood to make way for a new arcology, they'll bulldoze that neighborhood. If they want to buy out a rival's chain just so they can shut down a dozen locations, allowing their spots to dominate the market, they'll do that. Some buildings may stay put, but ownership will change hands, names and signage will alter, and so on.

- This happens more when there is open competition for business, like spots Downtown. In a subdivision solely owned by one corporation, or inside an arcology, things are more permanent, as the ownership corps don't feel they need to do anything to win the business of the people inside, and they don't really care about impressing them.
- Sunshine

Meanwhile, at the bottom of the social structure, the Barrens in general may look like a bombed-out war zone day-in, day-out, but the particular details of its devastation change from week to week, or even day to day. Street peddlers migrate from place to place looking for business while avoiding former customers they might have inadvertently poisoned, people squatting in shipping containers move to a new block because someone meaner and tougher than them decided the container should be theirs, and gang territory shifts due to the changing fortunes of the various groups of thugs strewn across the area. In both Redmond and Puyallup, the term "permanent address" is laughable, and you usually have to track down residents of the area the way a lion tracks a wildebeest.

Some things seem permanent—Dante's Inferno, the Pike Street Market—but Seattleites have learned to treat them like the exception, not the rule.

Openness: If we remember that there is no such thing as a perfect utopia where everyone is accepted for their skills and character rather than their appearance, then we'll see that Seattle, despite its imperfections, tends to be very accepting of a wide variety of people. Now, I can hear orks and trolls chortling as they read that, and I can hear the protests from people saying it's tough to claim you're accepting when a pretty dedicated

racist has been at the head of the government for years on end, but remember it's a sliding scale. Did it take the Ork Underground a long time to get recognition, leaving tens of thousands of people disenfranchised in the interim? Yeah. But it happened, in a democratic way that would never happen in most of the other cities in the world. So you'll find Humanis and other racists in Seattle, and you'll find every kind of prejudice metahumanity can imagine, but you'll also see orks and elves on the same runner team, trolls and humans in the same bar or the same gang, and humans and dwarfs manning the same roadside work crews. And you won't be surprised to see any of it, and they won't act like it's a big deal. Seattleites are often willing to see what you've got instead of judging you.

Now, there's a downside (or upside, depending on your perspective) to this. The "live and let live" attitude often leads to people not wanting to rush to judgment about others, so when they see something that appears suspicious or even outright criminal, they may tell themselves that they don't know just what's going on and don't have all the facts, and it's probably none of their business anyway, so they'll just go about their business. This is a problem if someone is beating on you in the street and you'd like someone to jump in and stop it, but it can be beneficial if you're the one committing the crime.

- Note that this primarily applies to the average person on the street, not to law enforcement or security guards. It's not a good idea to count on them being lax just because of the culture of the city.
- Ma'Fan

The Seattle Freeze: This sometimes seems like a contrast to the openness quality, but a certain chill toward outsiders sits side by side with an acceptance of those same outsiders. That is to say, just because Seattle residents won't necessarily judge you on your appearance doesn't mean that you'll instantly be friends. You're not just going to stroll into a bar, start up a conversation with strangers, and immediately find yourself part of their runner team. Social networks are important. Getting an introduction from someone who knows someone can help thaw out the freeze, so use them. Remember, just because Seattleites are not always immediately friendly doesn't mean they're mean.

- Don't press your luck, though. I'm not going to introduce you to all my friends in Seattle just because you ask. You have to earn it.
- Sunshine

- There's some of that warmth to outsiders, right there!
- Ma'Fan

Loyalty: Loyalty is a quality in short supply in the Sixth World, but there is perhaps a bit more of it in Seattle than you'll find elsewhere. I'm not talking about the megacorps here—they have draconian contract terms and lifelong servitude agreements whose sole purpose is to keep them from having to worry about whether their employees will ever leave them. But if we move beyond the corp drone world, we find people who are somewhat more likely to stick with something they are building rather than jump ship. Runner teams won't disband just because a job goes pear-shaped, street gangs will hang together through lean times, and Mr. Johnson is often more interested in finding a team he can trust than in screwing them over. That loyalty tends to be more to an individual's clique than to the over-arching city organizations, which means Knight Errant has a devil of a time finding people to inform on others or act as confidential informants. The police focus a whole lot more on gathering physical evidence than attempting to find witness testimony, since witnesses are often difficult to come by. They are more loyal to their own people and neighborhood than to the law.

Remember that this has limits. The loyalty of Seattleites doesn't mean Mr. Johnson will never turn on you, or your teammates will never sell you out for a nice pile of nuyen. This is the Sixth World, after all, and those are the sort of things that happen in the shadows. And if they happen in the shadows, they happen a *lot* in Seattle.

That's the city, in broad strokes. But what the city really is, is the districts, thirteen divisions that in many ways act like separate city-states, each with its own culture and a mayor. Here's a briefing on all of them.

DOWNTOWN

Downtown is the heart of the sprawl. When people think of Seattle, they think of Downtown's skyline in its chrome-polished, neon-infused, never sleeps, AR-enhanced glory.

Downtown is where the biggest biz in the Sprawl happens. Other districts have their own action, but it pales in comparison to what's happening Downtown. Only the best can handle operating here, and if you can't deal with that fact, then get the hell out.

What makes Downtown so fragging special? Well, it's got more corporate, business, and government real estate per square kilometer than anywhere else in the Sprawl. Five of the Big Ten megacorps have regional HQs in Downtown, which makes the area ripe for running opportunities.

> And let's not forget all the overlapping security zones. Each corp or government agency defends its own patch of turf in

different ways. The government is usually legally bound not to kill you outright for stepping on their lawn. But with the corps' extraterritoriality, it's a totally different story.
> Slamm-0!

But all work and no play makes Downtown a dull boy. So when biz is done, Downtown is the place to go. Want to check out the trendiest shops? Need to find that hard-to-find item? Want to dance the night away in the hottest nightlife scene in the Pac-Northwest? Care to sample some of the finest in local or exotic cuisine? Are you a professional sports fan? Or maybe you're a touristy type who likes local flavor. Then guess what, *omae*? Downtown is for you!

> More shadowruns happen in Downtown than any other district. It's also the best area, IMHO, for mixing business with pleasure.
> Kat o' Nine Tales

DOWNTOWN TAGS
• ACHE • The Big Rhino • Corp heaven • Dante's Inferno • Halloweeners • Knight Errant is watching • Space Needle

BELLEVUE

If Downtown is where the rich and powerful go to work and party, then Bellevue is where they sleep at night, tucked away in tailored micro-arcologies and shuffled around the city in luxury APCs. "The Belle" got its nickname from longtime mayor Marilyn Shultz, who dubbed it "belle of the ball" and the most popular place to live in Seattle. A version of that name dug itself into the psyche of the residents.

The slogan, like Bellevue itself, is a complete fabrication. Nothing is genuine. Bellevue is based on every image we see on the trid of an idealized suburban enclave culture; a Horizon-scrubbed vision of the best stuff to emerge out of other parts of the city.

This false vision extends into the racial makeup of the area. Twenty years ago the ork population was close to twenty percent, but a long campaign of redlining and Tolkien-esque bigotry redistributed the population breakdown. Recent years took things one step further, triggering an influx of highly educated corporate types with disposable incomes looking to live in the next "it" part of the city.

The Belle is that place. Bellevue boasts rolling green hills, lakes, and million-dollar views of Downtown. The area is speckled with gated communities that are arcologies in everything but name. Several offer domes and purified air shipped in from the Canadian wilds. This style of living comes with a high price tag, and even if you have the money you also need to have the social capital to jump to the front of the waiting list.

Still, not everyone in Bellevue is white-collar wealthy. Virtually all of the population is corporate affiliated; yet sixteen percent of the people still live below the poverty level, most of whom are not affiliated with the corps. These are the workers who keep Bellevue running while living in a society entirely separate from their upper-echelon counterparts. The two sides rarely meet, but when they do it is usually back-alley affairs, black-market deals, or rich kids trying to play gutterpunk.

BELLVUE TAGS

- 405 Hellhounds • The Belle • Corporation Row
- High security • The Lake Acids • Mayor Jonathan Blake
- Wealthy suburb

TACOMA

Tacoma will forever be etched in memory as the place where the Night of Rage found its worst moments and some of its greatest heroes. When the violence peaked, the Sheraton Tacoma opened its doors to fleeing metahumans and protected them through the night. Once the tide shifted from rage to remembrance, sculptors erected a Crying Wall to commemorate the sacrifice. That wall became a symbol and eventually a tourist attraction that brought more attention to the area.

- ⦿ So by "attention," you mean "unwanted metahuman attention." I suppose that's the reason Tacoma went to hell?
- ⦿ Khan-a-Saur

Tacoma was an area on the rise—an area originally built around the very particular needs of Shiawase—but in recent times the tide quite literally shifted. The Nicaragua Canal diverted shipping from the area, and with it the shoreline commerce that powered the city's wealth dropped. Office Parks emptied. Tacoma fell victim to sagging real-estate prices and thriller gangs. The so-called City of Tomorrow faded into yesterday's news.

TACOMA TAGS

- Basil's Faulty Bar • Cathode Glow • Crying Wall monument
- Dockside smuggling • Seoulpa rings
- Silcox Island Correctional • Tacoma aroma

EVERETT

Not yet a barrens, not even definitively slated to become one, Everett is balanced on a teetering scale, waiting for one thing or another to shift the district into whatever it will become. There are high-tech corp facilities here, residences most of us can only dream about obtaining, but also areas of high abandonment, squatters' paradises, and traffic routes where smugglers outnumber law-abiding folks. The population of the district is growing, but it's unclear if this is people moving here as a staging ground for a better life or people falling to this district from something better. One large investment in a mixed-use complex may push the district into a long, upward growth trend; while a riot, other disturbance, or simply a persistent increase in violent crime may doom it to becoming the cousin of Redmond and Puyallup. My crystal ball isn't telling me how it will end up, but I can tell you this: Many people across the sprawl are plotting on ways to profit from whatever changes overtake Everett. But that's not exactly news.

The good news is that people like us don't need to wait for the district's fate to be decided to enjoy it. Have you ever been in Bellevue on a run and wished you could just travel a few blocks and lose yourself in the twisted ruins of Redmond's streets? Well, while Everett's highs do not approach Bellevue and their lows do not touch Redmond, you still have a chance to lift something from a corporate pad, travel a short distance, then hide out in an abandoned apartment complex full of squatters. Enjoy it while you can.

- ⦿ If I had to wager, I'd say the area is as low as it's going to get and will soon trace an upward, gentrifying pathway. Federated-Boeing has invested substantially in the area and is unlikely to sit on the sidelines while Everett becomes a barrens around it. They may have to wait until after the election, once Brackhaven or his successor has their feet under them, but I'd expect some major Everett redevelopment to be on the agenda for early 2079.
- ⦿ Mr. Bonds

EVERETT TAGS

- Bicson Biomedicals • Casino Corner • Ever-wet
- Independent Information Network • Naval station
- Not a barrens—yet • Rikki's Rathole • Shipping docks

RENTON

Considered by many to be "Seattle's Apartment," Renton was once one an example of Sixth World suburbia run amok. Compared to other districts such as Downtown, Tacoma, or even Redmond and the Ork Underground, Renton is almost forgettable. Simply put, Renton is the place that nice wageslaves and other working-class drones looked to as an example of "making it."

Renton isn't where business is done, it's the place that the nice, "good" people of Seattle call home and retire to when the working day is done. It's where families live and (try to) play in a nice wholesome, neo-WASPy, family-values state of domestic bliss. Or at least, that's the sales pitch.

> In other words, it's the kind of place that makes most runners (or anyone with the capability for independent thought) want to puke. Renton is so damn artificial and bland that it hurts!
> Slamm-0!

For decades, Renton was the home of several security services and small tech firms; the latter were hit hard after Crash 2.0, while the former got even bigger. In the following years, the local economy foundered and crime rose. In the past two years, however, the new Matrix has helped reinvigorate Renton's tech industry, and the district has been slowly returning to its former perceived glory.

Renton has an abundance of nice housing along with enough shopping and entertainment to keep residents satisfied. Throw in some green hills, lakes, and rivers for good measure, and it's little wonder why so many people want to live here. Too bad it has an undercurrent of anti-metahuman racism just below that wonderful middle-class façade, along with a few nasty local criminal elements.

Ever since the Night of Rage, Renton has been a Humanis stronghold, even though no one will admit it. Because of a combination of (slightly) shifting societal norms and increasing metahuman birth rates (especially among orks), hardliner racists and bigots in Renton have been forced to impotently watch as "metahuman encroachment" threatened their idea of domestic tranquility. But that just means they switched tactics.

> As much as I still hate Renton, I have to be honest for the sake of accuracy. Things aren't as bad as they used to be even a decade ago. Metahumans can walk the streets of Renton without too much fear of being assaulted on sight, because anti-metahumanism is seriously frowned upon—at least openly. Metahumans who live in Renton can expect more subtle attacks against them, however. Poor service at some shops/eateries/public services, being stopped in the street for no reason other than just being an ork, receiving less leniency by KE patrols, or just being silently shunned by the locals are just some of the public things metahuman residents of Renton can expect. Behind closed doors, it's worse.
> Bull

RENTON TAGS

• Homes for suits • Humanis stronghold • Knight Errant training academy • Meredith's Comfy Cubicle • Neighborhood Watch
• Seattle's apartment • Wanda's Witchery

AUBURN

The first thing people talk about when they get close to Auburn is the hum. The sound, like the famous Taos hum, seems to come from everywhere at once; a low-frequency buzz that can only be the result of 363 square kilometers of industrial equipment churning twenty-four hours a day. The people who live here put up with it, because that is who they are—survivors. They are the blue-collar wageslaves who keep the gears of Seattle spinning. This mentality results in a community that is extremely insular, preferring to take care of its own problems. Those problems are plentiful, including a budding race war and a Mafia family trying desperately to hold on to its claim.

On the bright side, real-estate prices here are excellent, which is why a handful of tech start-ups chose to make Auburn the new Silicon Valley. New capital and new attitudes have not gone well with the locals, leading to a cultural separation that mirrors the age-old separation of haves and have-nots.

> With all of the automated manufacturing, Auburn is the easiest place to acquire cheap gear and services, but the community isn't big on outsiders. You need to know someone in order to get anywhere in Auburn, so get real good at making friends and keeping them.
> Pistons

AUBURN TAGS

• Boeing Days • Ciarnello mob • Green River Arcology
• Stuck's Carnival • Supermall • Ultra Resort
• Wyneco Correctional Ultra-max ("The Hole")

SNOHOMISH

When most folks think of Seattle, they think of the hustle and bustle of the Emerald City, so the quiet country of Snohomish comes as quite a disquieting surprise. It's an old-fashioned community that managed to hold together when most of the changes occurred in Seattle after the Great Ghost Dance. Before and after that event, it has been the main source of locally grown produce for all of Seattle. Many have called it the Breadbasket of the Emerald City for its expansive wheat fields, but I don't want that to be the only image people have. Snohomish has wheat, corn, and soy fields in abundance, but it also has hundreds of apple orchards, berry farms of every variety, potato farms that rival the Idaho of old, and large greenhouses that grow everything from peaches to coffee, both out of season and out of their normal region.

Along with all this food production, the rest of what you would expect from agribusinesses came along for the ride. Underground growth testing sites; river pens full of modified salmon and seaweed; and massive soy processing plants to turn those bland little beans into delicious dishes and pastes. The megacorps have research and development work going on all over this region to develop better crops. And by "better" I mean producing more money for them, not healthier or anything crazy like that.

Beyond farms and fish, Snohomish is well-known for its antiques and has been for over a hundred years. The difference is, a hundred years ago the odds of an antique possessing accessible arcane potential were non-existent. Now, those looking for those rare items that have been infused with mana from powerful emotional events or pre-Awakening ritual magic often find them here. During the recent rush to find arcane artifacts, Snohomish became a popular location for folks to trade and make their deals, since it already had a reputation for arcane antiquities. Several individuals in this area have made names for themselves in the field of artifact identification and classification, making it a popular spot for artifacts to pass through or spend some time while these folks dig up their mysteries.

- What a pleasant view! Too bad that's not even close to the most shadowy aspect of Snohomish. While food and antiques may be big business, and thus important to runners, it's the corporate safehouses that bring most runners to this quiet district. The run-down farms, abandoned homes, and a few small mountain cabins on the outskirts are used by companies, governments, and shadowy organizations to lie low or stash important assets while the heat dies down.
- Traveler Jones

- The rare and lucky runner might get some training time at one of the several corporate black-ops training sites in Snohomish as well. Several corps that have safehouses here also have training grounds. The trainees are sometimes used as first responders (or only responders when they want it kept quiet). The sites are usually located on former farms where the ground can't sustain crops anymore.
- Hard Exit

- Can't finish this part up without mentioning that Snohomish is the most racist district in the 'plex. It's a regular spot for Humanis recruitment, and they're rumored to have a training facility for members of the militant arm of the Human Nation, the Flaming Sword. Metahumans are regularly assaulted, and murder investigations tend to be short and usually blamed on other metahumans.
- 2XL

SNOHOMISH TAGS

- Agribusiness • Blackstone's Museum and Zoo of the Paranatural • Coliseum cagefighting • Humanis Policlub
- Increased gang activity • Longest Night festival
- Quiet Death • Seattle's breadbasket • Thunderhorse Ranch

FORT LEWIS

Do you know what Fort Lewis is? Fort Lewis is your chance to look at a totally different dystopia than the one we have. Sick and tired of living in a corporate-controlled dystopia? Then head on down to Fort Lewis for a chance to look at an authoritarian military dystopia! Vive la différence!

One advantage of the military dystopia? It's cleaner. The military puts up with far less crap than Knight Errant cops tolerate, and soldiers in general are pretty good at keeping the place neat and not throwing garbage around.

- Cleanliness and order have always been some of the hallmarks of an authoritarian regime. It's part of their appeal—whatever their faults, they can at least keep things orderly.
- Goat Foot

It also is a lot prettier than most parts of Seattle, with its lush greenery and relative quiet. Honestly, it's downright eerie—go there some morning, when the fog is brushing the pines, and listed to the muffled quiet. A bird will chirp here and there, and then fly away as another sound slowly rises. You'll hear it before you see it, the sound of boots hitting the ground in unison as some patrol or another passes nearby. Freaks me out every time. And it's even worse in the evening, when they play "Taps."

- Man, do you ever have some weird problem with the army. It's pretty clear you never served.
- Hard Exit

Now, don't let me give you the wrong impression. Fort Lewis has a seedy side—it just does a lot better job than other places of keeping the criminality and debauchery behind closed doors. The place is populated with people, after all, and people are going to pursue their vices. It's what we do. The leaders of Fort Lewis would just rather such activities be kept in their proper place, out of the sight of children and the faint of heart.

And then, because nothing in the Sixth World is complete without a touch of the surreal, in the middle of this military state in miniature is one of the most popular family destinations in the sprawl, the Fort Lewis Zoological Gardens, with some of the most spectacular critters to be held in captivity on display in stunning replicas of their natural habitats. Of course, behind the scenes of the zoo, researchers are looking into how to tap into, alter, or even enhance the powers of the critters kept there, which means the friendliest part of Fort Lewis is also the one with perhaps the best odds of killing us all.

- Some of that depends on how much the military decides to share with others. Any general knows the value of having technology that the other side lacks, so any breakthroughs in critter-related research, especially when it comes to critter-based security, are likely to be kept under wraps instead of disseminated far and wide.
- Kay St. Irregular

- Yeah, so they won't sell their secrets, they'll just invent something so powerful that they'll lose control, break out, and start killing us in our sleep.
- Traveler Jones

FORT LEWIS TAGS

- The Drunken Non-Com • Fort Lewis Zoological Gardens
- Military base • Military Intelligence Brigade
- Parkland Mall • Urban Combat Simulator

REDMOND

If you've never lived in Redmond, you don't know Redmond. Wageslaves on day trips or rich thrill-seekers on weekend benders can never know what it's like here. Neither can runners who happen to have a safehouse here just to lie low for a while. Yeah, they see the same drek. They smell the same filth. The difference is, they get to leave. For those of us who were born into it and don't know anything else, it's not that easy to escape.

But sooner or later, every shadowrunner finds themselves in Redmond, where Seattle dreams come to die. Nothing thrives here. It's infertile. Unproductive. Toxic. That's why they call 'em Barrens. Once upon a time, Redmond was shiny. It was Seattle's new tech district, full of innovators and their money. But now, Redmond is like a perverse dreamcatcher, capturing and distilling the nightmares of the entire Seattle sprawl. After the tech crash of '29, Redmond lost everything. Eighty percent of its industry tanked overnight, along with its government. Everyone with means bolted. With no authorities to stop them, those who were left behind turned to rioting, looting, and every other form of lawlessness. Metahuman nature, chummers. The abandoned businesses and homes were irresistible to the addicted, destitute, and criminal from all over the sprawl, so while the rest of Seattle was getting cleaned up, Redmond was collecting society's detritus.

Even the "safe" areas of Redmond are more socially diseased than the worst parts of Seattle proper. Redmond is broken up into fiefdoms, separated by wastelands of decaying technology. Tribes of gangs, acting like warlords, each control their own slice of hell. What used to be high-density areas became the most sought-after real estate. The corp buildings and assets that remain are fortified with strong walls and heavy artillery. Most of the time, mercs or local gangers play security. Utilities like water, trash, sewage, and electricity don't function; anyone with those luxuries has jury-rigged their place to get them.

- The Matrix used to be nearly impossible to access in Redmond, but the new Matrix infrastructure has improved things a bit. Describing it as "spotty" is still generous, though.
- Slamm-0!

- You said it. The astral in the Barrens is fragged up pretty bad, too. Unless you have been raised there, slinging spells feels like swimming in jelly.
- Lyran

Astonishingly, Redmond has a government. Sonya Scholl is the mayor of Redmond. She's usually fighting with the corps here, but she's managed to choose her battles wisely. And she's won some (it helps that the corps don't care enough about Redmond to put their full heart into the fight). Unfortunately, no amount of winning can make any real difference here.

- Sounds downbeat, but it's accurate. If the Barrens gets anything—a new business that's making money, a runner who made a big score—the first thought is to get out. In Redmond, success is defined by leaving.
- Haze

- Nothing gold can stay.
- Man-of-Many-Names

Hope is the rarest thing in Redmond, and that's good, because hope gets you killed. Makes you think about tomorrow. Distracts you from surviving right now. And that's all that's left in the Barrens—survival.

REDMOND TAGS

- Barrens • Body Mall • Crimson Crush • Glow City
- No security • Plastic Jungle • Urubia's Funhouse

PUYALLUP

"Barrens," they say, lumping us all together. Redmond, too, like we're next-door neighbors, not sixty kilometers apart. Here in Puyallup, we're used to getting written off by outsiders. They figure we're just ashy gutters, Mafiosi and Yakuza thugs tearing each other apart, beetle dens and whorehouses competing for desperate nuyen, elves and orks killing each other over table scraps and corner deals.

We are all those things, but those things ain't all we are.

People friggin' live here, chummer. Always have, and always will. A hundred years ago this was farmland,

wide-open spaces, blue skies, and green hills. Then came Rainier and refugees, ash and assholes, the Night of Rage and Tír Tairngire's leftovers. After that, we layered on a couple generations of corrupt politicians and parasitic crime families sucking the place dry. Sprinkle with desperation. Add a pinch of hatred. Season to taste.

So we ain't like Downtown, sure, but people are still just people. Over half a million souls—just by official count—are trying to get by, wanting to live their life, put a roof overhead, fill their belly, have some kids.

If the corps would give us half a chance, just a fair shake, they could make some real money here. We've got space. We've got nothing but room for improvement, we've got people with nothing but hunger for a better tomorrow. They could build here, instead of always being teases about it. They could invest, and we could work, buy, sell. Everyone would win.

But that ain't what Puyallup's for, if you ask our neighbors. Nope. They come here to hide from the law, to buy drugs or chips, to rent joyboys or cred-slots, to bash some keeblers. They come here in tricked-out racers to compete, or souped-up rigs about to make the Route 7 smuggling run. They come here to slum it, to get a kick out of some real streets if Bellevue or Downtown are too safe for their liking.

Someone once said you don't pay a hooker for the sex, you pay 'em to leave you alone afterwards. To our neighbors, Puyallup's that working girl. They come here so they can leave again, and feel better about themselves for doing so.

PUYALLUP TAGS

- Ancients • Barrens • Bump and Sleep • Crime Mall
- Don Gianelli • No security • Tarislar • Yakuza

COUNCIL ISLAND

In the nineteenth and twentieth centuries, Council Island was known as Mercer Island, named for brothers Asa and Thomas Mercer who were the first white men to call it home. It grew into a thriving community, joining Seattle in 1960. With the signing of the First Treaty of Denver, the greater Seattle metroplex was retained as American territory, serving as the largest non-native reservation in North America, while Mercer Island was ceded to the Salish-Shidhe Council to serve as an ambassadorial residence and a general touchstone with other native nations. The Salish razed the modern buildings and stripped the roadways, spending over a decade restoring the land to a natural state while embedding power, water, and Matrix nodes well out of sight. Under the leadership of first Chief Jon Moses, then Chief James Grey Bear, the Salish ambassador to Seattle for decades, Council Island was turned into one of the prettiest areas of Seattle while also serving in a diplomatic capacity. The death of Grey Bear just before the negotiations for the third Treaty of Denver was devastating, as his seasoned experience as a negotiator was missed and talks eventually collapsed. As Denver has retreated, Council Island has stepped up, and now stands as the primary ambassadorial region for the NAN. The island is still adapting to this new status, and new buildings are springing up rapidly.

- Council Island's groaning under the weight of the Salish-Shidhe Battalion that was assigned there in the wake of the collapse of the Third Treaty of Denver negotiations. On top of this they have the expanded NAN-corp presence on the island, but it's the soldiers who have really done a number on the demographics, particularly in terms of bringing down the average of pay and education. Three quarters of the troopers are orks, with more than five hundred being drawn from the Cascade Ork tribe, where you can enlist as young as sixteen and without a high school diploma. With soldiers come higher levels of carousing and prostitution.
- SeaTac Sweetie

- The SS-Council has never been clear about that "other" population of about a hundred and fifty sentients. Do they count spirits in this number or not? Artificial intelligences? We know that there are shapeshifters and wendigo in the mix, but what else? Rumors are that there are intelligent fresh-water merrow present, or even a draco-forms. The only ones who know for certain are the Salish-Shidhe, and they aren't telling.
- Elijah

Council Island is left in a natural state—or more accurately is guided into a natural-seeming state—as much as possible. Greenery is ever-present, most obviously in tree coverage and shrubbery, but in the spring and summer months, there's a colorful explosion from the widespread flowers in bloom. Buildings are constructed to resemble the traditional dwellings of the Pacific Northwest Natives but are made of modern materials with a thin wooden veneer, rather than being actual wooden structures. It should be reminded that, all across the island, this theme will be seen repeatedly; citizens in native garb who're using cutting-edge NeoNET commlinks, wireless support is drawn from unseen points hidden in artwork or fountains, and while you'll never see a hint of modern wiring strung through trees, the roots share the ground with an impressive array of circuitry and pipes. The NAN are quite proud of their technical adaptability but always give a nod to tradition, and if you think of them as primitive due to their wearing of facepaint and feathers, the failure's on you, not them. The majority of the population is composed of bureaucrats, diplomats, and their families, but there are quite a few scientists around as well, including botanists and parabiologists.

- We Seattleites can forget this often, thanks to the NAN tourism boards always pushing for "NearCations" in Salish territory, and we all know somebody who was broken by the rat race, sold everything they owned, and joined an ersatz "tribe" to get back to nature. The vast majority of NAN citizens live in cities (former American cities at that!), drive cars, grumble about taxes, and check the news on their commlink, all before getting ready for today's meeting about the Running Deer account. There's a bit more environmentalism and the spiritual beliefs are different, but otherwise, they function in the city and share the same concerns, with same range of beliefs, as everyone else.
- Bull

- There are also those who fully walk the Old Path, but it is a choice that must be made, not an obligation to force upon another. It is a harder path, one fraught with danger, but what you see while walking it is glorious.
- Man-of-Many-Names

- While NAN drones and choppers can fly around, Council Island is officially NAN airspace and they are quite antsy about defending that airspace. If you aren't in a medivac chopper or on a pre-cleared diplomatic visit, expect spirits to land you gently in the lake.
- Kane

COUNCIL ISLAND TAGS

- Grand Council Lodge • Indigenous culture
- Nature preserve • Salish-Shidhe Territory
- Tight security • Totem Tower

THE UNDERGROUND

The Ork Underground has roots dating back to Seattle's ancient history. After the Great Seattle Fire of 1889, they decreed that new buildings must be made of fire-resistant material rather than wood. Since the city was built on a floodplain, which often, you know, flooded, they decided to lift everything by two stories as well. The lower levels of older buildings were used mostly for storage, and eventually they were just sealed off and ignored. In the late twentieth century, there was some interest in exploring them again, revealing that in the years between the undercity had been expanded by bootleggers and red-light workers, then expanded again by the city for underground transit. Some areas were refurbished and cleaned up for tourism, while most were left untouched.

- The underground was initially sealed off due to fear of disease back in 1907.
- Nephrine

When Mt. Rainier shook Seattle in 2017, the Underground was closed off again for fear of collapse and poison gas pockets (poison is far more dangerous than lava in an eruption, but lava gets all the airtime). Desperate people gradually opened small pathways down below, first the homeless, then the goblinized, as society turned a blind eye. "Out of sight, out of mind," after all. In 2039, Governor Victor Allenson rounded up every metahuman in Seattle and concentrated them into camps in the warehouse districts of Tacoma and downtown. On February 7, those warehouses all went up in flame. Thankfully, the goblins down below had already opened some passages for smuggling supplies up; those passages were then used to get thousands of people to safety. Not everyone, but a great many. If you ever wonder who's getting burned in effigy during the Night of Rage remembrances, it's Allenson.

- Rotting in Hell's too good for him.
- Butch

The city woke up from the madness and most of the metahumans were brought back into society, but many couldn't overcome the betrayal. They stayed below. Goblins and dwarfs worked together to expand the underground tunnels, shore them up, and establish places both large enough for a community to thrive and small enough to provide hiding places should they ever be needed again. They further discovered many tunnels created in the aftermath of the volcanic eruptions; science can't explain how they came to be, but to the creators of the underground, they were a blessing no matter the source.

- Obviously magical. Similar tunnels have been found all over the world. We don't know why or how they're created, but we're certain about the source.
- Ethernaut

- Alright Plan 9, let's have it. Secret dragon conspiracy? Bug spirits? Immortal dwarfs?
- Snopes

- No, just reverberations along mana lines, freshly awoken earth spirits checking out the surrounding area, and good ol' fashioned seismic activity.
- Plan 9

- I'm so confused.
- Sunshine

In the mid '40s, there was a big falling out between the ork and dwarf communities. There'd been many arguments in the past, but the trolls had always managed to keep the peace, but this time? It was too much. The dwarfs, who'd had the majority of engineering lore and college education, gathered up for a mass exodus, turning the Seattle Underground into the Ork Underground. Details are sketchy about what caused it, but the dwarfs have carried a grudge about it ever since.

Which brings us to today. The Seattle Underground, re-branded now that it's official, is the hottest property in the 'plex. Young artists and risk-taking investors are flocking to the area, marveling at the low cost of living and thriving local culture. Gentrification is a growing concern, but with it comes a massive overhaul of city services, with legitimate power and water lines instead of spotty, and illegal, taps. There was also work to improve schools, and Renraku will soon break ground on the first hospital in the Underground's history. Sanitation, police protection, and badly needed nuyen are flooding in.

- And orks are flooding out.
- OrkCEO

- When Prop 23 passed, making the Ork Underground an official city region, the dwarfs who'd left thirty years ago started streaming back, bringing with them documentation about ownership, hiring Hard Corps to toss hundreds of orks out of their homes. Women, children, families—it didn't matter. Gimli Harris (third-oldest dwarf in Seattle—there are lots of first-generation names like that) is the angry face of the "Reclaimers," driving a wedge through the heart of the Underground. They claim original ownership of great swaths of land, using strong-arm tactics to drive out the locals and establish settlements along prime territory. They claim it's about heritage. The orks claim it's hate.
- Sunshine

- Despite what you'll see in corporate media, most orks down there are ordinary people, working two or three jobs, trying to raise money to raise a family in peace. They're as worried about gang activity and crime as anyone else, but the dwarf incursion is agitating extremists to activity.
- Butch

- Of course, these counterattacks are recorded and rebroadcast by the media, who are all too happy to paint orks as violent brutes and savages. It keeps escalating and won't end well.
- 2XL

- The Underground's always been poor. Who's paying for this massive level of reconstruction? Renraku has to be taking a huge loss on this one.
- Riot

- Nope! Now that the city's made it official, Renraku's being paid while the city runs up the debt. Brackhaven'll be handing a giant pot of crap to any successor, and the budget crisis is being placed on the "uppity orks" rather than the corporation that's "just doing what it was hired to do." Telling you, those guys are artists.
- Haze

ORK UNDERGROUND TAGS

- The Big Rhino entrance • Dwarf incursion
- Lordstrung's entrance • Newest district • Orks and trolls
- Outlaw hideout • Skraacha • Smuggling • Tourist Highway

HAPPENING WORLD

This chapter contains thirty Contract Briefs, plotlines for games you can play. With the information in these briefs and the characters in the **Street People** chapter, you can quickly get a game going. Since there are some plot twists and other such info, we'll provide the following disclaimer:

IT'S PROBABLY BEST IF ONLY
GAMEMASTERS READ THIS CHAPTER.

Sorry, players. We love you, and we hope the rest of the book offers lots of fun for you, but the fun might be maximized if you keep yourself from knowing some of the material in this chapter.

So, gamemasters, now that we're down to just you, let's talk about what's here. The plot structures of the Contract Briefs are generally loose, often leaving room for the players to add their own twists and developments. Sometimes this means the ending is not set in stone; other times there are secrets that the gamemaster may eventually reveal, though the way the secrets come out may or may not follow the exact pattern outlined in the adventure.

The point is, the Contract Briefs are structures players and gamemasters can use to build games and plots from, but they should not be viewed as iron-clad gospel.

They are tools to get the story moving and to provide interesting story twists, but not strict outlines you must follow in order to avoid playing the game wrong.

Most of the Briefs in this chapter are a single page, and likely would take a single gaming session to cover (though given the creativity of shadowrunners, some of them may well go for multiple sessions). Toward the end of the chapter are Briefs with multiple parts to them, so that they form longer campaigns. Beyond these Briefs, some free-standing Briefs can be linked together to create campaigns as well. For example, the Bear spirit totem of **Onto the Path** (p. 158) might introduce the players to the fire spirit of **The Light Within** (p. 166), who, after that contract is over, might decide he wants the Fairy Flag to help him in his work with his cult, which leads players to **Let Your Flag Fly** (p. 160). The point is, whether you want standalone missions or longer campaigns, the tools are here to make them!

Note that each *Mr. Johnson's Pitch* contains the Karma payment offered by Mr. Johnson, stated as an amount of karma each player would receive. Players can always attempt a negotiation, and the payment can be adjusted by the gamemaster based on extenuating circumstances (like maybe they're doing a job because they owe Mr. Johnson a favor from a previous job, and thus they should be taking less pay). Generally speaking, though, payment should not dip lower than 3 Karma, and should not be negotiated to higher than 9.

BE CAREFUL WHAT YOU SEARCH FOR

MR. JOHNSON'S PITCH

The runners are hired by Jody Stubblefield, a high-level data analyst at Hildebrandt-Kleinfort-Bernal, one of the largest banks in the world. He's made a discovery that has placed his life in great danger. Strange things have been happening to him lately. He says he is being followed, that someone's been going through his garbage, and his family is getting strange calls. Jody needs to get to a safe location and be kept from harm until he can sell what he has. If he is kept safe, the PCs receive 4 Karma, with a 2 Karma bonus for keeping Stubblefield's data safe.

OBJECTIVES

- Help Stubblefield retrieve data from his apartment
- Get Stubblefield to a safehouse
- Repel gang attack

TAGS

- Dwarfs • Protection • Gang • Safehouse
- Conspiracy • Data

THE SETTING

The job starts in a pretty typical slice of Renton. The low-rent neighborhood all around is poor and a bit dangerous, but not controlled by the local gangs … yet. The Stuffer Shack down the block is the only source of food for a few kilometers, but even that monument to greed-by-way-of-junk-food looks pretty battered and neglected.

THE PLOT

SCENE 1

Suggested NPCs: Elite soldiers, Enemy Drones (Small)

Jody tells the runners that before they head to a safehouse, he needs to grab something from his apartment. He left a copy of his research data there and needs to destroy it so no one else can get to it first. Jody is paranoid, but the runners see no evidence of anyone out to get him.

After looking around for a bit, Jody becomes erratic. He can't find the other copy. As Jody continues to franticly look around for the data, a dwarf strike team ambushes the runners inside the house. These are not typical corporate security or even military. The dwarfs

seem to be an elite-ops group, although the only distinguishing feature is a small, almost unnoticeable (have the runners make a Perception test of Very Hard difficulty) patch on their sleeves which reads: "Zhigul M."

SCENE 2

Suggested NPCs: None

Jody's data is found after the fight, possibly on the body of one of the dwarf strike team members. Jody begs the runners to get him to the security of the safehouse, and on the way, he begins to ramble. Jody insists that while analyzing and archiving physical bank information from before the Matrix Crash of 2029, he came across a pattern of deposits and withdrawals that seemed curious.

Stubblefield claims to have found similar bank discrepancies from all over the globe, but much of the data had been tampered with. When he analyzed the net effect these discrepancies had on the global economy, it seemed twenty billion nuyen could not be accounted for. Digging deeper, he found the companies that were responsible for the discrepancies no longer exist, and the people supposedly serving as officers and board members can't be found on any records after 2029.

SCENE 3

Suggested NPCs: Gangers

While there may be digressions along the way, eventually the runners should get Jody to a safehouse. Once there, Jody's commlink rings and he shouts that he has a buyer for his data. Outside, a local gang has descended upon the safehouse. The gangers aren't tough, but there are a lot of them. This can be a bruising combat because of the sheer number of gangers, but at some point Jody interrupts it by yelling out that he has the money. The gangers' leader glances at a freshly received message and then orders a retreat. The gangers disperse and run back to their hovels.

Jody pays the runners and mentions that he has more work for them if they want it.

EPILOGUE

As the story unfolds, the players and GM might have developed some of the secrets about where the money went and who received it. Stubblefield certainly would like to pursue these leads (and perhaps gain a chunk of the missing money), so he can be the nudge the team needs to keep looking for answers. If no answers come up, have some of the money trail leading to shell companies around Biloxi, Mississippi, where an impressive new dwarf-owned tech university has recently opened.

BLACK STAR RISING

CONTEXT

Background: Black Star was a group of neo-anarchist shadowrunners. Over time, Black Star became militant and joined Amazonia in a war against Aztlan. The war took a huge toll on the group, and at this point only one member remains alive—a runner named Liberator.

MR. JOHNSON'S PITCH

The runners grab their gear and head to an abandoned airstrip. They're met by a winsome female elf and offered a job to board a plane immediately for Bogota, on the border of Aztlan and Amazonia. They'll help Mrs. Johnson liberate a weapons cache belonging to old friends of hers. If the runners accept the job, their new employer introduces herself as Rose Red (see p. 116). She offers 5 Karma for the runners' help.

OBJECTIVES

- Smuggle themselves into Zona Norte in Bogota
- Find the weapons cache
- Receive payment, survive counter terrorist forces

TAGS
- Neo-Anarchists • Bogota • Black Star • Aztlan
- Weapons Cache

THE SETTING

Bogotá is a city of extremes. High rises border shanty-towns while colonial churches face theaters, universities and cantinas. Spanish and Aztlaner culture commingle with abject poverty and untold wealth surrounded by the stench of destruction and conflict.

THE PLOT

SCENE 1

Suggested NPCs: Insurgents (use Gangers),

Security Guards (use Rent-a-cops), Enemy Drones (Small)

The plane lands outside of Bogota. Rose Red tells the runners that their destination is the Zona Norte section of the city. Aztlan remains vigilant against insurgent groups, so security is tight. To get in, the runners can get smuggled in, acquire fake SINs and talk smooth, use bribery, or figure out whatever their creative minds can develop.

SCENE 2

Suggested NPCs: Outpost drunks (use Gangers)

Once inside, Rose Red says a runner named Liberator was the last person to see the cache. Whether the runners use violence, persuasion, or bribes, someone in Zona Norte will point them to a bar called the Outpost, saying that Liberator has been known to hang out there. At the bar, the runners can gain information on Liberator's current whereabouts—namely, holed up in a nearby hotel.

SCENE 3

Suggested NPCs: None

The runners find the small hotel on the outskirts of Zona Norte. No one answers the door to Liberator's room; when the runners enter, they find him bleeding in a corner from multiple stab wounds. Seeing Rose Red, he smiles and relaxes. He tells her he thought he was the last of Black Star. Rose tells him, "there are still plenty of us out there; we just didn't want any part of a war." He smiles and says, "Me neither," and breathes his last. (Don't force this death. If the players try hard to save him, that is okay.)

After composing herself, Rose Red lifts the carpet to reveal a cellar full of weapons, armor, and intelligence. Satisfied, she pays the runners and says she'll stay with the cache, but the plane should be waiting for them.

FUTURE HOOKS

If the runners were professional, and not overly violent, Rose will extend an offer to join the renewed Black Star, a group of neo-anarchists-for-hire, with less of a terrorist orientation and more of a focus on helping people.

SCENE 4

Suggested NPCs: Aztlaner Counter-insurgent Soldiers

(use Elite Soldiers), Enemy Drones (Medium)

As the runners make their way to the plane, they find an Aztlan counter-terrorist group was tipped off to their presence. In order to leave Bogota, they will have to fight their way past the soldiers and onto the plane.

FOOD FIGHT

THERE'S NO MR. JOHNSON

Food Fight is meant to be a quick, combat-heavy, whirl-wind that you throw the players into as an introductory adventure (to test out new characters or *Anarchy* conversions), or that you add to an existing *Shadowrun*, hitting them when their armor is chewed up, they're beat down, and they're least expecting it.

OBJECTIVES

- Relax for once (just kidding!)
- Role-play and look into what everyone's favorite snacks say about them.
- Survive the robbery, and try not to spill your tasty beverage.

TAGS

- Stuffer Shack • Late Night Snacks • Robbery • Ultraviolence

THE SETTING

Stuffer Shack is a Sixth World classic, a temple to consumerism, garbage food being cheaper than anything healthy or fresh, and sugar as the true opiate of the masses. What's not to love?! With a bay of old-style arcade machines on one wall, a dizzying array of half-frozen drinks to dispense, and a plethora of salty, sweet, and soy products for consumers to kill themselves with, it's a fantastic late-night destination for the hungry runner on the go. Whether players go for a Nuke-a-Wave burrito like mom used to make, a Frozee-Treet slurry, or a CHOCO-PUNCH snack, have fun making up and describing a ridiculous assortment of over-processed garbage food.

THE PLOT

SCENE 1

Suggested NPCS: Use six Gangers with colorful names if you want to keep things simpler and easier. For a tougher fight, modify a few archetypes and jump in: Catcher (gang leader and instigator of the robbery, stats as Wagon, p. 130, minus the medical skills), Slicer Dicer (a wannabe samurai desperate for a duel, stats as Borderline, p. 88, minus ranged weapons), Wendy (a thrill-ganger psyscho gal and bad influence on Wylie, stats as Kix, p. 102), Static (a big cybered-up burnout, stats as Sledge, p. 82, with only a pistol), Wylie (a teen-aged shaman with a boyish crush on Wendy, stats as Coydog, p. 74), and Spike (the scared rookie, stats as a generic Ganger, who can maybe be talked down).

Wreck the consumer-idyllic scene with a spray of autofire, and a psycho screaming that this is a robbery. Simple criminals in the late 2070s don't have much cash they can demand (though they'll gladly take any corporate scrip from cowed shoppers), but they're eager to take physical goods (commlinks, jewelry, or even firearms) or to try to threaten Stuffer Shack patrons into initiating a nuyen transfer. Catcher and his Chiller Thrillers are in it for the fun of the slaughter; too much partying, too many fried brains, too little conscience to go around.

Don't forget to make the fight messy as the shelves of foodstuff absorb any shots fired, or as close combat attacks throw people into them. For some inspiration, roll 1D6 to consult the Food Fight chart, then a second 1D6 to get more details in just what kind of mess is made

AFTERMATH

The owners of this Stuffer Shack will effusively praise the runners for their help, wipe the security cameras if the team wishes to remain anonymous, and will hurry each of them away—before security responds—with a cart full of whatever they want, free of charge. Handling the laundry and bathing needed might require a real fixer, though!

FOOD FIGHT TABLE (ROLL 1D6)

1-2: LIQUID, ROLL 1D6	3-4: POWDER, ROLL 1D6	5-6: MUSH, ROLL 1D6
1) green and gooey	1) fine and blue	1) gross and soft
2) red and syrupy	2) thick and green	2) spongy and soft
3) clear and smelly	3) powdery and red	3) lots o' pieces
4) black and sticky	4) lumpy and white	4) gross and smelly
5) pink and gross	5) sudsy and blue	5) hard little chunks
6) roll twice	6) roll twice	6) roll twice

DON'T KNOW MUCH ABOUT ARCOLOGY

CONTEXT

Word Watch: Arcology n. Architectural Ecology. Massive building that houses a self-sustaining, densely populated habitat with no need for import or export.

A.C.H.E. n. Arcology Commercial and Housing Enclave. Ninth largest building in the world. Formerly the Renraku Arcology.

BACKGROUND

In 2059, a rogue artificial intelligence shut down the arcology and subjected those within to nightmarish conditions. Seattle stripped the Arcology from Renraku and turned the lower five floors into a shopping mall. Two hundred floors above are sealed off to house Seattle's welfare recipients, often involuntarily. The arcology's highest floors remain a mystery.

MR. JOHNSON'S PITCH

"My employer, Shiawase Corporation, has made a bid to purchase the ACHE. As a show of good faith, they have offered to provide a containment unit around it, to facilitate renovation without danger to the community. This dome prevents communication in or out, and has a contained EMP to shut down any cybernetic threats.

"My employer wants to take inventory of the arcology and its systems before work begins. Unfortunately, the UCAS government occupies the underground levels, where the nuclear reactors are located.

"You will break into the lowest levels, get past the UCAS soldiers, and install a program code onto the nuclear reactor network. The program will diagnose and record relevant info for twenty-four hours. When finished, collect the data and get out."

If the runners deliver the data to Mr. Johnson, they are promised payment of 6 Karma.

OBJECTIVES

- Break into the ACHE. Gain access to basement.
- Install program code onto nuclear reactor network.
- Collect data and escape.

TAGS

- Seattle • Arcology • Shiawase • Technology
- UCAS Soldiers • Artificial Intelligence?

THE SETTING

The mall's temporarily closed. It's eerily quiet and the runners can't help but feel dread as they head through the giant, empty hallways. A specter of hidden threats and mechanized terror still lingers here. Although nothing accosts them, they should feel like something will at any moment. An empty mall provides a number of opportunities for weirdness; help the players explore them!

THE PLOT

SCENE 1

Suggested NPCs: Rent-a-cops

Entering into the ACHE should be fairly easy. The mall area has been emptied and foundations for the dome have started. Getting past the construction workers and rental cops should be easy. Once in, they need to find the elevators to the lower floors.

SCENE 2

Suggested NPCs: Rent-a-cops,

Enemy Drones (Small), IC, Black IC (treat as IC, p. 179, with

Biofeedback program)

On the lower floors, UCAS soldiers are extremely hostile to anyone who isn't expected. Runners should use stealth to avoid setting off alarms. If the runners use stealth, it should be fairly easy to slip into the control room unnoticed. Allow the decker (if the team has one) to describe the scene inside the arcology's host and introduce IC for extra challenge.

SCENE 3

Suggested NPCs: Soldiers, Enemy Drones (Medium)

Once the program finishes, an arcology-wide alarm sounds. The UCAS soldiers are on high alert, and guards now block the exits. To add to the confusion, a few hundred of Seattle's poorest try to escape from the housing floors when the alarm sounds. On top of that, building systems begin operating in weird and unpredictable ways. By the time they escape, the runners should feel lucky and grateful to be out of the building.

ONTO THE PATH

CONTEXT

Word Watch: Mentor spirit n. Mysterious spirits that help Awakened individuals find and stay on a particular path. The nature of mentor spirits remain unclear, but whether they are active in an Awakened individual's life or passive, their influence cannot be denied. Also known as totems.

Note: The mentor spirit Bear is used here, but with minor tweaks, any other mentor spirit/totem can be used. This contract is broken into three parts, with three separate runs.

BEFORE THE PITCH

The night before the run, the mage/shaman/adept of the group is startled by a deafening roar. As they work to figure out what's going on, they come face-to-face with an impossibly large bear. The runner is unable to move as the gargantuan brown form speaks with an inhuman voice. It says the runner has been chosen to be the representative of Bear, if they are worthy. Once it finishes speaking, it opens its mouth and swallows the runner whole.

When the runner awakens for real, it is dawn, and a message on their commlink tells them to meet Mr. Johnson with the rest of the group.

MR. JOHNSON'S PITCH

Mr. Johnson hires the runners for a simple smash and grab. He represents a local jewelry store that wants its competition crippled. The runners are hired to break into Diamond Lux Jewelry and steal as much as possible. For this simple job, the runners are offered 3 Karma.

OBJECTIVES

> Smash and grab Diamond Lux Jewelry
> Escape the police
> Grab Bear's amulet

TAGS

• Spirits • Smash and Grab • Mentor Spirit
• Difficult Decision • Magic • New Contact

THE PLOT

SCENE 1

Suggested NPCs: Rent-a-cops (lots of Rent-a-cops)

Everything at Diamond Lux Jewelry should go smoothly at first. No alarms have sounded and the runners are making good time grabbing jewelry. About halfway into the grab, however, a random Knight Errant patrol spots them and calls for backup. By the time the runners notice, Knight Errant cops have them surrounded. The runners can fight or not, but at the most desperate moment, the runner who had the vision will have another. Bear appears and offers help if the runner accepts Bear as their mentor. If they accept, Bear will aid the runners, either by creating a diversion, or by having an actual Bear come from nowhere and maul some of the opposition. If Bear is not accepted, he leaves them on their own.

SCENE 2

Suggested NPCs: Rent-a-cops, Shadow Spirit
(use Greater Spirit of Man)

Weeks later, Bear appears to the PC again, asking that the runner retrieve an ancient amulet uncovered on an archeological dig. It resides in a museum acquisitions department. Security is light, but only if the runners are stealthy. When they arrive where the bear-shaped amulet is supposed to be, they find it in the possession of a shadowy spirit. They must defeat the spirit to take possession of the amulet.

SCENE 3

Suggested NPCs: None

Sometime later, the player dreams of handing the amulet to Benjamin Grey Fist. Research will show that Grey Fist works as a talismonger downtown. He gladly takes the amulet, thanking the runners genuinely. There will be no reward for this, but sometime in the future, Grey Fist will contact the runners through a fixer and offer them a job (possibly any of the Contract Briefs in this chapter). When that run is finished, Bear appears once more to the runner, thanking them for their service.

From this point on, Bear can be used as a spiritual Mr. Johnson, sending the player and the team on runs that are in Bear's interest, such as preserving nature, protecting the weak, or healing the sick.

EPILOGUE

Bear offers to continue as a mentor for the runner, with all the benefits and challenges that come with such a relationship.

SNATCH AND GRAB

MR. JOHNSON'S PITCH

This job's an extraction, plain and simple. Mr. Johnson wants a prominent researcher to be safely taken from the grasping hands of a rival corporation (along with his prototype reflex enhancement research), and is willing to pay the runners good money to get the job done. After the researcher—Jeremiah Singh—is clear of his NeoNET employers, get him to a pre-determined location for the transfer, and payment of 6 Karma will be made in full.

OBJECTIVES

- Get into the NeoNET facility.
- Gain access to Mr. Singh despite his security team.
- Grab the prototype and get away.

TAGS

- Human • Prototype cyberware
- Brilliant cyberneticist • Unwitting test subject

THE SETTING

This NeoNET facility is a sleek, modern, affair, all angular glass, soft lighting, and off-white hallways. There is a top-notch exercise facility, a perfectly serviceable cafeteria, and an oppressively overwhelming security presence. With expert technicians and engineers from the Transys Neuronet days, this facility houses high-end cyberware design and testing equipment—like the expert system that Singh is working on.

THE PLOT

SCENE 1

Suggested NPCs: Security Guards

The players will need to infiltrate the facility, first and foremost. They might try to hack themselves fake credentials, call in a favor from an appropriate contact, sneak in at night, pretend to be janitors, or a dozen other plans bubbling up from players' unique minds. Singh should be made available to them with whatever plan they like (he can work as late or as early as needed to make their plan work).

SCENE 2

Suggested NPCs: Security Guards, led by a Company Man (stats as Shades, p. 120)

Gaining access to Singh should be difficult, but hardly impossible. His executive protection detail is good at their job, but so are your runners. Singh himself is eager to leave, having long since negotiated with Mr. Johnson. He will take cover when the fight starts, unless told to do something else by the team. He is eager to comply and ready to get out of here.

SCENE 3

Suggested NPCs: Security Guards

The difficult part of this last scene is leaving with the prototype: It was just installed into another employee! David Chang is just a bottom-rung worker, and now he is saddled with a cutting-edge reaction enhancement program that a number of people would love to get their hands on. He's a low-wage meat puppet used to test new cyberware. Chang doesn't know anything about any deal, and as far as he knows he's just being kidnapped (and he may very well be, depending on how your team reacts).

AFTERMATH

Mr. Johnson is happiest to receive both Singh and the prototype, but he will be grudgingly content with just Singh (his knowledge, and extensive headware computer, will be quite a boon). Offer the team roughly two-thirds of their agreed-upon pay (meaning 4 Karma) if Singh makes it out but Chang and the prototype cyberware doesn't.

LET YOUR FLAG FLY

CONTEXT

Word Watch: Unseelie Court: A whisper. A rumor. A hint. Rebellion and revolt. As firmly as the Seelie Court (the mysterious power behind the government of Tír na nÓg, the nation formerly known as Ireland) believes in its right to exist for its own sake, the Unseelie Court, a broken mirror image of the Seelie Court, believes the schemes and machinations of its self-important counterpart must be thwarted. The Unseelie Court is impossible to define because its members are unknown, as are its ultimate ends, or even if there are any. Those sympathetic to the Unseelie, if you can find them, are convinced these rebels are freedom fighters and seekers of justice.

BACKGROUND

A powerful magical artifact, the Fairy Flag, has been stolen. Unseelie Dan, a Fomorian, is a shadowrunner-turned-druid in Scotland. He wants to smuggle the flag to the Unseelie Court to support their unseen conflict.

MR. JOHNSON'S PITCH

"Hello, I'm Mr. Johnson. I'd like to hire ye for a retrieval job—six Karma is in it for you if you succeed. An artifact known as the Fairy Flag was taken by from Scotland's Dunvegan Castle by operatives from Tír na nÓg. You must sneak into Tír na nÓg, track down the Flag, and bring it back to me.

"Getting into the Tír isn't easy, but I can help. Off the coast of Northern Ireland sits a series of basalt columns called the Giant's Causeway. They head toward Scotland, then disappear into the water. There's a counterpart off the Scottish coast.

"Head to the Isle of Staffa, where the Causeway connects to Scotland. A contact of mine, Green Gretchen, has an amulet called Fingal's Ring that can summon a mystical bridge that completes the path to Tír na nÓg."

OBJECTIVES

- Gain access to Tír na nÓg
- Find and retrieve the Fairy Flag

TAGS

- Magic artifact • Tír na nÓg • Seelie Court
- Unseelie Court • Magic • Celtic Isles

THE SETTING

Scotland's Staffa Island features breathtaking columns of basalt flanking deep caves, surrounded by beautiful blue sea. In the morning, the sun illuminates the hidden caves, and under moonlight, singing voices often echo from the largest cave.

THE PLOT

SCENE 1

Suggested NPCs: Tír Republican Corps soldiers (use Soldiers)

Arriving at the Isle of Staffa (via tour boat or any other way), the runners are met by Green Gretchen. She leads them across the bridge, where they are ambushed by a Tír Republican Corps strike team. In the fight, Gretchen's hit, and she falls into the sea with the amulet. The bridge's stability is now in question, adding an extra element of danger to the runners' journey.

SCENE 2

Suggested NPCs: Water Spirit, Air Spirit, Bean-Shidhe (use Greater Spirit of Air)

The Causeway sits at the convergence of powerful ley lines. Strange things happen there, including mana storms and the appearance of strange, otherworldly creatures. Once on the bridge, runners find themselves on the other side far quicker than should be possible. The strange creatures might intercept the runners at any part of their journey. The runners should be able to add descriptions of the creatures and troubles with the bridge to keep the adventure unpredictable.

SCENE 3

Suggested NPCs: Tír Path of the Sword Adepts (use Elite Soldiers), Tír Sword Adept (use stats for Rose Red, p. 116)

Once inside the Tír, the runners can track down the flag by following leads mentioned by Dan. The flag is at a run-down youth hostel in Belfast. They can take it by stealth or by force, and then must head back across the causeway. Once the runners make it to Staffa, the magic bridge fades.

HONG KONG CANNON

CONTEXT

Legendary ork decker William "Bull" MacCallister has a job for the runners, following up on work he did more than two decades ago. It'll take a journey to the wild runner haven of Hong Kong, but isn't globe-trotting adventure what shadowrunners dream about?

MR. JOHNSON'S PITCH

A grizzled ork fixer named William "Bull" MacCallister looks the runners in the eyes.

"Back in 2056, me and a few notable shadowrunners were hired to infiltrate the Ares Hong Kong facility and steal a prototype laser sniping cannon. I normally wouldn't take runs that took so much travel, but I had to pay off an old debt. Unfortunately, because of some embarrassing events, another shadowrunner team ended up taking the laser out from underneath us.

"Now, I'd like you to help me settle this old debt. I want that laser. My Matrix search bots picked up chatter about someone trying to sell a laser that matches the one I want, so I'm sending you to a market outside of Hong Kong, by the walled city of Kowloon."

Bull offers 7 Karma for this job.

OBJECTIVES

- Find the person selling the laser
- Follow the laser into Kowloon
- Defeat ambush and escape

TAGS

- Hong Kong • Bull • Ares • Prototype
- Red Dragon Triad • Kowloon Walled City

THE SETTING

Hong Kong is a powerful port in the political storm of the Sixth World. The Hong Kong Free Enterprise Zone is successful economically, as well as being home to many dangerous monsters, human and otherwise. Spirits and traditions are honored, but breaking the rules can make one rich.

THE PLOT

SCENE 1

Suggested NPCs: Gangers

The runners are treated with suspicion the moment they arrive. The locals don't like outsiders and don't even try to pretend to. If the runners ask around for the laser, or its seller, play up the tension. Everywhere they look, they see people staring at them and whispering in hushed tones. People on the street will give the runners two rumors about the laser. The first is that Gaichu might know about it, though no one seems to want to talk about Gaichu, however. The second is that the laser is being sold just down an ally from where the runners are standing—in the shadow of the wall that contains the Walled City of Kowloon.

SCENE 2

Suggested NPCs: Gangers

Approaching the alley, the runners are ambushed by members of the Red Dragon Triad. Once they defeat the Red Dragons, they see one of the gang members running away towards Kowloon. If they follow him, it should be a crazy, maze-like chase through Hong Kong streets. Allow the runners to describe all of the madcap things that might happen when the Hong Kong underworld and Hong Kong streets come between the runners and their payday. If the runners catch the ganger, he won't have the laser, but he will mention the name Gaichu. If they don't catch him, he will escape into the Walled City and the players will have to follow up on Gaichu anyway. After the runners have dealt with the Red Dragons, people are more willing to trust them and tell them Gaichu can be found inside Kowloon.

SCENE 3

Suggested NPCs: Gangers, Enemy Mages

Inside Kowloon is a no-man's land. People are packed in tightly and the squalor immediately assaults the runners' senses. After asking around about Gaichu, the runners gather that he is some sort of urban legend that the people spread in order to scare gangers away. Ask the runners to describe how they eventually find Gaichu. When they do, they learn he is a ghoul, wearing Red Samurai armor, and he is surrounded by Red Dragon thugs.

If the runners help Gaichu, he shows himself honorable and tells them that he does indeed have the laser cannon—a memento of an important time in his development, but that time is over, and he willingly gifts it to the runners. Once the laser is theirs, the runners must escape the maze of Kowloon and return to Bull.

NERPS RUN

MR. JOHNSON'S PITCH

"That son of a slitch must pay!" Mr. Johnson's all worked up tonight, but that's what happens when you mess with a metahuman's NERPS. A dishonest, hard-working, corporate shark can only take so much before they snap, and taking someone's NERPS is a step too far, even in this dangerous, dog eat dog, world. Johnson's corporate rivals sent company men to attack him and took his briefcase with all his NERPS in it. That case has to be recovered, no matter what, and Mr. Johnson will pay 6 Karma to make that happen.

OBJECTIVES

- Investigate the attack.
- Track down the Company Man responsible.
- Get back the NERPS!

TAGS

• NERPS! • Corporate • Betrayal • Bodyguard • Chase

THE SETTING

The mission kicks off at a Downtown intersection, where the team's client was set-upon while returning home. The trail of clues will lead to an idyllic city park, with well-manicured lawns, stylish pagodas, and a nefarious hand-off about to take place.

THE PLOT

SCENE 1

Suggested NPCs: Security

Mr. Johnson's bodyguard/driver was taking him home after a long day of corporate back-stabbing, rat-racing, and merciless jockeying for position (in other words, a Tuesday). As their GridGuide auto-stopped them at a red light, they were attacked by masked robbers (clearly wearing similar suits—more corporate security) who killed Mr. Johnson's driver, shot their way into his luxury sedan, pistol whipped him, and took off with his briefcase of NERPS.

This first scene should have the players investigating the scene (Knight Errant security will have received special orders to allow the players access, temporarily flagged as Independent Security Assets of Mr. Johnson). They can hack nearby cameras, talk to witnesses, or ask spirits for help, but eventually they should get a clear picture of four Corporate Suits with laser-like focus on the NERPScase and a distinctive black SUV.

SCENE 2

Suggested NPCs: Soldiers, Rival Johnson (stats as Ms. Myth, p. 80, plus a Eurocar Westwind sports coupe and Piloting (Ground) 4), Company Man (stats as Shades, p. 120), Security Mage (stats as Tommy Q, p. 126)

The players should be able to track the slick, corporate SUV to a Downtown park just in time to see the suit-clad killers handing over their ill-gotten gains to their employer. If Mr. Johnson is informed (kept in the loop via commlink call), he'll be heard smashing things and cursing in the background, out the opposing leader as a rival for an upcoming promotion, and demand his NERPS back, pronto. He doesn't want his rival dead, but his security detail are entirely disposable, "Let that tusky bastard slink back into the office with a few bruises, though!"

Rival Mr. Johnson will try to escape with the NERPScase as soon as any shooting starts, and this will likely turn into some sort of chase scene (either afoot, on wheels, or both). The Corporate Suit and Sec-Mage will, with a group of suit-clad thugs, try to stop the players from catching their lumbering, trollish boss, and if he can make it to his car, the players will have a tougher time of it. Luckily the Westwind has great security features (the rival Mr. Johnson will be left breathing), and the case is all but indestructible, so even a terrible car wreck won't bust it open or damage the precious cargo nestled within. NERPS survive.

AFTERMATH

Mr. Johnson won't care who's been hurt, maimed, or killed, as long as he gets his NERPs back and the rival Mr. Johnson lives to reek of failure in the office tomorrow. His rival's car being smashed up will earn a small bonus, though, as payback for his second-favorite luxury sedan's broken windows and bloodstains.

DATA/STEEL

MR. JOHNSON'S PITCH

Mr. Johnson needs a rigger for this one and is willing to pay 5 Karma to get the job done. He's after data and prototypes; an experimental drone signal booster is being worked on by an underground drone-racing outfit. A skunkworks of black and gray-market riggers is the target of tonight's job, and getting control of a swarm of light drones is tonight's mission.

OBJECTIVES

- Break into the facility.
- Get control of the swarm.
- Get the modified data-terminal and the obedient swarm to Mr. Johnson.

TAGS

- Headware • Datasteal • Hivemind • Muscle • Control

THE SETTING

The underground operation has taken over an abandoned warehouse down by the docks (presenting players with aquatic options if they prefer that). Shadows are long and the alleys between warehouses are narrow, and much of the warehouse floor is dark and cramped with the cast-off machinery the place once housed (in order to make room for the fabrication equipment and networking hardware). Contrast all of this with the burnished steel and lights of the drone swarm for maximum effect.

THE PLOT

SCENE 1

Suggested NPCs: Ork Gangers (use Gangers, increase Strength by 2)

The first line of defense is getting past the Steel Tusks, a gearhead gang who've been paid to guard the skunkworks. They're mostly able to just glower and scowl and keep legit street traffic away from the absolutely not-legit operation going on, but the PCs won't be so obliging.

THE DRONE SWARM

Hundreds of mini-drones are able to respond to a single command, swirling like a hive of bees or a school of fish instead of responding one machine at a time.

A RIGGER IN CONTROL OF THE SWARM TEMPORARILY ADDS:
- (AMP) Spy Drones III: +3 to Perception Tests
- (AMP) Armed Mini Drones III: +3 attacks per turn (only with Armed Mini Drones)
- (AMP) Shield Drones III: Reduce all damage taken by 3.
- (WEAPON) Armed Mini Drones (weapon): 7P, OK / OK / —

But the rigger controlling the swarm is so distracted by the incoming sensor data they may not take their standard attack in a round (and their defense tests should be described as the swarm swooping to protect them and deflect incoming attacks).

SCENE 2

Suggested NPCs: Rigger Alpha (stats as Shades, p. 120), Rigger Bravo (stats as Hardpoint, p. 78, armed with The Drone Swarm), Ork Gangers

The interior of the converted warehouse is a monster of light and shadow. The darkness of the docks and abandoned building itself is split by the probing lights of a rippling spiral of drones, hundreds of them, acting as one. Bravo is plugged into the customized rig and controlling The Swarm, Alpha is monitoring responses and recording everything, and another group of Steel Tusks is split between gawking at the swarm and standing guard.

SCENE 3

Suggested NPCs: Rigger Delta (stats as Fusion, p. 96), Ork Gangers (use Gangers, increase Strength by 2), Steel Tusk Lieutenant (stats as Sledge, p. 82, replace Intimidation with Piloting [Ground])

After securing The Swarm, the runners must protect their Rigger, get the bulky data-terminal/control center (a cobbled-together Frankenstein roughly the size of a mini-fridge) out of the warehouse, and make it to their drop-off point. Opposing them is the last racer in the network, and the members of the Steel Tusks who were out street-racing and only just got the call for help. The chase is on!

AFTERMATH

Mr. Johnson will pay handsomely if the customized data-term/control-center is in good shape and the drone swarm is mostly unharmed, but the players may have made enemies in the getaway driver/street-racer circuit.

PUYALLUP PROBLEMS

MR. JOHNSON'S PITCH

There's been a mobster Cold War in Puyallup for years, but—like always—it's threatening to heat up. The Ken-ran-Kai Yakuza and the Gianelli Mafia family have started to escalate their long-simmering feud, and Puyallup's locals are hoping outside help can nip it in the bud. The elven private investigator, Jimmy Kincaid, has offered a standing favor to anyone who can figure out what's going on today and smooth all the ruffled feathers. He's working with PI resources, meaning he's offering 4 Karma for the runners' help.

OBJECTIVES

- Investigate a recent drive-by site, looking for signs of what might happen next.
- Intercept the Blue Dragons go-gang before they wreck a Mafia joint.
- Stop some Gianneli thugs from their drive-by attack, minimizing the damage.
- Find out who's actually responsible for all this, and put a stop to it.

TAGS

- Barrens • Rising Fear • Vengeance • Misguided Retribution
- Syndicates

THE SETTING

Puyallup's had a bad go of it for the last few decades, and the rising tension has even the hard-bitten natives looking afraid and restless. The streets should be emptier than normal, in an eerie, "Old West before a shoot-out," sort of way.

THE PLOT

SCENE 1

The first scene is a shot-up sushi joint, indiscriminately blasted by autofire from slow-moving sedans with mirrored windows. Hitting the streets and asking witnesses what they saw will leave most signs pointing towards the Gianellis, but a few old-timer locals will shake their head in disbelief (and perhaps desperation?) insisting it can't be true.

SCENE 2

Suggested NPCs: Gangers

The investigation will be interrupted by the howling engines of a gaggle of blue-painted street bikes. Yakuza thugs will posture and brandish katanas and machine pistols, peeling out and roaring down the street with vengeance clearly on their mind. Runners familiar with the neighborhood (or syndicates, or shortcuts, or similar knowledge skills) can guess their destination; Sunny Salvo's, Enzo Gianelli's favorite joint! If they hurry they can beat the Yakuza go-gangers—the Blue Dragons—there or disrupt the pack of them en route.

SCENE 3

Suggested NPCs: Gangers, led by Kim Hyuk (stats as Kix, p. 102)

As the Blue Dragons are scattered, defeated, or re-routed, the situation immediately escalates again as a group of window-tinted sedans—the model from today's attacks, the same ones often used by the local Mafia—roll up onto the scene with autoguns pointed out the windows.

In the ensuing fight, the players will quickly spot the crude deception. The Divine Revenge Ring, a Korean syndicate, is behind the attacks in a simple, albeit effective, ploy to hurt their Puyallup rivals. The Divine Revenge are known to have a deep-seated feud going with Seattle's Yakuza, and—as the violence of the day shows—the situation in Puyallup is serious enough even their ham-fisted trick was enough to almost bring really big guns to bear.

AFTERMATH

The ruse will end with the Divine Revenge Ring's defeat, but the city's larger conflicts remain in place. The Ken-ran-Kai and the Gianellis will still be glaring at one another, and perhaps the best that can be hoped for is that the unsteady peace will be extended a little while longer.

THE HALLOWEENER UNDERGROUND

CONTEXT

For three decades, the Halloweeners gang has plagued downtown Seattle. No matter how often they seem down for good, they always come back. Now, someone has discovered one of the reasons. A long-forgotten tunnel system, designed as a public transit beneath Bellevue and Lake Washington, connects downtown Seattle to the Redmond Barrens. The tunnel terminates in the Barrens just a few miles from the Jackal's Lantern, the Halloweener's official bar, and allows the 'Weeners to escape the heat Downtown, regroup, and live to terrorize Seattle another day.

MR. JOHNSON'S PITCH

Unfortunately for the Halloweeners, a survey team, hired by Bellevue mayor Jonathan Blake, discovered the Halloweeners' tunnel while scouting the area for a future Saeder-Krupp facility. The runners are hired by Absinthe, the Halloweeners' second-in-command, to track down the survey team, ensure their silence, and make sure the survey report mentions nothing of the tunnel. Absinthe will pay extra if they are able to alter the report so that Mayor Blake and Saeder-Krupp no longer want to build anywhere close.

As a street gang Halloweeners are not the richest organization in the world, but their secret is important enough that they will pay runners 5 Karma to help them keep it.

OBJECTIVES

- Find the survey report
- Stop the information about the Halloweeners' tunnel from getting out
- Alter the report to make the area appear inhospitable

TAGS

- Sprawlgangers • Halloweeners • 405 Hellhounds
- Redmond Barrens • Downtown • Bellevue
- Underground Tunnel • Saeder-Krupp

THE SETTING

Bellevue is the upscale suburb where the families of wealthy Seattle business people sleep at night. With Downtown on one side and Redmond on the other, it shines brightly compared to the lawlessness of Redmond or the excess of Downton. Bellevue does its best to project well-manicured lawns, tidy living rooms, and nuclear families walking pets in the evenings.

THE PLOT

SCENE 1

Suggested NPCs: Construction Workers

(use gangers with no combat skills)

It shouldn't be too hard for the runners to find the survey team. They still have a temporary office set up at the site. Work is still continuing, but the project lead has vanished. The truth is, the head of the survey team, a dwarf named Mike Samuels, not only discovered the tunnel, but as a result of his investigations he figured out who was using it. Samuels has decided that this is too big to keep to the mayor of Bellevue and is taking the information to the Knight Errant police force.

His survey crew will gladly sell him out for nuyen or to avoid violence. Let the players have fun describing their interrogations. If pressed, the crew will tell the runners where Samuels' apartment is and where he said he was headed (to the Knight Errant precinct).

SCENE 2

Suggested NPCs: 405 Hellhounds gangers

(use gangers, add +2 Piloting (Ground) and Street Bikes)

The pressure is on to find Samuels before he tells the cops what he knows. He won't be at his apartment, but he will be close to a Knight Errant station. Unfortunately for the runners, the route they chose will take them through 405 Hellhounds territory. As the runners exit the 405 freeway, they are accosted by the Hellhounds, demanding tribute or just trying to destroy something, like they do. This could either be a stationary ambush or a vehicular one. Let the players decide and describe how they fight back.

SCENE 3

Suggested NPCs: Rent-A-Cops

Once the Hellhounds are dealt with, the runners reach the Knight Errant Precinct. If they spend any significant time scouting or doing any legwork, Samuels will have been taken back to see Detective Tonkovich, head of Bellevue's gang unit. Once there, it will be difficult to get to him and depending on how much he's said, the players might need to deal with Tonkovich as well to finish the run. If the players go straight in, without waiting, they will find Samuels, with the survey report, waiting to be seen by an officer. If the runners try to use force to get Samuels out, he'll kick, scream and do whatever he can to draw attention to the struggle. If this happens, the runners will have to be creative to finish the job. A brawl in the middle of a Knight Errant police station would be tough. Once the runners get to him, however, they find Samuels to be weak-willed and easy to manipulate.

EPILOGUE

Absinthe doesn't thank the runners, but he does pay them for "taking care" of Samuels. He gives them each a patch, a flaming Jack O' Lantern, and tells them they are welcome on 'Weener turf anytime. Lastly, he tells them if they want more work, they should head to the Jackal's Lantern in Redmond and talk to Carnevil.

THE LIGHT WITHIN

CONTEXT

Word Watch: Free Spirit n. A spirit that has been summoned to our world, but has been released. This is usually through the death of its master or summoner, and it is liberated to pursue its own ends.

BACKGROUND

The Light Within is a religious group that started in 2068, but it has gained a moderate following in that short time. It began with only their leader, Warwick Gulliver, his immediate family, and a small, but loyal number of families. Now, their compound outside the sprawl consists of well over two hundred members.

MR. JOHNSON'S PITCH

Your fixer hooks you up with an unusual Mr. Johnson—a free fire spirit. The fire spirit forgoes small talk and begins:

"The Light Within is a religious group that believes that the Great Light Spirit communes with the world's chosen few, by which they mean themselves, and grants them prophetic visions and ecstatic worship experiences. Recently, their group has been growing exponentially larger because their deity, that aforementioned Great Light Spirit, has been appearing physically among them. Here's the thing—the Great Light Spirit is me.

"It went well for a while, but now there's a problem, and that problem is the leader, Warwick Gulliver. Gulliver welcomed me at first, but some recent arguments over the vision of the group have made him resent me. I want you to infiltrate the Light Within as religious seekers. Once accepted, work to discredit Gulliver and cement my influence over the group by whatever means necessary. Five Karma is waiting for you if you do this right."

OBJECTIVES

- Infiltrate the Light Within
- Solidify the fire spirit's power base
- Discredit Warwick Gulliver and escape

TAGS

- Free Fire Spirit • New Religious Group • False Prophet
- Rival Runner Team • Infiltration

THE SETTING

The Light Within's compound is luxurious. However they got their money, it seems that almost all of it was used to make this place an urban paradise. Rooms for exercise, worship, recreation, and study surround the inner courtyard, with living quarters placed along the outer perimeter. The high walls keep out intruders without diminishing the spectacular view.

THE PLOT

SCENE 1

Suggested NPCs: The Light Within members
(Use Gangers with no active skills)

Infiltrating the group is not difficult. They are enjoying the new growth and popularity that has come with the spirit's presence among them. Gulliver will not be particularly suspicious of the runners and will try to make them allies. Allow the players to describe how they do this and encourage them to elaborate. Once they are in his confidence, he will reveal that he knows the spirit isn't really the Great Light Spirit. Gulliver is trying to show the community that the spirit cannot make accurate prophecies by pushing it to prove itself by making

difficult-to-fulfill predictions. It's up to the runners to describe how they make the spirit's prophecies come true … however unlikely they may appear. After two to three successful "prophecies," move onto Scene 2.

SCENE 2

Suggested NPCs: The Light Within members
(Use Gangers with no active skills)

After cementing the spirit's power base in the community, the runners now have to discredit Gulliver. If they look into his past, they will find that he legally changed his name from Henry Danforth after earning a doctorate in behavioral science. Snooping in Gulliver's office will yield his journals. They outline his plan to create a new religion using behavioral techniques to manipulate people's perception and emotions, in order to create a sustainable life for himself as a big fish in a small religious pond. If the runners describe finding other dirt on Gulliver, go with that as well! The most recent entries outline his plan to hire a mage to banish the spirit and take his group back.

SCENE 3

Suggested NPCs: Great Light Spirit
(use Greater Spirit of Fire), Rival Shadowrunner team
(choose one character from pages 74–133 for each runner.
One of these should have the Summoning skill)

Before the runners can act on any of this, a rival runner team forces its way into the Light Within's compound. The rival team is there to banish the spirit on Gulliver's behalf, placing leadership of the group back into his hands. If the runners want to get paid, they will have to defeat the opposing team and use what they found in the journal to destroy Gulliver's credibility.

URBAN BRAWL

MR. JOHNSON'S PITCH

The major league sport, urban brawl, began as a way for street gangs to settle their differences with ritualized, somewhat restrained violence. As a handful of gangs sold out into cutthroat affairs with chapters all over the world—criminal enterprises concerned with profit, rivaling organized crime syndicates—others have backslid, with smaller outfits concerning themselves with romanticized notions of respect, community protection, and loyalty.

Urban brawl as ritualized violence, a sort of sports-fueled trial of champions, has had a minor resurgence in recent years among these small-scale gangs. The Alder Street Avengers are one such small gang, with a scheduled brawl-bout against their rivals, Red's Rhymers, for dominance over half a city block. The Rhymers tagged over some Avenger graffiti, and this sort of insult can't stand!

Unfortunately, half of the Avengers can't stand, either. A wave of gastrointestinal distress has washed over Alder Street, thanks to Devil Dave's Deviled Devil Rats, a dodgy food truck. Alder Street's honor is on the line, and a team of shadowrunners are their only hope!

Standard pay for an urban brawl match is 3 Karma, so that's what the runners will get.

OBJECTIVES

- Move the ball through the abandoned warehouse to score goals against the Rhymers.
- Defend your goal against the Rhymers at all times.
- Maimings, knock-outs, and injuries are fine, but any deaths disqualify the offending team. No killing!
- Get away from the cops!

TAGS

• Gangs • Old School • Athletics • Pride • Knight Errant

THE SETTING

The brawl site is an abandoned prefab housing warehouse/display site, a wide-open space interrupted with half-finished walls jutting up almost at random, sections of faux-wall for mounting doors and windows, low fences, and an assortment of other neo-construction projects that will provide great cover, cinematic obstacles, and plexiglass-protected viewing stands behind each goal.

THE PLOT

SCENE 1

Suggested NPCs: Gangers, led by Red (stats as Strider, p. 122)

Brawl's on! Teams move the ball downfield with Athletics tests (running with the ball, kicking it, throwing it, etc.). After ten hits are scored by various players to represent getting the ball within range, a final Athletics test is made to attempt an actual goal (opposed by a dedicated goalie, rolling Close Combat to block). Regular combat skills (magic included) are fair game to wallop on the other team with, but remember to keep things nonlethal and avoid disqualification.

Set a target score (at least one point per PC, so everyone has a chance to shine), and the first team to reach it wins the bout.

SCENE 2

Suggested NPCs: Rent-a-cops, led by a single Elite Soldier

Knight Errant rolls up just as either team's about to score the winning goal. The real challenge begins as the streets unite to fight against The Man! The battle now isn't just for pride, but freedom, and differences get set aside as the two battered, bruised, teams struggle to fend off the cops and escape. A good showing here will let the PCs win the community's respect (and either overturn a match they were about to lose, or cement a victory they almost lost due to the interruption).

AFTERMATH

Figuring out how Knight Errant knew about the fight (or why they cared) could be a plot hook that starts a larger storyline. Win or lose, assuming your runners comported themselves well, they'll gain some respect on the streets, favors to call in, and a little money for their troubles.

UNKNOWN STUNTMAN

CONTEXT

Word Watch: Fall guy n. An actor who performs stunts and takes brutal beatings, which are recorded with simsense, and used to make summer blockbuster trideo. Simsense allows consumers see, hear, and feel the actions of the fall guy as if it were them.

MR. JOHNSON'S PITCH

"I'm your Mr. Johnson, but you probably know me as Colt Majors. I'm a 'fall guy,' currently working on an upcoming Optical Dreams trideo called *Dragon Down: Unsung Heroes of Aztlan*. Last week, I was injured on the set, which is common enough, but I believe this time was intentional. Two other employees from my company have also sustained injuries on set, and while I can't prove foul play, I'm not going to put them in danger anymore. Instead, I'd like to hire you to be temp fall guys and fulfill my crew's contract. While you are there, investigate and stop whoever is trying to sabotage the show.

"I can provide you with synthskin face masks to match the appearance of the actors, employee IDs for my company (which is called Unknown Stuntmen), and simsense recorders for your datajacks or trode recorders if you don't have datajacks. I need this straightened out so my company can function without any more injuries, so there's six Karma in it for you if you can help me out."

OBJECTIVES

- Participate in the film as directed
- Investigate the movie set for clues.
- Stop the behind-the-scenes terror.

TAGS

- Aztlan • Trideo • Simsense • Movies
- Stuntmen • Fall Guy • Actors

THE SETTING

The set of Optical Dreams' upcoming trideo called *Dragon Down: Unsung Heroes of Aztlan*, is created to look like Bogota and the surrounding jungle. Of course, outside of those particular lots, Optical Dreams' movie lot has all of the amenities common to trid studios. The actors, director, catering, costuming, and sound company, along with many others, all have their own custom trailers.

THE PLOT

SCENE 1

Suggested NPCs: Actors (use Soldiers without the Firearms skill)

On the set of *Dragon Down*, the runners meet the director, Heather Banks. She wastes no time in getting the runners in wardrobe. They are playing Aztlan Jaguar Guards, and in this scene, they infiltrate a secret Amazonian bunker and are discovered by the enemy. When the scene begins, a fire fight ensues. Banks encourages the runners to make it seem as real as possible, because this is what the fans pay for!

Unbeknownst to the runners, the Amazonian actors' weapons have been loaded with live ammo. As the shooting begins, have the runners make normal defense rolls, and if they are hit, they take damage as normal. Whenever the first runner takes damage, Banks yells, "CUT!"

SCENE 2:

Suggested NPCs: None

Banks is convinced that this was just a mistake by the prop department. She of course apologizes profusely but insists that the trid is on a tight schedule, and she doesn't want to waste any more time.

While on set, the runners will get to know a few notable people. First, the Star of the show is Monte Zuma, a trid star from the town of Bogota in Aztlan. Second, the company in charge of props is called Leather and Lace Costuming, with ties in Amazonia, the losers in the Amazonia/Aztlan war. Last, Phineas Bolton is playing the dragon Sirrurg, the villain of the movie. Bolton is gruff and complains often about being overlooked for the starring role.

SCENE 3

Suggested NPCs: Mechanical Dragon (use Young Dragon, but remove all Amps and Skills except Close Combat, Elemental Attack, and Natural Weapon)

After numerous scenes of jungle warfare and training montages, the runners prepare for the final scene. Phineas Bolton is fitted into a huge mechanical construct of a dragon, allowing him to operate it as if it were his own body. Some of the runners wait offstage for their cue, while the others (along with computer generated soldiers) act out Aztlan's final engagement with the dragon.

As the runners backstage wait for their cue, a thumping noise comes from a dressing room. Inside they find Phineas Bolton, bound, gagged, and definitely *not* inside the mechanical dragon. On set, the dragon is trying to kill the runners, and he isn't acting. To survive, they need to take down the mechanized monster. Once they do, they find Monte Zuma in the dragon. He defiantly screams that Aztlan killed his family in the war and he was trying to prevent this movie from making them look like heroes.

IS THAT A BUG IN YOUR POCKET?

CONTEXT

Word Watch: Bug spirit n. A race of hostile spirits resembling giant insects. They come from a distant realm, but desire to break into our world and consume everything. They can appear as bugs or even as metahumans.

BACKGROUND

Early in the 2020s, the sleepy town of Carlinville changed. Population loss caused them to invest in cattle to keep their dairy going. Soon, their cattle began dying of unknown causes, but Ares Macrotechnology saved them (of course, Ares secretly poisoned the cattle in the first place, because that's how the game is played). An Ares rep convinced the town to house a secret facility in exchange for help with the cows. They agreed, and the cows miraculously began to prosper. They quickly understood that they should steer clear of this new facility, and the runners will learn that this was very wise of them.

MR. JOHNSON'S PITCH

"I'd like to hire you to rescue a kidnapped woman, Nicole Brunson. I'm convinced she's somewhere in the town of Carlinville, just hours outside the Chicago sprawl. Here is her picture. Please bring her back safe."

Mr. Johnson offers 5 Karma for the safe return of Brunson.

OBJECTIVES

- Find the underground farm facility
- Rescue (or destroy?) the wasp spirit queen.

TAGS

- Chicago • Bug spirits • Creepy town
- Genetically modified food • Plot twist

THE SETTING

The sleepy little town of Carlinville is quaint, like something out of a movie from last century. It smells strongly of cows and manure. The runners might notice the folks of Carlinville look a bit sickly. Their skin has a slightly pale greenish shade. Raising cattle, for both milk and slaughter, is the main industry in town.

THE PLOT

SCENE 1

Suggested NPCs: Citizen (use Ganger)

The runners should do some legwork in the town to gain intel, but the townsfolk will be tight lipped. With any amount of force, or interrogating someone away from the others, they will break and tell the runners everything from the background above. If the runners don't ask to see the farm, have a conscience-ridden older person approach them instead.

They will also give the location of the underground farm. It should be clear that if people in town go missing, that's where they go.

SCENE 2

Suggested NPCs: Bug Spirits (Consider altering stats up and down to reflect the fact that bug spirits have merged with different types of animals), Rent-a-cops

When the runners break into the underground facility, they realize the horror Ares has brought to town. The huge facility holds a genetically modified wasp spirit queen, along with hundreds of animal/bug spirit hybrids. They are all in various stages of experimentation, from being milked to being dissected to being fed to others. This is torturous for the Queen and the hybrids, but they aren't human, so the town tries not to think of it. But they suspect Ares feeds them bug-spirit/cow hybrids.

SCENE 3:

Suggested NPCs: Bug Queen, Bug Spirits
(Hybrids, as above), Corp Security (use Elite Soldier)

The twist is the wasp spirit queen is the very picture of Nicole Brunson, the woman they've been hired to rescue. Depending on how they play it, the runners will be up against Ares security, freakish hybrid bug spirits, or both. Allow the team to narrate how they want this to play out—and what they're going to tell Mr. Johnson.

ASSASSIN'S GREED

MS. JOHNSON'S PITCH

The runners are approached by the contract killer Marie Grey, a known underworld figure renowned for her consistent kill rate and consummate professionalism. She currently is in a very bad mood, with a bullet in her belly. Scowling at the world from beneath the shadowy hood sewn into her armored long coat, she explains that she's recently completed a mission for a new employer, but now her patron has refused payment and, in fact, tried to kill Grey instead.

Grey is good at her job, but not cocky; she knows she needs backup! She's willing to give even splits of her promised payment to the team (meaning the team will get 5 Karma), it's the principle of collecting the money (and preserving her rep) that matters now.

OBJECTIVES

- Escort Grey to her safehouse
- Assault the fortified home while Grey provides fire support.
- Negotiate with Mr. Johnson on Grey's behalf (or just let Grey snipe him).

TAGS

- Double-cross • Assassin • Secret Armory
- Reinforced Mansion • Security

THE SETTING

Initially meeting characters at their favorite shadowrunner bar, Grey hurries the team to a safehouse/armory she maintains in the seedy side of town (unfortunately one that the people hunting Grey are watching and ready to ambush). From there they ride to the outskirts of town to the palatial estate of a middle executive.

THE PLOT

SCENE 1

Suggested NPCs: Soldiers, Grey

(stats as Shades, p. 120, with rifles instead of pistols)

The team escorts Grey to her safehouse, where she can recover her unhackable, hard-copy files on the Mr. Johnson who hired her, along with some guns. Her ultra-secure safe clashes with the squalor of the neighborhood, and shortly after she opens it (and allows the team to arm up, as well, at least within reason), a team of hitmen arrives.

This gang-riddled neighborhood is basically a free fire zone, and Grey's granting them access to her standing safe full of hardware, so let the players let loose blasting away at the black SUVs full of suit-clad thugs as they arrive.

SCENE 2

Suggested NPCs: Elite Soldiers, Grey

After the raucous shoot-out at the not-so-safehouse, there's a stark contrast to the clean and security-patrolled streets of Johnson's middle-upper-crust neighborhood. If the team doesn't think to take one of Mr. Johnson's security SUVs, Grey can provide them appropriately stylish transportation (albeit temporarily) to get the whole team to Johnson's home grounds.

Grey's basic plan—let the team supersede it if they have something cleverer!—is to linger at the rear and use her rifle to clear the way, so that the players get the tension of infiltration, the thrill of assault, or both. She's quite capable at providing fire support from a safe distance, but remember to use her to assist the team, not take the spotlight from them.

When confronted (lounging by his pool), Mr. Johnson won't show any remorse about short-shrifting the killer, nor of his security force's attack on the players. He'll constantly berate and belittle the players as simple thugs who understand nothing but violence, and that the law of the jungle applies to creatures like them. If a player works very hard at talking him down (or blackmail him with Grey's files), he'll transfer over the credits. If not, Grey will be content with Johnson's corpse as a means of repairing her rep.

AFTERMATH

Whether Johnson transfers the agreed-upon sum or not, Grey will pay up, and if they impressed her the team may gain a contact as well as the agreed-upon sum.

CLEANING HOUSE

MR. JOHNSON'S PITCH

Ghouls are infected with a special strain of the HMHVV (human/metahuman vampiric virus) that turns them blind, gives them claws and fangs, and forces them to live off raw metahuman flesh. Most fight their disease and try to stay relatively human. Some don't. It looks like a pack of ghouls—once content to feed off a street doctor's waste material—have gone violently crazy.

Cleaning out a feral ghoul nest is gonna be a real handful, but Mr. Johnson's got 6 Karma that says you'd be willing to do it.

OBJECTIVES

- Examine the ghoul warren in the sewers beneath "Doc Johnson's" shadow clinic.
- Find out what's made them go feral.
- Handle the problem, one way or another.

TAGS

- Street Doc • Ghouls • Recycling • Disease • Compromise?

THE SETTING

The sewers below Johnson's clinic are a mess. Drones handle most of the routine maintenance (enterprising deckers or riggers might be able to spy through hacked utility drones). The "warren" of ghouls itself is out of a nightmare; they live in filth and squalor, with some of their number gone mad from the disease and others desperately clinging to their metahumanity.

THE PLOT

SCENE 1

Suggested NPC: Doc Johnson

(stats as Wagon, p. 130, without combat skills)

Doc Johnson has thrown damaged/spare parts to a nest of ghouls for years, feeding them organs and tissue that can't be re-implanted (the ghouls, in exchange, dispose of evidence of his illegal clinic). Lately the ghouls have attacked people, though, and he needs the runners to go put a stop to things.

SCENE 2

Suggested NPCs: Feral Ghouls (stats as Gangers with no weapons or armor, just a Physical-damage Unarmed bite attack)

Feral ghouls will attempt to ambush the group after they've gotten near the sewer coordinates provided by Doc Johnson. Anyone bit by a ghoul (taking physical damage from an Unarmed attack) should feel terrible, feverish, and with their eyesight going blurry (–1 or more to all actions until they get to Johnson's for medical treatment).

SCENE 3

Suggested NPCs: Ghouls (Gangers equipped as normal, but also with a Physical-damage Unarmed bite attack), Ghoul Leader Rebecca (though not a troll, stats as Ms. Myth, add a Physical-damage Unarmed bite attack)

The camp of the ghouls is very different from the sewers the exiled ferals attacked from. Here there are blankets and sheets hung for privacy, pirated electricity powering small personal electronics for music, cots and sleeping bags, etc. This group lives like refugees, dealing with their disease, while Rebecca leads them and constantly contends with "The Hunger" driving so many of them mad.

The rise in ferals is no one's fault; Doc Johnson hasn't sent tainted meat, nor cut off their food supply. The ghouls have simply needed more meat lately to stay sane, and there has not been enough to go around. Rebecca's community grew too large, too fast, and The Hunger within the Infected has spiked in disturbing ways lately. The next steps are up to the players: Will they try to monitor or control this population, or ensure they get enough metahuman flesh to survive on? Other street doc contacts may be useful, or unsavory criminal types with bodies to dispose of.

AFTERMATH

Rebecca and her tribe could prove useful allies and informants if they are helped instead of attacked, and if peace is restored (no matter how) Doc Johnson will be good to his word and pay up.

STREET SWEEPER

MR. JOHNSON'S PITCH

The players get offered their payment from a community organizer this time, not a shadowy Mr. Johnson but Granny Smith, a sweet old lady that runs a food truck she uses to feed the homeless. As the mouthpiece of the neighborhood's plain-living civilian folk, she's worried about a spike in go-gang violence. What can the players do to sort things out, in exchange for 3 Karma, an awful lot of community goodwill, and maybe a few contacts?

OBJECTIVES

- Investigate the recent go-gang violence.
- Track down the auto shop headquarters of the culprit.
- Decide whether to put a stop to the Street Sweeper or to help them seek their vengeance.

TAGS

- Gathering • Gasoline • Guns • Gangs • Grief

THE SETTING

The run works best near the player characters' home turf, and the high-octane action can work in neon-drenched Downtown streets just as well as the pothole-strewn streets of the Barrens. Keep the story moving too fast for cops to be an issue and things will work just fine.

THE PLOT

SCENE 1

Suggested NPCs: Gangers

In their initial legwork, the players should get several leads that point them to the Road Dawgz, a classic biker go-gang that favors black leather, burly motorcycles, and shiny chrome. If confronted about the recent violence, they'll raise their hackles and likely brawl, but they will eventually admit to it; they're actually not the culprits, but the *victims*, of recent attacks.

SCENE 2

Suggested NPCs: Gangers, led by Mongoose (stats as Kix, p. 102)

Next up the ladder are the Quick Slivers, an up-and-coming go-gang that favors sleeker, lighter, bikes. Their leader, the razorgirl Mongoose, will rankle at any accusations, but they will grudgingly explain that they haven't been the instigators, either. They've lost a few Slivers to wrecks that they don't think the Dawgz are behind. If the PCs are convincing, she'll offer them a brief video feed from the latest attack. It's shaky and hurried—the commlink video of someone right before getting rammed off their street bike—but it shows a clearly customized muscle car, all chromed up, turbo-charged, and with mirror-chromed windshields lending it an eerie, otherworldly, appearance.

SCENE 3

Suggested NPCs: The Street Sweeper (stats as Fusion, p. 96, changing specialization and vehicle to muscle cars)

More legwork and research will lead the PCs to the Street Sweeper's headquarters, the only shop around capable of customizing a rig like that (not to mention one it's been seen coming and going from by reputable contacts). When the players confront the mysterious rider, though, they may be surprised; the Sweeper is a woman in her mid-twenties, paralyzed from the waist down, sporting fresh cranial scars and vehicle control-rig implants. She and her family were the victims of random go-ganger violence—the 405 Hellhounds attacked them at random on the highway—and now she's made it her life's work to wipe them all out.

AFTERMATH

How the players react is up to them. Will they stop the Street Sweeper (Louise Prescott), thinking it will restore some peace to the streets? Will they assist her in her quest for vengeance? Will they try to compromise with her, assisting in more directed attacks at specific gangs? Their choices can lead directly to more work, or can inform who comes after them and who helps them in future jobs.

TRIAD TAKE-OUT

MR. JOHNSON'S PITCH

Bing-Lei "Billy" Shen is an up-and-coming Red Pole (lieutenant) and hitman in the Octagon Triad. He's got style, panache, elven charm, strong Kung-Fu, adept abilities, and—right now—a few bullet holes in him and his tailored suit, with more incoming fire on the way!

Billy calls mid-chase, needing the players to run interference for him and then handle some errands. He needs some get-back against a rival Triad that tried to take him out. The Yellow Lotus are no joke, but Billy's got to handle them without leaning on his Triad for support. He's involved in an internal schism and could lose face if he asks his gang for favors. He needs the runners to scramble and deliver some justice for him; his superiors in the organization will respect his independence and initiative. His hoop's in a sling, and he'll pay 5 Karma to runners who can help him get it out.

OBJECTIVES

- Help Billy get clear and escape to his safehouse.
- Shoot up the Golden Blossom Wok, a Yellow Lotus-owned restaurant.
- Go after Fat Belly Chang, the Yellow Lotus Red Pole Billy blames for the hit on him.

TAGS

- Triads • Racers • Suits • Chinatown • Fireworks • Revenge

THE SETTING

This mission will tour Downtown neighborhoods dominated by Chinese immigrants and the criminal syndicates that recruit from and extort them. You can play up the contrast of old-style decorations (fireworks and paper lanterns) contrasted with the high-tech realities of the Sixth World (neon and augmented reality), in the same way there's a sharp contrast between the work-a-day citizens of Chinatown and the flashy, dangerous, mobsters that prey on them.

THE PLOT

SCENE 1

Suggested NPCs: Gangers

First thing's first, the players need to keep Billy Shen from getting finished off. As soon as they intercept the rolling chase/battle, have the bike-riding Triad killers adjust their fire from Billy (who floors it after a grateful farewell). Keep the action fast-paced and cinematic, with the Triad killers riding racing bikes and spraying autofire from sleek machine pistols.

SCENE 2

Suggested NPCs: Gangers

As soon as the action from the chase scene stops, have the players get another commlink call from Billy, grimacing in pain but in a safehouse. He wants the players to bust up a Yellow Lotus restaurant, Golden Blossom Wok, to send a message.

The fight at the Golden Blossom Wok can go a lot of different ways based on the players' ideas. They can keep it simple and pull an ugly drive-by, they can wade in and bust the place up with bats, or they can just whistle up a spirit and order it to smash the place. Triad thugs on-site will put up a token defense, but they're really not prepared to stop a full-on runner team with their hearts set on property damage.

SCENE 3

Suggested NPCs: Gangers, Fat Belly Chang (stats as Sledge, p. 82), Seven Thunders Raging (stats as Tommy Q, p. 126)

Finally, Shen will ask the runners to go after the Yellow Lotus boss behind the initial attack. Fat Belly Chang is an orkish killer who's gone to seed, plumped up by his success but still a formidable foe. The players can find him at a laundry's back-room gambling den. Chang is surrounded by a complement of suit-clad bodyguards, and also Seven Thunders Raging, a nattily dressed bodyguard and combat mage.

AFTERMATH

Billy Shen will pay the characters the promised price, and if they did a good job they earned something else—his trust. The elf's a decent guy for a mobster and can be retained as a contact, which might net the runners favor from Shen's Triad or access to some of their supplies.

TRUCKING WITH THE FAE

MR. JOHNSON'S PITCH

The Deireadh An Tuartheil, a hospital serving the people of the Tarislar elven ghetto, is in desperate need of supplies. A large delivery has been arranged (including some magical reagents and rare laés-based elven concoctions), but the cargo and driver have been seized by a branch of the Tír Tairngire government. The driver is one Harrison Stiobhard, a Seelie Court citizen, which has other factions within the Tír government concerned enough to break him out.

The Information Secretariat—the elven nation's spies and secret police—currently hold Stiobhard and his illicit cargo. Captain Loriel Taylor, a young combat mage in the Tír Peace Force, is eager to disrupt the rival organization's plans *and* help the Tarislar hospital all in one fell swoop. She wants outside help, and she's decided it's a job for shadowrunners. An elf-heavy group might be chosen because they'll blend in, a mostly human group could be justified because they're an unknown quantity, and so on—spin it however is needed to make your players sound like a good fit.

OBJECTIVES

- Travel through Salish territory and across the border with Captain Taylor.
- Free the elven smuggler Harrison Stiobhard and his load of pharmaceuticals and reagents.
- Escort Stiobhard back to Seattle.

TAGS

- Elf • Smuggling • Salish Ork • Information Secretariat
- Great Escape • Road Warriors

THE SETTING

The drive south through Salish territory is low-tech and rugged, and the countryside of the Tír itself is a forested wonderland, all of which may feel alien and discomfiting to city-born runners used to concrete Sprawl.

THE PLOT

SCENE 1
Suggested NPCS: Ork Gangers,
Captain Loriel Taylor (stats as Tommy Q, p. 126)

The young Captain Taylor will drive the players along an open-secret smuggler route. She's a Peace Force offi-cer, but that won't impress the Salish Orks that run the refueling camps along the way. They'll go easier on a team with lots of orks and trolls in it, but anyone else can expect a resentful shakedown and a brawl. The orks demand the group pay the usual cut for the lucrative "Daisy Eater Run" into elven territory, not just gas money.

SCENE 2
Suggested NPCS: Elf Soldiers, potentially
led by combat mage (stats as Coydog, p. 74).

Captain Taylor leads the team around border checkpoints by taking an overnight trek through the woods. She's a capable forester (anyone paying particular attention or asking her for help can get a +1 to Survival tests for the rest of the adventure), but unless the team takes remarkable steps to avoid detection, they should have a skirmish with the infamous Border Patrol or a band of rogue "Mistish Farad," xenophobic Paladins dedicated to elven supremacy.

If accosted by uniformed Border Patrol soldiers, Taylor will argue for nonlethal attacks and may even try to order the elves to stand down (with one or two calling her "Princess" in the excitement). Against the rogue Followers of the Hunt, though, she will be merciless, and any mention of her noble rank will come from those elves with an accusation of her being a race traitor. If pressed, she will admit to being the daughter of Prince Connal Taylor, but insists she's only a captain while on a mission.

SCENE 3
Suggested NPCs: Birdsong (12 Biotech dice), Soldiers

The team must find transport to Corvallis, the home to the shadowy Information Secretariat. They'll be crossing through verdant forest and fertile farmland to reach it (wild blackberries will make a hike tolerable).

Corvallis is a once-vibrant town turned tense, dominated by the oppressive knowledge that anyone, anywhere, could be spying for the Info-Sec. A motherly nurse, Birdsong, runs a safehouse here where the runners can rest and prepare. If the team is appropriately cautious, they can avoid a fight during this transition. Play up the sense of paranoia, with looming danger contrasting with the idyllic countryside.

SCENE 4
Suggested NPCs: Elf Soldiers, led by a Combat Mage (stats as Tommy Q, p. 126), and Info-Sec Hacker (stats as Gentry, p. 76)

The Information Secretariat's paramilitary base handles prisoners and evidence. Taylor's branch of the Peace

Force doesn't see eye to eye with the Information Secretariat, nor does her brand of patriotism agree with their methods. She will do what she can to help before parting ways with the team here, but make sure the team keeps the spotlight.

Whatever your team plans, remember to be a fan of it; they can be as loud or as subtle as your campaign decides, and the NPCs should react accordingly (either with an action-heavy shoot-out or a tense game of cat-and-mouse as they hack, lie, and sneak their way across the base).

Harrison Stiobhard is likely not what was expected. Once an elven scout of the Seelie Court, a sister metaplane to our own, his wanderlust led to him "adventuring" in the mortal realm, where decades of life as a long-haul trucker have overcome his elven metabolism. "Ol' Harris Stubby" always refers to himself in the third person, and he has traded away the glamorous Seelie Court for a UCAS drawl, a mesh ball cap, and morbid obesity that threatens to overwhelm his t-shirt at any moment.

Stubby's smuggling vessel, "The Orkchop Express" (complete with a fanciful airbrushing job that shows a leaner, meaner, Stiobhard fighting fantastic enemies) is sealed pending investigation not far from his holding cell. Once reunited with his noble steed, Stubby is a surprisingly capable driver who will cheerfully rocket the big rig onto the open road.

SCENE 6

Suggested NPCs: Trucks and bikes full of Ork Gangers, led by a tougher foe (stats as Sledge, P. 82), Harris Stubby (10 Piloting dice)

All that's left after the Great Corvallis Breakout is the ride home. For an easier run, have the team hear from Captain Taylor that the political infighting within the Tír has cleared the way, as has Harris' status as a citizen of a sovereign fae state (of sorts). For a tougher job, the team hacker or face may be very busy at a few checkpoints in the Tír. The end result should be a tense but safe drive out of the elven nation (either thanks to diplomatic immunity, forged e-papers, or bribes and fast talking).

None of which will help with the Salish Orks and their banditry on the way back! The open roads aren't safe at the best of times, but this band of orks are no fans of Harris Stubby and the Orkchop Express. Have cinematically appropriate swarms of orkish raiders attack the one-truck convoy as it moves through the northern mountain passes.

Stubby can either stick to the wheel when the action starts (if your team would rather fight than drive), or he can slurp a little too much from his oversized styrofoam cup filled with some laés-wine frozen concoction (if a player wants to drive the big rig into combat on the Faerie Road!).

AFTERMATH

With the Salish Orks off their back, the players only have one last threat to face: a long ride with Harris Stubby regaling them with stories of his fae heroics, his wild political ramblings, and his unique perspective about human/metahuman/Seelie relations.

At the end of the trip, they'll have payment from the good folks of the Tarislar hospital (including discounted medical care or access to goods), the vague thanks of some patrons in the Tír, and a favor to call on from an eccentric trucker.

ONE FOR ALL

OBJECTIVES

- Find where the captured team is being held
- Find a way into the holding site
- Rescue the team and retrieve paydata

THE SETTING

Much of this mission will be taking place inside the Najima Securities building, a fairly nondescript office building in uptown Seattle. The meeting with Mr. Johnson takes place in Damian's, an American-style restaurant in Downtown famous for large portions and overcooked steaks.

MR. JOHNSON'S PITCH

The blond crewcut in front of you calls himself Dancer. He looks every bit the professional, dressed in a presentable suit, but his face bears recent cuts and bruises, and his expression seems guilty.

"Thanks for coming on such short notice," he says, skipping further pleasantries. "Two nights ago, my team and I broke into a Renraku facility down on the docks. We were tasked with retrieving a set of data files, which our decker managed to do. Almost immediately after that, though, things went pear-shaped in a big way. With the exception of myself, my entire team was captured. I'm not completely sure how I managed to get away. It was ugly."

He takes a deep breath. "I need to rescue my team, but I don't know where they're being held, and even if I did, I can't do this on my own. I need your help, and I'm willing to pay 5 Karma to get it."

THE PLOT

SCENE 1

Suggested NPCs: Dancer (use Reese Frenzy, p. 114)

Once payment is agreed upon, the clock is ticking. The team needs to find out where the captured runner team is being held. There are a variety of avenues they can take to figure this out. They can hit up their contacts and see what's on the grapevine. They could take to the Matrix and hack their way into the Renraku host to find the prisoners. Socially adept characters can try cozying up to Renraku security personnel to sweet-talk the information out of them. They might come up

with ideas of their own. Player creativity should be encouraged and rewarded.

While this is going on, they can interact with Dancer, who eventually comes out and admits that he was the one who screwed up and brought security down on his team in the first place. They can also do some legwork to find out his bona fides; successful research tells them that while Dancer is relatively new to the shadows, his reputation is fairly solid.

SCENE 2

Suggested NPCs: Corporate Security, Corporate Suit

Eventually, the runners should discover that the captured team is being held in a sub-basement of the Najima Securities building further uptown. Through several layers of corporate and legal paperwork, it's easy to determine that Najima is a wholly-owned subsidiary of Renraku Computer Systems. Getting there isn't a problem. It's getting into the secure facility, and then down into the more highly secured sub-basement holding area that present a greater difficulty.

Again, player creativity is encouraged. The direct approach is contra-indicated, but there are a variety of alternatives ranging from impersonating a janitorial crew, to lifting a keycard off one of the guards, to the pure moxie of bluffing their way in.

SCENE 3

Suggested NPCs: Dancer's team (use Shades, p. 120, Sledge, p. 82, Coydog, p. 74, and Bit-Bucket, p. 86, but reduce Strength by 1, increase Willpower by 1)

The captured team is in three different places in the sub-basement. Two of them, a human woman and a male ork, are seated sullenly in a cell. In another cell is a female elf; her hands are bound with special handcuffs that surround and immobilize the entire hand, while her head is completely covered in a tight-fitting leather hood, with only her nose exposed to allow breathing. Any magical character, or those with backgrounds and knowledge skills that include law enforcement and/or magical security will recognize them as magecuffs and a magemask. She is also quite unconscious; Renraku security is taking no chances with a magician attempting to leave their gracious hospitality behind, so they tranqed her to the gills on top of their other precautions.

The fourth member of the team is in an interrogation room. She's a young dwarf woman, surrounded by a couple of medical types preparing to inject her with something. This is the team's decker, and she has a considerable amount of very important paydata locked carefully in her cybernetic headware implants. Her hosts are sparing no effort to get her to unlock her headware, and she's clearly terrified.

They've found the team. It's time now for some daring heroics!

COMPANY TOWN

BACKGROUND

Art Vogel, an environmentalist dwarf who owns nearly twenty-five percent of Ares Macrotechnology, spends most of his time on the corp's Daedalus space station. He's recently come back down to Earth, which has led to speculation that he is up to something.

OBJECTIVES

- Get biometric data from Cross Global Development
- Get employee RFID tag and access code from Gavilan Ventures
- Get ID card and voice recognition sample from Project Avalon

TAGS

- Ares • Detroit • Art Vogel • Cross Global
- Gavilan Ventures • Project Avalon

THE SETTING

Located on the eastern border of Michigan, north of Lake Erie, Detroit is a model of safety and prosperity. Ares might stumble and fall in other places, but in Detroit, they are everything. Even unemployment is under two percent. Oversight by civic and corporate entities merges well to govern this hyper-modern city. The eight-meter wall around the entire sprawl doesn't hurt, either.

MR. JOHNSON'S PITCH

The private room in the Eye of the Needle restaurant offers a spectacular view of the Seattle skyline. A human woman in her mid-thirties, attractive and professionally dressed, is seated at the table, her back to the window. "Thank you for coming this evening," she says once the team is seated. "My employer wants you to access three subsidiaries of Ares Macrotechnology. He needs access code information from employees of these three companies. Subtlety is a must; he wishes to use this information at a later time, and anything that would cause the companies in question to change the access information would make the mission a waste of time."

She pauses and takes a drink, then continues. "Transportation to and from Detroit will be provided, of course. Your compensation for the job will be 6 Karma."

THE PLOT

SCENE 1

Suggested NPCs: Rent-a-cop, Corporate Security, Corporate Suit

Cross Global Development used to be Cross Applied Technologies, a large and diverse umbrella corporation run by Leonard Aurelius. Currently, it is mostly concerned with finance. At Cross Global, biometric scans of both fingerprints and retinas are used to verify employee identification. The runners must somehow acquire samples of these without alerting anyone that there is a problem. Encourage players to come up with creative solutions to getting the ID information.

SCENE 2

Suggested NPCs: Corporate Security, Corporate Suit

Gavilan Ventures is a shell company that is home to twelve percent of Ares' stock. Since its headquarters is in Singapore, Gavilan's Detroit branch serves mostly as a hub for data and human resources. However, there is a large and well-protected server bank in the basement. Those in management are encouraged (read: contracted) to live on site, with their families occupying the upper levels. Managers have an RFID tag implanted on-site once they move in, and they are given a memorized access code. Both are needed to grant them access to Gavilan Ventures' offices.

SCENE 3

Suggested NPCs: Bug Spirits (at least 2 per runner)

Project Avalon was scrapped by Ares for reasons unknown. The facility that housed it is abandoned, and no information on anyone who worked on it is available. Talk around Detroit suggests that nothing was ever moved out of there, so there's a chance that employee records might still be on-site. Once they get in, the runners must head to the HR office to find employee records. Along the way, they find very curious prototype rifles (one per runner) left over from Project Avalon. Unfortunately, they also find an infestation of bug spirits. Once the runners have dealt with the bugs, they find remains of employees, with both ID cards and commlinks with recorded voice notes.

Prototype weapons use the following stats:

	Damage	Close	Near	Far
Project Avalon manatech rifle	12P/AA	OK	OK	–2

The weapons fire a sickly yellow-green bolt of energy and are only effective against bug (and other) spirits. After the first shot, the weapon grows noticeably, almost uncomfortably, warm; after the second shot, some of the components melt, and the weapon is useless.

MY FAIR LADY

MR. JOHNSON'S PITCH

Club Penumbra is hopping tonight. The pulse-pounding rhythms of the Fragging Unicorns are threatening to liquefy your eardrums when Mr. Johnson invites you into a booth and pulls the curtain. A tall elf with bleach blond hair and two datajacks on his skull makes his offer.

"Within my flesh, there is a soul that counts thee its creditor, lords and ladies, for meeting me at this late hour. I would procure thy services for an adventure of most wondrous importance. There remains, here in Seattle, a castle of steel and glass that hath used to hold the name Aneki Corporation. It has since become just another Renraku facility. I wilt be making a run into that same castle tonight. Thy job is to hack into yon computer server on the highest floor whereupon thou must download a file called 'Drake.' In order to distract mine enemies, wait inside yonder Matrix to be noticed, defeat at least one of the foul intrusion countermeasures, then jack out. Escape the castle, I wilt forward thee payment of 5 Karma, and our business wilt be concluded." You aren't sure why he was talking like that, but your fixer said he was good for the money.

OBJECTIVES

- Break into the old Aneki Corp building.
- Head to the top floor.
- Hack in, download the file, defeat at least one IC.

TAGS
- Dodger • Decking • Aneki • Renraku • Drake

THE SETTING

Downtown Seattle, where the old Aneki building is located, is alive with life, despite the pervasive rain that falls this time of year. The building no longer bears the Aneki logo; the blue, glowing letters high up on the west face instead read: Renraku. The building is U-shaped, with a courtyard full of greenery that contrasts with the ultra-modern transparent aluminum that now covers the entire surface of the building. Inside, there is a sterile environment with very few workers, almost as if they are there just to keep up appearances.

THE PLOT

SCENE 1

Suggested NPCs: Rent-a-cops, Enemy Drone (small)

The building is closed for the night, but there are drones and security guards walking the perimeter. The runners can go in with guns blazing or try for stealth. These obstacles won't pose much threat, but they will alert the corporate security inside. On the other hand, if they aren't blasting in, they will have to get past the maglocked doors. Allow the runners to be creative here, and reward sound planning.

SCENE 2

Suggested NPCs: Corporate Security, Security Spider, Enemy Drones (small and medium)

Inside the building, the runners will not face very much resistance unless they made lots of noise on Scene 1, or if they happen to come across a patrolling Corporate Security officer. They should be able to enter the elevator (or take the stairs) and arrive at the top floor with no problems. Once they reach the top floor, however, alarms begin sounding and they are in for a fight. Corporate security will come in waves of four, accompanied by two enemy drones each time. There is only one computer on this floor, and it is in the far north office. The decker could hack into the computer system while their team is fighting the corp, or they could shut down the alarms and stop the waves of security from coming before they hack in.

SCENE 3

Suggested NPCs: Outside the Matrix: Corporate Security, Security Spider, Enemy Drones (small and medium). Inside the Matrix: Intrusion Countermeasures (IC): See below.

Once the decker jacks into the server, the Matrix comes alive to them. This Matrix feels different somehow, like watching an old trid of what people thought the future would look like in the 2050s. All around are what looks like medieval Japanese buildings, but they are obviously upgraded with technology from twenty years ago. The intrusion countermeasures look like robot samurai wearing red armor. The file named "Drake" is located in a well surrounded by a pagoda, and is easy enough for the decker to grab. Once they do, however, the samurai come alive and begin to attack. The decker must defeat at least one, but defeating more would surely cement their reputation as a wiz decker! Once jacked out, the runners must escape the Renraku building, one way or another.

RENRAKU INTRUSION COUNTERMEASURES (IC) RATING 5

Firewall	Log
10	5

Skills: Hacking 3+L
Programs: Mugger: May reroll 1 dice in Cybercombat tests.
Condition Monitors (Matrix): 11

FREE-FOR-ALL

OBJECTIVES

- Survive meeting the Mudplugs
- Survive meeting the Jerk Monkeys
- Choose a side and wipe out the opposition

TAGS

- Gang warfare • Interference • Sewers • Protection

THE SETTING

You think the Tacoma Aroma is formidable on the surface? Wait until you go underground. The sewers are dark, confining, and rank. Not to mention inhabited by squatters, gangs, and critters both malignant and benign. We'll leave out the explosive gases for now.

MR. JOHNSON'S PITCH

Benjamin Tucker is not a very big man, but he doesn't appear all that nervous facing a tableful of shadowrunners. "My name's Mr. Johnson," he says. "Blah blah blah. Look, I'm going to get down to it. There's a gang problem near my place in Tacoma. Two gangs, the Mudplugs and the Jerk Monkeys, inhabit the sewer system, in sort of their own mini-Underground. They're starting to argue over turf down there, and it's spilling out into the streets and it's threatening local businesses. I need one or the other of them wiped out; I don't care which. One of them needs to survive and stay down there, though; there are other things that live down there, and the gangs keep them in check."

THE PLOT

SCENE 1

Suggested NPCs: Gangers (one per runner), rats, and devil rats.

A little bit of research shows that there are a couple of known entrances into the gang-controlled areas of the Tacoma sewers. It also shows that there's not really a lot known about the gangs. For the runners to decide which gang to back and which to help wipe out, they're going to have to go down and get to know them.

Choosing an entrance at random, they go down and encounter a small hunting party from the Mudplugs. This gang is mostly orks, but there are also some humans and dwarfs in their ranks. They're hunting rats and devil rats to fill up the gang's larder, which is growing a little thin. The Mudplugs are not fans of those who dwell on the surface, and are not happy to see the team impinging on their turf. With little hesitation, they're ready to rumble with the team.

SCENE 2

Suggested NPCs: Gangers, rats, and devil rats.
And a couple hellhounds.

After assessing the Mudplugs, it's time to go see about the opposition. One of the other entrances takes them into a different, but eerily similar, section of the sewer system. The ubiquitous hordes of rats are everywhere.

Hearing yelping and cursing, the runners follow the noises to find a gnarled-looking dwarf wearing the colors of the Jerk Monkeys, training a pair of largish hellhounds. He's using the expedient, but unpopular, "beat the stuffing out of them with a bat" method of training, and it may or may not be working. He's at least managed to not be roasted alive yet. He takes a certain amount of exception to being interrupted, especially if the runners have issues with his training methods. He'll give a sharp whistle, and a few more gangers will start to appear a narration or two after things start heating up. And they'll heat up, literally, since the imperfectly trained hellhounds will also join in the fray. Let them add a note of chaos to the fight.

SCENE 3

Suggested NPCs: Gangers. Lots and lots of gangers.

Now that they've had encounters with both gangs, the team needs to decide on which horse they're going to back. Then they have to go down into the sewers again and convince that gang's leadership that the enemy of their enemy is their friend. Which, considering how the introductions probably went down, isn't going to be all that easy. Once the leadership is convinced, it's time to marshal the troops—all of them—and go to war with the other side.

LEAKS AND PLUMBERS, PT. 1

CONTEXT

From *Cold & Hard* entry for Brackhaven, Kenneth: ... while Brackhaven had never exactly been a beloved governor, he had a talent for remaining liked enough to keep being re-elected, and that's all he needed. During his watch he had a serial killer, a copycat of the serial killer, a mass attack on his district attorneys, and more thrown at him, and he listened to the boos hurled at him by angry crowds but still stayed in office. He teetered when the Ork Underground became an official district of the city against his wishes, but he looked like he might retain enough corporate support to stay in place—until the revelations of just how far he went to bury the Underground came out. It's not clear what led to the corps removing their backing from him—whether it was disgust at his lack of morals, or disappointment that he went all-out and still couldn't bring home a victory—but whatever the cause, the closest allies Brackhaven had throughout his administration withdrew themselves, leaving Brackhaven alone, defenseless, and with no option besides retirement ...

BACKGROUND

Kenneth Brackhaven has resigned, and a forthcoming election will put a new governor into office. The candidates are numerous and jockeying for power, which makes it a great situation for shadowrunners. Some politicians have considerable warchests, and a portion of that money is going to make its way into the shadows.

MR. JOHNSON'S PITCH

Ms. Johnson is a young, earnest staffer working for frequent gubernatorial candidate Josephine Dzugashvilli, and she invites the runners to a nondescript diner to make the following pitch:

"We have a leak in our office. Every argument we test internally is getting out to our opponents, giving them a chance to lay the groundwork for refuting it before we even make it. We want to find the leak, but we also want to find out who's behind it—and put a little hurt on them for the way they've screwed us up. We're going to do some good in this city, but first we're going to have to play a little rough. We're ready for that, and we've got 5 Karma for each of you to make this happen."

OBJECTIVES

- Find the source of the leak.
- Discover which candidate the leaker is working for.
- Pull off a political dirty trick against the rival candidate.

TAGS

- Seattle • Politics • Brackhaven • Dirty Tricks • Governor

THE SETTING

Dzugashvili views herself as a woman of the people, so she has set up her campaign headquarters in western Renton, not far from Downtown. It's in a strip mall, in between a discount shoe store and a Stuffer Shack (natch). It's a busy place, with people constantly making calls, having policy meetings, and checking the latest polling data. The runners will be identified as volunteers, giving them freedom to wander around the headquarters. They should occasionally look busy to maintain their cover story.

THE PLOT

SCENE 1

Suggested NPCs: Campaign workers (use Corporate Suits)

The latest leak from the campaign involved some information about candidate and director of the Seattle FBI office Katherine Choi, who was alleged to be using many forms of torture, including magically based torture, in her office's interrogations. Before Dzugashvili could get an attack out, Choi released an ad portraying her as someone who would do literally anything to protect the citizens of Seattle, and the populace ate it up. Dzugashvili's attack was neutered before it was unleashed. The first step to find out who is behind the leak would be checking in on the team members who were working with the Choi oppo data and see who might have leaked it. Deputy speechwriter Ben Solondz, volunteer coordinator Maria Castille, and assistant campaign coordinator Beatrice Cornstone are all possible culprits; the runners will have to use their social and networking skills to identify who is the leaker.

SCENE 2

Suggested NPCs: Gangers

Finding the leaker is one thing; finding out what campaign they are working for is another. As it turns out, the obvious suspect, Katherine Choi, has nothing to do with the leaker. Again, the runners will have to rely on

their social and Matrix skills to try to make connections, but they can get a boost when a squad of gangers attacks them in an effort to shut them up. One of the gangers, it turns out, just signed up as a campaign volunteer for Downtown mayor Nikola Taul. It seems in Taul's efforts to build a big-time political machine, she has adopted some questionable means of getting ahead.

SCENE 3

Suggested NPCs: None

Once Taul has been identified as the source of the spies in Dzugashvili's office, Dzugashvili wants revenge. Any con will do, but if the runners are in need of an idea, Dzugashvili can suggest getting Taul to donate to a fake charity. Taul has a strong relationship with Knight Errant, so perhaps getting her to donate to a charity she thinks will support officers wounded in the line of duty but in reality funds a bunraku parlor run by and for Knight Errant officers would do the trick. The runners need to remember that Taul has already responded to their efforts with violence, and may do so again if she catches wind about what they are up to.

LEAKS AND PLUMBERS, PT. 2

CONTEXT

From *Cold & Hard* entry for Oaks, Dana: Possibly the last incorruptible thing left in the Sixth World, District Attorney Oaks has resisted dozens if not hundreds of attempted bribes, years of pressure from Kenneth Brackhaven before he left office, and an assassination attempt, all the while remaining convinced that her job was to dispense justice in a tough but fair manner. She is steely, determined, and humorless, and she is also tremendously good at what she does. If she ran a corporation, it would be on its way to AAA status, but she chooses to apply herself to government, so she is destined to remain a large, high-integrity fish in a small pond.

MR. JOHNSON'S PITCH

Mr. Johnson, a well-groomed dwarf, does not immediately identify his affiliation; instead, he uses the following approach:

"Believe it or not, a few of us are naïve enough to think that this election is our last, best hope to bring some sort of integrity to the governor's office, and to perhaps make Seattle a more honest city. Scoff if you want, but there is little point to putting a lot of work in some area if you don't think you can make a difference.

"What I'm saying is there are people who believe this election should be done *right*, and we are willing to do a lot to make it work better. If there are people out there who have done illegal things, or know of people who have done illegal things with this election, we might be looking to make examples of them. Unless they help us out.

"It's time to get on the right side and make this election work right. Luckily, I'm not asking you to be altruistic—you'd get 4 Karma out of the deal, while some of your recent exploits might be overlooked by people who would be in a position to make your life more difficult.

"We want to know what people are planning and use it to our advantage. Go get me some intel I can use.

OBJECTIVES

- Learn what shenanigans campaigns are planning.
- Determine what to do with information about a planned act of violence.
- Head off the violence and try to keep the streets of Seattle calm.

TAGS

- Seattle • Politics • Dirty Tricks • Governor • Humanis Policlub

THE SETTING

While gubernatorial candidate Josephine Dzugashvilli is based in Renton, the other candidates tend to keep their headquarters Downtown, the better to facilitate meetings with various city powers. Runners will be hopping back and forth between these rather simple offices, but eventually they'll have to head to the border of Redmond and Bellevue to head off a planned act of extreme violence.

THE PLOT

SCENE 1

Suggested NPCs: Campaign workers (use Corporate Suits)

This should be a fun spying scene, where the runners use spy gear, social skills, intimidation, and hacking to learn some of the numerous dirty tricks candidates are pulling on each other. From discovering that New Century Party candidate Alonso Solis is being propped up by the Katherine Choi and Howard Cannon campaigns in

an apparent effort to split the populist vote to learning that the Scholl campaign is manufacturing connections of UCAS Senator Charles Seaver to the mysterious Black Lodge, there should be plenty of dirt to discover. To cap it all off, the runners learn that the Choi campaign is funneling money (very indirectly) to the Humanis Policlub. And this is not just general support—they are helping the club buy arms and recruit members for a major gathering on the border of Redmond and Bellevue in one week. Looks like they have violence on their minds.

SCENE 2

Suggested NPCs: Campaign workers and Government bureaucrats (use Corporate Suits)

The runners have found information about one of the dirtiest of all possible dirty tricks; now they need to figure out what to do about it. They could approach Choi with what they know and either get her to stop the effort or give them a cut of the action; they could approach DA Oaks to help law enforcement crack down on Choi; they could inform her opponents; or one of many other options. This is where they need to figure out what their information can make happen, and how much it might be worth to the right bidder.

SCENE 3

Suggested NPCs: Gangers (and plenty of 'em)

Heading off the planned attack on Redmond won't be easy, because most of the other parties involved seem to want to let it happen. DA Oaks knows she can get several arrests from the attack, and she thinks the chance to clear scum off the street is too valuable to pass up. Choi's people have worked long and hard to plan this riot, and they are not inclined to call it off. Candidates whose constituents might be harmed in the planned attack, like Dzugashvilli and Redmond Mayor Sonya Scholl, would love to stop the attack but have little means to do so. The runners will have to act fast—intercepting arms, perhaps confronting Humanis personnel, and trying to keep the planned area of attack free of as many innocent passers-by as possible. It's likely they won't be able to fully stop the attack from happening, which will make them face another question: Intervene in the attack and try to keep the loss of life as low as possible, or stand back and let political nature take its course?

BENEATH THE SANDS, PT. 1

CONTEXT

Word Watch: Reagent n. A normally mundane item with a high concentration of mana. Reagents take many different forms, dictated by the tradition of the user. Examples could be ancient trinkets or pure elements for hermetic mages, or animal bones or rare plants for shamans. Most reagents from any given tradition do not work well for practitioners of other traditions, affording talismongers of the Sixth World a measure of job security.

Spirit whisperer n. A person engaged in the illegal rental of spirits. These individuals summon spirits, bind them, and rent them as slaves for others' use, often for shadowrunning purposes. Spirit whisperers often have a poor reputation in the spirit world and are often in partnership with disreputable talismongers.

BACKGROUND

The Apep Consortium comprises three companies; Nubian Insurance Company (NIC), the United Bank of Panama, and Jomakou Industries. They have been a major player in the hunt for ancient and magical artifacts since the early 2060 and are most successful in the Mediterranean, African, and Middle-Eastern regions of the world.

MR. JOHNSON'S PITCH

A local spirit whisperer called Alyosha Duska needs something stolen. One of his spirits tipped him off to a load of magical reagents coming into Seattle's harbor tonight. The runners need to find which crate the reagents are in, and then bring it back to Duska without bringing any heat down onto him. The proposed payment for the job is 4 Karma.

OBJECTIVES

- Find the crate with the reagents
- Bring the crate to Alyosha Duska.

TAGS

- Magic Artifact • Egypt • Spirits • Reagents
- Apep Consortium • Bug Spirits

THE SETTING

Even at night, Seattle harbor's Terminal 30 is alive with motion. Every product imaginable eventually finds its way onto a boat bound for the Emerald city. Dock workers and ship crews hustle to and from cargo freighters, moving massive shipping containers from boats on the sea to storage facilities on land. The smell of the ocean is commingling with the stench of the Seattle Sprawl.

THE PLOT

SCENE 1

Suggested NPCs: Rent-a-cops, Enemy Drones (Small)

The runners have arrived at Terminal 30 and have to find out which of the hundreds of possible shipping containers coming in tonight contains the crate Duska paid them to find. The runners need to be a bit sneaky unless they want corporate security making their night miserable. The crate is coming in on a ship called Snake Island Express, carrying goods from Mitsuhama Magical Services, a subsidiary of Mitsuhama Computer Technologies. The crate will be the only content in shipping container MMS204897. How the runners find out which crate that is and where it sits can be determined by the players and gamemaster unspooling the story together.

SCENE 2

Suggested NPCs: Corp Security (use Soldier),
Enemy Drones (Medium)

Once the crate is secure, they must transfer it somehow to their employer. Unless the runners take great care to be stealthy, attracting unwanted attention is likely. But the runners should be able to make it out of the harbor with little trouble. On the way, however, they are assaulted by a strike team from the Apep Consortium, who want the crate for themselves.

SCENE 3

Suggested NPCs: None

Once Duska has the crate, he opens it to confirm the goods. There aren't quite as many as he thought, but he concedes that the runners are not to blame for this. Rather, he is curious about another of the crate's contents. An ornamental scarab, gold and turquoise by the look of it, seems to have made its way from ancient Egypt and into this crate. Wanting to study it further, Duska pays the runners and politely shoos them away.

BENEATH THE SANDS, PT. 2

MR. JOHNSON'S PITCH

Alyosha Duska contacts the runners once again. The scarab in the crate is no ordinary artifact. Duska claims that it is the key to unlocking some sort of treasure horde from ancient Egypt. Duska tells the runners that the Apep Consortium has threatened his life if he doesn't hand it over, so he wants them to take the scarab, get on a plane to Egypt, and meet with Duska's Egyptian guide (Ammon Talib). They will then use the scarab to enter the Pyramid of Dimeh, which until recently was completely buried. They are to secure what treasure they can and escape. Duska promises he can fence the treasure and will give the runners a cut, which should amount to 5 Karma or so.

OBJECTIVES

- Meet with Duska's Egyptian guide
- Take the scarab to the Pyramid of Dimeh in Egypt.
- Use the scarab to enter the pyramid and take possession of the treasure.

THE SETTING

Egypt's Dimeh al-Siba is an isolated place, far from modern convenience. Permits are required to even get close. Thankfully, your guide, Mr. Ammon Talib, took care of that. Ancient temples, houses, underground chambers, and walls made of mud bricks show what used to exist here thousands of years ago, before the harsh sands and winds reduced them to ruins. Following a path that had long since been destroyed, the sands have been parted to reveal an enormous pyramid, rivaling the size of any you've seen before. The entrance is guarded.

THE PLOT

SCENE 1

Suggested NPCs: Rent-a-cops, Enemy Drones (Small)

The runners and Ammon must somehow deal with the guards or slip past them to enter the Pyramid. Inside, a dark hallway leads into the pyramid's interior and opens up to a large entrance chamber. All around are gargantuan statues of beetles. At a certain point, the runners notice the scarab artifact glowing and pulsing. Ammon seems giddy.

SCENE 2:

Suggested NPCs: Ammon (use Elite Soldier)

Ammon will point out that there appears to be a hidden nook below the largest scarab statue, which looks like a housing for the scarab. Upon placing the scarab there, a hidden door opens up, revealing a dark tunnel. If possible, Ammon attempts to open the door, take the scarab, and run into the hallway before the door closes behind him. But he will avoid revealing himself unless he is certain of success.

SCENE 3

Suggested NPCs: Hem'netjer Mages (use Enemy Mage), Beetle Spirit Queen (use Bug Queen)

The final hallway leads to what looks like a royal chamber. The hieroglyphics all around the room are illuminated by an unearthly glow. They depict a scene of abject horror. Robed priests stand around an altar, strapping down some unfortunate ancient woman. Priests with beetle masks gesture toward the altar as magic arcs toward the victim. In the next scene, the victim is transformed into the horrifyingly large and twisted form of a queen insect. In the next frame, the priests wail as the queen is buried by some magical force. After the runners have looked around, Ammon will reveal himself to be a servant of the Hem'netjer—mages who serve an ancient beetle spirit. Ammon greedily thanks them for their help. He tells them the scarab needed to be brought here so the queen could awaken once more. The ground shakes beneath their feet as the floor gives way to reveal a slowly awakening beetle queen. She is powerful, but after sleeping so long, she has not regained her full strength yet. The runners must stop her and Ammon before she fully awakens!

SCENE 4

Suggested NPCs: Apep Consortium Reps (use Elite Soldiers), Enemy Drones (Medium)

After the battle, the runners find very little of value in the chamber. The stories of wealth were overrated. When the runners leave, they are confronted by representatives of the Apep Consortium, who, in light of the runner's destroying the beetle spirit threat, offer to pay the runners a fair sum in return for the scarab.

ARABIAN KNIGHTS, PT. 1

CONTEXT

Arabian Caliphate: Until recently, King Kalim Ibn Saud was the caliph of the Arabian Caliphate. He, along with the tribal leaders of the various emirates, kept a tight rein on the population. The only thing that keeps them from outright war on metahumans and the Awakened is the Great Dragon Aden. In 2020, when Iran declared war on metahumans, Aden rampaged over Tehran, destroying everything within five miles of the Ayatollah's compound, making clear that aggression against metahumans would not be tolerated. Aden's action may have had the appearance of making the Middle East safer for metahumans and the Awakened, but in reality, the intolerance remained, simmering just below the surface.

New Islamic Jihad: Aden's actions may have made things safer for many, but it did not change many hearts or beliefs in the early years of the Awakening. In the last few decades, however, many minds have been changing. When Ibn Eisa united the Islamic world behind him in the 2060s, he called for jihad against metahumans, the Awakened, and a number of faiths and Middle-Eastern nations. However, when Ibn Eisa was subsequently revealed to be a shedim, or shadow demon, many of the devout began to question whether their current leaders were really sent by Allah. While this feeling has not led to revolution, it rekindled calls for reformation, which have been simmering since the 2050s. There are those, however, who continue to see war as the best way to deliver change.

IRM: Among the common people, the Islamic Renaissance Movement has been the most successful in shifting attitudes within the Islamic world, specifically around women, metahumans, and the Awakened. Their work has even yielded some small support within the Islamic Unity Movement. But for many, the progress has been too small and too slow.

GOAT FOOT

Goat Foot is a female satyr and Muslim scholar. She is a regular on JackPoint and is an operative for the Islamic Unity Movement (IUM), but her interests often dovetail with the Islamic Renaissance Movement. She wears a full hijab in dark colors, but her eyes are a striking violet color.

MR. JOHNSON'S PITCH

A shadowrunner known as Goat Foot has been working for the Islamic Unity Movement for decades. They push reform in the Islamic world and have succeeded on many fronts. One area they are not succeeding is within the leadership of the Arabian Caliphate, which retain prejudice against metahumans and have outlawed magic. Goat Foot has become impressed with the runners' reputations, and she needs out of town assets. Meeting her in Dubai, she makes the following pitch:

"Just last week, the Caliph, King Kalim Ibn Saud, was found dead in his bedroom. No reports have been released as to the cause of death, but the IRM believe that this event has provided an opportunity to create change within the Arabian Caliphate. Before the tribal representatives vote for a new Caliph, you need to get to at least four of the voting emirates and convince them to vote for Ibrahim Kamel, CEO of Caliphate-based AA holding company Haqibat Alqabida. He is Sunni but is sympathetic to Sufi Islam and the IRM. This will allow a more moderate leader to come to power and change the dynamics in the Middle East.

"The first emirate you need to convince is Jassim bin Joaan Al Thani, the voting emir of Qatar. Emir Jassim bin Joaan Al Thani is a decent man and loves his wife and two daughters more than anything else. That is why you are going to kidnap them and bring them to us. This might seem unsavory, but I assure you, it is necessary. We will keep them safe and treat them well until the vote is over. It is imperative that you do not harm or treat them poorly in any way. Doing so will negatively affect your pay. Speaking of pay, I am prepared to offer you six Karma for this job."

OBJECTIVES

- Kidnap Emir Jassim bin Joaan Al Thani's family.
- Escape Qatar
- Deliver Al Thani's family safe and unharmed to Goat Foot

TAGS

- Middle East • Arabian Caliphate • Kidnapping • Politics
- Islamic Renaissance Movement • New Islamic Jihad
- Global Sandstorm • Computer Virus • Break In

THE SETTING

Qatar is a relatively small emirate in the Arabian Caliphate. The waters of the Persian Gulf encircle all but its southern border with the Arabian Heartland. The jewel in Qatar's crown is the capital, Doha, with its brilliant skyline and ultramodern architecture. In the streets, souks, or Arabian markets/bazaars offer street food, along with all manner of art, silk, jewelry, and clothing. Runners take note: Qatar expects women to keep covered to the shoulders and knees, and magic is strictly prohibited.

THE PLOT

SCENE 1

Suggested NPCs: Emirate Security (use Soldiers),

Enemy Drones (Small)

Getting into Qatar is easy. Goat Foot can get the runners a plane or a boat into the emirate. Once there, the runners need to do some legwork and figure out where Emir Jassim bin Joaan Al Thani's family will be. When they are at home, security is overwhelming, and the runners will find it nearly impossible to reach them. However, rumor has it that Al Thani is out of the city, in Northern Qatar, for a few days this week. His wife Geri and his daughters, Gabrielle and Lola, will be visiting Doha's *Mathaf*, the Arab Museum of Modern Art. Allow the runners to formulate any plot they like, and as long as it is remotely plausible, then have some fun pulling it off.

Note: Given how magic is suppressed, a mage might be able to turn the advantage greatly in the runner's favor. Keep in mind, though, that the penalties will be harsh and swift for anyone caught wielding mana.

SCENE 2

Suggested NPCs: Smugglers (use Gangers)

Once the runners have secured Geri, Gabrielle, and Lola, all hell breaks loose. The city goes into lockdown, and not long after, airports, railways, and harbors halt all travel. The runners must now hide their precious cargo while finding some way out of Qatar and back to Goat Foot in Dubai. If the runners try to remain cautious but seek out help, they will find Doha's underground can provide them with smugglers who can get them out via boat. However, they should always feel that there is a decent chance that they are going to be betrayed, even by the smugglers.

During this whole scene, Geri, Gabrielle, and Lola should come alive with their own personalities, fears, and irritations, not simply as willing background noise in Jassim bin Joaan's life. Geri might be indignant and entitled, continuing to expound on how "the runners will pay for this!" Gabrielle would hide her fear using sarcasm and defiance. Lola will be worried but will gain boldness when the other two falter.

SCENE 3

Suggested NPCs: Smugglers (use Gangers),

Enemy Drones (Small)

This scene takes place as the runners arrive at a hidden dock in Dubai. The smuggler has put the pieces together about his cargo and informed associates of his to meet him when he arrives. They plan on taking Geri, Gabrielle, and Lola for their own ends, and so it falls on the runners to defeat them and get them to Goat Foot unharmed.

ARABIAN KNIGHTS, PT. 2

CONTEXT

Word Watch: Djinn \djin\ n. Free Elemental Spirits native to the Metaplanes. Most have kinship to fire or air, although earth and water djinn have been encountered. These free spirits are most often summoned by Islamic mages and bound carefully with licit Qur'anic magic to inanimate objects, as not doing so would invite evil onto the mage, according to Islamic tradition.

Corporate Court n. A body of arbitration for extraterritorial megacorporations. The Corporate Court (CC) has complete authority over disputes involving the AAA megacorps. Founded in 2023 by seven corporations, it is housed on the Zurich-Orbital space station. Currently the Court has thirteen justices representing ten corporations. The court's members (or "justices") are selected to represent the corporations' interests and ensure equity in judgement.

MR. JOHNSON'S PITCH

Goat Foot tells the runners that she has been in contact with an unnamed board member from the AAA corporation Mitsuhama Computer Technologies. Mitsuhama wants another ally on the international Corporate Court, and facilitating the creation of a new AAA corporation would do just that. Given that it would also play against Saeder-Krupp (the current second-largest AAA corporation, behind Mitsuhama), Mitsuhama is willing to help bring Global Sandstorm up to AAA status and sponsor them for entry into the Corporate Court if an opportunity arises. Global Sandstorm's board is willing to offer Emir Sulaiman Hamad Al Futtaim of the United Emirates the seat on the Court, provided he votes for Ibrahim Kamel as Caliph. Unfortunately, neither Mitsuhama nor Global Sandstorm has been able to contact Al Futtaim, although he clearly still runs the United Emirates. Goat Foot is concerned that his lack of communication and erratic behavior could mean disaster for her long-term plans. She hires the runners to track down Al Futtaim and get to the bottom of his behavior, and if possible, make Global Sandstorm's pitch in person.

OBJECTIVES

- Enter the United Emirates and locate the Emir.
- Break into his compound, doing as little damage as possible.
- Make Mitsuhama's pitch to Emir Al Futtaim

THE SETTING

Abu Dhabi is a world-class city whose luxurious beaches sit on the Persian Gulf. It has two hundred natural islands and four hundred kilometers of coastline. It's an adventurer's dream with falconry and dune bashing. It's a posh sanctuary of high-rise towers, glittering palaces and high-end shopping. And it's a historian's playground, with the world's largest mosques, desert camps, and oases. One of the coolest things about this Arabian haven is all of the ways available for you to explore all it has to offer—including hot-air balloons across the desert, helicopter excursions, and bus, camel, and boat tours. Whatever you choose to do in Abu Dhabi, rest assured that your time there will be filled with adventure and culture.

THE PLOT

SCENE 1

Suggested NPCs: None

The Emir's presidential palace is in the United Emirates' capital of Abu Dhabi. The runners should begin by gathering information about where the palace is and how best to break in. As this is happening, via Matrix legwork or hitting the streets, the runners should find out that Al Futtaim isn't in his palace much. In fact, while extraordinarily ambitious, he has become known as a man of the people. The next few days, he will be visiting the fire damage caused by an oil accident in the Motor City district.

SCENE 2

Suggested NPCs: Personal Guards (use Soldiers), Enemy Drones (Medium)

Let the runners come up with a plan to get Al Futtaim alone. Don't feel obligated to favor one course or another. Let them have fun (and if they spend enough Plot Points, let them pull it off). Al Futtaim will be heavily guarded at all times, so a direct approach might be difficult. A few options might be a) swapping out his limousine driver, b) the decker finding out his itinerary and waiting inside the home of a citizen he will visit, or c) creating a diversion and grabbing him out from under

his security. Reward the runners' creativity, and become a fan of whatever plan they come up with.

SCENE 3

Suggested NPCs: Personal Guard (use Elite Soldiers), Bound Djinn (use Greater Spirit of Air)

This final scene takes place once the runners have found a way to engage with Emir Al Futtaim away from his security, or perhaps in spite of them. Al Futtaim, even in this extreme circumstance, conducts himself with poise and does not ever appear weak or distressed. He simply introduces himself as Sulaiman Hamad Al Futtaim, Emir of the United Emirates, adding that, "you, my friends, have made a grave mistake." Now, Al Futtaim unleashes a bound djinn from his ink pen, which immediately attacks the runners. After the djinn's defeat, Al Futtaim seems like a different person. He reasons that the djinn that he held in his ink pen was supposed to protect him, but it was not what it seemed to be and instead had been influencing his mind. He is grateful to the runners and pleased to accept the offer. Al Futtaim offers them any immediate assistance they need, and releases them without further incident.

ARABIAN KNIGHTS, PT. 3

MR. JOHNSON'S PITCH

Goat Foot informs the runners of Jaber Al-Mishal Al-Sabah, emir of Kuwait. He cares little about anything besides oil revenue. Ruyat Baghdad Oil is the largest Iraq-based oil company, and Al-Sabah wants to know their secrets. The Arabian Caliphate is negotiating with (many say bullying) Iraq to join the Caliphate, and if they do, having insider information ahead of time will allow Al-Sabah to manipulate Iraq's oil future in his favor. If the runners can plant the Cl@$$yJinn virus in the Ruyat Baghdad host, Al-Sabah has assured Goat Foot that he will support Ibrahim Kamel for Caliph. Plus, the runners will earn themselves 5 Karma.

OBJECTIVES

- Break into Ruyat Baghdad Oil
- Install the Cl@$$yJinn virus onto a private host.
- Escape without leaving any loose ends.

THE SETTING

Baghdad is located on the Tigris River, and at one time was the center of the Muslim world. Baghdad, more than almost any other city in the Sixth World, is a city of turbulence. Every decade or so since the early 2000s, Baghdad achieves a measure of peace and vibrant nightlife and giant bazaars return, offering cultural gems, unique cuisine, and insights from an illustrious history. However, just when Baghdad gets back on its feet, conflict always seems to plunge it back into chaos. For the last few years, it has been in a chaotic cycle. Militants and insurgents, along with mistrustful law enforcement and military, roam the streets, making suspicion the order of the day. Bombings, unexploded mines, and marketplace violence make Baghdad the number three city on the Corporate Court's international do-not-visit list. Best of luck, chummers.

THE PLOT

SCENE 1

Suggested NPCs: Government Security (use Soldiers), Enemy Drones (Small), Enemy Drones (Heavy)

As the runners enter the city of Baghdad, they are hassled every step of the way. All government security is suspicious at borders, airports, and docks. The gamemaster may want to consider using a Plot Point to have a runner's fake ID flagged at a checkpoint. No matter how careful they are, it seems the government is more suspicious. Simply approaching Ruyat Baghdad Oil headquarters should feel like a spy movie, in that the building is easy to spot, but it has heavy guards in an office building that takes up four city blocks.

SCENE 2

Suggested NPCs: Corporate Security, Enemy Drones (Medium)

Breaking into Ruyat Baghdad Oil should be difficult. Any scheme the runners try should be met with some kinds of challenges. However, if the runners are discreet and ask the shadows, they will find rumors of a sewer line leading from a ravine right up into the bowels of Ruyat Baghdad. It will be heavily armored and difficult to break into, but once in, the opposition will be minimal if they are careful. A connection to Ruyat Baghdad Oil's private host is located on the fifth basement level, two levels above the sewer output. The threat of corporate security is real and should be in the forefront of the runners' minds, but teams going out of their way to keep silent (being creative, succeeding at skill rolls, spending Plot Points) should be able to do so.

SCENE 3

Suggested NPCs: Brutal Dogs gangers (Use Gangers)

Once the Cl@$$yJinn virus is installed in the Ruyat Baghdad private host, the runners should be able to easily slip back out the way they came. The only hitch is that the ravine where the sewers empty out is controlled by a local Baghdad gang known as the Brutal Dogs ("Kallab Wahashia" in Arabic). They will immediately attack the runners at the first sign of their exit. If not dealt with, these gangers might find a way to exploit what they have seen and complicate the runners' requirement of discretion. The runners should have no trouble returning to Goat Foot once the run is over.

ARABIAN KNIGHTS, PT. 4

MR. JOHNSON'S PITCH

Emir Talal bin Ali of Jordan is willing to entertain Ibrahim Kamel as Caliph, as he has a child who is Awakened, but only if they can help him eliminate a New Islamic Jihad cell that continues to target his family for death. They must do this without the Emir's support, as he will deny any involvement with the runners. The Emir believes the delicate peace could be disrupted by the hiring of foreign criminals to attack his rivals. The job is important enough that he offers 7 Karma.

OBJECTIVES

- Do legwork on the New Islamic Jihad group in Jordan
- Make sure that they are no longer a threat to Emir Talal bin Ali's family.
- Bring proof to Emir Talal bin Ali.

THE SETTING

Downtown Amman is a labyrinth of streets and markets, mosques, and coffeehouses, surrounded by hills. Ancient Roman ruins mix with museums, the magisterial Citadel, and modern life in Jordan. The locals often disagree about what it means to be Ammani, because there are so many true answers. Poor refugees rub shoulders with wealthy western-educated business folk. Muslims of many variations live as neighbors with Christians, atheists, and Nabatean revivalists. While they may often scoff at each other's ways, a hard-fought balance of peace has been achieved within the city.

THE PLOT

SCENE 1

Suggested NPCs: None

There are very few leads from Goat Foot or Emir bin Ali regarding the whereabouts of the New Islamic Jihad cell in Amman. This means the players must get creative in their search. However they go about their legwork, let them find out that the NIJ cell has been kidnapping awakened children. Ask the runners to describe what additional information they find about the NIJ's disruptive activities. Eventually, their investigation will lead to a recently fired member of the Emir's security guard.

SCENE 2

Suggested NPCs: None

If the runners track down the guard, they will find him at his home in Western Amman. The guard introduces himself as Moha. He was recently placed on leave for questioning the ability of the Minister of Security to protect the Emir's family. If the runners explain themselves or ask for help, Moha will tell them "the Emir's daughter, Nina, has secretly been in Prince Hamza Hospital for three days, being treated for an unknown ailment. The New Islamic Jihad cell in Amman plans to kidnap her, and may strike at any time. If you were to guard the Emir's daughter *and* capture the Jihadists, then they surely will convince the Emir to vote for Ibrahim Kamel as Caliph.

SCENE 3

Suggested NPCs: New Islamic Jihadists (use Soldiers)

The Prince Hamza Hospital is more guarded than normal. The runners should display some cleverness and creativity in developing a plan to get in. No matter how they eventually proceed, they will enter Nina's room in time to see a group of New Islamic Jihadists gathered around a sick child. After the runners deal with the kidnappers, they should make plans to exit. But security has significantly increased, and the runners now have a child along for the ride. At some point before or after they leave the hospital, the runners should notice (possibly with help of a biometric scan) that the child is not Nina.

This child, Clara, was planted by the NIJ in Nina's room as a decoy, and has been surgically altered to resemble the Emir's daughter. She was in the middle of being placed when the runners arrived. Nina has already been kidnapped and taken to the NIJ cell's base of operations. Clara, having not been treated well, is willing to help the runners. She tells them she can take them to the base, but they must hurry because the operatives are already in the process of moving.

SCENE 4

Suggested NPCs: New Islamic Jihadists leaders (use Elite Soldiers), Enemy Drones (Small), Enemy Drones (Medium), Enemy Drones (Heavy)

Clara leads the runners to the Eastern district of Amman, the more traditional and conservative of the two halves of the city. People here will be unlikely to help outsiders. But with Clara's help, they are able to find not only Nina, but almost two dozen other Awakened children being held against their will. The cell has been using pharmaceuticals and fear to keep them from using their abilities. Unfortunately, the runners must deal with the NIJ cell as well. When all is said and done, among the combatants, they find that Khalid Munif, the Emir's Minister of Security, was at the head of the cell.

EPILOGUE

Emir Talal bin Ali of Jordan, grateful to the runners, is true to his word. Goat Foot is also grateful, and she claims that, although the work was often unsavory, the future will be brighter due to the runners actions, which is not something that shadowrunners often hear. Months later, the runners will hear a news trid, informing them that Ibrahim Kamel has succeed King Kalim Ibn Saud as the new ruler of the Arabian Caliphate. Caliph Kamel promises a unified Caliphate, standing strong amid a world that has too long followed the path the West has set for it. Caliph Ibrahim Kamel's first act as ruler was to formalize the joining together of Syria and Iraq within the Arabian Caliphate, which had been slowly making progress since the early 2060s.

UN-SEELED FATE, PT. 1

CONTEXT

Yellowstone Calamity: Only called so by the pretentious Seelie Court, which views all foreigners to their realm with disdain. But indeed, the incident in Yellowstone has brought more than a few foreigners over. The "calamity" was a minor physical eruption coupled with a more significant explosion of mana on the astral plane, ripping a hole in the veil between our world and the world of the faerie. There may also be some truth to the rumor that the incident in Yellowstone has caused a breach in the mana reserve keeping the Seelie Court in its own, private, metaplane. If this proves correct, "calamity" may prove to be the correct word, both for the Seelie and for magic in the Sixth World.

MR. JOHNSON'S DEVICE

The device that Mr. Johnson gives the runners is a chest made of obsidian. It is cool to the touch and, aside from a power switch on the top center, has no other features. It is giving off a strong wireless signal and radiates strong magic.

MR. JOHNSON'S PITCH

"Good evening. Thank you for coming all the way to Denver for this meeting. Your team comes highly recommended. My name is Jefferson Tlazopilli, I represent a company known as Snake Mountain. If you accept this job, I would like your team to go north into the Sioux Nation, to the igneous butte known as the Devil's Tower. Getting into the Sioux Nation will require some skill, but getting near the Devil's Tower will be much more difficult, as the Lakota keep a close guard on the area. That is why I am hiring deniable assets. Please take this device and place it as close as you can to Devil's Tower. On top of the butte is ideal. The Lakota Warrior Society has orders to shoot on sight, so take caution. Once you have placed the device, turn it on, and the payment of 6 Karma will be automatically deposited to your account."

OBJECTIVES

- Cross the border into the Sioux Nation
- Sneak or fight onto the Butte of the Devil's Tower
- Activate Mr. Johnson's device

TAGS

- Seelie Court • Yellowstone Calamity • Unseelie
- Sioux Nation • Metaplanes • Yellowstone Anomaly • Niall O'Connor • Tarot • Arcana • Ebon Queen

THE SETTING

The Sioux Nation was created from what used to be known as Montana and Wyoming, with smaller parts of Idaho, Colorado, the Dakotas, Nebraska, Kansas, Alberta, and Saskatchewan. Driving through, the runners experience landscape ranging from mountains in the west to rolling foothills and high plains. Along its roads, most see only endless restored prairie or farmland. Farms are mostly automated, most people live in cities like Cheyenne, and those who wish to live off the land like their ancestors are permitted to do so, which accounts for the runners seeing so few people on the way.

THE PLOT

SCENE 1

Suggested NPCs: Border Agents (use Rent-a-cops)

Unless the runners are from the Sioux Nation already, they will find it difficult to cross the border out of Denver. The border is well guarded and monitored closely. Players should get creative in finding ways into the Sioux Nation, because there is no time for them to apply for legitimate access. Options for runners include being smuggled in, using forged SINs, Hacking the border guard commlinks, or using negotiation and gifts (read: bribes).

SCENE 2

Suggested NPCs: None

Once in Sioux territory, the runners have 1,900 kilometers to cross before they reach Devil's Tower. How they do so is up to them. Spirits may be able to carry them, they may have already paid a smuggler to take them (but perhaps the smuggler is caught at a checkpoint?), or they may purchase or hack/rig/steal transportation as soon as they have opportunity. There are plenty of chances for interesting encounters and action along the way; make sure something happens!

SCENE 3

Suggested NPCs: Lakota Warrior Society (use Elite Soldier), Lakota Shamans (use Enemy Mage)

Traveling through the Sioux Nation is occasionally beautiful, but mostly empty. There are few signs of metahumanity until the runners get close to city sprawls. Approaching their destination, the runners see Devil's Tower rise over what used to be Northeast Wyoming. This site is sacred to the Lakota tribe, and as the runners get closer, they see soldiers from the Lakota Warrior Society making regular rounds, armed with assault weapons. Awakened runners can tell that there are summoned spirits patrolling as well.

SCENE 4

Suggested NPCs: Lakota Warrior Society Soldiers (use Elite Soldiers), Lakota Shamans (use Enemy Mage)

Once on the butte called Devil's Tower, the runners switch on the device. When they do, a visual burst of magic resonates from it. If the runners check to see if they have been paid, the promised nuyen is in their account. However, from the west, a large burst of visible magic hurtles toward them and the device. This is the Yellowstone Anomaly, a quirk in the manasphere caused by the calamity. It envelops the runners, if they are all together, and transports them to the faerie realm (see **Un-Seeled Fate, pt. 2**). If the runners are not all together on the butte, the GM may allow the anomaly to engulf them as they leave together, or be more creative and have the Lakota soldiers overwhelm them, forcing the runners to use the Anomaly as an escape route.

UN-SEELED FATE, PT. 2

MR. JOHNSON'S PITCH

In this scene, there is no Mr. Johnson's Pitch. Rather, the runners have been drawn into the Yellowstone Anomaly and have emerged into the Faerie metaplane. See *The Setting* below for more detail of their surroundings. Technology works differently in this metaplane, and the runners will notice many changes to their gear (see sidebar). Karma awards for this adventure are not based on pay from Mr. Johnson, but on how well the runners accomplish the objectives—they should get 1 Karma for each objective they accomplish, 2 for each objective they accomplish with what the gamemaster judges to be a nice amount of style.

TECHNOLOGY AND CYBER ON THE FAERIE METAPLANE

Technologically advanced gear still functions in faerie realm using the exact same rule mechanics as normal. However, the metaplanes transform their appearance into more fitting forms. For example, commlinks and cyberdecks take the form of notepads on which information can be sent or received. Other gear is transformed in similar, imaginative ways. Guns become medieval ranged weapons, and cyberlimbs resemble steam-powered machinery. In addition, a rigger's drones or vehicles also transform. Once again, they keep the same function, but their form is more fitting the faerie plane. For example, a Doberman drone may become an actual dog, or a Fly-Spy drone may become a will o' the wisp.

OBJECTIVES

- Survive being attacked by the pukwudgies .
- Make their way towards cottage.
- Listen to Niall O'Connor's offer.

THE SETTING

The wild lands on the faerie metaplane, often referred to as Brocéliande, are mysterious and untamed. While beautiful, the great forest, rolling hills, glassy lakes, and sprawling thickets are every bit as dangerous as the wildlife that dwells within it. Whispers and strange sounds come from all directions at once, and from one moment to the next, singing and screaming can be heard in the distance, but never with any clarity. The air gives the impression of autumn, and a gentle, cool breeze blows in spite of the unmoving clouds.

THE PLOT

SCENE 1

Suggested NPCs: Pukwudgies (use Spirit of Beasts)

Have fun with this scene. The runners are completely out of their element and are bound to have a variety of reactions. This forest is the template for every fairy tale forest you heard as a child. Play up the wonder and mystery. Let them use their plot points to help you create

PUKWUDGIES

Pukwudgies are fae humanoids about one-third the height of a normal human. Their skin has a bright, grey tone, and their feet, fingers, and ears are disproportionately large. Though this gives them an endearing appearance, they are creatures of bitterness and rage. Their appearance makes their power somewhat comical to behold but no less deadly.

the scene, or simply ask them what *they* see. Once they have had a chance to do some exploring, a group of cute but bitterly powerful creatures known as pukwudgies ambush them.

SCENE 2

Suggested NPCs: Pukwudgies (use Spirit of Beasts)

Runners can see smoke rising up in the distance. "Drones" or other forms of aerial viewing show that the smoke is rising from a cottage not far from where the ambush took place. The cottage is empty, and the runners can rest there. Food is laid out when they arrive, wine, bread, and various cheeses. Remark about how hungry, thirsty, and sleepy the runners feel after their ordeal. Keep track of who eats the food or drinks the wine. If they do, they will fall into a deep sleep and awaken to Scene 3. If any runners do not eat or drink, they will be awake when Niall O'Connor knocks on the door. If the runners decide not to investigate the cottage, but go off in their own direction, that's fine! Just modify this scene and the next accordingly, having Niall track them down wherever they end up.

SCENE 3

Suggested NPCs: Niall O'Connor (use Enemy Mage, but raise Sorcery to 8, add Intimidation 6, and add any two spells).

When the runners answer the door, elf knocking on the door introduces himself as Niall O'Connor. He is a tall, handsome elf, whose appearance is rather dashing. He says he is glad to finally meet the runners and he has been looking forward to it for some time. If confused by this, Niall will explain where they are and how time works differently here, although he will dodge any direct questions about how he knew they were coming. Niall tells them all, once they are awake, that the food was to prove a point, and that the runners should be careful about what they eat and drink here, and should likely think through any other actions as well. As he explains further, Niall can get them home, but only if they do something for him first. Niall's offer is found in **Un-Seeled Fate, Pt. 3.**

UN-SEELED FATE, PT. 3

CONTEXT

Seelie Court: In the Shadows between our world and the worlds beyond, the Seelie Court blinks in and out of existence, moving from a hidden location within the elven

nation of Tír na nÓg to the fractured faerie metaplane, and back again. The Seelie Court is more than a collection of fae creatures, and more than a place that can be visited. It is a hierarchy of secrets and power, where terrible prices are paid and fortunes are altered by those who play the game well enough.

Note: The Seelie Court and its intrigue could provide story hooks and background for many adventures beyond this one. For more information on the Seelie and their Court, see the *Court of Shadows* sourcebook)

MR. JOHNSON'S PITCH

Niall O'Connor says he can get the runners home, provided they do some work for him. He offers the following pitch to the runners:

"The Seelie Court has long existed hidden from your world. And yet it holds great influence over your people that very few grasp. Now, however, the rules are changing. The Seelie Court is no longer so hard to reach, and its influence is teetering on the razor's edge between growing and losing it altogether. Those who can manipulate it now stand to gain much for their cause. I would like you to infiltrate the court. Say nothing of your affiliation with me, but rather listen, learn, impress the courtiers. Do errands, play games, and somehow get yourself invited to the Red Sun Ball a fortnight from today. There will be certain fae there with knowledge I need. Whether by skill, charm, guile, or your own inventive ways, listen for the phrases 'Gwyn,' 'Shadow Realm,' and 'Ebon Queen.' Bring everything you learn to me. I can renumerate you with 6 Karma for your efforts."

OBJECTIVES

- Go to the Great Hall of the Seelie and infiltrate the Court.
- Find ways to earn invitations to the Red Sun Ball.
- Play the crowd and pay attention for Niall's key phrases.

THE SETTING

The Great Hall of the Seelie Court: Past the intricately carved marble statues that form the archway into the Seelie Court is the Great Hall. Inside a vast chamber with no visible ceiling encircles one, lonely oak tree. Huge and impossibly high, the branches and leaves create a canopy of autumnal beauty. Below the canopy, yet still high, walls in myriad shades of purple stretch down the height of the Hall. Above the floor is the gallery, where the nobility of the Court and their càraidean (consorts) gather for session. The highest seat is opposite from the entryway, and that is where Lady Brane Deigh presides over her Court.

The Red Sun Ball: Located within the Hall of Night, this event conveys a sense of desperation and dread. The hall is completely black, with six staggered, transparent platforms rising above each other, stairs connecting them. For the Red Sun Ball, the newest and least important attendees find themselves on the top platform looking down. An air spirit with the appearance of a raven-haired elf keeps the drapes fluttering rhythmically. The lamps, which barely illuminate the room, are a deep, crimson red.

THE PLOT

SCENE 1

Suggested NPCs: Seelie Court Members (use Enemy Mage or any Awakened character from pp. 74–133)

Here, the runners approach and enter the Great Hall of the Seelie Court. Strangely, even if the runners stand out and look awkward, no one approaches them or even appears to take notice. In order for anything to happen, the runners must either do something to get noticed (leave it to their imaginations) or approach one of the courtiers for conversation. There are infinite ways to navigate this scene. Keep in mind that the Court values rules and decorum above all else. Getting noticed for covering for someone's misstep will likely give openings to the runners, while oafish behavior or showing off brazenly will be looked down upon. If the runners need hints, let an NPC mention a few of the activities in the Court's Favor sidebar. Gamemasters should let each of the runners narrate their runner's chance to shine.

COURT'S FAVOR

There is no manual for gaining favor in the Seelie court. But there are some good ideas. Things that bring honor to patrons will be rewarded with respect and reputation. The following is a list of possible activities that may gain the runners favor within the court.

- Saving a courtier from embarrassment
- Keeping/telling secrets about courtiers
- Acting as a second in a duel
- Speaking wisely when drawn into conversation
- Offering aid when aid was needed
- Returning a lost item to a courtier
- Poetry, dancing, or other craft exhibitions/contests

GMs and players are encouraged to think beyond this, and GMs should reward creative players.

This scene may last anywhere from hours to nearly two weeks for the runners.

SCENE 2

Suggested NPCs: Seelie Court Members (use Enemy Mage or any Awakened character from pp. 74–133)

In this transitional scene, the runners are approached in secret and given invitations to the Red Sun Ball. Alternatively, you may have a fewer number of runners invited, but they are allowed to bring guests. GMs may consult *Court of Shadows* to choose a suitable NPC or may create one based on what the runners did to garner favor in Scene 1. Either way, the courtier hopes they will continue to impress the courtiers at the ball. In the ways of the court, this will reflect well not only on the runners, but the courtier who invited them.

SCENE 3

Suggested NPCs: Seelie Court Members (use Enemy Mage or any Awakened character from pp. 74–133)

At the Red Sun Ball, the runners are escorted to the highest platform within the Hall of Night (see description above). Unfortunately for them, the real secrets will likely be discussed where the most honored guests are: on the ground floor. Allow the runners to stretch their social muscles. Deckers can attempt to gain information the same way they always do, via the Network of Keepers. If they continue to impress the Seelie, they may be moved to lower platforms. Be creative and allow them narrate the rumors and secrets they hear.

After they have mingled for half the night at the Red Sun Ball, there will be a moment where, on the fourth platform, an immaculately dressed elf, Walks-through-Tall-Grass, will be having a discussion with Plor na mBan, the Woman of Flowers. Walks-through-Tall-Grass is a càraidean under Lady Thisbe, the Queen in Exile, while Plor na mBan has been a càraidean for innumerable Seelie. Allow the runners to hear whispers from other courtiers about why these two would be talking, and why they would be so far away from the ground floor. This should clue the runners in that there might be something worth hearing.

When the runners can hear, Walks-through-Tall-Grass tells Plor na mBan, "Yes. It appears Gwyn is looking for her. A former Queen of the Court prevented her escape and quietly made a covenant with a shadow Got. She'll remain in Fauth-Doshgoi. Gwyn will be denied his Ebon Queen."

Now the runners have what they need to report back to Niall. Allow them to finish off the Red Sun Ball however they wish, and then proceed to **Un-Seeled Fate, pt. 4.**

UN-SEELED FATE, PT. 4

MR. JOHNSON'S PITCH

Niall congratulates the runners on doing what not many can: successfully navigating the Seelie Court. The next day, Niall informs them the information they gathered requires immediate action. "There is an artifact known as the Ashen Mirror within the Seelie Court. It has been used in times past to spy upon darker realms home to creatures who wish the end of all life. The mirror has switched hands many a time, so where it resides now is a mystery. But I need you to find it and use it. By concentrating, you will be able to see the Ebon Queen's location. Leave the mirror, but confirm what you heard about *Fauth-Doshgoi* and its prisoner. If the Ebon Queen is there, we are most eager to know her fate. This is the last task I will ask of you.

OBJECTIVES

- Seek out rumors of the Ashen Mirror within the Seelie Court
- Find and use the mirror to view the Ebon Queen
- Give Niall the information gathered and return to Earth.

THE SETTING

Beyond the Great Hall of the Seelie Court, the very foundations and structures on which the Court is built upon shift from day to day. There are those who are competent in navigating the ever-changing labyrinth, but to outsiders, the pathways of the Court will appear without rhyme or reason. And they may be right. However, when the Court, or its Queen, wants you to be somewhere, the way will always be clear. Rooms and hallways within the Court range from vast, sylvan landscapes to indescribably ornate and lavish reception halls. Allow the runners to describe where they find themselves in any given change in location.

THE PLOT

SCENE 1

Suggested NPCs: Seelie Court Members

(use Enemy Mage or any Awakened character from pp. 74–133)

Returning to the Seelie Court, the runners find themselves once again in the Great Hall. This time, the Queen is holding her Morning Hearing, where she listens and responds to a limited number of her subjects' complaints and requests. There are always those who get their requests granted, and there are a few who have

been bringing the same request for decades or longer and continue to be rejected. One example is a mushroom-headed Seelie who has been asking for thirty years for help to keep certain leshii from eating his family. The runners interrupt this time at their own peril, but afterwards, there will be many Seelie to speak with, and some may just be bitter enough to speak honestly. The runners should discreetly begin asking about the Ashen Mirror. Allow the runners to describe who they speak to and what they say. If they come up with a great idea for where the mirror is, go with that! Otherwise, Scene 2 describes a possible location for the mirror.

SCENE 2

Suggested NPCs: Seelie Court Members

(use Enemy Mage or any Awakened character from pp. 74–133)

A disgruntled courtier tells the runners that he was gardening two moons ago, and he observed Queen Alachia's personal guard (but not Alachia herself) move a blurry, long, black mirror from somewhere near Alachia's quarters to an unknown room bordering the Geocache. If the runners ask, the Geocache is the newest room in the court, and it is vast. It acts like something the mortals call a matrix. In truth, it functions exactly as the Sixth World Matrix, as it was modeled after the 2050s version.

ALACHIA

No one from the Seelie Court knows, or is willing to discuss, why Alachia is called a Queen. It is rumored that she served as a prince of Tír Tairngire, but there is no hard evidence to back up this claim. What Alachia is known for in the Court is her tutelage of Lady Brane Deigh. Perhaps more important is that there is no single fae more feared in all of the Seelie Court than Queen Alachia, although even when pressed, no one has been able to answer why.

SCENE 3

Suggested NPCs: Geocache Intruder Countermeasures (IC) (p. 179), Black IC (IC with Biofeedback program), Seelie Court Guards (use Enemy Mage, but add 3 to Close Combat skill, add Seelie Guard Sword DV 6P, and Armor 12 [Seelie Woven Armor])

Using the information gained in Scene 2, the runners can attempt to find the mirror in the Geocache. Any runners without the Hacking skill will be useless in the Geocache, but a decker will shine. They can use Hacking to find the mirror in the Large Stepped Temple floating in the virtual, geometric world of the Geocache.

Once they have located it, those in the Geocache will find themselves attacked by IC. Those standing guard outside will also find themselves under attack by Court guards for trespassing.

SCENE 4

Suggested NPCs: Niall O'Connor

If the runners steal the mirror, they will be fugitives. If they simply use the mirror to look for the Ebon Queen, they will be forgotten. If a runner looks into the mirror and desires to see the Ebon Queen, have them roll a perception test. On 3 or more, they will see a dark-skinned, white-haired elven woman. She appears to be trapped in some sort of dirty, grey crystalline prison. She isn't moving, but her face appears defiant. When focused on the woman, the observer feels defiant and hopeful, in many ways the opposite of the way they feel among other courtiers. After this glimpse, have the runner(s) who looked into the mirror make a Willpower + Body test. With 4 or more successes, they feel ill and depressed afterwards, but with no other ill effects. With 3 successes, they should feel weak, overwhelmed with sadness about something they cannot place, and take 4 Stun damage. If they get 2 or fewer successes, ask the runner to narrate the moment of their life that caused them the greatest pain and they will be plagued with this in dreams for the next two months, feeling hopeless and afraid, along with taking 8 Stun damage.

FINAL SCENE

Returning to Niall at the cottage, the runners find him overjoyed at this news. He thanks the runners and offers them a special reward in addition to his promise of returning home. The reward is a tarot card, which radiates with strong magic. It pictures a mirror in the form of an ouroboros. Outside the mirror, a young girl looks into the mirror and touches the face of what looks to be a humanoid with wings. Niall indicates that this is a priceless gift, but he is sure it belongs with them—at least for now.

If the runners should wish to remain in the Court, Niall will sponsor their bid for regular admission. If they leave, Niall says they should look up a contact of his, a Scottish Fomorian named Dan. With a spark in his eye, Niall opens the cottage door and escorts the runners out, back into their world.

ANARCHY & FIFTH EDITION

ANARCHY AND SHADOWRUN, 5E

If *Shadowrun: Anarchy* is your first introduction to role-playing in the Sixth World, or your re-introduction to it after a long absence, there are two pieces of good news: First, this book is all you need for many, many hours of *Shadowrun* awesomeness. Second, if you want to learn more about the Sixth World and introduce more elements to your game, there are many, many books out there. Some of those books are quite stat-heavy, meaning they would take more effort to translate to *Anarchy*; others are full of plot, setting, and character information, offering plenty of inspiration, story hooks, and campaign ideas for *Anarchy* players with little effort at converting them. Here is a quick rundown of the types of books you'll find in the *Shadowrun* line, the information they provide, and what kind of effort may be needed to bring the content of those books into *Anarchy*.

Core rulebooks: Each of the major areas of the *Shadowrun* setting—magic (*Street Grimoire*), combat (*Run & Gun*), the Matrix (*Data Trails*), augmentations (*Chrome Flesh*), rigging (*Rigger 5.0*), and critters (*Howling Shadows*)—has a core book that focuses on it, and there is also a book full of character options (*Run Faster*). As core rulebooks, these naturally have lots of rules and stats that may not be of the most interest to *Anarchy* players, but there are still concepts and plot ideas that might be useful. *Run Faster* in particular might provide a range of character ideas for players looking to bring the full range of Sixth World personalities into *Anarchy*.

Plot sourcebooks: Since these are full of plot and setting information, they very easily translate over to *Anarchy* and can provide useful information and plot hooks. *Market Panic*, for example, provides detailed information on each of the ten AAA megacorporations, as well as background on the Corporate Court and its judges.

Deep Shadows books: These books combine plot and setting information with a focus on a particular type of shadowrun. While they have some gear, spells, or other rules that may need translation to *Anarchy*, the plot, setting, and tactical information can be very useful. *Stolen Souls* focuses on extractions, *Hard Targets* on wetwork, and the forthcoming *Cutting Aces* looks at con games.

Setting books and boxes: These offer details about a particular place, providing info on getting into and out of those locations, the powers-that-be in the area, the geography, notable spots, important people, and so on. The information about Seattle in this book gives a quick overview of the setting, but the *Seattle Sprawl* box set offers many more details, along with a wealth of characters and plot hooks to use in your stories.

Campaign Books and Adventures: Both of these types of books can be very useful in helping generate story and campaign ideas for *Anarchy* sessions. Non-player characters will need some translation to *Anarchy*, but as we'll discuss below, a quick-and-dirty translation can be done easily. Campaign books like the corporate-focused *Bloody Business* have a looser structure, enabling gamemasters to combine plot elements as they see fit, while adventures like *Serrated Edge* or

False Flag have a more defined storyline to reduce the amount of planning a GM must do.

So since we mentioned translating characters from *SR5* to *Anarchy*, let's look at how that's done.

MOVING FROM SR5 TO ANARCHY

There are two basic ways to bring characters—the quick-and-dirty method, and the detailed way. When using an NPC from a *Shadowrun* book, use the quick-and-dirty method, while the detailed way can be used for bringing a player character over from *SR5*, or if there is a prominent NPC that needs to be fully fleshed out.

Note that often neither of these full methods need to be used. For quick, on-the-fly rolls, the same Skill + Attribute combos used in *Anarchy* can be used with *SR5* characters. Just do steps 1 and 2 of the quick-and-dirty method, and you'll be able to generate rolls that keep the story moving.

For times when you need a little more detail, here's how to quickly bring an *SR5* character over to *Anarchy*.

THE QUICK-AND-DIRTY METHOD

STEP 1: TRANSLATE ATTRIBUTES.
Use the Strength, Agility, Willpower, Logic, Charisma, and Edge of the character.

STEP 2: TRANSLATE SKILLS
Use the skill ranks exactly as presented. If the skill no longer exists in *Anarchy*, put it in the skill most closely associated with it, likely the skill with the same name as the group into which that skill fits in *SR5* (such as making Gymnastics in *SR5* into Athletics for *Anarchy*). If the character has multiple skills that fit into the same *Anarchy* skill, use the highest rating.

STEP 3: TRANSLATE QUALITIES
Select up to two positive and one negative quality that the character has (note that many NPCs do not have qualities, making this step easy). Eliminate any excess qualities, and do not add any extra if they do not have the full complement. If the quality matches one of the ones listed on p. 204, use that. Otherwise, the default assignment is to make the two positive qualities into +2 dice bonuses for a relevant skill, and the negative quality into a -2 dice penalty to a relevant skill.

STEP 4: NOTE IF THE CHARACTER IS AWAKENED OR EMERGED
Carry that status over.

STEP 5: TRANSLATE WEAPONS
Some weapons can be found on p. 206, listing weapons for this game. If an item is not found there, make the following changes: For melee weapons, adjust the Strength part of the damage rating to (Strength / 2). For ranged weapons, generally reduce the damage by 2. Assign range based on the ranges provided for a similar weapon. At this stage, don't worry about weapon modifications; many of those (like recoil compensators) do not have an effect in *Anarchy*, while others will be handled in step 6.

STEP 6: TRANSLATE AUGMENTATIONS, SPELLS, POWERS, GEAR, AND SO ON INTO SHADOW AMPS
The listings on p. 202 can help make this translation; if an item a character has is found there, simply add the *Anarchy* equivalent and move on. Remember that characters cannot have more than six Amps, so for some characters, some items/spells/abilities/specialized weapons may need to be dropped. Focus on what is key to the character's archetype, and then reduce redundancies (a mage in *Anarchy* may not need both Manabolt and Powerbolt, for example).

If an Amp does not exist in the **Anarchy Catalog**, then powers need to be assigned. For most Amps, the easiest thing to do is assign one, two, or three re-rolls to tests made with a specific skill. Spells may have somewhat different effects, but they can follow the patterns established by existing spells. When in doubt, find something close and copy it.

STEP 7: CALCULATE NEW ESSENCE
The character's Essence should be based on subtraction from their current Shadow Amps, not their Essence in *SR5*.

STEP 8: COPY CRITICAL GEAR AND CONTACTS
Select the most important pieces of gear and contacts the character has and copy them over. It's best if there are no more than six items between these two categories, but exceptions can be made for particularly advanced or powerful characters.

STEP 9: GENERATE CONDITION MONITORS
The Stun Condition Monitor should be the same as it is in *SR5*; the Physical Condition Monitor should be [(Strength / 2) + 8].

The detailed way follows the same basic structure as the quick-and-dirty method while adding some more steps, as well as more detail to some steps.

THE DETAILED WAY

STEP 1: TRANSLATE ATTRIBUTES

Use the Strength, Agility, Willpower, Logic, Charisma, and Edge of the character. For every two points (rounded down) that the character's unaugmented Body is higher than Strength, increase the Strength by one. For every two points (rounded down) that unaugmented Reaction is higher than Agility, increase Agility by one. For every two points (rounded down) that the character's Intuition is higher than Logic, increase the Logic by 1. This means that a character with an Intuition of 5 and a Logic of 2 goes into Anarchy with a Logic of 3. In all cases, Attributes remain capped by racial maximums; any prospective points that would go above that maximum are lost.

For every two points (rounded down) that Magic is higher than Willpower, Willpower is increased by one. If Willpower hits its racial maximum and there are still points that could be added, add those points on the same two-to-one basis to the magic-based skill of the

player's choice. These points can be divided among multiple skills.

For every two points (rounded down) that Resonance is higher than Logic, Logic is increased by one. If Logic hits its racial maximum and there are still points that could be added, add those points on the same two-to-one basis to the Resonance-based skill of the player's choice. These points can be divided among multiple skills.

STEP 2: TRANSLATE SKILLS

Use the skill ranks exactly as presented. If the skill no longer exists in Anarchy, put in the skill most closely associated with it, likely the skill with the same name as the group for the SR5 skill (such as making Gymnastics in SR5 into Athletics for Anarchy). If the character has multiple skills that fit into the same Anarchy skill, use the highest rating initially. Then take the other skills in that group, add them together, and divide by three (rounding down). Add the resulting number to the new skill, remembering to not go above 12.

STEP 3: TRANSLATE QUALITIES

Select up to two positive and one negative quality that

the character has (note that many NPCs do not have qualities, making this step easy). Eliminate any excess qualities, and do not add any extra if they do not have the full complement. If the quality matches one of the ones listed on p. 204, use that. Otherwise, the default assignment is to make the two positive qualities into +2 dice bonuses for a relevant skill, and the negative quality into a -2 dice penalty to a relevant skill. If players do not want the default, they can work with their gamemaster to develop an acceptable quality.

STEP 4: NOTE IF THE CHARACTER IS AWAKENED OR EMERGED

Carry that status over.

STEP 5: TRANSLATE WEAPONS

Some weapons can be found on p. 206, listing weapons for this game. If an item is not found there, make the following changes: For melee weapons, adjust the Strength part of the damage rating to (Strength / 2). For ranged weapons, generally reduce the damage by 2. Assign range based on a similar weapon. At this stage, don't worry about weapon modifications; many of those (like recoil compensators) do not have an effect in *Anarchy*, while others will be handled in step 6.

STEP 6: TRANSLATE AUGMENTATIONS, SPELLS, POWERS, GEAR, AND SO ON INTO SHADOW AMPS

The listings on p. 202 can help make this translation; if an item a character has is found there, simply add the *Anarchy* equivalent and move on. Remember that characters cannot have more than six Amps, so for some characters, some items/spells/abilities may need to be dropped. Focus on what is key to the character's archetype, and then reduce redundancies (a mage in *Anarchy* may not need both Manabolt and Powerbolt, for example).

If an Amp does not exist in the **Anarchy Catalog**, then powers need to be assigned. For most Amps, the easiest thing to do is assign one, two, or three re-rolls to tests made with a specific skill. Spells may have somewhat different effects, but they can follow the patterns established by existing spells. When in doubt, find something close and copy it.

STEP 7: DEVELOP DISPOSITIONS AND CUES FOR THE CHARACTER

Using your knowledge of the character, write down Dispositions and Cues to help you use the character in gameplay.

STEP 8: CALCULATE NEW ESSENCE

The character's Essence should be based on subtraction from their current Shadow Amps, not their Essence in *SR5*.

STEP 9: COPY CRITICAL GEAR AND CONTACTS

Select the most important pieces of gear and contacts the character has and copy them over. It's best if there are no more than six items between these two categories, but exceptions can be made for particularly advanced or powerful characters.

STEP 10: GENERATE CONDITION MONITORS

The Stun Condition Monitor should be the same as it is in *SR5*; the Physical Condition Monitor should be [(Strength / 2) + 8].

MOVING FROM ANARCHY TO SR5

Some players may decide they want to port their *Anarchy* characters to *SR5* in order to use the more detailed ruleset of that game. Note that this is a summary; the *Shadowrun, Fifth Edition* core rulebook will be needed to make this process work and help with some of the details. As is the case with the previous processes, this follows a step-by-step process:

STEP 1: TRANSLATE ATTRIBUTES

Use the Strength, Agility, Willpower, Logic, Charisma, and Edge of the character and copy them directly. Make the Body equivalent to Strength, Reaction equivalent to Agility, and Intuition equivalent to Logic. Based on their metatype, characters get the following points they can use to increase attributes on a one-to-one basis.

ATTRIBUTE TABLE

METATYPE	POINTS	RESTRICTIONS
Human	—	—
Elf	1	Cannot be spent on Edge, Charisma, or Agility
Dwarf	2	Cannot be spent on Edge or Agility
Ork	2	Cannot be spent on Edge or Agility
Troll	3	Cannot be spent on Edge or Agility

Make sure the character also receives the metatype bonuses listed on p. 66, *SR5*.

STEP 2: TRANSLATE SKILLS

When skills have a direct equivalence, translate ranks over from *Anarchy*. For skills that are equivalent to groups in *SR5* (Athletics, Biotech, Close Combat, Conjuring, Electronics, Engineering, Firearms, Sorcery, Stealth, and Tasking), select one skill from that group and receive it at the level of the *Anarchy* skill. Then select two other skills from the group and receive them at half (rounded down) the level of the *Anarchy* skill.

STEP 3: ADD KNOWLEDGE SKILLS

Knowledge skills play a stronger role in *SR5* than they do in *Anarchy*, so more of them are needed. Add Intuition + Logic and multiply the result by 2; the final product is the number of Knowledge skill points the character has, and they can be spent at a rate of 1 point per 1 level of skill. The player should start by selecting a native language at no point cost, then they should assign some points to the Knowledge skill the character already has. They may then add more Knowledge skills to help them spend their points.

STEP 4: TRANSLATE QUALITIES

Anarchy qualities will generally have same-named equivalents in *SR5*. Simply give the character that quality. When a quality has multiple levels (such as High Pain Tolerance or Insomnia), select the quality at the lowest level.

STEP 5: NOTE IF THE CHARACTER IS AWAKENED OR EMERGED AND CARRY THAT STATUS OVER

Give Awakened characters a Magic rating equal to their [(Sorcery + Willpower) / 2], rounded up. Give Emerged characters a Resonance rating equal to their [(Tasking + Logic) / 2], rounded up.

STEP 6: TRANSLATE WEAPONS

The equivalent weapon to *Anarchy* weapons exist in *SR5*, so characters should receive those weapons in their standard versions, with no additional modifications.

STEP 7: TRANSLATE SHADOW AMPS INTO AUGMENTATIONS, SPELLS, POWERS, SPECIALIZED GEAR

As with weapons, Shadow Amps exist in some form in the game, so players should simply receive those items/spells/power/whatever. Many augmentations with mul-

tiple levels, such has wired reflexes, have that level noted in the Amp's name (e.g., wired reflexes 2), so they would receive the augmentation at that level.

Any characters with a cyberdeck should select three programs if they do not currently have three. Any technomancers should select three complex forms. Spellcasters should have at least four spells, and adepts should ensure they have adept powers whose power points add up to their newly calculated Magic rating.

STEP 8: CALCULATE NEW ESSENCE

The character's Essence should be based on their new augmentations, not their *Anarchy* Essence. If, somehow, this newly calculated Essence goes below zero, give the character just enough alphaware or betaware to keep them from becoming a cyberzombie.

STEP 9: COPY CRITICAL GEAR AND CONTACTS

Gear and contacts should be ported over wholesale, and players should look at the rules effects of their gear. The player should multiply their Charisma by 3 and assign that many points in Connection and Loyalty ratings to their various contacts.

STEP 10: GENERATE CONDITION MONITORS

The Stun Condition Monitor should be the same as it is in *Anarchy*; the Physical Condition Monitor should be [(Body / 2) + 8].

STEP 11: FINAL CUSTOMIZATION

The character receives 15 Karma and 10,000 nuyen for final touches, generally following the **Spending Your Leftover Karma** rules on p. 98, *SR5*. Karma can be translated into nuyen at the customary rate of 2,000 nuyen for 1 Karma. There is no limit on how much of this Karma may be translated to nuyen. No more than 5,000 nuyen from this process can be brought into the actual game.

STEP 12: CALCULATE LIMITS

Limits in *SR5* should be calculated as normal:

Mental = [(Logic x 2) + Intuition + Willpower] / 3 (round up)

Physical = [(Strength x 2) + Body + Reaction] / 3 (round up)

Social = [(Charisma x 2) + Willpower + Essence] / 3 (round up)

ANARCHY CATALOG

Below is a list of Amps—including spells, adept powers, and augmentations—qualities, weapons, and gear that can be used in *Shadowrun: Anarchy*. This should not be taken as an exclusive list of the only things you can use in the game, but rather an easy list to pick items from and also a source of inspiration for designing your own Amps and whatnot. Peruse and enjoy!

SPECIAL AMPS

Awakened (Amp Level 2): Has access to magical amps.
Emerged (Amp Level 2): Has access to technomancer amps.

MAGICAL AMPS

SPELLS

Accident (Spell) (Amp Level 3): Effect. Each combat turn, may add 1 glitch die to (WIL rating) rolls.
Acid Stream (Spell) (Amp Level 2): Combat. Damage of 6P/AA, +2 damage to Armor.
Analyze Truth (Spell) (Amp Level 1): Effect. Caster can determine whether or not subject is telling the truth.
Antidote (Spell) (Amp Level 2): Effect. One target is able to overcome the effect of a toxin.
Armor (Spell) (Amp Level 2): Effect. While sustained, the spell adds three points of Armor to the target.
Chaotic World (Spell) (Amp Level 2): Effect. Mass hallucination/distractions. Targets must reroll 1 successful die per roll.
Clairvoyance (Spell) (Amp Level 1): Effect. The caster can see distant locations as if they were there.
Confusion (Spell) (Amp Level 2): Effect. Target's senses are confused. Target rolls 1 less die per action while the spell is sustained.
Control Thoughts 1, 2, 3 (Spell) (Amp Level 2, 3, 4): Effect. +1/2/3 dice to Intimidation and Negotiation Tests.
Detect Magic (Spell) (Amp Level 1): Effect. Magical objects and active spells glow in a way the caster can perceive.
Fireball (Spell) (Amp Level 3): Combat. Damage of 6P. Defense = A + L. Damages multiple targets.
Heal (Spell) (Amp Level 2): Effect. Heal one box of Physical or Stun damage per hit on a Sorcery + Willpower test (remember to adjust for the Essence of the target).
Improved Invisibility (Spell) (Amp Level 3): Effect. Mass invisibility, and targeted group may reroll 2 failed Stealth dice.
Invisibility (Spell) (Amp Level 2): Effect. Solo invisibility, targeted person may reroll 1 failed Stealth die.

Lightning Bolt (Spell) (Amp Level 3): Combat. Damage of 6P/AA. May reroll one failed Sorcery die. Defense = S + W.
Manabolt (Spell) (Amp Level 2): Combat. Damage of 6P/AA. Defense = S + W.
Physical Mask (Spell) (Amp Level 3): Effect. Mass illusion/disguises, and targets may reroll 2 failed Disguise dice.
Stunbolt (Spell) (Amp Level 2): Combat. Damage of 8S/AA. Defense = S + W.

OTHER

Protective amulet (Amp Level 2): (Talisman) Usable once per day, reduces damage from one attack in half (round up).
Spirit trust (Amp Level 2): Spirits summoned by you allow other players to give them commands.
Summoning focus (Amp Level 2): (Focus) You may summon one additional spirit.
Sustaining focus (Amp Level 2): (Focus) You may sustain one additional spell.

ADEPT AMPS

Attribute boost 1, 2, 3 (Choose Attribute) (Amp Level 2, 3, 4): Adept power. Add 1/2/3 dice or 1/2/3 damage when using (attribute).
Critical strike 1, 2, 3 (Amp Level 2, 3, 4): Adept power. Add 1/2/3 damage to melee attack.
Enhanced perception (Amp Level 2): Adept power. Reroll 1 die on a Perception test.
Improved reflexes 1, 2, 3 (Amp Level 2, 3, 4): Adept power. 1 = Gains +1 attack. 2 = +1 attack, 1 Plot Point per Scene. 3 = +1 attack, 2 Plot Points per Scene.
Killing hands (Amp Level 2): Adept power. Your unarmed attacks may inflict either Stun or Physical damage (player's choice).
Light body (Amp Level 2): Adept power. +2 dice for jumping tests.
Mystic armor (Amp Level 3): Adept power. Ignore 1 point of Armor damage each time your Armor is about to absorb damage.
Voice control (Amp Level 2): Adept power. You may change your voice to mimic others voices to the point of fooling voice detection systems.
Wall running (Amp Level 1): Adept power. Run up/across vertical surfaces during a movement.

BIOWARE AMPS

Bioware arms 1, 2, 3 (Amp Level 3, 4, 5): Bioware. May reroll 1/2/3 dice on Agility-related rolls. –0.5 Essence

Cerebral booster (Amp Level 3): Bioware. Reroll 1 die on Logic-related tests. –0.5 Essence

Dynamic facial hair/tattoos (Amp Level 2): Bioware. You can quickly manipulate your facial hair and/or body tattoos. –0.5 Essence

Dynamic handprints (Amp Level 2): Bioware. Fingerprints can change to avoid leaving prints, or leave someone else's. –0.5 Essence

Muscle augmentation 1, 2, 3 (Amp Level 3, 4, 5): Bioware. May reroll 1/2/3 dice on Strength-related rolls. –0.5 Essence

Muscle toner 1, 2, 3 (Amp Level 3, 4, 5): Bioware. May reroll 1/2/3 dice on Close Combat tests. –0.5 Essence

Synthacardium 1, 2, 3 (Amp Level 3, 4, 5): Bioware. May reroll 1/2/3 dice on Athletics tests. –0.5 Essence

Tailored pheromones (Amp Level 3): Bioware. Reroll 1 die on all in-person Charisma-related tests. –0.5 Essence

CYBERWARE AMPS

Aluminum bone lacing 1, 2, 3 (Amp Level 2, 3, 4): Cyberware. Reduce damage taken by 1/2/3. –1 Essence

Audio Analyzer (Amp Level 1) Cyberware. –1 Essence

Control Rig 1, 2, 3 (Amp Level 2, 3, 4): Cyberware. Control vehicles by VR, +1 die to vehicle actions, may reroll 1/2/3 dice on vehicle actions. –2 Essence

Cyberarms 1, 2, 3 (Amp Level 2, 3, 4): Cyberware. May reroll (1/2/3) dice on Agility-related rolls. –1 Essence

Cybereyes 1, 2, 3 (Amp Level 2, 3, 4): Cyberware. Ignore vision modifiers, may reroll 1/2/3 failed dice with ranged attacks. –1 Essence

Cyberleg 1, 2, 3 (Amp Level 2, 3, 4): Cyberware. 1 = Gain 1 extra movement per narration, may re-roll 1 die on Athletics tests. 2 = Gain 1 extra movement per narration, may re-roll 2 dice on Athletics tests. III = Gain 1 extra movement per narration, may re-roll 2 dice on Athletics tests, reduce damage taken by 1. –1 Essence

Cyberlimb Armor Plating (Amp Level 2): Reduce damage taken by 1. –1 Essence

Cyberspurs (Amp Level 2): Weapon, may inflict Physical or Stun damage with Unarmed attack. –1 Essence

Datajack and Headware (Amp Level 1): May access the Matrix via full VR, +1 die to Matrix actions. –1 Essence

Dermal Plating 1, 2, 3 (Amp Level 2, 3, 4): Reduce damage taken by 1/2/3. –1 Essence

Reaction Enhancers (Amp Level 2): +1 Plot Point at the beginning of combat. –1 Essence

Retractable Hand Razors (Amp Level 2): Weapon. Inflicts Physical damage with Unarmed attack, may reroll 1 die. –1 Essence

Skill Wires 1, 2, 3 (Firearms) (Amp Level 2, 3, 4): Add 1/2/3 dice to Firearms rolls. –1 Essence

Smartlink (Amp Level 2): +1 die to Firearms or Heavy Weapons rolls. –1 Essence

Synthlink (Amp Level 3): Gains +2 dice to Con rolls. –1 Essence

Wired Reflexes 1, 2, 3 (Amp Level 2, 3, 4): 1 = Gains +1 attack. 2 = +1 attack, 1 Plot Point per Scene. 3 = +1 attack, 2 Plot Points per Scene. –1 Essence

MATRIX AMPS

Cyberdeck 1 (Amp Level 2): May reroll 1 die on Matrix actions, Firewall +1, Matrix Condition Monitor 6, may run 1 program at a time. (Erika MCD-1, Microdeck Summit, Microtrónica Azteca 200, Hermes Chariot)

Cyberdeck 2 (Amp Level 3): May reroll 1 die on Matrix actions, Firewall +2, Matrix Condition Monitor 9, may run 1 program at a time. (Novatech Navigator, Renraku Tsurugi)

Cyberdeck 3 (Amp Level 4): May reroll 2 dice on Matrix actions, Firewall +3, Matrix Condition Monitor 9, may run 1 program at a time. (Shiawase Cyber-4, Sony CIY-720)

Cyberdeck 4 (Amp Level 5): May reroll 2 dice on Matrix actions, Firewall +3, Matrix Condition Monitor 12, may run 2 programs at a time. (Shiawase Cyber-5, Fairlight Excalibur)

Biofeedback (program) (Amp Level 2): Deal Cybercombat damage to your opponent's physical or Matrix condition monitors.

Exploit (program) (Amp Level 2): May reroll two dice on non-Cybercombat hacking tests.

Hammer (program) (Amp Level 3): +2 damage in Cybercombat.

Mugger (program) (Amp Level 2): May reroll 1 die in Cybercombat tests.

Track (program) (Amp Level 2): May reroll 2 dice on Matrix Tracking tests.

TECHNOMANCER AMPS

Cleaner (complex form) (Amp Level 1): Erase your 3 most recent Matrix actions from being seen by G.O.D.

Diffusion (complex form) (Amp Level 2): Effect. Choose an attribute of enemy in Matrix. Make a cybercombat attack against target. Until combat ends, target's chosen attribute is –1 for each net hit (min. 1).

Infusion (complex form) (Amp Level 2): Effect. Choose an attribute of ally in Matrix. Make a Tasking + Logic test. Target's chosen attribute is +1 for each net hit.

Pulse Storm (complex form) (Amp Level 2): Effect. Make a cybercombat attack against target. Until combat ends, all actions are at –1 die for each net hit.

Resonance Spike (complex form) (Amp Level 2): Cybercombat. Matrix damage = 8. Defense = Logic + Firewall.

Stitches (complex form) (Amp Level 2): Make a Tasking + Logic test. Target sprite heals 1 damage box for each hit.

DRONE AMPS

GM-Nissan Doberman Drone (Amp Level 2): Gain +1 attack (only with Doberman drone). [A6, D9]

Custom Gun-Drones 1, 2, 3 (Amp Level 2/3/4): Gain +1/2/3 attacks/movements (only with gun-drones). [A6, D6]

Drone/Vehicle Mounted Assault Rifle (Amp Level 1): Acts as weapon, but only provides additional attack per turn with increase Amp Level.

Drone/Vehicle Mounted Grenade Launcher (Amp Level 1): Acts as weapon, but only provides additional attack per turn with increase Amp Level.

MCT Fly-Spy Aerial Drone (2 drones) (Amp Level 3): +2 dice to Perception tests. [A3, D3]

GEAR AMPS

Custom Lined Coat (Hidden Compartments, Bug Scanner) (Amp Level 4): 10 armor. -3 dice to Perception tests for items in coat.

More Where That Came From (Amp Level 1): Gain additional 2 weapons. May trade melee weapon for ranged weapon.

SOCIAL/OTHER AMPS

Fear (Amp Level 4): +2 dice to intimidation rolls, melee opponents must roll 2 hits on Cha + Wil or run away.

I Know Everybody (Amp Level 2): Gain (Cha rating) contacts

Jack of All Trades (Amp Level 2): Reroll 1 failed die when you're rolling a skill you don't have.

Team Player (Amp Level 2): You may freely gift your own Plot Points or Edge to other players.

CRITTER AMPS

Accident (Critter Power): Effect. Each combat turn, may add 1 glitch die to (WIL rating) rolls.

Animal Control: Mundane animals in Near range obey simple commands. Limited to swarm of tiny creatures, three dozen small creatures, or 6 large creatures.

Concealment (Critter Power): May reroll 3 dice on Stealth tests when not moving.

Control Thoughts (Critter Power): Effect. +3 dice to Intimidation and Negotiation Tests.

Dragon Sorcery (Critter Power): Dragons may choose from any spell in the list of Spell Amps.

Dragonspeech (Critter Power): May speak and be understood without the use of audible words.

Elemental Attack (Cold) (Critter Power): Combat. Damage of 6S/AA. Defense = S + W. +2 damage to Armor.

Elemental Attack (Fire) (Critter Power): Combat. Damage of 6P/AA. Defense = A + L. +2 damage to Armor.

Elemental Attack (Earth) (Critter Power): Combat. Damage of 8P. Defense = A + L.

Elemental Attack (Water) (Critter Power): Combat. Damage of 8S. Defense = A + L.

Elemental Attack (Electricity) (Critter Power): Combat. Damage of 6P/AA. Defense = S + W.

Engulf (Critter Power): Combat/Effect. Damage of 4S/AA. Defense = S + W. Target Cannot move.

Enhanced Senses (Critter Power): Gain +3 dice to any Perception test.

Essence Drain (Critter Power): If used on incapacitated enemy, permanently lowers essence of target by 1.

Fear (Critter Power): May reroll 2 dice on Intimidation tests.

Immunity (Choose) I, II, III, IV, V (Critter Power): Reduce damage taken by 1/2/3/4/5 (choose).

Infection (Critter Power): If an Essence Drain action would take the target to 0 essence, target is infected with the same virus as the attacker.

Insect Chemicals (Critter Power): Give +1 Plot Point/turn to ally bug spirit.

Natural Weapon (Critter Power): Weapon (claws, teeth, tail) damage of (STR/2 +3)P.

Mist Form (Critter Power): Critter may slip through cracks its normal body could not pass through.

Regeneration (Critter Power): Every combat turn, Critter regains 2 boxes of damage, in the following order: stun, physical, armor (if Natural Armor).

Vampire Sorcery (Critter Power): Vampires may choose from any spell in the list of Spell Amps.

Vermin Control (Critter Power): May give orders up to Charisma x 5 animals of a specific type in Near range.

QUALITIES

POSITIVE QUALITIES

Ace Pilot: +2 dice to Piloting (Other) tests.

Ambidextrous: +2 dice when using two melee weapons.

Animal Empathy: +2 dice on any test involving influence or control of an animal.

Better Feared Than Loved: You have leverage on someone important. Add this blackmailed person to contacts.

Biocompatability: Ignore 1 point of Shadow Amp Essence cost.

Black Market Pipeline (Narcotics): Add a reliable fence for Narcotics to contacts.

Brand Loyalty (Choose Corp): +1 die to tests when using (Choose Corp) gear. -2 dice when making a test using gear not produced by (Choose Corp).

Bruiser: +2 dice to Intimidation tests.

Catlike: +2 dice for Stealth tests.

Codeslinger: +2 dice to Hacking tests.

College Education: May choose 2 additional Knowledge skills.

Combat Pilot: +2 dice to Piloting (Other) tests.

Contortionist: +2 dice to Escape Artist tests.

Exceptional Attribute (Choose): Increase your (Chosen Attribute) cap by +1.

Fame (Choose Location and Reason): +2 dice to Charisma-based tests if recognized.

Gearhead: When pushing the limits of vehicles or performing difficult maneuvers, +2 dice to roll.

Go Big or Go Home: –2 dice when making a cybercombat test, but may re-roll all misses once.

Guts: May reroll 2 dice when resisting fear or intimidation.

Hawkeye: +2 dice for Perception tests.

High Pain Tolerance: Does not take dice penalties for damage until second row of damage boxes is filled.

Home Ground (Selected Home Ground): Gain +1 Plot Point when entering or waking up in (Chosen Home Ground).

Indomitable (Selected Combat Skill): When attacking with (Choose Combat Skill), may reroll exactly 2 dice.

Iron Will: May reroll 2 dice during Conjuring tests.

Leader of the Pack: Add 1 group/organization/gang to list of contacts.

Lucky: Increase your Edge value by +1.

Mentor Spirit (Bear): + 1 damage to melee combat damage, using First Aid does not cost a Plot Point.

Mentor Spirit (Cat): +1 die for Athletics or Stealth tests, may reroll 1 die when casting effect spells.

Mentor Spirit (Coyote): +1 die for Con tests, may reroll 1 die when casting effect spells.

Mentor Spirit (Dog): +1 die for Survival tests, using Take the Hit does not cost a Plot Point.

Mentor Spirit (Eagle): +1 die for Perception tests, may reroll 1 die when Conjuring.

Mentor Spirit (Rat): +1 die for Escape Artist and Stealth tests, may reroll 1 die when casting effect spells.

Mentor Spirit (Raven): +1 die for knowledge tests, using Live Dangerously does not cost a Plot Point.

Mentor Spirit (Wolf): +1 die for tracking rolls, may reroll 1 die when casting combat spells.

Natural Athlete: +2 dice for Athletics tests.

Natural Hardening (Technomancers Only): Reduce Matrix damage taken by 2.

Silver Tongue: May reroll 2 dice on Charisma tests.

Spirit Affinity (Chose Spirit Type): +2 dice with (Chosen Spirit Type).

Spirit Whisperer: When making a Conjuring Test, may reroll 2 dice

Street Racer: +2 dice for Piloting (Ground) tests.

Tough as Nails (Physical): + 1 to Physical Condition Monitor.

Tough as Nails (Stun): + 1 to Stun Condition Monitor.

Toughness: All damage taken is reduced by 1.

NEGATIVE QUALITIES

Allergy (Specify): When affected by allergy (GM decision), –4 to all dice rolls.

Codeblock: –2 dice to all Hacking tests.

Combat Junkie: Must use a Plot Point to avoid using violence as first response to any given problem.

Combat Paralysis: Act last on the first round of any combat (that isn't you specifically initiating an ambush).

Distinctive Style (Choose): Always seen wearing (Chose Style). Opposition is at +2 dice to recognize or remember you in Perception tests.

Distaste for Violence: Player attacks do 2 less damage.

Elf Poser: When making social tests about/with elves, always add a Glitch Die that cannot roll an Exploit.

Emotional Attachment (Specify): Must spend a Plot Point to avoid prioritizing (Specify) above anything else.

Gremlins: When using high-tech items, always add a Glitch Die that cannot roll an Exploit.

Lifelong Thief: At times, you must spend a Plot Point to avoid prioritizing petty (or grand) larceny over other concerns.

Low Pain Tolerance: Increase penalties due to damage by 1.

Paranoia: Must reroll successes (max 2) when making social tests.

Phobia (Specify): When in the presence of (Phobia Source, GM decision), –2 to all dice rolls.

SINner, National (Choose Nation): Character is a legal citizen. Their data is available through the Global SIN Registry.

SINner, Criminal: Character is known to Law Enforcement. Their data is available through the Global SIN Registry.

SINner, Corporate (Chose Corp): Character is a corporate citizen. Their data is available through the Global SIN Registry.

Stubborn Loyalty (specific, Choose Corp): –1 die when using a drone/vehicle that isn't (Choose Corp)-crafted or that you haven't customized.

Unsteady Hands: –2 dice to all Agility-based tests.

WEAPONS

CLOSE COMBAT

	Damage	Close	Near	Far
Unarmed Combat	STR/2	OK	—	—

Knives/knucks/spurs (STR/2 + 1)P OK — —
(Survival knife, combat knife, hand spurs, hand razors, brass knuckles, densiplast knuckles, hardliner gloves)

Staff/baton/club (STR/2 + 2)P OK — —
(Staff, baton, telescoping staff, baseball bat, escrima sticks)

Stun baton/staff 7S OK — —
(Shiawase/Nemesis Arms Maul stun staff, stun baton)

Swords/axes (STR/2 + 3)P OK — —
(Ares "One" Monosword, katana, vibrosword, sword, chainsaw, combat axe, polearm, rapier)

PROJECTILE WEAPONS

	Damage	Close	Near	Far
Thrown weapon	STR/2 +1P	OK	-2	—

(Chakram, boomerang, spear, javelin, rocks, harpoon, shuriken, throwing knife, tomahawk)

Bow and arrow STR/2 +1P -2 OK -2
(Compound bow, traditional bow, dynamic tension bow)

Crossbow 5P OK -2 —
(Heavy, light, medium, ranger sliver pistol crossbow)

Grenades 12P OK* OK* —
*Player(s) damaged as well at GM discretion
(Fragmentaion, high explosive)

Stun grenades 8S OK* OK* —
*Player(s) damaged as well at GM discretion
(Stun grenade, gas grenade)

FIREARMS

	Damage	Close	Near	Far
Tasers/tranq pistols	6S	OK	-4	—

(Cavalier Safeguard, Defiance EX Shocker, Tiffani Defiance Protector, Yamaha Pulsar, Narcoject Pistol, Parashield Dart Pistol)

Light Pistols 5P OK -2 —
(Colt New Model Revolver, Streetline Special, Ares Light Fire, Beretta 201T, Colt America L36, Fichetti Security 600, Taurus Omni-6)

Heavy Pistols 6P OK -2 —
(Ares Predator V, Browning Ultra-Power, Colt Government 2066, Remington Roomsweeper, Ruger Super Warhawk)

Machine Pistols 6P OK -2 —
(Ares Crusader II, Ceska Black Scorpion, Steyr TMP)

Submachine Guns 6P OK OK —
(Colt Cobra TZ-120, FN P93 Praetor, HK-227, Ingram Smartgun X, SCK Model 100, Uzi IV)

Assault Rifles 8P OK OK -2
(AK-97, Ares Alpha, Colt M23, FN HAR, Yamaha Raiden, Shiawase Arms Monsoon)

Sniper Rifles 9P -4 -2 OK
(Ares Desert Strike, Cavalier Arms Crockett EBR, Ranger Arms SM-5, Remington 950, Ruger 100)

Shotguns 9P OK* -2 —
*By taking -2, may attack two targets at half damage.
(Defiance T-250, Enfield AS-7, PJSS Model 55)

HEAVY WEAPONS

	Damage	Close	Near	Far
Machine guns	8P	OK	OK	OK

(Ingram Valiant, Stoner-Ares M202, RPK HMG)

Cannons/launchers 12P OK* OK* OK
*Player(s) take damage as well at GM discretion
(Ares Antioch-2, ArmTech MGL-12, Aztechnology Striker, Krime Cannon, Onotari Interceptor, Panther XXL Assault Cannon)

VEHICLE/DRONE WEAPONS

	Damage	Close	Near	Far
Drone melee attack	8P	OK	—	—
Assault rifle	8P	OK	OK	-2
Machine gun	6P	OK	-2	—
Cannon/launcher	12P	OK*	OK*	OK

*Player(s) take damage as well at GM discretion

ARMOR

Actioneer Business Clothes: 6 (+1 skill point)
Armor Clothing: 6 (+1 skill point)
Synthleather jacket: 6 (+1 skill point)
Armor Vest: 9
Lined Coat: 9
Armor Jacket: 12 (-1 skill point)
Body Armor: 12(-1 skill point)

GEAR

The gear below represents just a sample of what the Sixth World has to offer. Players are encouraged to create their own unique gear or recreate a piece of gear they have found in previous Shadowrun products.

- Area signal jammer
- Bag of smooth rocks
- Commlink
    (Meta Link, Sony Emperor, Renraku Sensei, Erika Elite, Hermes Ikon, Transys Avalon, Fairlight Caliban, Common Denominator Element, EvoTech Himitsu, FTL Quark, Leviathan Technical LT-2100, Xiao Technologies XT-2G, MCT 3500, MCT Blue Defender, Microtronica Azteca Raptor, PULSE Wave, Sony Emperor, Shiawase Kawaii Shugenja, Spinrad Industries Trompe L'Oeil)
- Courier bag
- Crowbar
- Enhanced vision goggles
- Fake SIN
- Fake license (specify)
- Fifty drams of reagents
- Frag grenades
- Goggles/glasses (image link, thermographic vision, vision magnification)
- Hard shell briefcase
- Keepsake, memento, heirloom, antique
- Magical lodge materials
- Mechanic toolkit
- Medkit
- Metal restraints
- NERPS
- Plastic restraints
- Smoke grenades
- Stim patches
- Survival kit
- Trauma patches
- Vehicle (listed with Armor, Durability ratings)

(Harley-Davidson Scorpion Bike [A 9, D 8], Eurocar Westwind [A 9, D 10], Suzuki Aurora Street Bike [A 6, D 5], Shiawase Karuma Sports Car [A 6, D 10], Toyota Gopher Truck [A 9, D 14], GMC Bulldog Step-Van [A 12, D 16], Yamaha Rapier street bike [A 6, D 5]
- White noise generator

SPELL EFFECTS AND COSTS

EFFECT	COST
Base damage 6P or 5S+AA	1
AA	1
Extra effect	1
Multiple targets	1
Extra damage	1 per +1 damage

INDEX OF ANARCHY

A

Accuracy, 72
Acid and toxic waste, 50
Action, 37
Adept
  amps, 202
  powers, 33
Aetherpedia, 25
Agility, 29, 32
Air travel, 26
Airless vacuum, 50
Alachia, 195
Alamos 20,000, 23
Allied German States, 23
Amazonia, 23
Ammo, 41-42
  reloading, 41-42
Anarchy to SR5 conversion, 200-201
Ancients, 21
Arabian Knights (contract briefs)
  Pt. 1, 186-87
  Pt. 2, 187-88
  Pt. 3, 188-89
  Pt. 4, 189-90
Ares Macrotechnology, 16-17
Armor, 30, 67-68, 206
  improving, 71
  regaining damage, 43
  repair payment, 43-44
Asamando, 23
Assassin's Greed (contract brief), 171
Assistance, 38
Astral combat, 32, 47
Astral projection, 47
Athletics, 32
Atlantean Foundation, 24
Attack
  limits, 40
  from vehicle or drone, 48
Attitude modifiers, 38
Attribute(s), 29
  dice, 29, 37

improving, 70-71
maximums, 64, 70
-only tests, 38
points, 63-64
tests, 38
Auburn, 147
Augmentations, 13
Augmented reality (AR), 25, 44, 47
Awakened/Awakening, 15, 63
Aztechnology, 17
Aztlan, 23

B

Barrens, 144
Be Careful What You Search For (contract brief), 154
Bellevue, 145-46
Beneath the Sands (contract briefs)
  Pt. 1, 184
  Pt. 2, 185
Big Ten, 16-20
Biotech, 32
Bioware, 33
  amps, 202-3
Bit-Bucket, 86-87
Black Star Rising (contract brief), 155
Bleeding Edge, 10
Blood payments, 13-14
Borderline, 88-89
Boston quarantine, 16
Breathing, 48
Bug
  queen, 134
  spirit, 134
Building Street Cred, 10
Buses, 26

C

Campaign books/adventures, 197-98
Carry limits, 41
Cars, 26
Character(s)
  advancement, 70-72
  death, 44
  illustration, 29
  movement, 42
  sample, 74-140
  sheet, 27
Character creation, 27, 61
  armor, 67-68
  attribute points, 63-64
  Awakened or emerged, 63
  background, 69
  cues, 69
  game level, 62
  gear, 68-69
  metatype, 63
  name, 62
  qualities, 67
  shadow amps, 65-66
  skill points, 64-65
  theme, 61-62
  tweaking, 69-70
  weapons, 68
Charisma, 29, 32
Chrome Bison, 90-91
Cinematic initiative, 54
Cleaning House (contract brief), 172
Close combat, 32
  damage bonus, 41
  weapons, 206
Clubbing, 25
Clues, 59
Cognitive fragmentation disorder (CFD), 16
Collaborative narration/storytelling, 35, 56
Comando Verde, 21
Combat, 40
  armor, 30

modifiers, 40
options, 60
spells, 46
Company Town (contract brief), 178
Complex forms, 46
Con, 32
Condition monitor, 30, 64, 70
flowchart, 43
regaining damage, 43
Confederation of American States, 23
Conjuring, 32
Contacts, 31, 68-69
Context, 28
Contract brief(s), 34-35, 154-96
selection, 28-29
Controlling Anarchy, 10
Conversation, 34
Cooldown, 57
Core rulebooks, 197
Corporate Court, 13
Corporate scrip, 26
Corporate security, 134
Corporate suit, 134
Corporations, 13
Council Island, 150-51
Coydog, 74-75
Crash 2.0, 16
Crashes, 25, 48
Critter
amps, 204
powers, 33
Cue System, 27, 55-56, 59, 60
Cues, 29, 30, 35, 69
Cumulative wound modifiers, 43
Cutters. 21
Cybercombat, 44, 45
defense, 46
Cyberdecks, 33
Cyberware, 33
amps, 203

D

Daktari, 92-93
Damage, 42-43
repairs, 43
value, 42
Darkness, 50
Data/Steel (contract brief), 163
Deep Shadows books, 197
Devil rat, 135
Dice, 27
pools, 37
rolling, 27, 37
Disguise, 32
Dish best served cold, 36, 44, 53
Dispositions, 29, 69
Distractions modifiers, 38
Don't count me out just yet, 44
Don't Know Much about Arcology (contract brief), 157
Double time it, 36, 52
Downtown, 145
Draco Foundation, 24
Drone
amps, 204
combat, 47-48
damage, 48

swarm, 163
weapons, 206
Dunkelzahn, 16
Duska, Alyosha, 84-85
Dwarf
parkour adept, 122-23
security rigger, 78-79
spirit whisperer, 84-85
street doc, 92-93
street fighting adept, 104-5

E

Edge, 30, 39
points conversion, 66
Effect spells, 46
Electronics, 32
Elf
brute force decker, 100-101
combat archaeologist, 108-9
mystic adept, 116-17
razorgirl, 102-3
street shaman, 74-75
Emerged, 63
Enemies, 29
Enemy drone
heavy, 135
medium, 135
small, 135
Enemy mage, 136
Engineering, 32
Entertainment, 26
Environment

modifiers, 38
conditions, 48, 50
Escape artist, 32
Esprit Industries, 22
Essence, 29
loss, 33-34, 37
Essence loss, 37
Everett, 146
Evo Corporation, 17
Exploits, 39-40
Extraterritorial status, 13

F

Faerie metaplane, 192
Firearms, 32, 206
First aid, 36, 52
Food, 26
Food Fight (contract brief), 156
Forces of Chaos, 10
Fort Lewis, 148-49
Fourth, 94-95
Free-for-All (contract brief), 180
Fusion, 96-97

G

Game, 70
level, 62
making more or less lethal, 42
Gamemaster, 34
designation, 27-28
earning points, 35
Karma, 70
plot points and, 36-37, 52-53
pointers, 55-60
Gang(s), 21-22
Ganger, 136
Gang-level game, 62
Gear, 30-31, 68, 207
amps, 204
buying/improving, 72
using, 44
Gentry, 76-77
Glitch die, 39, 53
Glitches, 39
Goat Foot, 186
Goblinization, 15
Go-gangs, 22
Great Ghost Dance, 15
Grid Overwatch Division (GOD), 25
GridGuide, 25

H

Hacking, 32, 44, 45
Halloweener Underground (contract brief), 165-66
Halloweeners, 21
Hand of Five, 23
Happening World, 10
Hardpoint, 78-79
Hawk, 98-99
Heavy weapons, 32, 206

Hellhound, 136
History, 15-16, 69
Hits, 37
Hong Kong Cannon (cb) 161
Horizon Group, 17-18
Hot/noxious gas, 50
Human
arms dealer, 110-11
combat decker, 76-77
combat medic, 130-31
former company woman, 120-21
former wage mage, 126-27
ganger razorgirl, 88-89
infiltration expert, 106-7
street samurai, 98-99
technomancer, 128-29
vigilante, 124-25
Humanis Policlub, 22-23

I

IC, 179
I'll never be the same, 44
I've had better days, 44
Illuminates of the New Dawn, 24
Initiative
cinematic, 54
rolling for, 53-54
seizing, 44
Injuries, 37
Intimidation, 32
Is That a Bug in Your Pocket?
(contract brief), 170

J

Japanese Imperial State, 23
Jinn, 100-101
Johnson, Mr.
corporate, 136
device, 191
pitch, 28
street, 137
Just give me a minute, 44

K

Karma, 70
payment, 43
Kenya, 23
Killed in action, 43
Kix, 102-3
Knight Errant, 22
Knowledge skills, 32, 64
Knox, 104-5
Koshari, 21

L

Lambeth Martyrs, 23
Law enforcement, 22
Leaks and Plumbers (contract briefs)

Pt. 1, 181-82
Pt. 2, 182-83
Let Your Flag Fly (contract brief), 160
Lethality, 72
Light Within (contract brief), 166-67
Liquid metals/rocks, 50
Live dangerously, 36
Logic, 29, 32
Lone Star, 22

M

Mafia, 20
Magic, 12-13
amps, 202
groups, 23-24
Malfunction, 36
Maneuvering, 48
Marks, 45
Matrix, 15, 24-25
amps, 203
damage, 46
optional rules, 45-46
Metatype, 63
Micro-gamemaster, 56
Mind control, 50
Mitsuhama Computer Technologies, 18
Modifiers, 37-38
Money, 26
Mooks, 60
Movement, 42
Ms. Myth, 80-81
My Fair Lady (contract brief), 179

N

Narration, 34, 35, 51-52
abuse, 56
cue system, 55-56
player hints, 58-59
player interactions, 57-58
Native American Nations, 23
Negative qualities, 205
removing, 71
Negotiation, 32
NeoNET, 18-19
NERPS Run (contract brief), 162
Night of Rage, 16
Ninetails, 106-7
Noise, 45
Noncombat gear, 31
Non-player character (NPC) sheet, 31
Nuyen, 26

O

Objectives, 28
Obstacles, 29
One for All (contract brief), 177
Onto the Path (contract brief), 158
Opposing dice, 38
Opposition, 16
Ordo Maximus, 24
Organized crime, 20-21

Ork
decker, 86-87
illusionist, 112-13
reporter, 94-95
rigger/ganger, 96-97
rocker/face, 114-15
street samurai, 82-83
Ork Rights Commission, 23
Ork Underground, 151-52

P

Panopticans, 23
Parashield, 22
People's Party, 23
Perception tests, 38-39
Personal data, 29, 69
Personality, 69
Petrovski Security, 22
Physical damage, 42-43, 64
Piloting, 32
Play segments, 34-45
Player
interactions, 57-58
options, 57
earning points, 35
narration tips, 51-52
spending plot points, 35-36
Plot
points, 35-37, 52-53
sourcebooks, 197
Politicos, 22-23
Positive qualities, 204-5
Price, 12
Prime runner game, 62
Programs, 33
Projectile weapons, 32, 206
Promise a favor, 43-44
Pueblo Corporate Council, 23
Pukwudgies, 192
Putallup Problems (contract brief), 164
Puyallup, 150

Q

Qualities, 29, 30, 38, 67
negative, 205
positive, 204-5
Questions, 56-57
asking good, 58

R

Raider, 108-9
Range, 72
penalties, 40
Raspberry Jam, 110-11
Razzle dazzle, 112-13
Redmond, 149-50
Reese Frenzy, 114-15
Refereeing, 56
Renraku Computer Systems, 19
Rent-a-cop, 137
Renton, 146-47

Resource Rush, 15
Retreat, 60
Roleplaying banter, 58
Rose Red, 116-17
Ruckus, 118-19
Rules, additional, 48-50
Rules of the Street, 10

S

Saeder-Krupp Heavy Industries, 19
Sakura Security, 22
Salish-Shidhe Council, 23
Scene(s), 29, 34
Seattle, 141-42
    change in, 144
    coldness in, 144
    culture, 142
    Downtown in, 145
    loyalty in, 145
    openness, 144
    secrets of, 141-52
    shape of, 142-43
Second Matrix Crash, 16
Secondary effects, 42
Security spider, 137
Seelie Court favor, 194
Setting, 29
    books/boxes, 197
Shades, 120-21
Shadow amps, 30, 32-33, 65-66
    cost table, 65, 71
    Edge points conversion, 66
    effects, 38
    effects, added, 66
    Essence effects, 66
    Essence loss, 33-34
    improving/adding, 71
    level, 66
    types, 32-33
    weapon effects, 40
Shake it up, 36
Shiawase Corporation, 19-20
Shiawase Decision, 15
Sioux Nation, 23
Sixth World, life in, 24-25
Skill(s), 30, 31-32
    dice, 37
    improving/adding, 71
    points, 64-65
Sledge, 82-83
Snatch and Grab (contract brief), 159
Snohomish, 147-48
Social amps, 204
Soldier, 137
Sons of Sauron, 23
Sorcery, 32
Sounder, 141
Special amps, 202
Specialization(s), 31-32, 64-65
    adding, 71
Spells, 202
Spells, 32, 46, 202
Spirit(s), 47
    of air, 138
    of beasts, 138
    of earth, 139
    of fire, 139
    of man, 139
    of water, 139

Sports, 25
Sprites, 46
SR5 to *Anarchy* conversion
    detailed way, 199-200
    quick-and-dirty method, 198-99
    sourcebooks, 197-98
Staggered, 43
Stealth, 32
Sternschutz, 22
Storytelling, 48
    derailment, 59-60
    refocusing, 59
Street gangs, 21
Street people, 10
    characters, 74-133
    non-player characters, 134-40
Street runner game, 62
Street Sweeper (contract brief), 173
Strength, 29, 32
Strider, 122-23
Stun damage, 42-43, 45, 64
Stunts, 48
Sudden Unexplained Recessive
    Genetic Expression (SURGE), 16
Surprise threat, 36
Survival, 32
Synchronicity, 4-9

T

Tacoma, 146
Tags, 28, 62
Take the hit, 36, 44, 52
Talk time, 58
Target tokens, 57
Tasking, 32
T-bird, 26
Teamwork tests, 39
Technomancer(s), 45-46
    amps, 203-4
Telesma, 33
Thunder, 124-25
Tommy Q, 126-27
Tracking, 32
Trains, 26
Transportation, 25-26
Treaty of Denver, 15
Triad Take-Out (contract brief), 174
Triads, 20-21
Troll
    bruiser, 118-19
    face, 80-81
    gang leader, 132-33
    street samurai, 90-91
Troubleshooting, 37
Trucking with the Fae
    (contract brief), 175-76
Turns, 34

U

Unarmed combat damage, 41
Underwater, 50
United Canadian and American States
(UCAS), 15, 23
Universal Brotherhood, 16

Unknown Stuntman (contract brief), 169
Un-Seeled Fate (contract briefs)
    Pt. 1, 191-92
    Pt. 2, 192-93
    Pt. 3, 193-94
    Pt. 4, 195-96
Urban Brawl (contract brief), 168

V

Vampire, 140
Vector, 128-29
Vehicle
    combat, 47-48
    damage, 48
    movement, 47-48
    weapons, 32, 206
Virtual reality (VR), 25, 44, 47
Virtually Induced Toxic
    Allergy Syndrome (VITAS), 15
Vory v Zakone, 21

W

Wagon, 130-31
Weapon(s), 30, 40-42, 68, 206
    buying/improving, 71-72
    customizing, 72
    dice, 40
    ranges, 40
Wheezer, 132-33
Willpower, 29
Wuxing Incorporated, 20

Y

Yakuza, 20
You're gonna love this!, 58
Young dragon, 140

SHADOW SLANG

When you hit the streets, sling the lingo like a pro with this handy guide.

amp *n.* Short for "amplification," broad term to cover just about anything that gives you an advantage over opposition.

breeder *n.* Ork slang for a "normal" human.

chill *adj.* Good, cool, acceptable.

chip truth *n.* A fact or honest statement.

chipped *adj.* Senses, skills, reflexes, muscles, and so on, enhanced by cyberware.

chrome *n.* Cyberware, especially obvious enhancements.

chummer *n.* Friend, used in the same sense as "pal" or "buddy."

clip *n.* A box magazine for a firearm.

comm *n.* Short for commlink, your phone, handheld computer, music player, game device, and more in the palm of your hand.

corp *n.* Corporation. *adj.* Corporate.

cred *n.* Money. Reputation, especially good reputation.

dandelion eater *n.* (vulgar) An elf.

dataslave *n.* Corporate decker or other data-processing employee.

datasteal *n.* Theft of data from a computer, usually by decking.

deck *n.* A cyberdeck. *v.* To use a cyberdeck, usually illegally.

decker *n.* A person who illegally uses a cyberdeck.

deckhead *n.* Simsense abuser.

drek *n.* (vulgar) Feces. A common curse word.

dump *v.* To be involuntarily ejected from the Matrix.

dumpshock *n.* The painful sensation of being forcibly ejected from the Matrix while deeply involved in multi-sensory interactions.

frag *v.* (vulgar) Common swear word referring to the act of copulation. fragged *adj.* (vulgar) Broken, in trouble.

geek *v.* To kill.

go-gang *n.* A vehicular gang.

hacker *n.* Someone who illegally interacts with the Matrix, either by using a cyberdeck (as a "decker") or with the power of their mind (as a "technomancer").

halfer *n.* (vulgar) A dwarf.

hoi *interject.* (Dutch) Hi, a familiar form of greeting.

hoop *n.* (vulgar) A common curse word referring to a person's backside.

ice *n.* Security software. From "intrusion countermeasures" or IC.

jack *v.* To connect or disconnect to the Matrix or other device via a jack. "Jack in" means establishing the connection, "jack out" means breaking a connection, "jack" by itself refers to changing from one state to the other.

jander *v.* To walk in an arrogant yet casual manner; to strut.

jing *n.* Money, usually cash.

keeb *n.* (vulgar) An elf.

meat *n.* A physical body. Pertaining to the physical world. Organs harvested for sale.

mojo *n.* (Caribbean) Magic. A spell.

Mr. Johnson *n.* Refers to an anonymous employer or corporate agent, regardless of gender or national origin.

mundane *n.* (vulgar) Non-magician. *adj.* Non-magical.

nutrisoy *n.* A cheaply processed food product derived from soybeans

nuyen *n.* The world's standard currency.

omae *n.* A close friend. Can be used sarcastically.

organlegging *v.* Trading in organs or cyberware harvested from formerly living people.

pawn *n.* (derogatory) Street slang for Knight Errant officers

paydata *n.* A data file worth money on the black market.

pixie *n.* (vulgar) An elf. An elf poser.

plex *n.* A metropolitan complex, short for metroplex.

poli *n.* A policlub or a policlub member. *adj.* Pertaining to a policlub.

prets *n.* Generally complimentary term referring to a combination of courage, toughness, and strong motivation.

razorgirl/razorguy *n.* A person with extensive combat enhancements.

samurai *n.* (Japanese) Mercenary or muscle for hire. Implies an honor code or a good reputation.

sarariman *n.* (Japanese) A corporate employee. From a mispronunciation of salaryman.

screamer *n.* Credstick or other ID that triggers alarms if used.

scrip *n.* A currency that is not nuyen, usually referring to currency issued by a megacorporation.

simsense *n.* A sensory broadcast or recording that lets the viewer feel and experience what the participants feel and experience.

SIN *n.* System Identification Number. Identification number assigned to each person in the society.

SINless *adj.* Lacking a SIN. *n.* A SINless person.

SINner *n.* A person with a SIN. An honest person.

slot *v.* To insert a chip or credstick into chip or credstick reading device.

slot and run *v.* Hurry up. Get to the point. Move it.

so ka (Japanese) I understand. I get it.

soykaf *n.* Ersatz coffee substitute made from soybeans.

sprawl *n.* A metroplex (see plex); *v.* fraternize below one's social level.

squat *n.* Abandoned urban area used for housing. (vulgar) A dwarf.

squishy *n.* (vulgar) A dwarf, elf, or human. Usually used by orks and trolls.

Star, the *n.* The police. Originally referring to Lone Star specifically.

static *n.* Trouble, usually social in nature.

swag *adj.* Awesome.

trideo *n.* The three-dimensional successor to video. Trid for short.

trog *n.* (vulgar) An ork or troll. From troglodyte.

tusker *n.* (vulgar) An ork or troll.

vatjob *n.* A person with extensive cyberware replacement, reference is to a portion of the process during which the patient must be submerged in nutrient fluid.

wagemage *n.* A magician (usually mage) employed by a corporation.

wageslave *n.* A low-level corporate employee.

wetwork *n.* Assassination. Murder.

wired *adj.* Equipped with cyberware, especially increased reflexes.

wiz *adj.* Wonderful, excellent.

wizworm *n.* A dragon.

Yak *n.* (Japanese) Yakuza. Either a clan member or a clan itself.

zaibatsu *n.* (Japanese) A megacorporation.

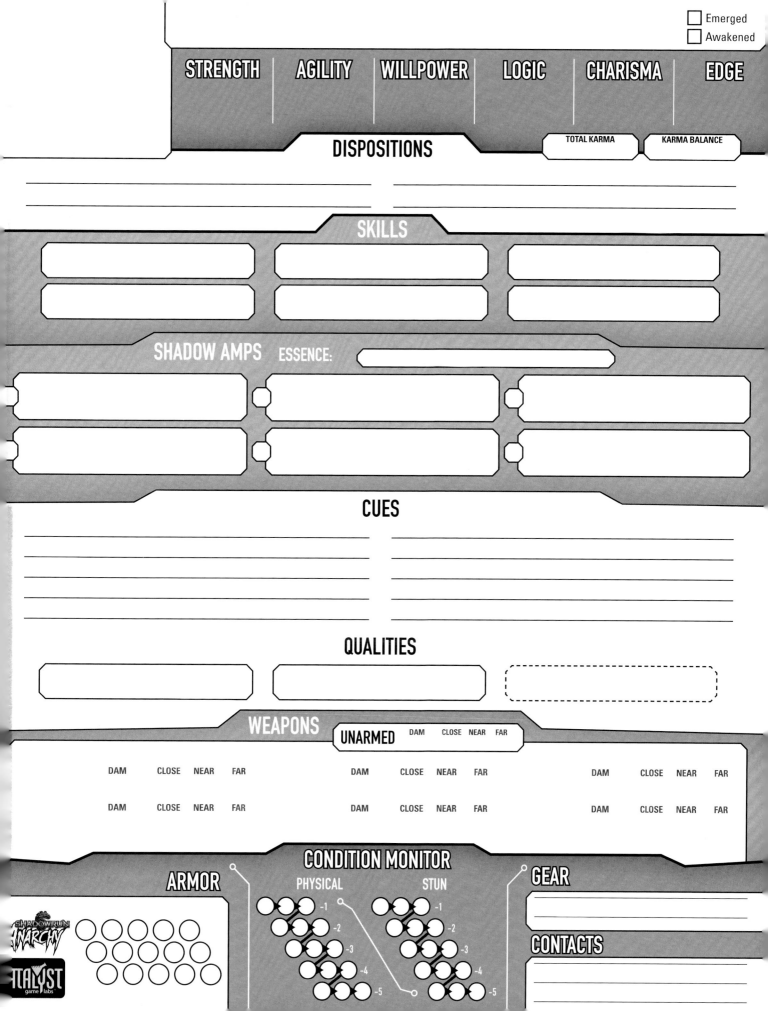

| STRENGTH | AGILITY | WILLPOWER | LOGIC | CHARISMA | EDGE |

☐ Emerged
☐ Awakened

DISPOSITIONS

TOTAL KARMA   KARMA BALANCE

SKILLS

SHADOW AMPS   ESSENCE:

CUES

QUALITIES

WEAPONS

UNARMED   DAM   CLOSE   NEAR   FAR

| DAM | CLOSE | NEAR | FAR | | DAM | CLOSE | NEAR | FAR | | DAM | CLOSE | NEAR | FAR |

| DAM | CLOSE | NEAR | FAR | | DAM | CLOSE | NEAR | FAR | | DAM | CLOSE | NEAR | FAR |

CONDITION MONITOR

ARMOR   PHYSICAL   STUN   GEAR

PHYSICAL: -1 -2 -3 -4 -5
STUN: -1 -2 -3 -4 -5

CONTACTS

SHADOWRUN ANARCHY

CATALYST game labs